Ways of Remembering

Ways of Remembering tells a story about the relationship between secular law and religious violence by studying the memorialisation of the 2002 Gujarat pogrom—postcolonial India's most litigated and mediatised event of anti-Muslim mass violence. By reading judgments and films on the pogrom through a novel interpretive framework, the book argues that the shared narrative of law and cinema engenders ways of remembering the pogrom in which the rationality of secular law offers a resolution to the irrationality of religious violence. In the public's collective memory, the force of this rationality simultaneously condemns and normalises violence against Muslims while exonerating secular law from its role in enabling the pogrom, thus keeping the violent (legal) order against India's Muslim citizens intact. The book contends that in foregrounding law's aesthetic dimensions we see the discursive ways in which secular law organises violence and presents itself as the panacea for that very violence.

Oishik Sircar is Professor of Law, Jindal Global Law School, and Associate Member, Institute for International Law and the Humanities, Melbourne Law School. He is the author of *Violent Modernities: Cultural Lives of Law in the New India* (2021) and co-director of the documentary film *We Are Foot Soldiers* (2011).

Law in Context

Series editors
Professor Kenneth Armstrong
University of Cambridge

Professor Maksymilian Del Mar
Queen Mary, University of London

Professor Sally Sheldon
University of Bristol and University of Technology Sydney

Editorial advisory board
Professor Bronwen Morgan
University of New South Wales

Emeritus Professor William Twining
University College London

Since 1970, the Law in Context series has been at the forefront of a movement to broaden the study of law. The series is a vehicle for the publication of innovative monographs and texts that treat law and legal phenomena critically in their cultural, social, political, technological, environmental and economic contexts. A contextual approach involves treating legal subjects broadly, using materials from other human- ities and social sciences, and from any other discipline that helps to explain the operation in practice of the particular legal field or legal phenomena under investi- gation. It is intended that this orientation is at once more stimulating and more revealing than the bare exposition of legal rules. The series includes original research monographs, coursebooks and textbooks that foreground contextual approaches and methods. The series includes and welcomes books on the study of law in all its contexts, including domestic legal systems, European and international law, transnational and global legal processes, and comparative law.

Books in the Series

Rowbottom: *Democracy Distorted: Wealth, Influence and Democratic Politics*

Sauter: *Public Services in EU Law*

Scott & Black: *Cranston's Consumers and the Law*

Seneviratne: *Ombudsmen: Public Services and Administrative Justice*

Seppänen: *Ideological Conflict and the Rule of Law in Contemporary China: Useful Paradoxes*

Siems: *Comparative Law, 3rd Edition*

Stapleton: *Product Liability*

Stewart: *Gender, Law and Justice in a Global Market*

Tamanaha: *Law as a Means to an End: Threat to the Rule of Law*

Tuori: *Properties of Law: Modern Law and After*

Turpin & Tomkins: *British Government and the Constitution: Text and Materials, 7th Edition*

Twining: *General Jurisprudence: Understanding Law from a Global Perspective*

Twining: *Globalisation and Legal Theory*

Twining: *Human Rights, Southern Voices: Francis Deng, Abdullahi An-Na'im, Yash Ghai and Upendra Baxi*

Twining: *Jurist in Context: A Memoir*

Twining: *Karl Llewellyn and the Realist Movement, 2nd Edition*

Twining: *Rethinking Evidence: Exploratory Essays, 2nd Edition*

Twining & Miers: *How to Do Things with Rules, 5th Edition*

Wan: *Film and Constitutional Controversy: Visualizing Hong Kong Identity in the Age of 'One Country, Two Systems'*

Ward: *A Critical Introduction to European Law, 3rd Edition*

Ward: *Law, Text, Terror*

Ward: *Shakespeare and Legal Imagination*

Watt: *The Making Sense of Politics, Media, and Law: Rhetorical Performances as Invention, Creation, Production*

Wells & Quick: *Lacey, Wells and Quick: Reconstructing Criminal Law: Text and Materials, 4th Edition*

Young: *Turpin and Tomkins' British Government and the Constitution: Text and Materials, 8th Edition*

Zander: *Cases and Materials on the English Legal System, 10th Edition* Zander: *The Law-Making Process, 6th Edition*

International Journal of Law in Context: A Global Forum for Interdisciplinary Legal Studies

The International Journal of Law in Context is the companion journal to the Law in Context book series and provides a forum for interdisciplinary legal studies and offers intellectual space for ground-breaking critical research. It publishes contextual work about law and its relationship with other disciplines including but not limited to science, literature, humanities, philosophy, sociology, psychology, ethics, history and geography. More information about the journal and how to submit an article can be found at http://journals.cambridge.org/ijc.

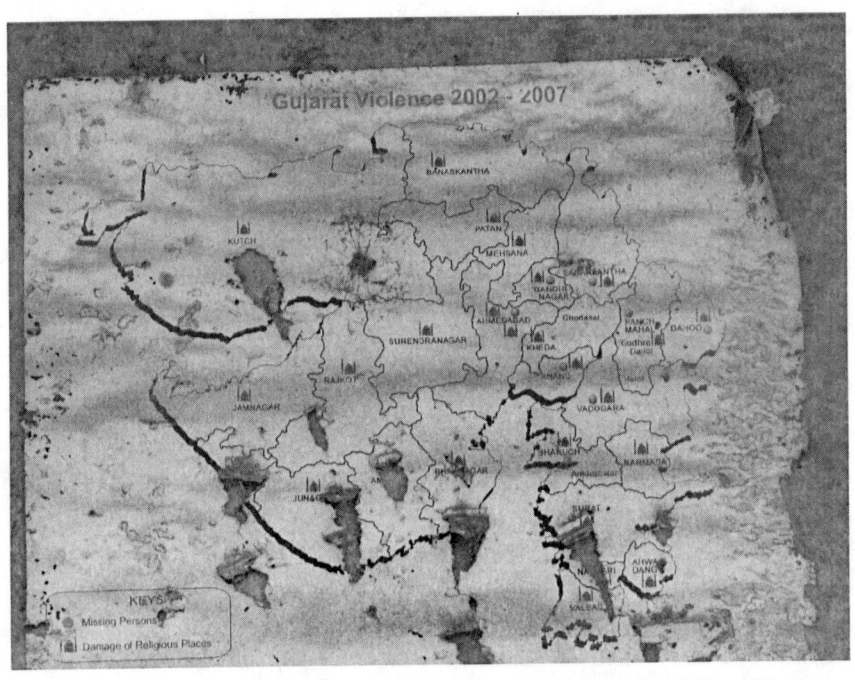

A map of the state of Gujarat pasted on a wall in Gulberg Society, Ahmedabad
Source: Photo by author.

Ways of Remembering

Law, Cinema and Collective Memory in the New India

Oishik Sircar

CAMBRIDGE
UNIVERSITY PRESS

Shaftesbury Road, Cambridge CB2 8EA, United Kingdom

One Liberty Plaza, 20th Floor, New York, NY 10006, USA

477 Williamstown Road, Port Melbourne, vic 3207, Australia

314 to 321, 3rd Floor, Plot No. 3, Splendor Forum, Jasola District Centre, New Delhi 110025, India

103 Penang Road, #05–06/07, Visioncrest Commercial, Singapore 238467

Cambridge University Press is part of Cambridge University Press & Assessment, a department of the University of Cambridge.

We share the University's mission to contribute to society through the pursuit of education, learning and research at the highest international levels of excellence.

www.cambridge.org
Information on this title: www.cambridge.org/9781316512814

© Oishik Sircar 2024

First published 2024

Printed in India by Avantika Printers Pvt. Ltd.

A catalogue record for this publication is available from the British Library

ISBN 978-1-316-51281-4 Hardback

To
Misha, for making me experience the joy of the unconditional
Maa and Babi, for everything you do and don't for love

What matters is not the fact that we remember ... but the way in which we remember.

—Asmal et al., *Reconciliation through Truth:*
A Reckoning with Apartheid's Criminal Governance (1996)

Contents

Figures

Acknowledgements

May I live conscious of my debt to all the people who make life possible.

—Audre Lorde, *Zami: A New Spelling of My Name—A Biomythography* (1982)

The writing of this book began during my doctoral work at the Melbourne Law School (MLS) in 2012. However, it started its life in 2002—unbeknownst to me that it will ever become a book—when as a law student at ILS Law College, Pune, I went to Ahmedabad, the capital city of Gujarat, as part of a fact-finding team put together by the South Asia Human Rights Documentation Centre to record survivor testimonies in the wake of a pogrom directed singularly at Muslims. I was 21 years old and it was my first ever 'field' visit as an aspiring human rights lawyer and campaigner. Every day I would take an autorickshaw from the Judges Bunglow Road—an upmarket and Hindu part of the city that represented the advances of modern India—and arrive at the visibly Muslim Shah Alam Dargah (a shrine converted into a makeshift refugee camp), whose squalid atmosphere of grief and devastation was a study in cruel contrasts between two diametrically opposite worlds in the same city divided by a river. These auto rides back and forth comprise one of the most abiding memories of my time in Ahmedabad—although I never thought about them at that time. Every autorickshaw that I would take inevitably had interiors decorated with big hand-painted images of Bollywood stars who became my daily companions alongside a really heavy hardbound copy of *Criminal Major Acts*.

I returned to Ahmedabad (and Vadodara) in 2014 during my research. I wanted to come back to the city to see if there were public remnants of the 2002 pogrom. I thought that it would be ethically wrong to write a thesis on 'Gujarat 2002' without gaining some affective sense of how memory resides at the scenes of violence. During this visit, too, the numerous autorickshaw rides I took provided the companionship of hand-painted Bollywood stars. The only difference was that alongside the veterans now the insides of the autos were adorned by many new faces. It struck me, quite serendipitously, that the remote connection between Bollywood cinema and law that began as a subliminal one in those auto rides in 2002 has now become a palpable one in my research that aimed to read the texts of judgments and cinema as a shared narrative of collective memory of the Gujarat pogrom.

After completing my trip to Gujarat, I was returning to Calcutta through Bombay. This was a few months into the Bharatiya Janata Party's (BJP's) win in the national elections in 2014. On the way to Santa Cruz airport, I passed a huge procession of the Bajrang Dal—the militant youth wing of the Sangh Parivar (Collective Family of Hindu Right Wing outfits) of which the BJP is also a part. A resounding slogan in Hindi being shouted on loudspeakers by those in the procession was *Katwa pachtayega Ram Ram chillaye ga*, which translates as 'Circumcised Muslims will repent; they will have to cry out Lord Ram's name'. The fascist insinuation was unambiguous, and in several more recent incidents of anti-Muslim violence, variations of this slogan have become chillingly common.

*

As this book goes into print 20 years after the Gujarat pogrom and two decades of my life as a scholar-activist that was fundamentally shaped by my visit to Ahmedabad in 2002, it is important that I tell you the names of those without whose mentorship, friendship, companionship and solidarity this book would not be possible.

*

Since a majority of the writing of this book took place at MLS, I acknowledge the Wurundjeri people of the Kulin Nation as the unceded custodians of the land on which MLS stands. I pay my respects to their elders' past, present and future.

*

I thank my supervisors Dianne Otto (Di) and Sundhya Pahuja (Sun) for their generosity, friendship, intellectual investments in this project and the care with which they have mentored me. Sun's invitation to keep simplifying ideas without diluting them, Di's insistence on never losing grip on the thread of my argument, and their collective encouragement to find my own voice were essential lessons in writing in the genre of thesis and dissertations. Their training challenged my thinking, gave me courage to step out of my comfort zones, helped me rediscover the worth of academic humility and finitude, and appreciate anew the responsibilities of the critical legal scholar in the academy and the world. Di and Sun went beyond the conventional supervisor–supervisee relationship to open up their homes for me (and my partner Debolina) to live in, for which I am very grateful.

Peter Rush, who I was fortunate to have as a supervisor for six months and as the academic assessor on my completion committee, introduced me to a completely new world of jurisprudence and aesthetics. Every discussion with Shaun McVeigh was provocatively insightful. In response to my confirmation seminar presentation in 2013, an incisive comment by Ann Genovese about the relationship between memory and history remained an important conceptual insight that has helped me think through the idea of collective memory.

Friends, comrades and academics at the University of Melbourne, and in Australia, made the journey especially comfortable and engaging. We were all living with our own aspirations and anxieties but were joined by a shared sense of vulnerability. To work in a community of fellow travellers, where your vulnerabilities are not considered inadequacies, was remarkably buoyant. Those I would particularly like to mention are Tsegaye Regassa Ararssa, James Parker, Cait Storr, Corrine Tan, Maria Elander, Julia Dehm, Sara Dehm, Tom Andrews, Ben Silverstein, Jordy Silverstein, Madeline Chiam, Monique Cormier, Laura Petersen, Luis Eslava, Jake Goldfien, Shantanu Mehra, Sagar Sanyal, Joseph Kikonyogo, Sadaf Aziz, Florence Adora, Gashahun L. Fura, Robyn Honey, Maree Pardee, Robi Rado, Dolly Kikon, Sandeep Kirpalani, Bina Fernandez, Maddy Clarke, Rose Parfitt, Sophie Rigney, Robin Jeffrey, Rajdeep Roy, Irfan Ahmad, Shakira Hussein, Samia Khatun, Souresh Roy, Rajgopal Saikumar, Mangesh Padmawar, Priti Tagalpallevar. I want to especially acknowledge Claire Opperman's friendship as a huge source of support and comfort both through and beyond my research work.

Among MLS faculty members, I acknowledge the collegial support extended by Pip Nicholson, Tim Lindsey, Jenny Morgan, Farrah Ahmed and Andrew Harding. The work of the Asian Law Centre's India programme at MLS, the Australia India Institute (particularly Amitabh Mattoo) and the Melbourne South Asian Studies Group offered opportunities to remain connected to discussions on Indian law, politics and cinema and as venues to share half-baked ideas without inhibition. The jurisprudence and feminist theory reading groups at MLS became regular venues to collectively read texts, learn, eat, drink and laugh.

Outside of the academic sphere in Melbourne, getting to know and spend time with Joan Nestle, Jeremy Baskin, Ananya Baskin, Om Pahuja, Asha Pahuja and Monica Pahuja has been like finding a family away from home. Playing beach cricket with Joan, breaking into a spontaneous dance with her in the middle of the night and listening to her voice of poetic wisdom has been a source of huge inspiration. Every bit of the time spent with Ananya, be it failing miserably to read her to sleep or watching *Matilda* together, has been a joy.

I have been lucky to find friends who took the time to read, comment on and discuss different parts of the book at various stages. This includes a very thoughtful group of scholars at the writing workshops of Harvard Law School's Institute for Global Law and Policy (in Doha, Cambridge, USA, and Geneva). I am grateful for their engagement and support: James Parker, Rajshree Chandra, Aziza Ahmed, Pooja Parmar, Jothie Rajah, Charlotte Peevers, Vik Kanwar, Mohammad Shahabuddin, Mathew Craven and Vasuki Nesiah.

If it were not for the keen reading eye and exactitude of Aruna Ramachandran and the research assistance of my former students Siddharth Saxena, Katyayani Suhrud and Smruti Bhutada, this book would not be completed. I would like to especially thank my dear friend Adil Hasan Khan for his wicked humour, easy affection and generous support both through and beyond the writing of the book. We met for the first time in 2010 at a very crowded and noisy Cambridge bar. Our indefatigable attempt to shout over deafening music to have a conversation about protest politics has turned into a friendship for life.

During my travels to Gujarat in 2014—so lovingly hosted by Nishant, Jagruti and Neerja Lalakiya—I wanted to see if there were any public remnants of the pogrom. It was an important and very disturbing visit. While there were no visible scars of the pogrom on the cityscape, my conversations with activists, lawyers, academics, some victim-survivors and the drivers of autorickshaws and taxis that I hired revealed how insidious the anti-Muslim prejudice in Gujarat is and how deep it runs through people's minds and hearts, businesses and state institutions. I thank the following people—in Ahmedabad, Vadodara, Mumbai and Delhi— for sparing time to speak with me, because these conversations strengthened my conviction in the political worth of this book: Mihir Desai, Johanna Lokhande, J. S. Bandukwala, Ayesha Khan, Pravin Misra, Pratik Sinha, M. M. Tirmizi, Mallika Sarabhai, Tridip Suhrud, Amrish Patel, Rohit Prajapati, Lancy Lobo, Justice Hosbet Suresh, Yusuf Shaikh, Imtiaz Khan Pathan, Uma Chakravarti, Shabnam Hashmi. I must acknowledge the help extended by Teesta Setalvad, Rakesh Sharma, Raheel Dhattiwala and Zahir Janmohamed for putting me in touch with some of those mentioned here. I am deeply saddened that Justice Suresh and J. S. Bandukwala have passed on before the publication of the book. Both of them were very generous with their time when I met them in 2014.

I completed writing alongside teaching at the Jindal Global Law School, and I could not have asked for a more supportive environment for this purpose. C. Raj Kumar has been a most sympathetic dean, and so has S. G. Sreejith been a very accommodating executive dean. A very special group of friends and colleagues made living, teaching and writing in Sonipat possible. I could not have survived without Rohini Sen's and Saptarshi Mandal's care and camaraderie (and Saptarshi's exquisite culinary skills). They have been sources of intellectual succour, mindless banter and Bengali parochialism in equal measure. Dipika Jain and Shilpi Bhattacharya are friends whom I relied on (and continue to) in spirit even if I am rightly accused of not staying in touch (*mea culpa!*). Sannoy Das, Mohsin Alam Bhat, Prabhakar Singh, Arun Sagar, Sanskriti Sanghi, Reeju Ray, Arpita Gupta, Sandeep Kindo, Albeena Shakil, Aashita Dawer and Aman offered opportunities for stimulating and comforting conversations that made institutional life bearable. My colleagues at the *Jindal Global Law Review* took on an unfair share of my responsibilities that allowed me to complete writing. I acknowledge the labour of Mamtarani, Asha, Padmarani, Puspa Roy, Sanju, Kabita di and Jhuma Khatun, our domestic workers, for taking care of us at our Sonipat home.

A key period of intense writing and revisions was carried out in Boston in the most wonderful apartment of Bryan Gangemi that my partner, Debolina Dutta, had rented during her residential fellowship at Harvard Law School. To be able to travel to the US on a dependent visa, away from the quotidian demands of life in Calcutta/Sonipat (especially after the devastating second wave of COVID-19 in India) and to live in such a comfortable apartment like Bryan's was plain lucky. If it was not for the months of uninterrupted writing in Boston, this book would have been poorer in rigour.

My small but very tight group of friends from school, college and beyond—Sakya Deb Chowdhury, Deepti Mohan, Trina Nileena Banerji, Garga Chatterjee, Biswarup Chakrabarty, Sayanti Sinha, Debabrata Sanyal and Alivia Dey—have been the most unconditionally supportive companions through the last 30 years of my life. They possibly do not know how important they are to me and how much I love them. I draw immense comfort from their presence in my life, even if we are not always keeping up with what is happening in each other's lives.

My family members had to bear the idiosyncrasies that come with the pursuit of a writing life. I am not the best of communicators even in the best of times, and that was only exacerbated through the period of writing. They have, however, always egged me on, sometimes leaving me alone, sometimes helping me de-stress by making light of my tension and, at others, being excited about when I will finally complete this book. To them, I say, thank you for your unwavering love and patience: Swapna Sinha (Tua), Amal Kumar Sinha (Pisho), Ratna Gangopadhyay (Pia), Roma Sarkar (Thia), Ishika Sircar (Raka), Shayak Sircar (Ron), Sayak Datta, Ashima Saxena, Shreya Khastgir (Tia), Pratima Dutta (Mummy), Manjula Chatterjee (Mashimoni), Pradip Khastgir (Chhotomama), Kanishka Basu (Rajib Babu). Tua has always been a source of righteous wisdom and unconditional love. I especially treasure her encouragement in times of loss and sadness, which ensured that I remained focused on the writing.

If there is one person whose commitment to a practice of aesthetics as a craft and life practice has been a constant source of encouragement for me, it is Mummy (Pratima Dutta)—my mother-in-law. Her passion for art and music, her stories about her teachers at Santiniketan and my heated disagreements with her about our takes on art (and life) have been inspirational. I am honoured and proud that her painting entitled 'Feathered Foes' (a rendition of Chang Xiufeng's *Copy of Ancient Indian Painting*), from her Kalabhavan days now adorns the cover of this book. The art is so powerfully apposite and prescient for the book's subject matter, especially its metaphorical charge in conveying the intimate contestations between violence, memory and justice. I am grateful to her for the permission to use it. I cannot be happier, and I hope she is too.

Ricco, my little human-nephew, and Poppy, my dog-nephew, have effortlessly provided much happiness and calm through the final months of writing. Watching videos of their hilarious histrionics offered much respite from a gruelling writing schedule.

Since before and through the years that I have been writing the book, many of my dearest people passed away. I regret not being able to share this moment with Krishna Narayan Khastgir (Dadubhai), Prafulla Kumar Sircar (Dadumoni), Santosh Kumar Sarkar (Kakadadu), Ajit Dutta (Daddy), Dolly Khastgir (Diu), Purnima Bhattacharya (Bordimashi), Ranjan Khastgir (Boromama), Alok Sarkar (Jetha), Bani Sircar (Dia), Tota Gangopadhyay (Pito) and Tapan Khastgir (Mejomama). Dia's and Mejomama's absences have left a gaping hole in my heart, and it pains me to not have them with me during this moment of putting the book out in the world.

Nothing in my life over the past decade and a half would have been meaningful if it was not for the love, care and companionship of Debolina Dutta (D), with whom I share a life of immense joys, critical contradictions and deep sorrows. D has been the kindest and fiercest interlocutor for all my scholarly projects. With her intellectual sharpness, she has read, rejected and helped me revise some of the most difficult portions of the book. It is her honest feedback about my ideas and writing that kept my overindulgences under check. It has been a brilliant experience to have shared this journey—through writing, cooking (with me as the sous chef!) and obsessively watching Scandinavian noir.

This journey of ours has a new member now in a mini monarch called Misha whose crying commands rule our lives! We are overwhelmed with joy and fatigue in equal measure but are loving—despite the sleeplessness—every bit of this life-altering experience called parenting. Misha, our dear daughter, has come into this world and to us at a time when the planet is in an intensified state of crisis and devastation in unprecedented ways. D and I marvel at her mischievous smile, and I hope against hope of being adequate to the task of protecting and preparing her for the promises and perils that our futures hold. Giving the final touches to the book in Misha's presence in my life makes this an especially happy moment. I dedicate this book to Misha, with all the love from her Abu.

I also dedicate this book to my parents—Anjana Sircar (Maa) and Anjan Sircar (Babi)—for things that they have taught me, consciously and unconsciously, through active directions and impositions, and wise and troubling silences. I owe my love for watching films, reading and writing to them. When I was growing up, I do not know of any child who was taken to see as many films as they took me to watch at movie theatres. Since I was an introverted child, my mother gave me a writing pad for my sixth birthday and told me that I could write stories for myself. My father's voracious appetite for reading passed on to me through the delight of just watching him read. I have grown up not seeing eye to eye with them on many crucial things, and yet I cannot not acknowledge my contradictory inheritances of their many selves that have fundamentally shaped who I am. My parents have been flawed, inspirational and beautiful. This book is a tribute to their love for each other, the love with which they fill up my life. I know it is an inadequate reciprocation, but it is a heartfelt one.

*

This work would have never become the book that it has if it was not for the editorial care of Qudsiya Ahmed, Anwesha Rana and Priya Das at Cambridge University Press. I am grateful to the editors of the Law in Context series for making it a part of their list which is nothing short of an honour.

The book has gained immensely from the detailed and considered reports by the two anonymous reviewers and my doctoral thesis examiners, Upendra Baxi and Rebecca Johnson. Upen's and Rebecca's works are also key intellectual inheritances writ large over the orientation of this book.

No words of thanks would suffice for the generosity with which Peter Goodrich, Jasbir K. Puar, Sunera Thobani and Achin Vanaik have written the endorsement blurbs for the book. I only hope that the book is able to take forward, in a modest way, the scholarly and political commitments present in their rich oeuvre that I continue to learn so much from.

*

It is a cruel coincidence that I am publishing this book at a time when the regime under whose watch the Gujarat pogrom was orchestrated is now the democratically elected ruling government in India—in its second term. In the current climate in India, where anything remotely critical of the state is being labelled 'seditious' and a new normalisation of gender-, caste- and religion-based violence has emerged, I wonder whether to think of this moment of publication as an achievement or a curse. It has been a privilege to have carried out this research in relative safety, especially given how, under grave threats to their life and work, lawyers, academics, writers, journalists, students, filmmakers, peasants and labourers in India are continuing the good fight—failing, sustaining, resisting, repairing, repeating. This book draws 'dark hope' from their fragility and resilience.

Abbreviations

BJP	Bharatiya Janata Party
CBFC	Central Board of Film Certification
CBI	Central Bureau of Investigation
CJP	Citizens for Justice and Peace
CM	chief minister
FIR	first information report
FTC	fast-track court
INC	Indian National Congress
J-A	jurisprudential-aesthetic (approach)
NHRC	National Human Rights Commission
RSS	Rashtriya Swayamsevak Sangh
SIT	Special Investigation Team
SLP	special leave petition

1 | Law and the Aesthetics of Atrocity

It is when we think of the world the aesthetic of indifference might bring into being that we recognize the urgency of remembering the stories we have not written.[1]

For several weeks in the early months of 2002, a pogrom singularly targeting Muslims was executed in the western Indian state of Gujarat. The violence resulted in deaths numbering in the thousands, egregious forms of sexual harm against women, massive displacements and loss of property, hearth and home.[2] 'Gujarat 2002', as the pogrom has come to be popularly called, is independent India's most litigated and mediatised[3] event of anti-minority mass atrocity.[4] In the two decades since 2002, there has been much contestation over memory and forgetting related to the pogrom, played out in multiple sites such as litigation, films, literature, art, reportage, the economy and, of course, electoral politics. Of these sites, this book engages with judgments and films, by far the most 'publicly available commemorative symbols, rituals, and technologies'[5] of collective memory of the pogrom.

The pogrom's legal and cinematic representations continue to provoke debates regarding state impunity, minority rights, liberalism, justice and the very meaning of India as a secular, constitutional democracy. Central to these post-pogrom debates is a concern with collective memory: the ways in which the pogrom and its aftermath are remembered through 'shared meanings'[6] in public discourse, how these memories are invoked through 'circuit[s] of culture' like law and films,[7] by whom and to achieve what end.[8]

This book reads judgments and films—two key narratives of India's secular legal imagination[9]—as a posteriori sites of collective memory where the contestations about the Gujarat pogrom have been most pronounced. The first of these two narratives is written into the texts of four judgments of the Best Bakery case—a landmark criminal trial related to the massacre of a Muslim family in the city of Vadodara on 1 March 2002. The second narrative is framed in the images and sounds of three Bollywood films about the pogrom, namely *Dev* (2004), *Parzania* (2007) and *Kai Po Che* (2013).

These two narratives have had a shared temporal journey—the three films span a period of nine years (2004–13), coinciding closely with the years through which the trial in the Best Bakery case ran (2003–12) (Figure 1.1). Both the trial and the films have been the cause of several controversies that were widely reported in the media, notably on issues of witness intimidation, faulty police investigation and censorship. These controversies have given the trial and the films a cultural and political traction that has made both the narratives and the event live on in collective memory since 2002. This book focuses on the decade-long post-pogrom period because it offers a concentrated insight into the consolidation of Hindu right-wing nationalism, or Hindutva,[10] and neoliberalism in the wake of the pogrom.[11] I refer to this consolidation as the 'New India'. Attending to this consolidation will throw light on how the relationship between secular law and religious violence is understood and articulated in postcolonial India by the judiciary and in cinema.

The judicial narrative reconstructs the pogrom as a matter of 'fact' to get to the 'truth', convict the wrongdoers and deliver justice. The cinematic

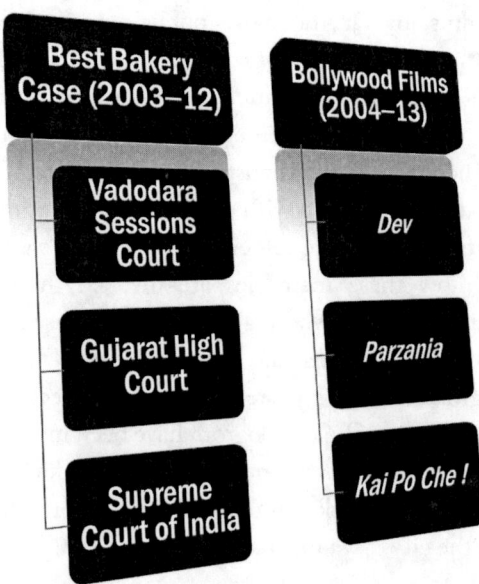

Figure 1.1　Judgments and films: A shared narrative of collective memory
Source: Prepared by author.

narrative uses the scaffolding of facts to offer fictionalised accounts of ordinary human depravity and compassion in the face of mass violence. When read together (rather than in opposition), the shared narrative of the judgments and the films engender ways of remembering the pogrom in which a faith in secular law offers a resolution to the crisis of religious violence. In both the legal and cinematic imaginations, the pogrom is reconstructed as a conflict between secular law and religious violence, in which secular law ultimately emerges victorious.

The book argues that the shared narrative of law and cinema participates in the ordering of collective memory, which produces ways of remembering that acknowledge the horror of the pogrom and simultaneously rationalise it as aberrant. Such ordering is made possible through the workings of a particular kind of rationality that masks secular law's complicities with religious violence. I call this a 'state-making and state-preserving' rationality that demonstrates how 'popular sovereignty takes the paradoxical form of inclusion [of Muslims] and unspeakable violence [against them]'.[12] In the public's collective memory, then, this rationality, as recorded in the shared narrative of law and cinema, considers Muslims as citizens and condemns the pogrom while always already exonerating secular law from having played any role in fomenting the actual violence—thus keeping intact the violent (legal) order against India's Muslim citizens.

To pursue this argument, I develop a 'jurisprudential-aesthetic' (J-A) approach to the reading of the judgments and the films. The J-A approach enables me to pay particular attention to the intertextual form of the judgments and films—to look for 'the *way* something is said in contrast to [merely] *what* is said'.[13] I do this by foregrounding the aesthetic dimensions in the texts of the judgments and the jurisprudential dimensions in the texts of the films.[14] Despite working in different genres, judgments and films are both public sites and records of storytelling that share a 'commitment to narrative as a central organizing principle'.[15] The development and deployment of the J-A approach helps to understand law not only as an autonomous body of rational knowledge with its own self-referential norms, rules and principles but also as one that shapes and is shaped by aesthetics—passions, emotions, sentiments and the senses.[16]

When the judgments of the Best Bakery case and the three films are read using the J-A approach, we can see two things: first, how the legal and the cinematic work together to produce collective memory; and second, how the shared narrative of the judgments and the films order the collective memories of the pogrom. This ordering engenders ways of remembering that condemn the violence while rationalising it as aberrational—a temporary crisis that can be overcome by restoring faith in secular law. My J-A reading will make visible a particular rationality at work in ordering collective memories of the pogrom—a state-making and state-preserving one. This rationality reconstructs the pogrom as an event in which secular law is understood to be rescuing the postcolonial nation-state from the destructive effects of religious violence.

This state-making and state-preserving rationality embeds the ideas of legalism, secularism and developmentalism in a national constitutional imagination, which is endorsed consistently by the Supreme Court of India.[17] These attributes—interpreted into the Constitution of India—work as markers of Indian modernity, considered by many to be in opposition to the so-called nativist ideology of Hindutva.[18] And yet, as this book will demonstrate, this triad of legalism, secularism and developmentalism operates discursively to both condemn and normalise violence against Muslims by advancing seemingly secular critiques of the pogrom, as represented in both the judgments and the films.[19]

In this double-play of normalisation and condemnation, anti-Muslim violence is rationalised—by references to the 1947 Partition of the subcontinent—as an a priori condition of the postcolonial Indian nation-state's coming into being.[20] In the constitutional imagination, India as a secular, rule-of-law abiding democracy exists because of the Partition—in contradistinction to the theocratic Pakistan.[21] For the Hindu Right, India and its Hindu citizens carry a distinct identity because of a traumatic history of violence (against Hindus by Muslims) that has to be constantly avenged through the 'weaponisation' of Partition memory to keep the Indian nation safe from Muslim outsiders.[22] Both these imaginations, as my J-A reading will show, are animated by the aforementioned triad. Embedded in the narrative subtexts of the judgments and films is a Hindutva discourse that aims to fashion India into a Hindu *rashtra*, or nation—the holy land of Hindus.[23] This triad thus becomes germane to the idea of the New India, which is marked by the symbiotic rise of neoliberalism and Hindutva.

In the rest of this chapter, I will offer a short account of Gujarat 2002—the event and its contexts—and explain how the relationship between law and cinema has worked to produce collective memories of the pogrom. I will then introduce the orientation and scope of the book. The purpose of this section is to provide an outline of the bodies of literature that I am drawing from and the scholarly field that I am contributing to, and to introduce the terms that form the conceptual base of the book.

Gujarat 2002: A 'Small' Retelling

Legal and aesthetic records of Gujarat 2002 have played an important role in shaping collective memories of the pogrom. This is the case especially for those like me who experienced it from a safe distance, consuming the unfolding of the violence on television screens or in newspapers, and then through films. The pogrom's contested narratives are best captured by a set of iconic photographs—like Qutubuddin Ansari begging for mercy with folded hands, or a saffron bandana-clad Ashok Mochi brandishing an iron rod with outstretched arms[24]—and landmark criminal trials of highly localised massacres, like the Best Bakery and Gulberg Society cases.[25] These images have not only produced a surfeit of reportage but also offered templates for popular culture and aesthetic reconstructions in film,[26] literature[27] and art.[28]

In my retelling of the Gujarat pogrom—both in this section and in the rest of the book—I do not claim to reveal the 'neutral truth' about the event.[29] I attend to a practice of reading that does not consider meaning to be bound entirely to 'real' authorial intent (of the judges or the filmmakers) and instead acknowledges that 'every text is embedded in an interrelated network of other texts whose boundaries are porous'.[30] My account maintains fidelity to the texts I will read,[31] rather than trying to establish interpretive superiority.[32] In a tradition of critical legal scholarship,[33] my account critiques what I disagree with, but without rejection,[34] recognises the partiality of my own views[35] and prioritises the question of suffering, without sentimentalising it.[36] The version of the events of the pogrom and the narrative that I hold on to through this book is aimed at foregrounding the 'small voices'[37] which struggle to keep alive a certain memory of the pogrom even as they are constantly being 'drowned in the noise of statist [and corporatist] commands'[38] that propagate a dominant memory.

It is now two decades since Gujarat experienced one of independent India's most violent mass atrocities against its Muslim minority population.[39] Postcolonial India has experienced many incidents of anti-minority mass religious violence since the Partition in 1947,[40] including the ones that have come before and after Gujarat 2002: notably, the ongoing persecution of

Muslims by the occupying Indian army in Kashmir;[41] the 1983 massacre of Bengali Muslim immigrants from Bangladesh in Nellie, Assam;[42] the anti-Sikh violence of 1984 in Delhi;[43] the anti-Muslim violence of 1992 in Bombay;[44] the anti-Christian violence in Kandhamal, Orissa (now Odisha), in 2008;[45] the anti-Muslim violence in Muzzaffarnagar, Uttar Pradesh, in 2013;[46] and most recently, the anti-Muslim violence in northeast Delhi, in 2020.[47] All of these events, among many others that are lower in scale and intensity, have been part of a larger script that animates the violence of postcolonial state-making.[48]

The Gujarat pogrom takes ahead the history of anti-minority mass violence in India[49] and offers a new template for normalising the Hindu nationalist project of both symbolically and materially reconfiguring India as the holy land for Hindus.[50] The Gujarat pogrom was distinct in certain specific ways in comparison to previous events of anti-Muslim mass violence.[51] The success with which Muslims were targeted was marked by the sophisticated planning and execution of the pogrom, the macabre forms of brutality and the unprecedented extent of state involvement, police inaction and judicial complicity.[52]

Although official estimates state that the violence lasted for three days, many Gujaratis who lived through it say that it lasted for as long as three months.[53] The killings, rapes, arson and destruction continued unabated, yet despite a complete breakdown of law and order and grave instances of police inaction, a constitutional state of emergency was not declared by the president of India. It can be argued that such a decision reveals how the federal government—which at that time was the National Democratic Alliance, led by the Hindu nationalist Bharatiya Janata Party (BJP)—condoned the event.[54] This failure to impose president's rule rendered the violence as not deserving of federal attention in political and public consciousness, even though it could be considered to be a situation where there was a complete breakdown of the constitutional machinery.[55]

Starting on 28 February 2002, groups of militant Hindus—with active support from Hindu right-wing outfits like the Rashtriya Swayamsevak Sangh (RSS), the Vishwa Hindu Parishad and the Bajrang Dal—singularly targeted Muslims across rural and urban Gujarat: killing close to 2,000 people (which included some Hindu, Christian and Parsi casualties as well), 'disappearing' an estimated 2,500 people and driving tens of thousands from their homes.[56] Sexual violence was used to murder Muslim women, including pregnant women, in order to humiliate the Muslim community.[57] Homes and property owned by Muslims were pillaged and burnt. Several mosques were desecrated and razed to the ground, and roads paved over them overnight.[58] The violence targeted Muslims irrespective of their class status and residential locations.[59]

That Muslims could be attacked in such a systematic manner without much resistance from the community was not only because of the state administration's complicity and police inaction. The sophisticated organisation was also made possible because an attack on Muslims had been planned over a long period of time. This planning included the advance accumulation of arms by Hindu militant groups[60] and the legislative planning of the city of Ahmedabad over many years, which resulted in the creation of Muslim ghettos whose captive populations were easy to attack.[61] The violence, thus, was not akin to a 'riot'—a spontaneous conflagration—but the result of long-term and systematic planning aided through state support that characterises a 'pogrom'.[62]

Even over a decade after 2002, many Muslims continued to be displaced,[63] and many victim-survivors still await compensation for damages.[64] The criminal justice processes trying some of the perpetrators have been under threat of being compromised by political interference,[65] intimidation of witnesses and judges,[66] and faulty investigations by the police and special investigation agencies.[67] By the Gujarat government's own admission made to the Supreme Court of India, of a total of 4,252 cases that victim-survivors registered with the police, nearly half were summarily closed by the police and thus never progressed to the trial stage.[68] For the few cases that did get to trial, some in the first instance resulted in full acquittal of all accused due to lack of evidence, reflecting the police's tardy investigation.

State impunity in India, especially for mass anti-minority violence, is strengthened by the active cooperation of the criminal justice system, and local political and patronage networks.[69] If lower conviction rates in the post-pogrom trials are one way to measure state impunity, then Gujarat has been particularly notable. As of 2012, in comparison to the national conviction rate of 18.5 per cent for cases related to riots, the conviction rate in cases related to the pogrom in Gujarat was 1.2 per cent.[70] Despite the failures in investigation and prosecution related to criminal trials arising out of the pogrom, the judiciary continues to be considered an able and willing neutral arbiter of justice that is not complicit with the deep structures of Hindutva's anti-Muslim prejudice. This has been called the 'impunity effect': 'how a majoritarian regime conducts farcical legal proceedings that allow it to acknowledge, yet benefit from, state-backed violence against minorities'.[71]

The normalisation of state impunity in the wake of Gujarat 2002 has not, however, gone unchallenged. Despite the failures of the state to effectively carry out prosecutions, activists, journalists, artists, academics and lawyers have spearheaded campaigns to seek justice for and with the victims and survivors of the pogrom. In these campaigns, they have expressed faith in secular law in the form of both the Constitution of India and international law as important tools for holding the state accountable.[72] From the initial characterisation of the event as a 'genocide' rather than a 'riot' in order to mobilise international attention by comparing it to the Holocaust,[73] to the campaign that led to the drafting of national legislation drawing on provisions in the Rome Statute of the International Criminal Court to include command responsibility in Indian criminal law,[74] secular and international legal standards have been the benchmark used to demonstrate both the Indian state's unwillingness to prosecute and the way its governance is being shaped by Hindutva ideology. The Hindu Right has, alongside, projected that it trusts the secular legal mechanisms of the country. Under the secular criminal justice system, leaders of the Hindu Right have been both convicted[75] and acquitted of wrongdoing for Gujarat 2002.[76] Since 2002, the Hindu Right has time and again cited these convictions and the acquittals as the triumph of secular law.[77] Secular law, thus, has been deployed in both the pro- and anti-Hindu Right narratives. While the parliamentary and ideological Left and the Liberals see the Constitution as a tool to resist the spread of Hindutva, the Hindu Right cite the Constitution to vindicate its commitment to secularism and consider Hindutva ideology to be in alignment with the secular constitution.[78]

After the 2002 pogrom, Gujarat, under the chief ministership of Narendra Modi (since 2014, the prime minister of India) of the BJP, has been celebrated as one of India's most developed states with unparalleled urban and industrial infrastructure, and has become a preferred destination for corporate investment by multinationals. Immediately after the pogrom, a group of influential Gujarati industrialists came together to form the Resurgent Group of Gujarat that organised an investors' conference in 2003 called Vibrant Gujarat. The aim was to simultaneously defend Gujarat as a business-friendly state and present Narendra Modi as a strong-willed business-friendly leader against the criticism that was directed at him by the Confederation of Indian

Industry for his role as chief minister during the pogrom. This inaugurated what has been called the 'Gujarat model of "development": violent Hindu nationalism underwritten by serious corporate money', resulting in a renewed relationship between Modi and Indian big business that propelled his prime ministerial ambitions and the current power and influence that the BJP wields drawing on the support of major industrialists and crony capitalism.[79] Due to the projections of rapid growth rates and the ease of doing business, the Gujarat Model has been showcased by political parties and industrialists as a template for development in the New India. These projections have been questioned by scholars who have argued that Gujarat's growth is built on the structural marginalisation of Muslims, Dalits and Adivasis. The Gujarat Model has been analysed as playing a role in consolidating the state's Hindu majoritarianism and has also been deployed to whitewash the memories of 2002.[80]

Modi's secular critics allege that he—along with other politicians in the Gujarat BJP—oversaw the planning and execution of the 2002 violence. It has been argued that the pogrom was meant to be a definitive step towards furthering the Hindu Right's vision of establishing India as a Hindu *rashtra*.[81] Hindutva's neo-fascist vision, fused with a Zionist sensibility, wants to establish India as the holy land for Hindus alone through both Hindu supremacist violence against religious minorities and secular 'constitutional accommodation'.[82] Muslims and Christians who are in the territory of India are not considered original inhabitants because their holy lands are elsewhere. According to Hindutva ideology, those who follow Islam and Christianity must assimilate, if they wish to stay in India, or their forced removal or killings will stand justified.[83] In the making of such an ideology against Abrahamic monotheism, Hindutva, ironically, advances an idea of Hinduism as 'political monotheism' tied to a single all-powerful Aryan god in the mythological figure of Ram.[84] In so doing, Hinduism is accorded a pseudo-historical status of a homogeneous and ancient religious order that is indigenous to an undivided territory called Bharatvarsha—the Constitution choosing its shortened version Bharat—which is both the fatherland and holy land of authentic Hindus.[85]

Gujarat has been called the 'Hindutva laboratory' that executed the pogrom as an experiment to teach Muslims in India 'a lesson'.[86] Modi and many of his ministers in Gujarat have been named in independent fact-finding reports,[87] survivor testimonies,[88] revelations by public servants about state complicity,[89] undercover investigations by journalists[90] and activist memoirs.[91] Statements by the Supreme Court of India have condemned the state government for ordering the police to step back and let the mobs rein free.[92] Many Hindu right-wing leaders (including Modi) have been recorded on camera instigating the mobs with their inflammatory anti-Muslim speeches and justifying the pogrom by citing the Godhra train-burning incident of 27 February 2002 that killed 58 *kar sevak*s (Hindu pilgrims) as a legitimate cause for this *pratikriya* (retributive action) by hurt, victimised and angry Hindus.[93]

The incident of the burning of compartment S-6 of the Sabarmati Express, carrying *kar sevak*s returning from Ayodhya,[94] allegedly by a Muslim mob at Godhra train station in Gujarat, has come to stand as the temporal and ideological justification for the pogrom, or as its 'precipitating event'.[95] In line with an explanation that Modi had provided as the then chief minister (CM)—'every "action" has an equal and opposite "reaction"'[96]—almost all references to the Gujarat pogrom until today continue to replay this cause-and-effect logic of 'who cast the first stone':[97] the violent Muslims burnt the innocent Hindus in the train, so now the tolerant Hindus are no longer able to remain silent.[98] They are avenging the deaths of their Hindu brothers and sisters by killing the intolerant and ungrateful Muslims.[99] In Teesta Setalvad's characterisation: 'Every act of violence of the majority Hindu is an act of retaliation of the perennially and permanently barbaric Mussalmaan.'[100] Collective memory of the pogrom has, thus, been mobilised through the marking of Godhra as a singular 'flashpoint'[101] moment that performs a 'moral inversion'[102] where India's majority Hindus become victims of its minority Muslims. Such a logic masks the deep and dispersed structures of Hindutva which enabled the planning of the pogrom well before the train caught fire.[103] It also masks the historical and economic antecedents of Hindutva in Gujarat that did not erupt only as a spontaneous and reactionary response to Godhra.[104]

The pogrom took place during Modi's time in office, and arguably, the violence consolidated the Hindu vote in Modi's favour, which led to him winning four consecutive state elections in Gujarat as CM since 2002.[105] In 2014, Modi was elected as the prime minister of India through a media-managed election campaign that wedded soft Hindutva with robust neoliberal developmentalism.[106] His election saw a clear majority emerge for a single party for the first time in independent India since 1984.[107]

During the run-up to his prime ministerial campaign, in 2012 Modi was exonerated due to the lack of prosecutable evidence—given a 'clean chit' in a closure report[108]—by the Special Investigation Team (SIT) appointed by the Supreme Court of India, which was tasked with specifically looking into three major massacres committed during the pogrom. The independence of this body has been questioned for procedural, investigative and ethical lapses.[109] In 2017, a protest petition by Zakia Jafri, a victim-survivor, against the SIT's exoneration of Modi was dismissed by the Gujarat High Court, upholding the clean chit. An appeal against this decision was dismissed by the Supreme Court in 2022.[110] In response to the 2017 judicial exoneration of his accountability as head of state, Modi had tweeted, 'Satyameva Jayate', or 'truth alone triumphs',[111] a Sanskrit expression from an ancient Hindu religious text (the Mundaka Upanishad) that has been secularised as India's national motto, accompanying the national emblem, the Sarnath pillar (which is of Buddhist origin), both of which adorn the original cover of the Constitution of India.[112]

In an interview with the news agency Reuters in 2013, Modi likened his feelings for the victims to the sadness that a person in a car would feel if the driver ran over a puppy.[113] Regarding continuing to fund relief camps for the Muslims displaced by the pogrom, Modi had expressed eugenicist panic about how they could turn into 'child producing centres' that will breed more Muslims.[114] Indeed, the possibility that Modi would express any remorse at all for the pogrom had, by 2013, become so absurd that one news outlet spoke of it in the form of an April Fool's day joke.[115] His standard refrain whenever asked about the 2002 violence has been to say, 'Why even talk about 2002? … It's the past. What does it matter?'[116]

It is Modi's and the Hindu Right's rhetoric of 'let's move on' that has animated much of the dominant legal and aesthetic discourse about how the Gujarat pogrom is collectively remembered.[117] This rhetoric, however, is not reflective of a practice of denial but one which, even while acknowledging the horror of the pogrom, either traces everything about it back to what it believes to be its originary cause, that is, Godhra, or relegates 'all violence to an amorphous "politics"'.[118] Such relegation works to guard against 'summoning a past that still vividly lurks in the present'.[119] As Ghassem-Fachandi notes:

> Such interpretations elide the more disturbing realization that not only
> do political parties manipulate constituencies for electoral gain, but

people themselves become complicit in this by inhabiting representations, participating in acts and thoughts that have effects beyond the mere political calculations of those who organize violence. The political machinations of the pogrom reveal only half the story.[120]

This book, thus, is interested in the other half of the story. In pursuing its argument, *Ways of Remembering* tries to work against this logic of amorphous politics by looking beyond the realpolitik of the memorial reconstructions of the pogrom to develop a method of reading the public lives of law and cinema as a shared narrative to understand their role in the production of different ways of remembering. What joins these ways of remembering is their unequivocal condemnation of the violence. However, embedded in these ways of remembering, as the application of my J-A approach will demonstrate, is a state-making and state-preserving rationality that leaves unquestioned the triad that constitutes this very rationality—legalism, secularism and developmentalism. This triad, which is foundational to the Hindutva justifications of the pogrom in the first place, continues to order the secular memorial aftermath of the violence.

Law in/as Aesthetics

The conceptual and methodological orientation of this book draws on and locates itself at the intersection of two fields of scholarship, namely, aesthetic jurisprudence[121] and cultural legal studies,[122] both of which are broadly concerned with the law's sensory, affective and narrative dimensions. I refer to this as the 'law in/as aesthetics' orientation that is interested in the relationship between law and the human senses: the law's appeal to the senses and how the senses perceive the law.[123] This body of scholarship is closely related to the law and literature movement that considers law as a narrative genre, inquiring into how literature, literary metaphors and rhetoric inform judgment writing, and how literary works represent the law.[124]

The focus of the law and literature movement grew over time through Western common law jurisdictions, overlapping with critical approaches to law, to include the humanities broadly (particularly art, cinema, photography, theatre and music) and to consider not only law's representation in these aesthetic forms but also how law was embedded in these forms and sometimes even resembled them, and vice versa.[125] This move marked a shift from interpretation as the primary critical legal method of reading the texts of law,[126] towards reading law's unconscious and affective intensities—passions, desires and fetishes—from psychoanalytical, postmodern and post-structural perspectives.[127]

Law in/as aesthetics can be considered a 'minor' jurisprudential tradition,[128] which is interested in some of the same questions—'what is law?' and 'what is the nature of law?'—that concern what has been called 'restricted jurisprudence': a jurisprudence that is narrowly focused on a hierarchy or pedigree of posited sources and considers law to be a self-contained and self-referential body of knowledge.[129] However, instead of trying to find a determinate answer only from posited sources of state law, law in/as aesthetics 'suspend[s] law's conventional conceptual, doctrinal, and institutional boundaries in an effort to imagine different modalities for understanding law'.[130] It ventures into the realms of the speculative, surreal, ephemeral, abstract, affective and experiential. To make this move, law in/as aesthetics delves into the feelings and emotions that we attach to law (or that the law attaches to us), and that are generated by law beyond its posited forms, by paying attention to the mythological, cultural, virtual, technological, architectural and affective avatars of law.[131]

Under the broad rubric of law in/as aesthetics, I have identified four types of scholarly works, which can be categorised as follows:

1. Representation: Works that are concerned with the representations of law in aesthetic genres—such as in art,[132] literature,[133] cinema[134] and television[135]—and use such representations to make larger arguments about law, politics and society.

2. Form: Works that study how the legal form can be an aesthetic category in itself (for instance, considering the literary composition of judgments,[136] a court's architecture,[137] the performative dimensions of judicial proceedings,[138] the sartorial authority of a judge's clothing[139] or the relationship between the forms of law, sound and music[140]).

3. Affect: Works that inquire into how aesthetic forms generate affective intensities that appeal to a legal imagination (for example, in the way in which cinematic narrative can give the audience a sense of authority to pass judgement, or how the tonality of the judge's voice in a courtroom can engender fear or sympathy for the accused).[141]

4. Technology: Works that study how visual, acoustic and haptic technologies impact and manipulate the senses in the realm of the juridical (like the administration of truth serum on an accused, or witnesses testifying

through videoconferencing, or the use of a vanished photo on Snapchat as evidence).[142]

What joins all the aforementioned law in/as aesthetics scholarship is their unsettling of the Manichean distinction between the categories of law and aesthetics, such that aesthetics is not considered the Other of law but rather that one cannot be imagined without the other.

In this book, I develop a theoretical orientation that combines these different kinds of scholarship to imagine law outside of its conventional or posited confines, and at the same time maintains a fidelity towards the materiality of the posited texts—judgments and films. In so doing, the book contributes specifically to scholarship in the area of law and cinema, and broadly to the fields of postcolonial law and Indian jurisprudence. This combination is itself unusual because the majority of scholarship around law and cinema has been oriented towards North America, the UK, Canada, Israel and Australia. Here, I take it to India, a non-Western and postcolonial location in the common law world, to speak to a specific event of mass violence. However, this is no simple transplant because this body of scholarship has itself almost never engaged with Indian law, nor the aesthetics of Bollywood cinema (let alone with other Indian cinema). Its references are primarily always Hollywood cinema, post-Holocaust cinema, Western European cinema and, if it has travelled to the non-West, Japanese and some South American cinema—but mostly those that have found world recognition through Hollywood. On the other hand, Indian film studies has had very little engagement with law's representation or law's affective dimensions in film, and Indian legal scholarship has remained hesitant to engage in studies of law's aesthetic dimensions.[143] Where this engagement is present, it has been limited to works that have focused on questions of censorship,[144] intellectual property[145] and, to a much lesser extent, pedagogy.[146]

My gesture of bringing a J-A frame developed using scholarship coming out of Western jurisdictions to explain an event in a postcolonial jurisdiction is not a work of an uncomplicated theoretical extrapolation but the recognition of a hermeneutical encounter. I am formally trained in Indian law and have subsequently acquired jurisprudential training in Canada and Australia. I am, thus, writing from the interstices of a disciplinary location that continues to be challenged and enriched through these encounters.[147]

I, therefore, write with a postcolonial legal and aesthetic sensibility that alerts me to both the possibilities and limitations of the theoretical bricolage that I have put together.[148] A part of this sensibility consists of the practice of responsibility towards the place, the peoples and the texts I am writing about, as well as towards the multi-jurisdictional disciplinary locations that I am writing from. This book demonstrates a mongrel heuristic that works through the oppositional and shared epistemologies that I have inherited.[149]

New India

The New India, in this book, is at once a temporal, cultural and ideological marker,[150] that describes the condition of the symbiotic rise of Hindutva and neoliberalism.[151] Beginning in the early 1990s—with the BJP's rise in national popularity and the consolidation of an upper-caste Hindu electorate that coincided with the liberalisation of the Indian economy—this condition combines the state's posturing as a champion of free-market economic policies, with an aggressive invocation of Hindu cultural conservatism that considers capitalist globalisation and Hindutva to be 'not only reconcilable but complementary'.[152] Instead of 'facilitating a moderation' of political movements driven by religious ideology, as has been the case in many other parts of the world, the embracing of neoliberalism has strengthened the Hindu Right.[153]

An instance of this is reflected in the findings of the Justice Rajinder Sachar Committee Report of 2005, which evidenced the widespread social, economic and educational disenfranchisement of Muslims across India.[154] The condition of Muslims today[155]—which has only worsened since Modi became the prime minister, with an alarming increase in hate crimes[156]— coexists with the celebratory projections of India's economic growth, military might and commitment to social and economic mobility captured appositely in the BJP slogans 'India Shining' and 'New India'.[157] Scholars have identified Gujarat 2002 to be paradigmatic of this condition.[158]

This book is particularly concerned with how the triangulated state-making and state-preserving rationalities of secularism (state regulation of religions in the language of freedom and tolerance),[159] legalism (strict constitutional adherence or constitutional foundationalism)[160] and developmentalism (state-organised political economy that weds socialism with neoliberalism in the service of growth)[161] have become part of the 'common sense'[162] of both the constitutional and popular imaginations of Indian democracy over the last 70 years. Court judgments and Bollywood cinema have been the two most publicly available memorial records of this New India in general, and of the Gujarat pogrom in particular. These two records have been previously researched separately, but not together.

Gujarat 2002 has led to the production of a vast body of literature that I have learned and borrowed from. This book is written in conversation with this body of literature and hopes to add its own insights from within the discipline of law.[163] The literature on which I have drawn has offered a powerful critique of the rise of Hindutva, its close affiliation with neoliberalism, how the combination of the two enabled the planning and execution of the pogrom, and how particularly the state of Gujarat served as the fertile ground for experimentation with the Hindutva vision of establishing a Hindu homeland, or *rashtra*, through the annihilation of the Muslim Other/outsider.

The disciplinary locations from where scholarly research on the pogrom has been carried out are anthropology,[164] sociology,[165] political science,[166] history,[167] media studies,[168] performance studies,[169] and marginally in law.[170] Alongside, there is a rich body of activist writings and journalism that has meticulously documented the violence of the pogrom, particularly its gendered and sexualised manifestations, the testimonies of victim-survivors and the arduous journey of justice-seeking processes in its aftermath.[171] Most of these studies place the event on a continuum with the history of both Hindutva ideology and anti-minority, particularly anti-Muslim, mass violence in independent India perpetrated by the Hindu Right.[172]

Law has been addressed in this literature broadly in three contexts: first, with regard to the struggles of the survivors for justice;[173] second, to highlight the failings of the criminal justice system;[174] and third, constitutional and human rights law standards have been used to challenge state impunity.[175] Law's role in this literature has been understood primarily as a remedial one, with the acknowledgement that it is the political and ideological dispensation of the government that determines the course that justice would take for victims of mass violence. That the legal process has been compromised, or has failed in responding adequately to mass violence, has been analysed to be an outcome of the Indian judiciary's structural limitations, particularly the anti-Muslim bias reflected both in the judiciary's composition and in practices of adjudication;[176] and also due to the lackadaisical workings of the police, either through fomenting violence through acts of commission and omission, or through faulty investigations.[177]

One abiding feature of this body of literature, especially works that engage with the law directly, has been the reiteration of faith in the constitutional values of secularism. There exists a very rich tradition of scholarly debates about secularism in India,[178] and in much of this literature there is a fair dose of suspicion about its avowed liberal virtues and Western antecedents,[179] even as some have tried to Indianise secularism.[180] The literature related to the Gujarat pogrom, or, for that matter, the literature related to issues of Hindu–Muslim violence in India, has tended to deploy constitutional secularism as a standard to argue against the politics of the Hindu Right.

Hindutva ideology has, from its formal inception in the 1920s,[181] considered India to be the holy land for Hindus and members of all other religions, especially Muslims, as a population of contaminants who need to either assimilate into Hindu ways of living or be ousted or annihilated.[182] With the BJP in power, the agenda to establish a Hindu *rashtra* has gained renewed vigour.[183] The founding 'fathers' of the movement have been influenced strongly by European fascism, with Adolf Hitler and Benito Mussolini being considered key figures of inspiration.[184] The contemporary Hindu Right is a dispersed group of outfits with an intellectual fountainhead in the organisation called the RSS.[185] The political consolidation of the Hindu Right as a parliamentary party in the BJP[186] has happened over a period of time due to a range of events, beginning notably with the 1947 Partition that created India and Pakistan as two sovereign dominions.[187] Once Pakistan established itself as an Islamic republic,[188] the Hindu Right expressed its discontent with M. K. Gandhi's opposition to forming India into a Hindu theocracy and one of their ideologues assassinated him.[189]

Since India's independence from Britain in 1947 (also the year of the Partition),[190] the other event cultivating a much stronger emergence of the Hindu Right was the constitutional Emergency, or president's rule, that was declared by the Indian National Congress (INC), or the Congress Party.[191] The Emergency lasted for 21 months through 1975–77, during which time an unprecedented political solidarity emerged between forces opposed to the INC, leading to the formation of the BJP in 1980, the Hindu Right's parliamentary force.[192] Since the Emergency, many other Hindu Right groups have emerged, including those that engage in parliamentary politics,[193] and

fringe non-formalised militant outfits.[194] Notable among these are regional
political parties like the Shiv Sena, and militant outfits like the Vishwa Hindu
Parishad and the Bajrang Dal. All of these groups consider themselves to be
a part of what they call the Sangh Parivar (the collective family of Hindutva
organisations).[195] The Sangh Parivar's popularity over the years has increased
due to its belligerent stand against Pakistan, particularly with regard to
nuclear bomb politics and India's constitutionally sanctioned military
occupation of Kashmir.[196]

Since the Hindu Right—through the BJP—has acquired nationwide
support and attained the formidable stature of a parliamentary party, its
position on constitutional secularism has become paradoxical. Currently, it
veers between rejecting constitutional secularism on the one hand[197] and
asserting Hindutva to be consistent with the Constitution on the other.[198]
The move towards the latter position offers justifications for a Hinduisation
of the idea of secularism. In this formulation, secularism is an intrinsic part of
Hindu religion, and thus Hinduism is in alignment with both the Constitution
and democracy.[199]

In developing and mainstreaming this argument, the Hindu Right has
found allies in Hindu liberals.[200] This tacit alliance of Hindu liberals and
conservatives argues in favour of establishing an ostensibly secular body of
family laws (to be based on codified Hindu laws) called the Uniform Civil
Code, which will deny constitutional validity to Muslim laws in the name of
saving the rights of Muslim women from Muslim men and their own
religion.[201] This alliance between liberal and conservative Hindus that
fortified the relationship between Hindutva and neoliberalism was a
moment in 1990 when affirmative action policies for non-Hindu 'other
backward classes' recommended by the Mandal Commission Report from a
decade earlier was implemented to increase the total reservations for
scheduled castes and tribes.[202] Upper-caste students, out of the imagined fear
of losing their caste privilege and the challenge that affirmative action posed
to caste hierarchy, touted this as marking the end of merit.[203] In time, this
led to a consolidation of the Hindu upper-caste electorate—against
emerging non-brahmin (Bahujan) political assertions[204]—which has been
the primary beneficiary and supporter of India's economic neoliberalisation
as well the intensification of Hindutva's secularised projections of Hindu
pride.[205] The Hindu Right's gradual appropriation of the idiom of
constitutional secularism received legal imprimatur in 1994 when its central

philosophy of Hindutva was characterised as a 'way of life' by the Supreme Court of India.[206]

My contribution to the legal literature on Gujarat 2002 is to offer a jurisprudential account that takes the Hindu Right's secular turn seriously.[207] This turn is illustratively captured in the Modi government's dual propositions of declaring the Constitution to be a holy book, and the Hindu holy book, the Bhagavad Gita, to be the 'national scripture'.[208] This turn, when it began, was accompanied by the consolidation of the Hindu upper-caste electorate in the wake of the implementation of the Mandal Commission recommendations in 1990, followed by India liberalising its markets in 1991 under pressure from the International Monetary Fund's structural adjustment programmes.[209] In 1992 came the demolition of the eighteenth-century Babri Mosque by Hindu militant mobs in Ayodhya to stake claim to a place that, according to the Hindu Right, was where the mythological Aryan-raced[210] Hindu warrior-god Ram was born.[211] In the legal disputes about the archaeological and historical accuracy of this claim,[212] the Indian judiciary, even while condemning the demolition of the mosque, has taken the side of Hindu mythology, effectively endowing a religious deity with legal personhood.[213] The demolition's aftermath saw widespread anti-Muslim violence in Bombay, whose main perpetrators are yet to be brought to justice.[214] These three temporal moments in Mandal, Markets and the Masjid—upper-caste Hindu electoral consolidation in 1990, economic liberalisation in 1991, and the Babri Mosque demolition in 1992 and its violent aftermath in Bombay, respectively— marked the beginnings of the Hindu Right's modern public persona, presented as one that seamlessly mixed neo-fascism with neoliberalism.[215]

This is where Gujarat 2002 gains significance, as a state that experimented with this mix, and executed it in a highly sophisticated way. The phenomenon of the Gujarat model of development that perfected the coming together of neoliberalism and Hindutva has also been documented and analysed in existing literature.[216] However, what impact this has had on the judiciary at both state and national levels, and in particular on the judiciary's response to Gujarat 2002, remains an area that offers scope for jurisprudential exploration. Given that the pogrom has been the most litigated of all events of anti-Muslim, or even anti-minority, mass violence in independent India, a focus on the judiciary's conduct gains special significance. This is more so because since the early 1990s, much like the Hindu Right, and connected to global trends, the Indian judiciary has also undergone a (neo)liberal turn reflected in many landmark judgments that bring together religious conservatism and free-market friendliness.[217]

Bollywood

The liberalisation of the Indian economy in 1991 also led to a drastic transformation in media and popular cultures.[218] This transformation was most palpable in the inauguration of 24/7 news media, cable television and the internationalisation of mainstream Hindi cinema or Bollywood.[219] These developments played a key role in the mainstreaming of a soft version of Hindutva ideology, presented as the celebration of a syncretic Indian culture that was secular in appearance and Hindu in sentiment, made palatable for the consumption of an emerging aspirational and liberal middle class, which included the Indian diaspora.[220]

India's state television, Doordarshan, had already begun the process of Hindu-ising the public and private spheres of Indian life through the production and broadcast of the dramatised versions of the Hindu epics Ramayana and Mahabharata through the early 1990s, coinciding with the demolition of the Babri Mosque and the national consolidation of the Hindu Right.[221] The new cable television channels began airing advertisements for multinational brands and producing soap operas celebrating Hindu tradition as modernist ethos.[222] Hindutva was being repackaged as rooted progressivism in popular culture, in contradistinction to representations of Islam as either fossilised or threatening.[223]

Bollywood cinema's reimagination of a New India that emerged after 1991 has played a particularly significant role in the naturalisation of a fused Hindutva and neoliberal ethos.[224] This ethos combined the progressivism of the developmental vision of a liberalising economy and an aggressive upper-caste Hindu nationalism in a syncretic and secular package.[225] The virtues of the rule of law in this cinematic imagination were embodied in hypermasculine figures such as the patriotic policeman or army officer, the aspirational entrepreneur, the rebellious lover who challenges authority but subscribes to patriarchy or the sacrificing and loyal wife in the joint Hindu family—all of which were deployed as secular tropes and plot devices that recovered and rehabilitated the Hindu foundations of the nation from degradation, decay and corruption.[226] An emerging trend in the task of advancing the fused narrative of Hindutva and neoliberalism in Bollywood cinema involves close relations between Bollywood actors and filmmakers with Narendra Modi, a direct involvement of the RSS with directors and produces, the work of certain actors in doing films that both subtlety and unabashedly tow the Hindutva line, superstars being spokespersons for Hindutva ideology in their public speeches and a growing fandom surrounding their ideological persona.[227]

Bollywood's legal universe is not restricted to the 'courtroom drama' genre in which law appears in its most obvious forms: lawyers, clients, litigants, accused, disputes, trials, judges and courts.[228] Although the courtroom, lawyers and judges have featured many times as part of films' diegetic narrative,[229] law as a normative idea of good has primarily inflected plots in the form of vigilante justice, moral conflicts, an end to suffering, the death or transformation of the villain or anti-hero, and as romantic/familial/patriotic love.[230]

In the two decades since the liberalisation of the Indian economy began in 1991, ideas of justice in Bollywood cinema have fetishised the secular rule of law and the entrepreneurial zeal as public virtues for the modern postcolonial nation-state.[231] However, even in this imagination, justice in Bollywood cinema does not come only from secular state law but also from *dharma*,[232] a juridico-moral ethic derived from Hindu scriptures that dictates the conduct of characters and frames the larger narratives that they are a part of.[233] On the occasions when any part of a film's plot—especially pertaining to issues around sex, religion and representations of the nation—goes against this juridico-moral ethic, such films inevitably end up being at the receiving end of both state and non-state forms of censorship.[234] Hindu right-wing political parties and its militant outfits have been especially active in deploying violence and have made use of the secular legal system and its laws on public decency, sedition and hate speech to censor such films (as well as works in other artistic genres).[235]

Political parties of all hues, buttressed by court orders, have time and again sought to regulate the spectatorial space of the cinema theatre in India as a location for demanding patriotic allegiance from audiences as a juridico-moral ethic of dutiful citizenship.[236] This has been done by making theatres play the Indian national anthem before the start of every film, thus making it de facto mandatory for all to stand up in reverence.[237] There have been several reported cases of audience members being abused and beaten for not standing up to honour the national anthem.[238]

It is for this reason that Bollywood as a genre and an industry has traditionally steered clear of developing stories on issues of an overtly political nature.[239] Doing that has been the domain of the independent feature and documentary film movements.[240] However, since the Bollywood aesthetic is potent in sentimentality,[241] melodrama[242] and music,[243] myriad films have been made about political events of mass suffering, such as the 1947 Partition; or, the Partition as a trope—where brothers get separated in childhood and get reunited in adulthood—has been deployed in stories that apparently make no references to the event itself. [244]

With the advent of 24/7 news media backed by private capital, infotainment has emerged as a particular narrative form.[245] In this genre, news channels use Bollywood background scores that appeal to the affective mood that the incident being reported is meant to create. At the same time, Bollywood cinema borrows the docu-drama model in making films that tell stories about contemporary political events as fiction.[246] In presenting a fictional narrative about politically charged events, such films defend themselves from the ire of the Hindu Right by using a standard opening disclaimer: that resemblance to any event, or persons living or dead, is purely coincidental.[247] From the filmmakers' point of view, these disclaimers also serve the purpose of insulating them from defamation and other anti-free speech suits for hurting popular sentiments.[248]

In the case of Gujarat 2002, a number of films—both feature and documentary—have been made over the decade following the pogrom. All these films have by and large taken a critical view of the violence. Regardless of their degrees of criticality, both feature and documentary films have been at the receiving end of legal and extra-legal censorship.[249] However, with regard to the Bollywood feature films on the Gujarat pogrom, as this book will show, the more fictional the account has claimed to be, the less the incidence of censorship has been.

Film studies scholarship on India is extremely sophisticated, and this body of work has produced critical accounts of film ideology and its interactions with secularism and nationalism, including cultures of censorship and spectatorship.[250] However, despite the fact that the Bollywood films on the pogrom constitute a key cinematic archive of collective memory, a scholarly study of the cinema of Gujarat 2002 is yet to be done.[251] *Ways of Remembering* studies three of the most popular (and controversial) of these films, which provide rich material for understanding how popular culture has been memorialising the pogrom, but also offer insights into cinematic imaginations of law and justice in contemporary India. This imagination is not restricted only to the way law is represented in these films but also includes the allusions, allegories and affects that cinema as a form of storytelling engenders. Legal scholarship in India has not yet extended serious thought to engaging with cinema and film studies. This book hopes to make a contribution in that area.

Collective Memory

Ways of Remembering, thus, brings a close study of the judgments of a landmark post-pogrom criminal trial into conversation with three major post-pogrom Bollywood films. The place where this meeting of the legal and the cinematic narratives take place is in the realm of collective memory. Collective memory provides a useful interface for a productive conversation between law and cinema, to address the overlaps between how their content, form and technique record memories of the pogrom.[252] For example, the rule of precedent is a memorial technique of adjudication in the common law, which can be compared to the use of narrative tropes in cinema: both cite their prior iteration as a way of justifying recurrence. Similarly, witness testimonies in a trial are akin to the use of flashbacks in a film: the unseen is made visible through the device of storytelling to aid in adjudication and narrative cohesion. While filmic and literary works on collective memory have featured centrally in feminist oral-history accounts of the 1947 Partition,[253] and in anthropological work on post-independence events of mass violence like the 1984 anti-Sikh violence,[254] and the 1992 anti-Muslim violence in Bombay,[255] Gujarat 2002 has not yet been studied using the analytic of collective memory.[256] This is the case in both film studies and law. Although scholarship on film and (mass) violence in India has engaged the question of memory,[257] Indian legal scholarship has rarely studied mass violence in the context of either film or memory.[258]

Collective memory—a term originally coined by sociologist Émile Durkheim, and subsequently developed by his student Maurice Halbwachs—is a mode of active remembering that is only possible to produce in groups, not individually. As Halbwachs notes in his classic work *On Collective Memory*: 'It is in society that people normally acquire their memories. It is also in society that they recall, recognise, and localise their memories.'[259] Within group formations, collective memory is not only generated through commemorative interactions between group members but also draws on publicly available material like cinema and judgments. Group interactions with these materials that record the history of violence happen at public locations like a cinema theatre or a courthouse, or through the publics that they mobilise. These continuous interactions in the present unsettle any possibility of collective memory becoming ossified, thus making it 'the *active past* that forms our identities'.[260]

In the context of the Gujarat pogrom, both law and cinema are publicly available material that are in continuous engagement with an active past: one whose meanings and truths are being revealed and regenerated through the ongoing investigations, trials, political rhetoric and aesthetic memorialisations. Legal and filmic reconstructions of the pogrom are archives that both lend to and derive meaning from their collective public reception and response.

In this book, collective memory is not an empirical claim about how the Gujarat pogrom is remembered in the New India. It is a metaphor which offers the possibility of thinking about Gujarat 2002 as it is remembered through both the factual and fictional narratives of judgments and films. The idea of the collective here is much like Benedict Anderson's description of how the 'imagined community' of the nation gained 'profound emotional legitimacy', facilitated by 'print-capitalism' under colonialism.[261] In a similar vein, this book will show that there is a national collective that the judgments and the films mobilise, and it is the shared public address of law and cinema that engenders particular ways of remembering the pogrom for this collective.

The texts of the trial judgments and the texts of the films are widely available and accessible as collective memorial records of the Gujarat pogrom. As such, through their 'address', the judgments and the films mobilise their national 'publics'.[262] These publics are formed through an 'assemblage' of the legal and cinematic narratives on the pogrom.[263] This assemblage is where collective memories of the pogrom are continuously being made and ordered.

Traditionally, one would consider the legal record in judgments to be factual accounts and the cinematic record as a fictional one. However, the lines between fact and fiction get blurred when we train ourselves to look at law and aesthetics not as Manichean categories but as porous and symbiotic ones.[264] When seen in this way, through the J-A approach that this book will develop, the judgments and the films can be understood as part of a shared narrative that engenders particular ways of remembering the pogrom. As my J-A reading demonstrates, the judgments and the films, even as they address their publics from a putatively secular location that condemns the pogrom in no uncertain terms, they simultaneously normalise, through their shared narrative, the very rationalities—secularism, legalism and developmentalism—that offer justifications for the pogrom's execution and order its memorial aftermath.

The Book Itself

The title of the book alludes to the work of British Marxist writer and critic John Berger's 1972 work *Ways of Seeing*, in which he wrote: 'The way we see things is affected by what we know or what we believe.'[265] *Ways of Remembering*, thus, aims to demonstrate that there is no incontestable memory of the Gujarat pogrom. What constitute collective memories of the pogrom are contestations between different ways of remembering, rather than a contest between memory and forgetting. These ways of remembering, as I will show, are affected by the state-making and state-preserving rationalisations implicit in the shared narrative of the judgments and films. What is collectively remembered—as knowledge and belief—about Gujarat 2002 is produced by a narrative through which judgments and films mobilise their national publics.

Chapter 2, 'A Jurisprudential-Aesthetic Approach', offers a description of my theoretical orientation. Here, I situate my J-A lens in the scholarship on which I have drawn and explain how it offers a novel way to read the judgments and films relating to Gujarat 2002. In this chapter, I will also describe the salient features of the politics and aesthetics of the Bollywood genre and locate my account of the pogrom in cinematic narratives of justice more broadly.

Chapters 3 and 4 form the crux of the book. Chapter 3, 'The Best Bakery Judgments: Aesthetics of Judicial Memory', focuses on a reading of a landmark post-pogrom criminal trial that ran from 2003 to 2012, heard across the full hierarchy of the Indian judiciary. In this chapter, I offer a close reading of the texts of the four judgments related to the Best Bakery case and then apply the J-A approach to read the judgments as records of collective memory. The chapter considers the aesthetic form in the judgments that engenders collective memories. By describing the life-worlds of the case, I show how an encounter between law and aesthetics shapes a particular way of remembering the pogrom. This way of remembering masks the role that secular law played in enabling the pogrom by positing the rationality of secular law and the irrationality of religious violence as oppositional. The judgments ultimately tell a story in which secular law saves the New India from religious violence.

Chapter 4, 'Bollywood's Law: Cinematic Justice and Collective Memory', reads three well-known Bollywood films on the pogrom—*Dev* (2004), *Parzania* (2007) and *Kai Po Che* (2013)—that were released through the post-pogrom decade when the Best Bakery case was in the courts. My J-A reading of the three films shows how the plots, narrative tropes and cinematic techniques of the films tell a story of the pogrom that simultaneously condemns and rationalises the event. As I will show, the films offer imaginations of cinematic justice (by remaining faithful to the Constitution of India and the juridico-moral ethic of *dharma*) through their representative and affective addresses that acknowledge the horror of the pogrom, while aligning with the state-making and state-preserving rationality of the New India. The films, thus, order collective memories of the pogrom to generate ways of remembering that condemn the visible violence of religious sectarianism, and at the same time they keep the deep-seated structural and ideological violence of the putative secular Indian nation-state against its Muslim minorities intact.

I conclude the book by outlining an important way of remembering the pogrom that has emerged through my J-A reading of the judgments and films. This way of remembering is unique to secular law's role in state-making and state-preserving practices in the New India. My readings will show that there is a particular kind of governmental rationality at work that valorises accelerated legalism and developmentalism as primary markers of secular constitutionalism. Such a rationality is simultaneously accompanied by a conjuncture of violence and violation against minority groups, which remains implicitly tied to the Indian state's secular performances and enactments of legalism. In this way of remembering, the pogrom becomes paradigmatic of an emerging alliance between the state that is working to preserve itself against an imagined threat by the Muslim 'outsider' and the responsibilised selves of secular Hindu citizens who perform this rationality, drawing authority from the secular law's promises of justice and development.

2 A Jurisprudential-Aesthetic Approach

Law tells stories, just as stories are told about law.[1]

This book studies two narratives of collective memory of the 2002 anti-Muslim pogrom in Gujarat from a law in/as aesthetics perspective. The first is written into the texts of the judgments of the Best Bakery case, a key criminal trial related to the pogrom, and the second is captured in the images and sounds of three Bollywood films that make the pogrom central to their plots. I have developed the jurisprudential-aesthetic (J-A) approach as a lens for reading the texts of the judgments and films not as discrete narratives but as a shared one. My J-A reading will show that collective memories of the pogrom are shaped by the workings of a postcolonial state-making and state-preserving rationality.

This chapter describes the J-A lens as a critical legal approach to interpret my material.[2] To discuss how I constitute the J-A approach, first, I explain why it is necessary to understand law's aesthetic dimensions as a minor jurisprudence. Second, I argue in favour of considering this minor jurisprudence of law and aesthetics as a narrative compact. Third, I animate the workings of the narrative compact as law *in* aesthetics and law *as* aesthetics. This chapter shows how law permeates cinema's imagination and how the J-A approach becomes necessary for an appreciation of cinema's lawscape. To do this, I indicate the key concerns that a study of law in/as cinema addresses, connect law in/as cinema scholarship and Indian film studies to describe the aesthetic specificities of the Bollywood genre and discuss what work the J-A approach will do to show how law and justice feature in Bollywood's cinematic imagination.

Constituting the J-A Approach

Law and cinema are, arguably, the two most publicly available records of collective memory of Gujarat 2002. The pogrom has been one of postcolonial India's most litigated events of mass violence, and by far the most mediatised of all anti-minority religious conflagrations. The Best Bakery case—whose judgments are the focus of Chapter 3—attracted huge media attention as the first high-profile trial related to the pogrom. The three Bollywood films (which I study in Chapter 4) released across theatres all over India are now available on DVD, have been broadcast on television and are streaming on online platforms. The public reach of both these records of the pogrom have, thus, continued to significantly shape collective memory. The judgments and films, when read together, offer a concentrated insight into the way the written judgments of the trials and the release of the films engender ways of remembering the pogrom, including the imaginations of justice that have accompanied these practices of collective memory making.

Minor Jurisprudence

To understand law from both inside and outside its conventional locations of the courts and their judgments, I will draw out the aesthetic dimensions in the judgments and the jurisprudential dimensions in the films. The imperative for doing so is to move away from the binary of the internal/external approaches in legal scholarship. While the internalists 'theorise the process of argumentation and reasoning used in institutional discourse', the externalists 'treat reasons, arguments and justifications as "facts" to be incorporated in wider non-legal explanatory contexts'.[3] For internalists like the legal positivists, the 'point of view of the judge or lawyer' is of primary significance, while externalists like scholars of sociology of law would develop critiques as 'corrective to the excessive formalism of [major] jurisprudence'.[4] Instead of pitting the internal and the external as oppositional,[5] I develop an approach that considers both the conventional inside and the outside of law to be inflected by aesthetics—an intensity that appeals to the senses. Thus, the texts of both the judgments and the films will be considered on par as (minor) jurisprudential knowledge.

    One way to explain my proposition is through a reference to Franz Kafka's parable 'Before the Law' from his novel *The Trial*.[6] In this well-known parable,[7] a villager ('man from the country') approaches the gate of law, which is guarded by a gatekeeper who decides who gets to enter the law and who does not.[8] A plain reading of the parable, independent of the larger work, might suggest that the story is about how inaccessible the law is to ordinary people who, in the hope of gaining access, spend a lifetime and eventually die at law's gate, never being granted the promised entry. In the parable's imagination, the law's authority both keeps the villager out and at the same time induces a desire for knowing or accessing the law. The gate of (positive) law protects the legal from the non-legal, which is traditionally considered to be the realm of morality and politics. 'This distinction between the inside and outside', writes Margaret Davies, 'is one which is absolutely fundamental to law', but 'as much as lawyers attempt to exclude an outside, it is always there *in* the law'.[9]

I understand both sides of the gate, including the villager, the gatekeeper and the gate itself as part of what Andreas Philippopoulos-Mihalopoulos calls a 'lawscape': '… so thick with law that, just like air, the law is not perceived…. It becomes an *atmosphere*—there but not there, imperceptible yet all-determining.'[10] The inside and outside can be said to be held together by the technology of jurisdiction,[11] which is exemplified by the gate and its keeper. The mise en scène of the parable—the gate, the gatekeeper, the villager, and the inside and outside of the law on either side of the gate—is part of this lawscape. The internal and external divide thus becomes permeable.

In Kafka's parable, when you are before the law, law is both a fear-inducing and a seductive enigma. The gate to the law is always open, we are scared of what is inside, we are always eager to look through the gate and yet we do not know what is on the inside. When the villager steals a moment to see through the gate, the gatekeeper says, 'If it tempts you so much, try it in spite of my prohibition. But take note: I am powerful. And I am only the most lowly gatekeeper. But from room to room stand gatekeepers, each more powerful than the other. I can't endure even one glimpse of the third.'[12] I would like to reimagine the gate not as the divider between the inside and outside of law but rather as the conduit that joins different laws in a lawscape. If we are to go by what the gatekeeper says, as we pass through this gate, there will be other jurisdictional encounters with other laws.[13] What we need to 'take note' of is what happens to the way in which we understand a law at the point of these encounters with other laws.

For my purposes, 'before the law', thus, does not signify a teleological prior but a temporal in-front. Similarly, 'after the law' would not mean what comes after we have passed by the law but what other laws we meet when we have crossed the gate of a law. I am interested in both the jurisprudence of positive law—the law read in the texts of judgments—and cinema's lawscape—the visual texts of the Bollywood films—that we encounter outside of the courtroom. The positive law of the state, which is in front of us, speaks to the gatekeeping rhetoric that has traditionally been the task of (major) jurisprudence to maintain the epistemic autonomy of legal knowledge from its non-legal outsides.[14]

Aesthetics, particularly cinema, thus enters this story not as an outside of state law but as Peter Goodrich's version of a 'minor jurisprudence'[15] that challenges 'the dominance of any singular system of legal norms' and 'neither aspires nor pretends to be the only law or universal jurisprudence'.[16] In crossing through the gate of positive law—as embodied in the texts of the judgments—we encounter another law, the minor jurisprudences that are embedded in the judgment form, and those captured in the sounds and images of cinema. These textual and cinematic minor jurisprudences of the Gujarat pogrom can also be characterised as 'microjurisprudences'—that one needs to zoom in close to see—which can create alternative imaginations of justice that challenge the knowledge hegemony of 'normal (positive) law'.[17]

In keeping with the orientation of this book, I do not treat 'minor' as the opposite of 'major', or in the sense of 'lesser'. Minor jurisprudence, for me, foregrounds the possibility of a miscegenation of laws that do not work with a foundational law of normative authority like Hans Kelsen's 'Grundnorm'[18] and H. L. A. Hart's 'Rule of Recognition',[19] or even like Lon Fuller's understanding of law with a self-referential 'inner morality'.[20] I also do not think of minor jurisprudence as equivalent to legal pluralism.[21] I use the concept to talk not about a diversity of legal imaginations but about how law needs to be understood as an assemblage. This assemblage is a lawscape that Deleuze and Guattari have called (in the context of Kafka's writing) 'the machine of justice'.[22] Every gate and room of law that we pass through, every minor jurisprudence that we encounter—in this case, cinema and the aesthetics of judgments—forms a part of this machine. A recognition of law as an assemblage of minor jurisprudences is a way to reimagine the relationship between law and aesthetics as co-constitutive, rather than considering aesthetics to be outside the gate of major (positivist) jurisprudence.[23]

Yet my aim is not to valorise minor jurisprudence in my archive of judgments and films as a romantic category of resistance to hegemonic state law. Creating a hierarchy between law and aesthetics defeats the very aim of thinking about their conjoined habitus in the making and ordering of collective memory. Rather, my account of minor jurisprudence is a story of complicities—between law and aesthetics, their inflections, seepages, contaminations and epistemic instabilities. Borrowing an expression from film studies, this can be called the 'narrative compact'[24] between law and aesthetics.

'Narrative Compact'

Central to the J-A approach is interpreting the texts of the judgments and the films as a narrative compact that will be seen both within the two genres and across them. This will be done by specifically attending to three elements in the form of the texts: record, judgment/image and mnemohistory. Here, I briefly explain how these elements will feature in my J-A reading of the judgments and films.

As Peter Goodrich has written, 'the common law has historically presented itself as a system of memories', which draws legitimacy from precedent.[25] Precedents are records of law that have been archived, or 'filed', to enable retrieval after the event.[26] Recording is a technology that applies to the filing or archiving of the texts of judgments pronounced in the court of law, as well as to the storing of (moving) images on a camera. It can also be considered as a form of remembering—actively or subconsciously[27]—the legal-event[28] and the media-event.[29] The pogrom is a legal-event—both in terms of its highly litigated aftermath, and the national and international legal precedents that have been used to characterise it as a riot or genocide. As a media-event, the widespread coverage of the pogrom made Gujarat 2002 the first event of mass violence in postcolonial India to be reported on 24/7 news channels.[30] These recorded images, along with the facts and description of specific incidents of violence in the legal record, have later become templates for art direction and screenplay writing in Bollywood cinema's fictional accounts of the event. As explained, this book will lend equal jurisprudential value to the judgments and the films. This will be done not only because cinema is the repository of popular cultural representations and imaginations of law and justice[31] but also because of the role that the narrative compact of law and cinema plays in the shaping and ordering of collective memories of mass violence.[32]

Judgments and images are mirrored categories of records that form the fulcrum of the narrative compact of law and aesthetics that keeps them in balance. This fulcrum can be considered as the meeting point of law and aesthetics—at the gate of law. It is this encounter that invites evaluations that either distinguish law from aesthetics or consider them as co-constitutive. The J-A approach treats this encounter as a narrative compact which allows a reading of this productive tension between the imagistic tropes in the written text of the trial judgments and looks at how images (and sounds) in the films mobilise spectatorial judgment about the pogrom. In so doing, I show how the narrative compact of the judgments and the films shapes collective memory, which 'is concerned not with the past as such, but only with the past as it is remembered'.[33] This is what Jan Assman calls 'mnemohistory': 'the ongoing work of reconstructive imagination' where 'the past cannot be stored but always has to be "processed" and mediated'.[34]

The Best Bakery judgments and the Bollywood films form the lawscapes of collective memory that I consider to be mnemohistorical in nature. Together, the narrative compact of the judgments and the films, as they continuously mobilise their publics—through images of law and the aesthetics of images—are engaged in contestations and convergences about the ways in which the stories of the pogrom are actively reconstructed and remembered.

Law in/as Aesthetics

The imperative for analysing the collective memories of Gujarat 2002 as produced by a narrative compact between law and cinema lies in my characterisation of the event as a 'pogrom', instead of a 'riot' or 'genocide'. While all three words are overlapping categories that describe forms of collective or mass violence, in the specificities of their methods and objectives they can be differentiated. A riot is spontaneous violence provoked by a situation or an event which is not pre-planned. It may or may not target a specific group. A genocide is a planned offensive that has the clear aim of eliminating an identifiable racial group or tribe, which may or may not have been aided by the state.[35] While the violence of Gujarat 2002 carried aspects of both, it is most appropriately described as a pogrom, which is planned, aimed at destroying an identifiable group of people and their properties, and aided by the state through acts of omission and commission.

In the particular context of Gujarat 2002, Parvis Ghassem-Fachandi notes: 'A pogrom is driven by words and images as much as by the associations and invocations that accompany it. The enactment of the Gujarat pogrom followed a script collectively shared on the streets and in media representations.'[36] In his detailed ethnographic study of the 2002 violence, Ghassem-Fachandi observes that the pogrom was an enactment of an 'imaginary script' of Hindu disgust and hatred towards the Muslim that was already being performed in Gujarat much before the actual violence began on 28 February 2002. This script was a 'symbolic repository to imagine [and enact] violence' against Muslims, continuously animated in aesthetic products like print news, photographs and a mainstream Hindi feature film.[37] Thus, in the case of a pogrom, the role of prior aesthetic propaganda using images and words by state and private actors to foment hatred against a particular community is fundamental.

Ghassem-Fachandi's analysis does not engage the law. Yet the law, as matter and metaphor, is a major collaborator in the imaginary script that provided a rationale for the enactment of violence. Law has a significant presence in the way the reconstructions of Gujarat 2002 have been framed in the images of Bollywood cinema. For this reason, it is necessary that law is understood as a discursive category that is not restricted to the written word in legislations and judgments in its shaping of collective memory. Rather, the idea of law needs to be 'made supple' by an imaginative engagement with the visual dimensions of justice both inside and outside these conventional sources.[38]

Historically, law and image have shared 'a troubled relationship'.[39] Cornelia Vismann identifies jurists as those who are most uncomfortable with images: 'After all, they are expected to establish order, a mission they see frequently challenged by the ambiguity of images.'[40] As Peter Goodrich observes, 'Law ... is a text that negates its images and denies the figurations of fluidity in its texts.'[41] The image, or the realm of the aesthetic, as Costas Douzinas and Lynda Nead argue, 'is the antithesis of law'.[42] Commenting on the 'aesthetic question' in law, they write: 'Modern law is born in its separation from aesthetic considerations and the aspirations of literature and art, and a wall is built between the two sides.... Art is assigned to imagination, creativity and playfulness, law to control discipline and sobriety.'[43]

Despite these attempts, the law cannot keep the aesthetic outside of its gate. As Desmond Manderson insists, the aesthetics in law is 'everywhere' in its material constructions and metaphoric imaginations.[44] If the task of jurisprudence is to 'obsessively address' the question as to what law is and thereby 'uncover' and 'pronounc[e]' the truth about it,[45] a jurisprudent cannot not take the aesthetic seriously. To engage in an analysis of law in the age of 'visuality'[46] means to think of law beyond its documents and written words, to open up to the image and imaginaries of law, and its myriad forms of aesthetic transmission. According to Goodrich, 'The law of print, the law of black and white spaces, has collapsed. It is time to move on and consider seriously the spectacular character of the legal enterprise and the mediated character of the transmission of law.'[47]

The J-A approach, then, takes the aesthetic seriously. To take the aesthetic seriously, as Robin West remarks, we need to recognise that 'because legal theories are in part a product of our literary [or filmic, photographic, televisual and digitised] imagination, they must be read and understood, in part, as art'.[48] Peter Rush and Andrew Kenyon identify these aesthetic forms and modes that archive and transmit law's imaginations—'the textual, the imagistic and the affective'—as the 'alter-egos of law'.[49] The study of these alter-egos in all their complexity forms a part of what Manderson calls '[l]egal aesthetics', an approach in jurisprudential scholarship which acknowledges that 'the discourse of law is fundamentally governed by rhetoric, metaphor, form, images and symbols'.[50] In his view, 'aesthetic dimensions … lie at the heart of law and justice. Aesthetics is the faculty which reacts to images and sensory input to which we are constantly exposed, and which, by their symbolic associations, significantly influence our values and our society.'[51] Law inhabits the aesthetic archive in both representative and affective forms.

The J-A approach enables me to read law's alter-egos in the texts of judgments and films by attending to law *in* and *as* aesthetics.[52] By *law in aesthetics*, I mean the images and imagination of law in texts conventionally considered to be non-legal, like film. By *law as aesthetics*, I mean law's aesthetic dimensions within its conventional texts like judgments. I understand aesthetics to mean two things: first, feelings—'meanings and values as they are actively lived'[53]—that the conscious activities of reading, seeing, listening and smelling generate; and second, the affective intensities that are provoked in the way our bodies interact with the textual, the visual, the aural, the haptic and the olfactory.[54] The first meaning is concerned with identifiable representations of law and the second with sensory invocations of law, even when law does not appear in its conventional forms.[55]

In conceptually understanding law's presence in visual culture, Richard Sherwin writes:

> If law is to be treated as part of contemporary visual culture, and of that need there be no doubt, it is not enough to consider the way in which law partakes in various aesthetic, cognitive and cultural codes that different visual media deploy. Law also shares in the various normative aspirations and afflictions that are bound up in the culture at large. For this reason, we must also be attentive to *cultural conditions.*[56]

Cinema in general, and Bollywood cinema in particular—with its massive popular appeal, commercial success and ideological impact[57]—is a cultural condition which plays a productive host (or an inviting gatekeeper, rather than a fear-inducing one) to the encounter between the minor jurisprudences of law and aesthetics.

The J-A approach, as I have discussed in this section, is an interpretive tool that considers texts as a narrative compact between the minor jurisprudences of law and aesthetics. The approach orients my reading of the judgments and the films to specifically look for law *in* and *as* aesthetics. I will now focus specifically on the lawscape of cinema as a subcategory of law in/ as aesthetics scholarship and introduce some key particularities of Bollywood aesthetics that my J-A lens will engage.

Cinema's Lawscape

Law in/as Cinema

The J-A reading seeks to avoid two standard approaches in law and film scholarship. It seeks, first, to not 'reduce film to a resource for specific legal issues, points or questions' and, second, to not let 'each medium retreat … to its own corner relatively unscathed and looking pretty much as it had before the encounter'.[58] In other words, the J-A approach combines conventional representational analysis of films, with reading film in what has been called the 'affective register':[59] one which attends to how the techniques of the film form make film watching a tactile activity. This is because a film impacts our spectatorial experience beyond the plot. The impact is also kinaesthetic, due to, for example, a film's colours, darkness, sounds, silences, atmospherics, editing techniques, camera angles, location of viewing.[60] The three Bollywood films, thus, will be read for both the stories of the pogrom that they tell and the intensity they generate through their affective dimensions.[61]

By reading in the affective register, the J-A approach enables an appreciation of how the experience of watching the moving images of the cinematic narrative of the pogrom is similar and/or distinct from reading a narrative of written words in the text of the judgments. In doing this, I do not mean to suggest that the image and the word are incommensurable categories. Rather, the word and the image are read as both scripts and visuals.[62] Such a reading might also be described as 'intertextual jurisprudence' that reads the texts of judgments and films as a narrative compact that 'recontextualise[s] jurisprudence from the specialist to the generalist interpretive community' in which collective memory is shaped.[63] This shift is in keeping with a broader direction, as mentioned in Chapter 1, in which legal scholarship is moving from a restricted to a 'general jurisprudence'.[64]

Another motivation behind legal scholarship's ongoing engagement with the aesthetic archive of cinema lies in the understanding that the 'moving image provides a domain in which legal power operates independently of law's formal institutions'.[65] The operation of legal power within the texts of cinema is not restricted to the genre of the courtroom drama alone. Films which are not specifically about the legal process and its identifiable actors and symbols, as Richard Sherwin notes, 'may provide insights into analytical methods, social values, and community aspirations that lie at the heart of the legal mind and culture'.[66] Law and film also share a relationship in which they use their distinctive and discursive narrative styles to make powerful symbolic gestures towards the ideas of witnessing and truth-telling. According to Jessica Silbey:

> The affinity of law and film lies in their mutual manufacture of truth through strategies of representation and storytelling and also in the power of these truth claims to structure and regulate social relations. Film, no less than law, changes our perceptions of reality; it shapes our understanding of the world. The power of both film and law derives at first from the intensity of the personal faith in believing what we see (*bearing witness and judging based on the act of witnessing*).[67]

This relationship between law and film opens up the space of affective reception such that the act of embodied witnessing and the responsibility of judging coalesce in the spectator. Attending to this relationship can offer 'an alternative view of legality, one every bit as likely to undermine ruling ideas about fairness and formal legal equality as to reinforce them'.[68] This is how, for Alison Young, 'cinema is jurisprudence'.[69]

The aforementioned double play that simultaneously undermines and reinforces imaginaries of justice is what the interpretive work of the J-A approach achieves in its reading of the judgments and the films. The J-A approach enables us to pay attention to the aesthetic dimensions of formal legal texts such as judgments, as well as the jurisprudential dimensions of a conventionally aesthetic text such as film. The approach considers the representative and affective work that such public records are doing together, in making and ordering collective memories of the pogrom. The J-A reading shows that, despite their difference in narrative form, at work in the texts of both the judgments and the films are tropes—images, figures, symbols—that become 'the constitutive and performative dimension of law's contexts'.[70] Paying attention to them makes visible the particular kind of governmental rationality at work which shapes and orders collective memories of the pogrom.

It is necessary to mention here that in my J-A reading, I privilege the visual over the acoustic and the acoustic over the haptic. Films, of course, have a major acoustic dimension, and I make some allusions to that in my reading in Chapter 4. The judgments also contain metaphorical references to the acoustic that I will point out in Chapter 3. Both the written text and the visual text do have haptic dimensions as well—we touch the paper that we are reading, or the bass of the music touches us when watching a film; similarly, law, in the form of handcuffs, or the administration of lie detector tests, can touch us when apprehended for a crime. However, what compellingly brings the texts of the judgments and the films together for me is the primary medium of their public circulation and reception—which is visual.

Law in the Bollywood Aesthetic

Since 2002, a number of Bollywood films have been made that have used the Gujarat pogrom as central to their plots, or as a key historical and dramatic peg in the narrative. I focus on the three most notable of these films[71]—*Dev* (2004), *Parzania* (2007) and *Kai Po Che* (2013).[72] These films do not conventionally fit the courtroom drama genre, but law can still be read into the tropes that are deployed in their narrativisation of the pogrom. In the forms of storytelling that each of the films uses, memory features both in terms of the text of the films as a memorial record and through cinematic devices—like flashbacks or diegetic/non-diegetic sounds—in assembling the reconstructions of the pogrom.

The three films are a part of the commercial Hindi cinema of Bombay, popularly known as Bollywood.[73] According to Ashish Rajadhakshya, contemporary Indian cinema has undergone 'Bollywoodization' with the liberalisation of the Indian economy: it has been turned into a 'culture industry' that is constantly 'being created and marketed' as an aesthetic genre, industrial product and economic practice.[74] In its culture industry avatar, Bollywood cinema occupies an extremely significant place in India's cultural, political and public life, and, in the wake of Bollywoodisation, in its transnational economic lives.[75]

M. Madhava Prasad has called Indian cinema 'a site of ideological production ... as the (re)production of the state form'.[76] Bollywoodisation has entrenched this further, with the emergence of 'techno-nationalism' as '*the* Bollywood thematic'.[77] This thematic proffers 'a discourse of love and a discourse of law—the two fundamental registers of universality'[78]—that have made Bollywood cinema 'indispensable to the State'.[79] It has made the film industry win 'for itself, a distinct, even unique, space for spectatorial address and spectatorial attention that even today is not shared by any of its other ancillary industries [like] ... television'.[80]

Bollywood's spectatorial affects, both inside and outside the theatrical space, and across geographical locations, are sutured through the cinema's address that produces publics of cinematic citizens,[81] where the 'ticket-buying [or DVD-buying] spectator assumes certain rights' like that of 'the right to enter a movie theatre, to act as its privileged addressee'.[82] As a community of cinematic citizens, 'spectators were, and continue to be, symbolically and narratively, aware of these rights, aware of their political underpinnings, and do various things ... that constitute the famous "active" and vocal Indian film spectator'.[83] 'The spectator is invited to be out there', writes Ravi S. Vasudevan, 'in that imaginary domain of the cinema, and to constitute a public not only as addressee and audience but *as imaginary component of the fictional field*'.[84] By virtue of this status, the cinematic citizen carries the authority to pass judgment on a film's form, content and context.

The three Bollywood films on the Gujarat pogrom, in bearing surrogate witness to an event of mass atrocity, contribute to a 'mythopoesis of a particular national imaginary'[85] by offering distinct ways of remembering the

Gujarat pogrom. These ways of remembering exemplify the role secular law plays in generating aesthetic imaginations of justice. The films offer a rich record of popular sentiments that weave fictional reconstructions of violence with realist narratives of the everyday and ordinary that Bollywood's publics of cinematic citizens can connect with at the level of the quotidian and not the exceptional.[86] The use of music and songs, typical of the Bollywood genre, adds texture to the fictional narrative that enhances their affective appeal, especially in the conjuring of a 'national imaginary' in the New India.[87]

From 1991, when the Indian economy began liberalisation and privatisation, Bollywood's form, content, reach and consumption started appealing to an audience that cut across class, caste, religion, gender and national barriers. What was once, in the words of Ashis Nandy, 'a slum's eye view of politics' changed to a *haute bourgeoisie* view of politics.[88] In post-liberalisation Bollywood, there does not remain an older 'binary opposition between a "low", popular, resistant Hindi cinema and a hegemonic "high" literary culture in India'.[89]

What gives Bollywood cinema such wide-ranging appeal is what Ranjani Mazumdar refers to as its 'techno-folk form'—like Rajadhyaksha's 'techno-nationalism' mentioned before—which is achieved '[by] combin[ing] folk traditions with new cinematic technology [that offers an] unabashedly hybrid cultural form that narrates the complicated intersection between tradition and modernity in contemporary India'.[90] This hybridity is sustained by invoking symbols of developmentalist desire on the one hand—democracy, rule of law, wealth, the market, glitz, fashion, technology, urbanity, exotic foreign locales, the good life—and by appealing to mythopoetic tropes of secular relationality in the family, community and, most importantly, the nation.

The complicated intersection between developmentalist desires and tropes of relationality does not always happen through neat categorisations of the former as markers of modernity and the latter as tradition. This is particularly the nature of a postcolonial political economy, where the lines between the state (politics), market (economy) and nation (culture) are increasingly blurred.[91]

Bollywood primarily produces privately funded cinema, so while the films can be said to have deep investments in a nationalist ethos, until recently they did not have a direct connection with promoting state propaganda.[92] Yet, as filmmaker Saeed Akhtar Mirza has sharply noted, '[a] certain kind of cinema exists only because a certain kind of state exists'.[93] M. Madhava Prasad considers 'cinema as an institution that is part of the continuing struggles within India over the form of the state'.[94] Although written in 1998, within a few years of India liberalising its economy, Prasad's observations still carry trenchant currency:

> Cultural production too registers this reality through the recurring allegorical dimension of the dominant textual form in the popular cinema.... What the allegorical dimension of texts represents is the continuing necessity to conceive the state form which will serve as the ground for cultural signification. Through the allegorical scaffolding, texts register the instability of their ground of practice and signification, as well as the continuing possibility of struggles *over* the state, of struggles to reconstitute the state.[95]

The most potent site for contests over allegories of the state form is cinema in general, and Bollywood cinema in particular. In the New India, the state and the nation merge seamlessly as a dominant allegorical trope in this kind of cinema, which, as many have claimed, has historically been 'an exemplar of secularism' with 'Islamicate roots'.[96] As Jyotika Virdi writes in her analysis of representations of the 'nation' in mainstream Indian cinema:

> Popular films touch a major nerve in the nation's body politic, address common anxieties, and social tensions, and articulate vexed problems that are ultimately resolved by presenting mythical solutions to restore an [*sic*] utopian world. The situation, complication, action and resolution in all popular film narratives both creates and is created by a collective social imagination.... The concept of nation subtends that imagination in Hindi films, and centres its moral universe. All ethical dilemmas revolve around the nation; good and bad, heroes and villains are divided by their patriotism and anti-patriotism.[97]

Law, in its discursive forms, is the scaffolding that plays the role of framing the allegories of the nation-state form.[98] Bollywood cinema has developed an aesthetic in which 'the old dramatic courtroom confrontations seem to have lost their place', replacing state law as one of the fundamental registers of cinematic universality with a rise in an Anglicised register of love.[99] This replacement, however, as I understand, is that of law's identifiable statist symbols like the courthouse and the courtroom. But even in this new discourse of love, the meta-trope of the nation, and the sub-tropes of community and family, draw on *dharmic* thinking (traditions of Hindu law founded on the *Dharmaśāstra*)[100] in moments of 'acute crisis' (Virdi's ethical dilemmas) 'to close the gap between the fallible world of human law and a divine ontology of justice'.[101] As Anustup Basu, writing about imaginations of justice in the Bollywood aesthetic, explains, 'Law, it must be remembered, is for judgment, not justice. The former is an earthly discursive phenomenon, prone to error and adjustment; the latter is a divine ideal toward which historical procedures of judgment aspire but never quite reach.'[102]

This juridico-mythical rendering of justice in Bollywood cinema seems to coincide with what has been referred to as the 'dream life of law' or the 'mythic discourse' in the law film genre in the West, where 'inasmuch as legal legitimacy is derived from society's perceptions of historical and cultural truths, generating myth is crucial to building legitimacy'.[103] To quote Sherwin: 'The battle to control the constitutive norms of myth by taking over the means of cultural production is crucial to many aspects of law and politics.'[104]

Myth, as Silbey notes, plays a role in connecting law, film and memory: '... film, like memory can be mythic.... This mythic memory is law's popular consciousness.'[105] In the New India, this popular consciousness is 'a marker of the readiness to enter the "modern" age, and the modern person produced as "Indian" was the free, agentive, romantic subject of liberal humanism'.[106] This modern cinematic citizen is also a mythic construction: '... while allegedly a neutral category, [they are] invariably marked invisibly as middle class, upper caste, Hindu and male.'[107]

Keeping this specificity of the Bollywood aesthetic in mind, the J-A lens attends to the mythic in the cinematic allegories of law and justice. The work that *dharmic* thinking does in Bollywood's legal imaginary, as I will show, affectively marks the Hindu-ness of the nation-state and its secular Constitution. Keeping this myth alive, even when fractures and fragments on the nation's filmic canvas contest it, is the ideological script for popular Hindi cinema. This mode of *dharmic* address in the three films that this book studies is directed at the spectatorial publics of a community of cinematic citizens for whom the secular nationalist language of Hindutva ideology is held up as a rationalising force to simultaneously condemn and normalise religious violence against Muslims.

3 The Best Bakery Judgments

Aesthetics of Judicial Memory

The forms and methods by which a trial or decision is recorded, and remembered, are variegated and often in competition. How those different records or stories are revealed is the preliminary step in recognising that a decision explains more than doctrine.[1]

[T]o read the genre of judgment as only legal is to miss the most important aspects of its operation. In particular, it is to miss the constitutive and performative dimension of law's contexts; contexts which are not decorative or ornamental, but rather provide the horizon and limit for the possibility of law's action.[2]

Sensory images and symbolism convey meaning ... not only in terms of the discourse of a particular trial ... but, more generally, through the legal environment in which the trial takes place.[3]

This chapter uses the J-A approach to read the memory of the pogrom that is recorded in the texts of the judgments of the Best Bakery trial, one of the most publicised and controversial cases arising out of the Gujarat pogrom. The Best Bakery case, as it has come to be popularly called, ran from 2003 to 2012, covering the whole hierarchy of the Indian criminal justice system. This chapter will focus specifically on four judgments: one by the sessions court in Vadodara, one by the Gujarat High Court in Ahmedabad and two by the Supreme Court of India in New Delhi.

While the reasoning and outcomes of the judgments differed across the courts, they were unanimous in their condemnation of the violence. My reading identifies a set of words as aesthetic tropes—'rhetorical or figurative'[4] expressions that 'are a feature of all [legal] discourses'[5]—which recur in the judgments. The use of these tropes valorises legalism, secularism and developmentalism as part of a particular state-making and state-preserving rationality.

I begin by providing a detailed re-description of the Best Bakery case and its judgments. The judges have organised the writing of all the judgments under two heads—judgment and reasons. I specifically attend to this organising structure of the texts to signpost the aesthetic tropes that each of the judgments deploys to build their narratives. I then use the J-A approach to read the texts of the judgments by paying particular attention to their forms of writing. These forms are categorised as record, image and mnemohistory.

My J-A reading will show how these aesthetic tropes are deployed as narrative devices in the judgment form that might not appear to have any direct relevance to judicial reasoning but are central to the way the judgments shape and order collective memory.[6] This collective memory that is shaped by the narrative compact of law and aesthetics bolsters faith in secular law for its triumph over religious violence, even as the New India's ideological foundations against its Muslim minorities are kept intact. Condemnation and normalisation of the pogrom thus happen simultaneously in the way of remembering that the judgments mobilise through their public address.

The Best Bakery Case and Its Judgments

The Best Bakery incident took place in Vadodara city on 1 March 2002. Vadodara is the third-largest city in Gujarat and is considered to be the state's cultural capital. Prior to 1974, the city was called Baroda, a name that was given by the British. Many Gujaratis refer to it as *sanskari nagari*, or the city of culture.[7] According to the 2011 national census, Muslims constitute 11.40 per cent of the city's total population and are the largest minority group.[8] This percentage has remained more or less consistent if one considers the 1971 census, which calculated Muslims as constituting 12 per cent of the total population. A majority of Muslims in Vadodara are poor—which is also a national trend.[9] The Hindu population stood at 85.39 per cent in 2011.[10] Historically, Vadodara has been a communally sensitive city, with major events of Hindu–Muslim violence having erupted in 1969 and 1981.[11]

The Best Bakery was housed in an ordinary two-storeyed building, located in the labyrinthine lanes of Hanuman Tekdi, a Hindu-majority working-class area located to the east of Vadodara city. The bakery was run by the Sheikh family. Best Bakery had been set up by Habibullah Sheikh, who died of a heart ailment a month before the pogrom. At that time, he was survived by his wife and three children, including two daughters and a son.

In the evening of 1 March 2002, an armed mob set the bakery on fire and killed a total of 14 people, of whom 9 were from the Sheikh family, including Habibullah Sheikh's elder daughter. Three of those dead were Hindus, and the others were Muslims. The dead included 4 children, 3 women and 7 men. A total of 25 people had taken refuge in the bakery building to escape the killings that were taking place across Gujarat at that time (Figure 3.1). Five of those who tried to escape the building were killed by the mob. The next day, dead bodies were found at a ground close to the bakery.[12]

This was the second attack on Best Bakery on 1 March. The first one, which took place earlier in the day, had been interrupted by the police. However, the police were not present when a mob carried out the second attack, setting the building on fire.[13] The mob had set fire to and looted several other Muslim-owned properties before arriving at Best Bakery.

Figure 3.1 The remnants of the Best Bakery in 2014
Source: Photo by author.

The Best Bakery incident took place three days into the pogrom, which began on 28 February 2002. By this time, the mass killings in Ahmedabad, particularly the massacres in Naroda Patiya and Gulberg Society, had already taken place, killing 97 and 69 Muslims respectively.[14] In comparison, the numbers killed in the Best Bakery incident were much fewer. Yet it was the twists and turns that the trial would take, more than the number of people killed, that made the Best Bakery case the first high-profile and one of the most publicised trials related to the pogrom. The case has set precedents that have had far-reaching political and legal consequences for mass violence jurisprudence in India. The judgments related to the Best Bakery case have received widespread media coverage because they led the Supreme Court of India to intervene. The Supreme Court called out the political atmosphere in Gujarat in the aftermath of the pogrom—with witnesses turning 'hostile' due to threats, the poor investigation by the police and the judiciary's blatant biases—that compromised the conduct of the trial, resulting in all the accused being acquitted in the first instance. The Supreme Court also ordered that a retrial be conducted in Mumbai in the neighbouring state of Maharashtra—outside the jurisdiction of the courts in the state of Gujarat where the killings had occurred. This was an unprecedented move in the history of litigation related to religious mass violence in India.

In this section, I do not intend to analyse the veracity of the judicial reconstruction of the facts of the Gujarat pogrom in general and the Best Bakery incident in particular, or to offer a critique of the case and its judgments. What I aim to achieve through my re-description is more modest: to narrativise the complex story of the legal journey of the case and to signpost a set of tropes in the judgments that have been used as narrative devices in the writing of the texts. In the next section, I will use the J-A approach to read these tropes to analyse how in their address the judgments reconstruct, recognise and rationalise the pogrom. I use the texts of the judgments as the primary source for re-describing the Best Bakery incident and its public life. I make references to academic, activist and media sources on the Best Bakery incident, the case and its judgments, not to offer correctives but as a means of providing additional information that can make my re-description thicker.

The Best Bakery case has given rise to a total of six judgments across original and appellate jurisdictions, traversing the full hierarchy of courts in the Indian judiciary and lasting a period of nine years from 2003 to 2012.

The first judgment was delivered by the Vadodara Sessions Court in June 2003, where all the accused were acquitted. The star witness, Zahira Sheikh, turned hostile at the trial by failing to recognise the accused in court.[15]

This judgment went to appeal at the Gujarat High Court in Ahmedabad, which dismissed the appeal, upholding the sessions court verdict in its judgment of December 2003. The high court's judgment was appealed to the Supreme Court of India, which delivered its judgment in April 2004, ordering a retrial of the Best Bakery case in Mumbai. The retrial judgment was delivered by the Court of Sessions of Greater Bombay in February 2006, which convicted nine people. Zahira Sheikh turned hostile again during the retrial. In March 2006, the Supreme Court delivered another judgment convicting Zahira Sheikh of perjury. The Mumbai retrial was appealed to the Bombay High Court by those convicted, which delivered its judgment in July 2012, acquitting five of them. There were no further appeals. Of the six judgments, I specifically focus on the texts of four judgments: the Vadodara Sessions Court (J1), the Gujarat High Court (J2) and the two Supreme Court judgments (J3 and J4).

The police investigations in the Best Bakery case were brought into motion on the day of the incident through a first information report (FIR) filed by one Raizkhan Amin Mohammed Pathan, a resident of Hanuman Tekdi.[16] On 4 March 2002, Zahira Sheikh, the 18-year-old woman survivor and younger daughter of the owner of Best Bakery, filed a second FIR with the police. Zahira was in the Sir Sayaji General Hospital in Vadodara on the morning of 3 March, where an inspector from the Panigate Police Station recorded her statement, which along with statements by other witnesses and injured persons were put together as the FIR for the Best Bakery killings. As part of the inquest and post-mortem, Zahira named and identified the deceased.[17] A few weeks later, on 21 March 2002, Zahira also appeared and deposed before the National Human Rights Commission's (NHRC) team visiting Gujarat to record testimonies of victim-survivors and gauge the aftermath of the violence.[18]

The courts pronouncing judgment in the Best Bakery cases have called Zahira the 'star witness'.[19] It was her testimony that was of the utmost importance because she had recognised the accused at the identification parade carried out by the police during investigation. One of the most controversial components of the Best Bakery case was Zahira's repeated recantations of the statements she had made to the police, to the NHRC and also under oath to the courts about her inability to identify the accused in court.[20]

Acquittal: *The Vadodara Sessions Court Judgment*

The first judgment in the Best Bakery case, *State of Gujarat v. Rajubhai Dhamirbhai Baria and Ors*, was based on the trial that began on 20 February 2003.[21] It was delivered by Additional Sessions Judge H. U. Mahida of the Vadodara Sessions Court, in Fast Track Court No. 1, on 27 June 2003. The sessions court is the court of first instance in the judicial hierarchy of the criminal justice system in India.[22] The proceedings were held on a fast track for speedy delivery of justice, as is evident from the name of the court, and the fact that the judgment was pronounced in 44 days.[23] This was also the first ever fast-track court (FTC) that tried and delivered judgment on a case of religious mass violence in India. The objective behind using the FTC mechanism was to lay emphasis on 'prosecution and conviction of those involved in the violence in order to demonstrate in the most visible way that action is being taken by the state to redress the harm experienced by a significant section of its citizenry'.[24] *Speed* as a trope—one that is part of the structural organisation of this judgment—will be deployed to do a particular kind of narrative work in the text of the next judgment.

The sessions court tried a total of 21 people—all of them with Hindu names—who were accused of carrying out the burning and killings at Best Bakery. The accused were charged under several criminal law provisions covering rioting, unlawful assembly, murder and breaking public peace, amongst others. The judgment is divided into two parts, as is with all the later judgments in the case as well. The first part is titled 'Judgment' and the second 'Reasons'. This is in keeping with Section 354 of the Code of Criminal Procedure, 1973, which lays down the requirement that all judgments 'shall contain the point or points for determination, the decision thereon and the reasons for the decision'.[25]

In its opening paragraphs, the judgment states on record that the accused were part of a 'fanatic crowd' or an 'illegal crowd' comprising '1000 to 1200' people who, 'armed with weapons and inflammable liquid', shouted 'beat, cut, drive away the Muslim … burn—set fire to houses of Muslims'.[26] This crowd, the court noted, was driven by 'their common intention to damage the lives and properties of the persons of Muslim community'.[27] The *crowd* is a trope that remains vital to the narrative reconstruction of the Best Bakery killings in the text of the judgment.

In the 'Judgment' section of the text, the court lists the names of the dead and the injured, provides a brief backstory about how Best Bakery was set up by the Sheikhs after they migrated from Uttar Pradesh many years back and introduces the members of the Sheikh family and the employees of Best Bakery (who were also migrants from Uttar Pradesh, and included Hindus as well). It describes the modus operandi of the attack, including the kinds of weapons used by the mob both to kill those inside Best Bakery and to set fire to the building. All these details are preceded by the explanation that the Best Bakery incident was a 'reversal action' to the burning of compartment S-6 of the Sabarmati Express at Godhra Station on 27 February 2002,[28] in which Hindu pilgrims were killed. The judgment further emphasises that because of the 'heinous' incident at Godhra,[29] communal riots broke out in Gujarat, which led to 'a tense atmosphere in the city'.[30] Through this explanation, the court both locates the Best Bakery incident as part of the larger event of violence unfolding in Gujarat at that time and identifies Godhra as the originating cause of that violence.

After contextualising the circumstances and the cast of characters involved and describing the mise en scène in which the Best Bakery incident took place, the judgment lays out the facts regarding how the case came to this court and then goes on to list the three points on which the court had to decide. These were: first, whether the prosecution had been able to prove that the Best Bakery incident took place at the alleged time and place by a crowd driven by the common intention of targeting Muslim lives and property; second, whether the prosecution could prove the charges framed against the 21 accused persons; and third, what order to pass.[31]

The second part of the judgment titled 'Reasons' offers the 'findings' of the court in response to these three points.[32] With regard to the first point, the judgment says that 'from the evidence recorded in this case it is clearly proved that in this incident of Best Bakery 14 persons were killed' and 'properties of [lakhs] of rupees were damaged and looted'.[33] In other words, the court ruled in the affirmative on the first issue, that is, that available evidence sufficiently confirmed that the killing, looting and burning did take place. To arrive at this decision, the court first relied on the depositions and reports by the doctors who had examined the injured and performed post-mortems on the deceased. Second, it relied on the depositions by 'witnesses of

Muslim community', stating that while this proved the extent to which property had been damaged, these witnesses were not able to identify or name people who were in the *crowd* that carried out the violence.[34]

Based on this finding, the judgment segues into a response to the second point on which the court had to decide. On this, the court stated that while the Best Bakery incident had been 'undoubtedly proved', the prosecution, however, '[had] not led any least evidence or acceptable legal evidence to prove that the accused or any of them before the Court had committed any such offenses'.[35] It then went on to list a select set of eyewitnesses—on whose statements to the police the prosecution had built its case—who denied seeing any of the 21 accused carry out the killings, looting and burning.[36]

Of the total 120 witnesses, 73 deposed in court.[37] Indeed, of these 73 prosecution witnesses (which included the injured witnesses and eyewitnesses), 41 recanted their statements. Of these, three eyewitnesses said to the court that they had never made any statements to the police.[38] The judgment makes special mention of star witness Zahira Sheikh's eyewitness account and discredits it as an inadmissible FIR, stating that Raizkhan Amin Mohammed Pathan's FIR was filed first.[39] It notes that 'it is not safe to rely upon the police statements of the star witness', because the court believed that the police had manufactured these statements after their investigations were over, and since none of the other witnesses had stood by their statements as recorded by the police, the same should be the case with Zahira.[40] Zahira had 'denied the contexts of her statement made to the police on 2 March 2002 but admitted [to the court] that the signature below the statement was hers'.[41]

However, of all the eyewitnesses, it was the deposition by one Lalmohmad Khudabax Shaikh, a witness produced by the defence, which the court chose to cite at length because it considered it to be 'in the interest of justice'.[42] There are two key components in the portion from Lalmohmad's deposition that the judgment quotes. First, the judge reiterates the court's previous concern about the mob, that it was too big for Lalmohmad to identify who all were a part of it. Second, and unlike the other eyewitnesses who recanted their statements, Lalmohmad identified all the 21 accused—not for having carried out the violence but for saving the lives of the survivors. He credited the accused, who according to him lived cordially with everyone in Hanuman Tekdi, saying that it was they, along with their family members, who had made calls to the police when Best Bakery was attacked. Lalmohmad further noted that if those who sought refuge from the mob within Best Bakery had come out, the chances were that they would have also been saved by the accused as well.[43]

Unlike the statements by some of the other witnesses that were recorded by the police, the judgment did not provide any reason to doubt Lalmohmad's deposition. It was Lalmohmad's witness testimony that was considered admissible evidence or the legal truth about what had happened at Best Bakery; the other judgments similarly organise their reasoning in ways that link justice and truth in a teleological relation—that it is in the interest of justice to rely on truth. *Justice* and *truth* are two other narrative tropes in this judgment that will also feature in the appeal decisions.

The judgment then goes on to point out that the prosecution had failed to prove its case because the statements of witnesses that they were relying on as evidence had been fabricated by the police. The court, though not in so many words, indicated that this was the result of a failure on the part of the police to carry out their investigation properly. The judgment mentions that the police had wrongly accused people in the locality to serve its cause and that it was because of such intimidating practices by the police that 'truthful witnesses' did not appear before the police.[44] The judgment declares that the witnesses who recanted their statements in court 'have turned hostile to the prosecution and they do not support at all the prosecution case'.[45] The court, thus, considered the slippages in the police investigation and the discrepancies in the prosecution's arguments as the reasons for witnesses turning hostile, 'rather than ... any shortcomings in the conduct of the trial or in the management of the witnesses'.[46]

The consequence of this, the judgment states in a tone of disappointment, was that while it had been proved that the 21 accused were innocent, it was still not known who the 'real offender' was. The court emphasised that 'it is not within the jurisdiction of the court' to find that out because '[t]he court of law or judiciary in the true meaning and sense, is *not the court of justice but the court of evidence*'.[47] To the tropes of justice and truth that I had signposted earlier gets added the trope of *evidence*. The teleological connection between justice and truth that the judgment had referred to is now qualified in a way where justice is replaced by evidence, which equals truth.

After delimiting the court's role as a court of evidence, the judgment takes on a didactic tone to offer an elaborate meditation on the causes and consequences of 'riots' in India.[48] This portion of the judgment marks a clear shift in the form of writing, where, having provided the legal reasons in a clinical voice, the judge decided to engage in a charged polemical exposition. Drawing on references from Hindu mythology, the judge blamed British colonialism and a failure of India's industrial and affirmative action policies for the Gujarat pogrom.[49] He emphasised that there 'is necessity of rekindling patriotic feelings'[50] in these circumstances and explained why '[t]he word "secular" cannot incarnate the feeling of our culture'.[51] He lamented that the Best Bakery incident had affixed 'black stigma' to 'cultured Baroda city' and how riots can lead India to 'jungle raj instead of development'.[52] Two key tropes appear in this densely written section of the judgment—*secularism* and *development*.

It is this section of the judgment that takes on immense significance in the way it offers a closure to the trial. The question of *closure*—as an end of the writing of a judgment, as completion of the trial, as well as the closing of law's record of memory—turns into a trope in the next judgment and it is worth signposting at this stage. In this judgment (J1), the act of closure is effected through a return to the trope of the *crowd* and holding up an image of it as one that is able to explain why riots are an affront to development. The court points out how individuals who are part of a mob lose their mind because of the collective anger of the crowd: 'The psychology of the fanatic mob is dangerous and senseless.'[53] The court substantiates this assertion by noting that it was because of 'fanatic anger' that the 'Hindu crowd itself killed three Hindu youths considering them Muslims'.[54] Collective rage, thus, according to the judgment, rendered the 'Hindu crowd' blind to the religion of those who were killed.

The Vadodara Sessions Court judgment ruled in the affirmative as to whether the Best Bakery incident had taken place and ruled in the negative on the culpability of the accused.[55] In other words, it recognised that the violence had occurred, but held that the evidence on record was insufficient to prove that it had been carried out by the accused. Its final order, pronounced in open court—accessible to the public at large and the media—acquitted all the 21 accused.[56]

The acquittal was met with severe criticism from the national English-language media. Major English newspapers across the country unanimously berated the judgment with editorials, some of which were titled as follows: 'Charred Justice'; 'Fixing Witnesses?'; 'Justice Blindfolded'; 'Half Baked Justice'; and 'A Mockery of the Law'.[57] When this case went to appeal at the

Gujarat High Court in Ahmedabad, these media reactions were brought under scrutiny in that judgment.

On 7 July 2003, a few weeks after the Vadodara Sessions Court judgment was delivered, Zahira Sheikh, along with the civil society group called Citizens for Justice and Peace (CJP), which was providing legal aid to her and her family, issued a press statement from Mumbai. The statement said:

> Lack of moral and legal support through the court hearings, coupled with an *atmosphere* of direct threat and intimidation, had led her and family members to deny recognition of the accused sitting in court the day she was summoned for deposition—May 17, 2003. She and her family had been directly threatened that they would all be killed by the key accused and their mentors from the Hanuman Tekri area in Vadodara.[58]

Of note in the statement is the use of the term *atmosphere*, which would be deployed as a trope in later judgments. By pointing to the atmosphere of intimidation, in the statement Zahira and CJP demanded that there should be a retrial of the Best Bakery case outside Gujarat because the trial as it was concluded in Vadodara 'epitomised the abject failure of the state administration and law and order machinery to protect the lives and properties of innocent citizens'.[59] Zahira was reported in the media to have been at the receiving end of intimidation by a BJP legislator named Madhu Srivastava, 'who had even escorted her to court and back while giving the testimony as he had desired'.[60] She also charged Raghuvir Pandya, the public prosecutor in the Best Bakery trial, with 'not even meeting her before she stepped into the witness box. When key witnesses turned hostile, Pandya did not exercise his right to cross-examine them.'[61]

At the press conference organised to issue this statement, Zahira was accompanied by activist Teesta Setalvad from CJP. In August 2003, along with Zahira, CJP filed a special leave petition (SLP) in the Supreme Court of India praying,[62] inter alia, for a retrial of the Best Bakery case outside of Gujarat in the interests of carrying out a fair trial, for providing protection to the witnesses and for directing the Central Bureau of Investigation (CBI) or any other independent agency to carry out investigations monitored by the Supreme Court.[63] In July 2003, the NHRC had also petitioned the Supreme Court to 'set aside the judgment of the trial court and to direct re-investigation and retrial of the case outside the State of Gujarat on the grounds that the victims had not been able to depose freely and that therefore the trial was unfair'.[64]

On 7 August 2003, the Gujarat government lodged an appeal against the Vadodara Sessions Court judgment in the Gujarat High Court in Ahmedabad. The appeal was accompanied by two applications seeking the court's permission to produce 'additional evidence in the form of witness affidavits and documentary evidence, and for an order for retrial and quashing of the entire proceedings' of the sessions court judgment.[65] This was followed by an amended application on 29 September 2003, because the Supreme Court, unhappy with how badly the appeal had been drafted, asked the Gujarat government to amend it.[66]

The media response in the aftermath of the Vadodara Sessions Court judgment and Zahira's press statement about witness intimidation was reflected in the exclamatory titles of the several newspaper editorials mentioned earlier. These characterisations by the media of the judicial proceedings in Gujarat can be read as an indication of the outrage provoked by the unanticipated conduct of the Indian judiciary, which was expected to be incorruptible in offering speedy justice to the victims of the killings.

Before moving on to describing the appeal in the Gujarat High Court, it is necessary to provide some context in terms of the political ramifications of the sessions court decision. The political ramifications are connected to what journalist Manoj Mitta, in his study of the police and judicial investigations in the wake of the violence, has called 'the Gujarat model of justice'.[67] This model was on display in the immediate aftermath of the pogrom, in the way the several incidents of mass killings were being prosecuted by courts in Gujarat. The Gujarat government was readying itself for elections in 2002, building on the historical trend that religious violence would have consolidated the Hindu vote in its favour.[68] In the run-up to his electoral victory, Modi popularised 'justice for all, appeasement for none' as his campaign slogan.[69] To demonstrate that the judiciary in Gujarat was responding efficiently and thus living up to the slogan's promise, courts in Gujarat trying cases related to the pogrom started handing out judgments in record time—*speed* was the marker of the efficiency of the judiciary. In October 2002, three FTCs acquitted all the accused in cases related to massacres in Kidiad and Pandarwada, where 70 and 40 Muslims were killed, respectively.[70] On the use of FTCs as the preferred forum for post-pogrom justice delivery in Gujarat, Mitta notes:

Though there were several ingredients to the Gujarat model of justice, one key element was a misuse of the then newly introduced fast-track courts, an initiative of the Central government across the country. The misuse lay in achieving speed at the expense of justice, thereby defeating the objective of the fast-track courts. It showed that the stress was more on clearing the docket and generating impressive statistics on the disposal of cases. The imbalance between speed and justice was by no means unintentional.... The innovation of the Gujarat model lay in pressing for a hurried trial even when the investigation was far from complete.[71]

Each of these cases were 'a casualty of rapid-fire justice'[72] that reconfirmed the 'urgent recommendations' made by the NHRC in its 1 April 2002 report, where serious concerns were raised about the poor quality of FIRs that the police were recording and how investigations were being 'influenced by extraneous considerations or players'.[73] The NHRC repeated these concerns in its final report on the pogrom released on 31 May 2002. In the light of these concerns, the NHRC recommended that five major cases related to the pogrom 'be entrusted to the CBI for independent investigation'.[74] The Best Bakery case was one of these five cases and, in being listed separately for independent investigation by the CBI, was brought to the attention of the national media.

As I have already discussed, the Vadodara Sessions Court's verdict acquitting the accused was immediately followed 10 days later, on 7 July 2003, by Zahira Sheikh's public statement at a press conference, where she was accompanied by activist Teesta Setalvad. In the light of these revelations, the NHRC, under the chairmanship of a former chief justice of India (A. S. Anand), approached the Supreme Court directly (instead of appealing to the Gujarat High Court) through an SLP. The petition prayed for a reinvestigation of the case by the CBI—as previously recommended by the NHRC—and for the case to be retried at any other location apart from Gujarat. This was a 'radical step', unprecedented in the history of the NHRC's existence since 1993. According to Mitta:

> The intervention was unusual, in that the NHRC did not just seek to be impleaded as a party but it also bypassed the regular appeals process, due to the exceptional circumstances of the case. The NHRC took the

'miscarriage of justice' in the Best Bakery case as a reflection of the environment prevailing in the whole of Gujarat. By approaching the Supreme Court directly, the statutory body ran the risk of appearing to have no confidence in the Gujarat High Court.... The suggestion clearly was that the extreme situation in Gujarat had called for an extreme solution.[75]

The judgment of the Vadodara Sessions Court was, thus, used as an exemplary instance of the communalisation of the judiciary in Gujarat in the aftermath of the pogrom. This move by the NHRC provoked Narendra Modi to write to the then president of India, A. P. J. Abdul Kalam, in August 2005. Modi wrote an open letter to the president attacking the NHRC, 'accusing it of falling prey to the "propaganda" of "vested interests"'.[76] The letter challenged the NHRC's move by raising the three classic concerns of governmental rationality: 'development, security and federal democracy'.[77] First, Modi cited statistics—a long-utilised tool of the postcolonial state-making and state-preserving rationality[78]—to show that Gujarat's growth rate was much higher than the expected rate for the country fixed by the Planning Commission of India.[79] Using statistical evidence as the basis of his argument, Modi's letter stated: 'Vested interests are trying to obstruct the path of progress. They are identifying stray incidents and exaggerating them with the sole objective of slowing the pace of development.'[80]

Second, Modi used the defence of India's federal governance structure, and the mandate of his democratically elected state government, to 'doubt' the 'intentions' of the NHRC for not respecting 'democratic values'. He wrote:

Nothing can be more harmful than the efforts of some groups to weaken the collective strength of the democratic institutions ... such self-appointed and so-called champions of human rights groups do not even hesitate to point fingers, with the help of a section of media, at institutions like the judiciary in the state.[81]

Third, he played the national security card to say that 'NHRC's alleged folly needed "serious attention because Gujarat being a border State [with Pakistan] has a strategic importance for the Nation's security"'.[82] Noting that Gujarat was committed to 'help usher in "an era of security, justice and prosperity"', Modi questioned the NHRC's motives by asking why it singularly sought to focus on Gujarat when 'group clashes and communal riots occur in many parts of the country'.[83] He returned to a statistical defence in closing: 'Facts on record will unveil the truth ... thereby exposing the vested interests that have targeted not only Gujarat, but have tried to weaken the democratic fabric and reputed institutions of the country.'[84]

Modi's letter offered the script that the Vadodara Sessions Court and the Gujarat High Court (as I will show next) enacted with precision. Both courts waxed eloquent on how people with vested interests had undermined Gujarat's *asmita* (pride) by accusing its administration of compromising the trial in the Best Bakery case and raising doubts about the independence of its judiciary. The Gujarat High Court, in addition to criticising the NHRC, also cast aspersions about human rights activist Teesta Setalvad and lawyer Mihir Desai of CJP for taking advantage of Zahira Sheikh with ulterior motives. In almost identical fashion, both judgments had much to say about Gujarat's commitment to development and prosperity. The High Court judgment even went on to say: 'The nation will suffer if Gujarat is made to suffer.'[85]

Modi's open letter seemed to have had a sway on the Supreme Court of India as well. In response to the NHRC SLP, the Supreme Court asked the Gujarat High Court to hear it as the first court of appeal. In fact, 'just a day after Modi's letter to the President on 5 August 2002, the prosecution filed an appeal before the Gujarat High Court against the Best Bakery acquittals'.[86] However, the appeal was so poorly drafted that the Supreme Court called it a 'complete eyewash',[87] and summoned two high-ranking officers of the Gujarat police and got them to state on record that 'rather than being declared hostile, [the witnesses] should have been re-examined by the prosecution and that the appeal filed by the government in the High Court ought to have sought a retrial'.[88] Justice V. N. Khare at the Supreme Court also had some pretty harsh words for the Modi government. He said: 'You should quit if you cannot prosecute the guilty. Democracy does not mean you will not prosecute.'[89] The Gujarat government, thus, was left with no option but to amend the appeal before the High Court at Ahmedabad.

Appeal: The Gujarat High Court Judgment

The second judgment in the Best Bakery case—*State of Gujarat v. Rajubhai Dhamirbhai Baria and Ors*[90]—emerged out of the appeal that the Gujarat government had filed against the Vadodara Sessions Court decision that acquitted all the 21 accused. The two-judge bench of the Gujarat High Court, comprising Justices B. J. Sethna and J. Vora, started hearing the appeal on 19 December 2003 and delivered judgment on 26 December 2003. This was approximately three months from the time when the appeal was lodged. The judgment was authored by Justice Sethna.

The judgment opens by stating the causes for the appeal—a demand for retrial, the quashing of the Sessions Court proceedings and placing further evidence on record. The judges then invoked the trope of *speed* and likened their work to that of the functioning of an FTC by emphasising how their high court had 'immediately started hearing the appeal'[91] when the matter was placed before it, and that it heard the defence and the prosecution in 'marathon hearings'[92] for about a week, and had now arrived at its judgment 'at the fag-end of the day'.[93] That the proceedings were conducted with such expedience, the court mentioned, was '[a]s per the hope expressed by the Hon'ble Supreme Court', which in its response to the NHRC petition had issued an order on 17 November 2003 stating: 'We hope that the hearing of the appeal will commence on 1st December, 2003 and the matter will be decided expeditiously.'[94]

The judgment was delivered in two separate parts on two separate dates, but published in law reports in its entirety, with part one titled 'Judgment' and part two titled 'Reasons'. This form is similar to the one followed by the sessions court in Vadodara. The high court noted that after hearing the appellant (represented by S. N. Shelat, advocate general of Gujarat) and the respondents-accused (represented by Senior Advocate Sushil Kumar), it was 'fully convinced that there is no substance in all these matters including the appeal, and therefore, they are required to be dismissed'.[95] In keeping with the fast-track spirit of the sessions court, after 'continuously' hearing the appeal for four days, while delivering the first part of the judgment 'dismissing all these matters' on 26 December, the judges clarified that they 'would have liked to assign reasons and passed the detailed judgment in the open court, but today being the last day before the Winter Vacation', the reasons were deferred to after the court reopened on 12 January 2004.[96]

Under part two titled 'Reasons', before arriving at the specifics of the Vadodara Sessions Court ruling, the Gujarat High Court spent a fair amount of space establishing its jurisdiction over the appeal. Such explanation was occasioned, as the judgment notes, because the advocate representing the respondents-accused 'vehemently submitted' that 'the State of Gujarat has filed the appeal ... only because it was challenged by National Human Rights Commission before the Supreme Court'.[97] According to the judgment, advocate Sushil Kumar had argued that the NHRC had no *locus standi* in the instant matter, and thus should not have filed the SLP against the Vadodara Sessions Court decision in the Supreme Court of India. He had added that since the Supreme Court had admitted the SLP, which was pending before it, the high court 'should not hear and decide this acquittal appeal'.[98] Kumar had further noted in his submissions that 'the NHRC had directly approached the Supreme Court', instead of waiting for the standard appeal process to reach the high court, 'only because of media hype, though the impugned judgment and order of acquittal passed by the [Vadodara] trial court is just, legal and proper'.[99]

In response to these submissions by Sushil Kumar, the high court clarified that in Gujarat the period of limitation for filing an appeal was 90 days, and that the instant appeal by the government had been filed within that period. Thus, 'by no stretch of imagination, can it be said that under compulsion or duress the State has filed the acquittal appeal in this case'.[100] It further stated that despite the fact that 'the Supreme Court has not adjudicated the question', in response to the SLP filed by the NHRC, this court is 'of the considered opinion that merely because the case is pending before the Apex Court, that fact itself should not debar us from hearing and deciding the said appeal'.[101] The judges noted that such a line of thinking 'undermin[ed] the independence of this court'.[102] Further, the judgment refused to comment on the NHRC's *locus standi*, because that was a matter pending before the Supreme Court, and that this court was not 'a proper forum, where such questions can be raised'.[103] It also withheld from expressing any opinion on the media reaction to the Vadodara Sessions Court judgment because according to the judges, the '[m]edia is not a party before this court'.[104]

The judgment, thus, emphasised the impartiality of the high court (in response to the criticism raised against the Vadodara Sessions Court), and that it had jurisdiction in the matter at hand, given that it was the superior court in the hierarchy, to competently hear the appeal. The judgment repeated:

[B]y no stretch of imagination it can be said that because of the media, this Court is likely to be swayed away and decide the appeal not on merits or not in accordance with law. It is undermining the independence of the Judges of this court, who have always decided cases without fear or favour and without being influenced by anything, *strictly in accordance with law.*[105]

This insistence by the high court on how its conduct was *strictly in accordance with law*—and that such legalism worked as a powerful means to preserve its independence—is a trope that we will see repeated both in this judgment and that of the Supreme Court. The high court's axiomatic emphasis, which would seem like a redundant repetition of common sense—what else should courts have strict accordance with, if not law?—gains prominence in the context of post-pogrom Gujarat. This was especially the case after the acquittals by the Vadodara Sessions Court that led to the media criticism of the Gujarat judiciary's conduct compromising justice. In fact, by saying this, the high court seems to concur with the sessions court's belief that courts should be driven by evidence, rather than justice. As I will show in the re-description of this judgment, the trope of *evidence* will be deployed by the judgment in both framing its reasons justifying the dismissal of the appeal and reconstructing the narrative of the Best Bakery case.

The high court expressed strong doubts about the prosecution argument that there had been no fair trial in Vadodara because the injured witnesses would not have recanted their statements in court if they had not been threatened and made to feel fearful about speaking the truth. S. N. Shelat, the advocate representing the appellants, requested the high court to consider the sessions court judgment 'as an exceptional case, which requires a retrial in view of the lapses on the part of the Investigating Agency, prosecution and the learned trial Judge'.[106]

The high court rejected the possibility that witnesses had been threatened and could not depose fearlessly 'for the simple reason that there may be more than one reasons for the witnesses from resiling from their so-called statements before the police'.[107] The judges identified three such other reasons. First, the judgment doubted the fact that those witnesses who were declared hostile had in the first place made any statements to the police. The court said: 'If they had not made any statement before the police, then, there was no question of resiling from their so-called statements either under threat or coercion.'[108] It may be recollected that a similar concern was raised by the sessions court to reject Zahira Sheikh's statement, saying that the police had manufactured the statements after the completion of investigation—so that it did not amount to recantation at all.

Second, the court noted that the 7 witnesses (who were victims and eyewitnesses) from among the 37 who had turned hostile did not speak or read Gujarati, because they were from Uttar Pradesh. This was a reference to the survivors of the Sheikh family, who, as the Vadodara Sessions Court judgment had recorded, were migrants from Uttar Pradesh. Their language inability was connected to the fact that their police statements were recorded in Gujarati and were not 'read over and explained to them in Hindi'.[109] The court's consideration, thus, was that they did not know what the police had recorded by translating their oral statements given in Hindi to Gujarati. Hence, for the court, it could not be said that they had recanted their statements because it was not possible to fully ascertain that what they had said to the police was what the police actually recorded.

Third, the judgment observed that because these seven eyewitnesses were also injured in the attack on Best Bakery, and had lost their family members, they had the 'best opportunity to depose against the accused' since 'there was no threat or coercion' in the sessions court. The judgment, however, added that 'if at all [these seven eyewitnesses] had seen the respondents-accused taking active part in the incident with other persons of the mob of more than 10000 to 15000 [*sic*] then they would have definitely identified the accused persons, who were very much present in the court'.[110]

Through these three points, the Gujarat High Court, as I read it, invoked two tropes: first, the Vadodara Sessions Court judgment was an outcome of a fair trial because the *atmosphere* in the court was such that the witnesses could have deposed fearlessly—they had the 'best opportunity', the judges wrote. Second, it returned to the trope of the *crowd*, to cast a shadow of concern, if not a doubt, about whether the witnesses could have at all identified the 21 accused from a huge mob. The underlining cause for this case to have reached a situation like this, the judgment noted, concurring with the sessions court, was the poor quality of the investigation carried out by the police.[111]

In responding to another submission by the lawyer for the state, S. N. Shelat, that the prosecutor and the judge in the Vadodara Sessions Court did not try to find out, by asking questions to the witnesses, why they were turning hostile while the trial was on, the high court delimited the scope of their conduct thus:

> The Prosecutor is the guardian of the society, who is concerned with punishing the guilty and saving the innocent. He has to protect the

interest of the society and has to see that wrong-doers must be punished, but at the same time, innocent persons should not be punished wrongly. Similarly, neither the Public Prosecutor nor the learned Judge can put any leading questions to the witnesses. *Neither the Prosecutor not the learned Judge can cross their limits and become persecutor.*[112]

This remark inaugurates the trope of the *role*, and I will point at its recurrence and the work it is deployed to do in the Supreme Court judgments as well. In the high court, the prosecutor/persecutor difference as a matter of legitimate roles seems to map on to the trope of *strictly in accordance with law*.

Holding on to its concern about resiling witnesses, the judgment makes special mention of the incident of Zahira Sheikh turning hostile. The judges raised 'serious doubts' about whether Zahira was threatened, as a consequence of which she recanted her statements in the sessions court.[113] The high court wondered why, if Zahira could make a public statement to the press about the threats she had received on the very next day after the trial court judgment was delivered, she did not do the same when the trial was on. The court asked: 'The question is that, how come that all of a sudden after the judgment was pronounced by the learned trial Judge, the effect of the threat had vanished and on the next day Zahira got courage of telling the truth?'[114] The trope of *atmosphere* makes its appearance here to identify the space of the court as one that enables truth-telling. Thus, if the courtroom whose conduct is organised in *strict accordance with law* has not led to Zahira speaking the truth, the court wondered, how was that even possible outside of the courtroom space?

That the *atmosphere* of the space outside the courtroom was a contaminated one is made apparent when the judgment noted 'a definite design and conspiracy to malign *the people* by misusing this witness Zahirabibi, who is hardly 19 years old. She can easily fall prey to anyone and play in the dirty hands of *anti-social and anti-national elements*'.[115] The trope of *the people* is a reference to the people of Gujarat. Teesta Setalvad had accompanied Zahira when she made the statement to the media, and CJP was the organisation which had filed (with Zahira) a petition in the Supreme Court asking for a retrial. They are identified as *anti-social and anti-national elements*. This trope speaks to the call for *patriotism* that was invoked by the sessions court judgment.

The high court's understanding of what it considered to be a vitiated atmosphere outside the courtroom was inferred from the fact that Zahira left

Gujarat after the Vadodara Sessions Court judgment, and spoke of the threat she had received during the trial to not identify the accused and recant her statement, on a 'public platform in presence of others', and that this was covered by a national English daily, the *Indian Express*.[116] This series of events is assessed by the judgment as 'a deep-rooted conspiracy of misusing witness Zahira, victim of unfortunate incident, by some people, with an ulterior motive, and unfortunately, poor people like Zahira and others, have easily fallen in their prey'.[117]

I would like to re-emphasise here that while the high court considered questionable the statement Zahira made to the police and then to the press, it did not raise similar doubts about what she had said in the court during the trial. In other words, the high court reconfirmed its belief that the *atmosphere* of the trial in the Vadodara Sessions Court was free of any threat or coercion, unlike the *atmosphere* outside the court where Zahira recorded her statement with the police, or where she made her statements to the press. The judgment's reasoning recognised Zahira's vulnerability but considered that it was only outside the *atmosphere* of the sessions court that such vulnerability could have been exploited by *anti-social and anti-national elements*.

The judgment then dismissed the submissions, one at a time, made by the advocate for the state. Notable among these was the state's submission that the Vadodara Sessions Court should have conducted the trial *in camera* and not in an open court; that Judge Mahida of the sessions court should have used the powers vested in him under the Code of Criminal Procedure and the Indian Evidence Act to recall and re-examine the resiling witnesses and ask questions to the witnesses to obtain further proof; and that the judge should have also postponed or adjourned the proceedings when he understood that the witnesses were turning hostile.

The high court said that the argument about the witnesses being frightened and not speaking the truth because at the trial the accused were present 'is nothing but a gross contempt'.[118] Invoking the trope of *atmosphere*, the judgment emphasised that the 'trial was conducted in open court in the presence of many including the relatives of the witnesses', and thus, the question of fear stopping them from speaking the truth was unfounded.[119] It clarified that under the law Judge Mahida had the discretion to not conduct the trial *in camera*, and that the high court had not been able to find any convincing reason why the witnesses should have been recalled and re-questioned. The high court reminded the advocate for the state that the trial was being conducted by an FTC—*strictly in accordance with law*—which is why adjourning or postponing the trial could not have been done without any 'solid reason', and if Mahida had done so, 'he would have been subjected to severe criticism for delaying the trial'.[120]

Having dismissed the submissions by the state in which questions were raised about the conduct of both Judge Mahida and the public prosecutor, the high court, in agreement with the sessions court, strongly criticised the police. It said:

> We are at pains to note that in the instant case, right from the beginning, the investigation carried out by the police was absolutely dishonesty [*sic*] and faulty. When the police did not find the real culprits, they have falsely involved the respondents in the case as accused, who were none else but the neighbours of the victims.[121]

That the accused were not the assailants, but neighbours who saved many of the victims, was considered by the court as an undisputed fact by relying on the testimony of Lalmohmad Khudabax Shaikh, the witness who deposed for the defence in the trial court. The judgment said: 'We have no reason to discard the testimony of Lalmohmad who has clearly stated before the Court that it was the accused persons who saved not only him, his family but also saved about 65 to 70 other Muslims of the locality.'[122] The court reasoned that this had to be the case because if the accused were part of a mob—the *crowd* trope—that was out to kill Muslims and destroy their property, 'they would not have spared' those who were alive.[123] The fact that '65 to 75 Muslims survived unhurt during that incident shows that they were saved and protected by the accused'.[124]

Along with the police, the media also came in for heavy criticism by the high court, despite the fact that at the beginning of the judgment it was stated that since the media was not a party in the appeal, the court would not comment on it. The judgment singled out the English-language newspaper *Indian Express*, which reported on Zahira's public statement on the threats that had made her turn hostile in the sessions court. The judgment considered this report to be the reason that the NHRC lodged the SLP in the Supreme Court. The judgment said: 'This [the newspaper report] was accepted as gospel truth, and thereafter, the matter is taken up by the N.H.R.C., and others before the Supreme Court.'[125] The judgment contrasts this with a report published in the *Times of India* a day after the high court judgment was pronounced on 27 December 2003. This report quoted Yasminbanu and her mother Rashidabibi, both Muslim residents of Hanuman Tekdi, who told the newspaper, the court noted, that the complaint by Zahira and her family against the 21 accused was 'totally false'.[126] Given the differing views about the Best Bakery incident that two separate newspapers carried, the court said that post a judgment, the media can 'make any type of statements, but no importance can be accorded to it in judicial decision-making, otherwise it would be "nothing but [a] mockery of justice"'.[127] In saying this, as I read it, the court emphasised what it considered credible evidence—the tropes of *evidence, justice* and *truth* recur—and equated Zahira's statement to the press to that of Yasminbanu and Rashidabibi, also quoted in the press, but who were not themselves witnesses in the Vadodara trial. In fact, in drawing this equivalence, Zahira's revelations about the threats she had received to recant her statement in court, stood negated by the judgment.

Having dismissed the status of media reports as evidence, the judgment turned to respond to the submission about considering Zahira's affidavit that had been filed before the Supreme Court as part of the CJP petition as additional evidence in the appeal. The court questioned the need for a retrial based on considering such an affidavit as evidence:

> Is there any guarantee that whatever [is] stated in the affidavit, after trial is over, is true because it is on oath, and nor what [was] deposed before the trial Court, which was also on oath? Is there any guarantee that the witness may not once again change his [*sic*] version before the trial court on retrial for any other reasons and tell [a] different story? What importance [can] be attached to the evidence of such witness [if] examined again before the trial court on retrial? What is the guarantee that the witness may tell the truth and nothing but the truth, on retrial before the trial court … and once again may not support the prosecution for any reason[?] Last but not the least, what would happen if such witness, on retrial, states that his or her affidavit filed in appeal was false? Or he or she was misguided?[128]

The court—invoking the tropes of *evidence, truth* and *justice*—thus rejected the application to bring affidavits on record, dismissed the plea for a retrial and upheld the judgment of the Vadodara Sessions Court's acquittal of the 21 accused. Deploying the trope of *closure*, the judgment emphatically stated:

> Everything has an end, including the trial. One cannot be tried endlessly for an indefinite period when his personal liberty is involved.... On the facts of the present case we are of the confirmed opinion that no retrial can be ordered as it may seriously prejudice the interest of the accused, whose personal liberty is at stake.[129]

Much like the sessions court judgment, the high court also turned contemplative to offer detailed comments on how those who were 'misusing poor persons like Zahira' were obstructing 'the development and progress' of Gujarat.[130] Note the trope of *development*. In this part of the judgment, the high court, like the sessions court, traced the origins of the 'riots' to Godhra and expressed concern about how they had adversely impacted the image of Gujarat as a peaceful, secular, progressive state. The court also offered some ideas about how to establish Hindu–Muslim harmony. These comments seem to offer the foundations on which the court built its thinking and reasoning in the judgment. In the next section, I read this portion of the text of the judgment in detail for the way the high court used these tropes in its narrative reconstructions.

In 'dismissing the appeal and rejecting the prayer for retrial', the judgment returned to recounting the events of the Best Bakery incident, thus recognising that the violence and the killings had indeed taken place, but not considering the sessions court judgment to be unfair or marred by any 'irregularity of illegality' that might have resulted in the 'miscarriage of justice'.[131]

Retrial: The First Supreme Court of India Judgment

On 12 March 2004, the Supreme Court of India in New Delhi admitted the state of Gujarat's appeal against the Gujarat High Court judgment upholding the decision of the Vadodara Sessions Court which acquitted all the 21 accused in the Best Bakery case. The appeal was joined by Zahira Sheikh and CJP, through the NHRC, which had filed an SLP in the Supreme Court against the sessions court judgment on 11 July 2003.

The Supreme Court judgment was delivered on 12 April 2004 by a two-judge bench comprising Justices Doraiswamy Raju and Arijit Pasayat. Justice

Pasayat authored the judgment. In the Supreme Court, the state of Gujarat was the respondent, and Zahira Sheikh was named the appellant. The case was called *Zahira Habibullah Sheikh and Another v. State of Gujarat and Others*.[132] It is in this judgment that the Supreme Court stated that the 'case is commonly to be known as "Best Bakery Case"'.[133] The judgment identified the Best Bakery incident as one of 'macabre killings allegedly as a result of communal frenzy'.[134] While the judgment does invoke the trope of the *crowd*, unlike the Vadodara Sessions Court, the Supreme Court did not identify the *crowd* as 'Hindu'.[135]

The judgment opened by noting that the appeals 'have several unusual features and some of them pose very serious questions of far reaching consequences'.[136] The circumstances that led to Zahira appealing to the Supreme Court against the Gujarat High Court judgment—'being forced to depose falsely and turn hostile on accounts of threats and coercion' at the Vadodara trial—the judgment noted, 'raise[d] an important issue regarding witness protection besides the quality and credibility of the evidence before the Court'.[137] The two other 'unusual features' that the judgment identified were those of 'improper conduct of trial by the public prosecutor' and the 'role of the investigative agency [the police]' as 'perfunctory and not impartial'.[138]

The judgment summarised the 'prosecution version which led to the trial', highlighting specifically that it was a 'ghastly incident'; that the 'attacks were stated to be a part of retaliatory action to avenge killing of 56 persons burnt to death in the Sabarmati Express'; and that '[f]aulty and biased investigation as well as perfunctory trial were said to have marred the sanctity of the entire exercise undertaken to bring the culprits to books'.[139]

The Supreme Court listed four grounds on the basis of which the state of Gujarat and Zahira Sheikh had prayed for a retrial in the appeal. These grounds, as the judgment noted, were: First, 'reasonable suspicion' should have arisen when witnesses were turning hostile during the trial, and the public prosecutor should have taken steps to protect Zahira.[140] Second, the public prosecutor under the circumstances did not request the sessions court judge to conduct the trial *in camera*. Third, the Vadodara Sessions Court did not exercise its powers under the Code of Criminal Procedure and the Indian Evidence Act to recall and re-examine witnesses 'to arrive at the truth and a just decision', and to accept affidavits from Zahira and four new witnesses who were injured, as additional evidence.[141] Fourth, the public prosecutor did not examine the injured witnesses who were not able to depose at the trial. In light of these circumstances, the Supreme Court stated that at every stage of the trial process, there had been a compromise in conduct and procedure. The judges wrote: 'When the investigating agency helps the accused, the witnesses are threatened to depose falsely and prosecutor acts in a manner as if he was defending the accused, and the Court was acting merely as an onlooker and there is no fair trial at all, justice becomes the victim.'[142]

The judgment then summarised the arguments made by the lawyers for the appellants and respondents, with a focus on whether the Gujarat High Court was bound by Section 391 of the Code of Criminal Procedure that empowers appellate courts to summon additional evidence. It is this contention that would form the foundation of the Supreme Court's decision about whether to order a retrial of the Best Bakery case.[143] The rest of the judgment builds on this point to offer an excursus on why the 'discovery, vindication and establishment of *truth*' is the foundational *role* of courts in the criminal justice system in the common law world.[144] In building on the trope of *role*, the judgment repeatedly speaks of three interconnected issues that form a part of what it considers the responsibility of the judiciary: the pursuit of truth, fair trials and witness protection. In framing these issues, the Supreme Court invoked the set of tropes that have already been in circulation now through the narratives of the previous judgments: *evidence*, *truth* and *justice*. My description of this judgment will elaborate on the connection between these three tropes as imagined by the Supreme Court.

The responsibility of the judiciary, the judgment explained, emerges from an understanding that '[c]ourts have always been considered to have an over-riding duty to vindicate and uphold the *"majesty of the law"*'.[145] It further states that for criminal courts to be able to effectively dispense justice, 'the Presiding Judge must cease to be a spectator and a mere recording machine by becoming a participant in the trial'.[146] The court here was referring back to the sessions court judgment in which it was stated that the trial court was a court of evidence and not of justice. In contradistinction to the sessions court's delimitation of a court's *role*, for the Supreme Court, it seems, drawing on the history of judicial activism in India,[147] this role had to go beyond merely being a court of record. The objective of taking on this role, as per the Supreme Court, was to uphold *the majesty of the law*—which is being equated with the achievement of justice.

The judgment further emphasised, now making references to reasons that the Gujarat High Court had stated for not admitting the affidavits: 'Since the object is to mete out justice and to convict the guilty and protect the innocent, the trial should be a search for the *truth* and not a bout over technicalities.'[148] Thus, the court noted: 'The fair trial for a criminal offence consists not only in technical observance of the frame and form of law, but also in recognition and just application of its principles in substance, to find out the *truth* and prevent miscarriage of justice.'[149] For such a process to be carried out, the judgment notes, a 'congenial *atmosphere* for a fair and impartial trial' is required,[150] which was allegedly absent during the trial in Vadodara, leading to the repeated cases of witnesses turning hostile.

We thus see the enmeshing of a range of tropes in the narrative of the judgment's text: the *role* of the judiciary is to search for the *truth* which will result in *justice* and ultimately uphold the *majesty of the law*; and that such a process is only possible in an *atmosphere* of impartiality. Noting that the present appeal would be approached in recognition of these connections, the judges wrote: '… we must approach the facts of the present case without excitement, exaggeration or eclipse a sense of proportion'.[151] In doing this, as I read it, the Supreme Court was qualifying the way it hoped to conduct the proceedings of the appeal, in clear contradistinction to the way the trial had been conducted by the Vadodara Sessions Court and the Gujarat High Court. More significantly, the Supreme Court was also calling attention to the fact that the *atmosphere* of 'mob action',[152] which was present during the violence in Gujarat, was not only restricted to its streets but also entered the courtrooms, both metaphorically and otherwise—and that is what had led to the witnesses turning hostile.

Building on the trope of the *crowd*, the judgment emphasised that '[m]ob action may throw out of gear the wheels of the judicial process' and that '[e]ngineered fury may paralyse a party's ability to present his [*sic*] case or participate in the trial'.[153] However, expressing belief in the conduct of the judiciary, the court also stated that it could not agree entirely with the appellants' argument 'that calm inside the court is beyond restoration'. In other words, it offered a means to restore public trust in the judiciary, despite the performance of the courts in Gujarat. The judgment avers, referring to the violence in Gujarat: 'Perhaps there was some rough weather but it subsided', thus recognising the compromised *atmosphere* of the judicial proceedings in Gujarat on the one hand, and affirming that courts were capable of conducting themselves impartially on the other, that is, if they took their *role* of ensuring a fair trial and search for *truth* seriously.

Speaking about the importance of protecting witnesses from undue influence, the judgment quoted Jeremy Bentham on witnesses being 'the eyes and ears of justice', and as such, '[i]f the witness himself [*sic*] is incapacitated from acting as eyes and ears of justice', the court noted, 'the trial gets putrefied and paralysed, and it no longer can constitute a fair trial'.[154] Here the Supreme Court deploys the trope of *role* to characterise the witness. Stating that it is a paramount responsibility of the state and the courts to protect witnesses to depose fearlessly, the judgment re-emphasises:

> Time has come when serious and undiluted thoughts are to be bestowed for protecting witnesses so that *ultimate truth* is presented before the Court and *justice triumphs*.... The State has a definite role to play in protecting the witnesses.... If ultimately *truth* is to be arrived at, the eyes and ears of justice have to be protected so that the *interest of justice* do not get incapacitated in the sense of making the proceedings before Courts mere mock trials as are usually seen in movies.... In this courts have a vital role to play.[155]

Reiterating several times the importance of 'arriving at the *truth*' or 'the real *truth*' as the 'ultimate objective'—the court itself considered such repetition 'ad nauseam'—the judgment explains why the high court ought to have used its powers under Section 391—a 'salutary principle' of the Code of Criminal Procedure, 1973—'to find out the *truth* and dispense justice impartially'.[156] It admonishes the Gujarat High Court for having failed to do that:

> The entire approach of the High Court suffers from serious infirmities, its conclusions lopsided and lacks proper or judicious application of mind. Arbitrariness is found writ large on the approach as well as the conclusions arrived at in the judgment under challenge, in unreasonably keeping out evidence from being brought on record.[157]

Further, the judgment stated that despite the sessions court having acquitted the accused, and the same being upheld by the high court, such decisions were based on 'tainted evidence, tailored investigation, unprincipled prosecutor and evidence of threatened/terrorized witnesses' and did not amount to an 'acquittal in the eye of the law and no sanctity or credibility can be attached to the so-called findings'.[158] According to the judges: 'It seems to be nothing but a travesty of *truth*, fraud on legal process.'[159] Despite strong disagreement with the decisions of the sessions and high courts, the judges also relied on the trope of *accordance with law* or *majesty of the law* to distinguish their own conduct from the previous judges.

Very much like the previous two judgments, the Supreme Court also devoted a fair amount of space to offering comments on the causes and consequences of religious violence in a meditative mode. The judges expressed dismay about how the 2002 violence in Gujarat posed a danger to the minorities in a country like India with its 'heterogeneous religions and multiracial and multilingual society [*sic*]'.[160] The court was concerned that such 'internal disturbances' could 'undermine the unity and security of the nation' and 'strike … at the very root of an orderly society, which the founding fathers of our Constitution dreamt of'.[161] I understand the tropes being alluded to here as *secularism* and *development*. That the violence had taken place 'in the land of Mahatma Gandhi' led the court to say that 'some people have become so bankrupt of their ideology that they have deviated from everything which was so dear to him'.[162] Emphasising a Gandhian refrain, the judgment stated that 'no religion teaches violence', and '[t]he golden thread passing through every religion is love and compassion'.[163] Making a reference to those who carried out the violence, the court said: 'The fanatics who spread violence in the name of religion are worse than terrorist [*sic*] and more dangerous than alien enemy.'[164] Having said this, the judgment reproduces a poem titled 'Little Things' by American educator Julia A. F. Carney,[165] and writes with poetic fervour:

> The little drops of humanness which jointly make humanity a cherished desire of mankind had seemingly dried up when the perpetrators of the crime had burnt alive helpless women and innocent children. Was it their fault that they were born in the houses of persons belonging to a particular community?[166]

One might be able to infer the reference to the Best Bakery incident in this paragraph of the judgment. However, the way the court framed the incident of violence here, speaking of the burning alive of innocents, and suggesting that they were targeted because they belonged to a particular community, might even be read as a reference to the whole of the Gujarat pogrom, including the Godhra incident.

The judgment strongly criticises the conduct of the police, the public prosecutor, the Gujarat judiciary and the Gujarat state in the Best Bakery case and, as mentioned earlier, says that they had reduced it to a 'mock trial'.[167] It is necessary to note that the idea of the mock trial is likened to the representation of judicial proceedings in cinema. In so doing, the court, it can be argued, considered cinema's representations of the legal system in general to be a falsity that had become a perverse reality in the Best Bakery trial.

In response to such a situation, the judgment recommends that the judiciary be cleansed of the kind of political interference that had influenced the proceedings of the case in the Gujarat courts. This 'whimsical political will', the court noted, was 'prohibited by the mandate of the Constitution',[168] the Constitution thus being likened to the *majestic* pinnacle of law. The court, then, in unflinching words, indicted the Gujarat government, and its investigative and judicial apparatus, in what has come to be the paragraph most cited and quoted by the media:

> Those who are responsible for protecting life and properties and ensuring that investigation is fair and proper seem to have shown no real anxiety. Large number of people had lost their lives. Whether the accused persons were really assailants or not could have been established by a fair and impartial investigation. The modern day 'Neros' were looking elsewhere when Best Bakery and innocent children and women were burning, and were probably deliberating how the perpetrators of the crime can be saved or protected. Law and justice become flies in the hands of these 'wanton boys'. When fences start to swallow the crops, no scope will be left for survival of law and order or *truth* and *justice*. Public order as well as public interest become martyrs and monuments.[169]

The Supreme Court made clear that this was a 'fit and proper case' for the application of Section 391 of the Code of Criminal Procedure (appellate court's power to take additional evidence), read with Section 311 of the same code (power to summon and examine witnesses),[170] and Section 165 of the Indian Evidence Act (judge's power to put questions or order production).[171]

None of this was done by the courts in Gujarat, because of which the Supreme Court felt that pursuant to Section 406 of the Code of Criminal Procedure (power of Supreme Court to transfer cases and appeals),[172] a 're-trial is a must and essentially called for in order to save and preserve the justice delivery system unsullied and unscathed by vested interests'.[173] This decision, in the way it cited specific sections of legislations, followed the trope of *strictly according to law* as a way to build the 'confidence of reasonable and right thinking citizen[s], in the justice delivery system'[174]—in other words, to restore faith in the *majesty of the law*.

Before passing its final order, the judgment makes a mention of three further concerns regarding the Gujarat High Court judgment. First, it admonishes the judges for hurrying to pronounce their order and keeping the reasons waiting till after the court vacations—the trope of *speed* at work. Second, it berates the judges for failing 'to maintain judicial balance and sobriety in making unwarranted references to personalities'.[175] This was in reference to the high court indicating that Teesta Setalvad, Mihir Desai and CJP had been instrumental in taking unfair advantage of Zahira and making her deliver a public statement about how threats had made her recant her statement. Third, it relegates concerns about this having been a 'media trial' for 'an appropriate case where the media is duly and effectively represented'.[176]

Allowing the appeals, the judgment passed the order for retrial by a court under the jurisdiction of the Bombay High Court, for which a new public prosecutor was to be appointed by the state of Gujarat, and stipulating that victims and witnesses should have a say in this appointment given the circumstances that had led to this appeal. Inter alia, the judgment entrusted the state of Gujarat with ensuring the production of witnesses at the fresh trial in Bombay and providing them with protection to enable them to depose without fear of threat or coercion. The director general of police in Gujarat was directed to monitor the reinvestigation if such was required, and to do so with urgency and utmost sincerity.

In closing, in what reads like an emphasis on the Supreme Court's authority as the highest court of the country, the judgment notes: 'We would like to point out that the orders passed by this Court are final and no further appeal lies against them. The Supreme Court is the final court in the hierarchy of our courts.'[177] The trope of *closure* in the text of this judgment, thus, is framed as one of judicial authority and its power to rewrite the narrative of the Best Bakery case by purging the abuse of authority by the lower judiciary.

The same Supreme Court bench, in another judgment accompanying this one—which emerged out of a separate SLP filed by Teesta Setalvad against the state of Gujarat (*Teesta Setalvad and Anr v. State of Gujarat and Ors*[178])—directed the Gujarat High Court to expunge from its judgment portions that cast aspersions on the intention of Setalvad and Mihir Desai of CJP in moving the Supreme Court against the Vadodara Sessions Court judgment. The bench noted: '... we direct that the observations of the high court, as against the appellants ... shall stand expunged and deleted from the judgment of the high court, and consequently must be treated as having never existed or being part of the high court judgment.'[179]

The Supreme Court judgment ordering a retrial of the Best Bakery case drew celebratory responses and had its share of detractors as well. *Outlook* magazine wrote, 'SC Makes the Best Possible History',[180] and the *Hindustan Times* concurred that the 'SC [had] stepped in for justice'.[181] A lawyer for Zahira Sheikh said that it was 'a victory for justice, secularism and the Indian constitution'.[182] Human rights lawyer Colin Gonsalves called it the 'judiciary's finest hour'.[183] K. T. S. Tulsi, a lawyer for the defence in the Best Bakery case, 'deplored the idea of shifting the case to another state' and called it a 'weak remedy'.[184] The Bar Council of Gujarat adopted a resolution calling on the Supreme Court to review its decision to transfer the case because 'the morale of legal fraternity and whole judicial administration of Gujarat was quite likely to be adversely affected'.[185]

Conviction: The Second Supreme Court of India Judgment

This second judgment of the Supreme Court came in 2006, two years after it had ordered the retrial of the Best Bakery case by a trial court in Bombay. The Bombay retrial judgment was delivered on 8 March 2006 by Additional Sessions Judge A. M. Thipsey, a month after the Court of Sessions for Greater Bombay retried the Best Bakery case, and convicted 9 of the 17 accused tried.[186] All the convicted persons received a life sentence. During the retrial in Bombay, Zahira Sheikh turned 'hostile' again.[187]

On 3 November 2004, a day before she was supposed to appear before the court in Bombay to depose at the trial, Zahira spoke to the press in Vadodara in the company of Gujarat government officials and the police. At the press conference, she claimed that she had been forced to level false charges against the 21 accused in the original trial in Vadodara.[188] She accused Teesta Setalvad of having kidnapped her and her brother, and keeping them in solitary confinement for seven months.[189]

In response to this second incident of Zahira recanting her statement, the Supreme Court ordered that a committee be set up to enquire into the allegations that Zahira had levelled against Teesta Setalvad.[190] The investigations by the committee revealed, as per an undercover investigation carried out by the news magazine *Tehelka*, that Zahira had accepted an amount of 5 lakh rupees (5,00,000 rupees) from three men connected to the BJP.[191] The allegations against Teesta Setalvad were declared baseless. The committee's findings were read out by a Supreme Court bench comprising Justices Arijit Pasayat and H. K. Sema, in which Zahira was called a 'self-condemned liar'.[192]

On 8 March 2006, in the Supreme Court case of *Zahira Habibullah Sheikh and Anr v. State of Gujarat and Ors*,[193] Justice Arijit Pasayat opened the judgment by quoting two stanzas in Sanskrit from the ancient Hindu scripture Manu Samhita (*The Laws of Manu*),[194] on the *role* of witnesses. The court offered English translations as follows:

> Stanza 14: 'Where in the presence of judges "dharma" [duty] is overcome by "adharma" [dereliction] and "truth" by "unfounded falsehood", at that place they (the judges) are destroyed by sin.'

> Stanza 18: 'In the adharma flowing from wrong decision in a Court of law, one fourth each is attributed to the person committing the adharma, witness, the judges and the ruler.'[195]

In this judgment, the Supreme Court verbatim repeated major portions from its previous judgment in the Best Bakery case, particularly those on the importance of fair trials, witness protection and the pursuit of truth. The court held Zahira Sheikh in contempt. The judgment, deploying the trope of *role*, noted: 'Serious questions arise as to the role played by witnesses who changed their versions more frequently than chameleons.... [T]he criminal justice system is likely to be affected if persons like Zahira are to be left unpunished.'[196]

In substantiating its decision to convict Zahira, the court offered an explanation for why it was necessary to do so to keep the integrity of the judiciary—or what it had previously called the *majesty of the law*—intact.

The court said that if Zahira was not convicted for contempt, people's faith in the efficacy of the judiciary would be 'destroyed'.[197] Along with Manu, the judgment also cites a range of eclectic non-Indian authorities from Lord Denning to Justice Cardozo to John Salmond to Jonathan Swift, and emphasises the principle of 'open justice'[198] by quoting Lord Bowen's patriarchal dictum from an 1889 decision (without attribution) that '[j]udges like Caesar's wife should be above suspicion'.[199] The judgment further said, citing precedents from the Supreme Court of India and invoking the trope of *role*: '… the role to be played by Courts … has to be focussed when eyebrows are raised about their roles'.[200]

The judgment convicted Zahira of perjury and ordered that she would undergo 'simple imprisonment' for one year,[201] and pay 50,000 rupees as fine. In the event that Zahira defaulted on payment within two months, she would have to undergo an additional year of imprisonment. Her bank accounts were ordered to be attached for a period of three months for inspection by the income tax authorities.[202]

At 6:30 p.m. on 10 March 2006 (two days after the Supreme Court's decision convicting her), Zahira Sheikh surrendered at the sessions court in Bombay and was remanded to judicial custody.[203] In an application declaring that she was surrendering, Zahira had requested not to be imprisoned in Gujarat because she was fearful of threats to her life there.[204] During the period of incarceration, Zahira appealed against the order and the Supreme Court dismissed the appeal. During this appeal hearing, when Zahira's lawyer mentioned that she had 'lost ten kilos in jail', 'the entire court packed with lawyers laughed'.[205] Zahira served a year at a jail in Nasik, Maharashtra, and was released on 14 March 2007. The fine and the additional sentence for defaulting on payment were waived because of her poor financial condition.[206]

On 9 July 2012, a decision on the appeal by those convicted in the Best Bakery retrial was delivered by the Bombay High Court, in which of the nine convicted, five were acquitted for want of evidence, and the life sentences against the other four were upheld.[207] This judgment was delivered by a division bench of Justices V. M. Kanade and P. D. Kode. The acquittals were not appealed further by any of the victim-survivors or the state of Gujarat. It brought about the closure of the judicial proceedings in the Best Bakery case.[208]

Judgment and Its Forms

The Best Bakery case's journey from 2003 to 2012, and the texts of its four key judgments across the full hierarchy of India's courts, offer insights into the interpretive and narrative role of the judiciary in the making of collective memories of the pogrom. This collective memory is actively generated through the address of the judgments. The address mobilises publics that simultaneously acknowledge the event's horror and valorise the very institutions that are foundational to the structural exclusion of India's Muslim citizens. To rehearse Robert Cover, legal interpretation happens within what he has called 'a system designed to generate violence',[209] even as the law speaks of legal interpretation as a 'practical activity'.[210] Thus, as I will show in this section, the four judgments of the Best Bakery case provide a dense narrative of the juridical investments in the workings of a postcolonial state-making and state-preserving rationality comprising the triad of legalism, secularism and developmentalism.

In the previous section, I offered a re-description of four key judgments in the Best Bakery case. The re-description was aimed, first, at detailing the textual contents of the judgments, with particular attention to the way in which the event and its aftermath have been narratively reconstructed in judicial memory; and second, at signposting the tropes that recur across the four judgments in the way the story of the event—the incident and the case—is narrativised. In this section, I will elaborate on these tropes and reread some specific portions of the texts of the judgments to foreground their aesthetic dimensions. I will look at the work that the narrative compact of law and aesthetics is doing in the making and ordering of collective memories. This exercise will employ the J-A approach to specifically do two things: first, pay attention to the narrative forms of interpretation that emerge in the judgments; and second, identify the aesthetic expressions, iconography or imaginaries that are deployed in the judgments as tropes of memorial reconstruction.

We might recollect that in the first Supreme Court judgment that ordered the retrial, the court emphatically commented on how the conduct of the judiciary ought not to be like 'mock trials' in movies.[211] This differentiation is an emphasis on the cinematic being fictional, and law being real and procedural. For the court, while cinema makes a mockery of judicial proceedings, real court proceedings must adhere to legal procedure. However, as I will discuss in this section, when the judgments are read as aesthetic texts, we see that there is a lot more than a strict adherence to technical legal procedure—or legalism—that constitutes its content and form.

In reading the texts of the judgments using the J-A approach, I will string together the tropes that I have signposted in the previous section. This stringing will be done by organising the tropes through the classification of the judgment form as a *record* of the Best Bakery incident; as expression, iconography or *image*; and as the assemblage of the legal record, the event and the image in narrating a *mnemohistory*. These three typologies in the organisation of the tropes will identify the narrative work that the judgments are doing as, borrowing from Cover, 'bonded [legal] interpretation'.[212] As Cover writes: 'Legal interpretation, therefore, can never be "free"; it can never be the function of an understanding of the text of the word alone.'[213] Cover insists that legal interpretation needs to be understood through the triad of word, deed and role.[214] His argument considers legal interpretation as the deed words enable through the speech of someone in the role of authority figure like the judge. In this way, words of a judge, when uttered as speech or text mobilise action and identity.[215] To quote Cover again: 'We begin, then, not with what judges say, but with what they *do*. The judges deal pain and death.'[216] This doing, as I understand from my reading of Cover, can be seen not through a mere content analysis of judgments but by paying attention to what judges draw on to build 'the *template* for transforming language into action, word into deed'.[217] As I will demonstrate through my J-A reading of the judgment and its forms, the template that will emerge by paying attention to the tropes is that of the working of a particular state-making and state-preserving rationality. It is this rationality—the triad of secularism, legalism and developmentalism—which serves as the base for the memorial reconstructions of both the Best Bakery incident and the legal case.

Judgment as Record

The open access availability of the Best Bakery judgments as a record of judicial memory and the incident's wide media coverage are resources for *a posteriori* narrative reconstructions of both the incident and the case. The four judgments from the Best Bakery case—seeking the same end, that of achieving convictions—offer connected yet contested narratives. The ways in which the judgments record the event of the Best Bakery killings and reconstruct it from the time and place of the legal proceedings and pronouncements work on multiple registers of collective memory.

The judgments pronounced in the courts offer a sense of *closure* through conviction, thus fixing culpability and lending primacy to what the law's recorded memory considers as *the truth*. The contestations in the ways in which the judgments have recorded the reconstructions of the Best Bakery incident are not about whether it took place or not. From the Vadodara Sessions Court to the Supreme Court of India, all the judgments are in agreement about the date, time and place of the incident, about the modus operandi of the killings, the number of dead people. As the first Supreme Court judgment noted: '... it is nobody's stand that the [Best Bakery] incident did not take place'.[218] All the judgments also concur, at least in their chronological reconstruction of the facts of the case, that the violence that spread across Gujarat beginning on 28 February 2002, leading to the Best Bakery incident on 1 March 2002, was provoked by the killing of Hindu pilgrims in Godhra on 27 February 2002. The Vadodara Sessions Court characterised the Best Bakery incident as a 'reversal action',[219] and the Gujarat High Court identified the 'communal riots' as having been carried out 'due to Godhra carnage'.[220] The first Supreme Court judgment, in stating the facts of the case, puts on record the prosecution version to note that the Best Bakery 'attacks were stated to be a part of retaliatory action to avenge killing of 56 persons burnt to death in the Sabarmati Express [in Godhra]'.[221]

The recognition of the happening of the event is accompanied by an acknowledgement of its horror. Even while acquitting the 21 accused persons, the Vadodara Sessions Court judgment called the incident 'cruel' and 'brutal' and considered it to be a 'black stigma' attached to 'cultured Baroda city'.[222] The first Supreme Court judgment called Gujarat's administrators 'modern day "Neros" [who] were looking elsewhere when Best Bakery and innocent children and women were burning'.[223] The contestations arise in the context of whether the 21 accused were the ones who carried out this act of violence. To ascertain that, the Vadodara Sessions Court relied on the eyewitness testimony of, among others, Zahira Sheikh, the star witness, who deposed for the prosecution, and that of Lalmohmad Khudabax Shaikh, who deposed for the defence.

While Zahira's statement as recorded by the police confirmed that she had identified the 21 accused persons as having carried out the burning and the killings, in court she recanted. The sessions court judgment declared her hostile, without raising concerns about whether this could be an outcome of any threats or coercion she might have faced. The same judgment also placed on record Lalmohmad's eyewitness account, which countered the statement Zahira had made to the police. Lalmohmad had said that the accused were in fact neighbours who had saved several Muslims in Hanuman Tekdi from being killed by the violent mobs. The sessions court strongly criticised the conduct of the investigation by the police for this evidentiary discrepancy and acquitted all the accused for lack of evidence.

In justifying its reasons, the judge wrote: 'The court of law or judiciary in the true meaning and sense, is *not the court of justice but the court of evidence.*'[224] In stating this, the Vadodara Sessions Court marks a distinction between *evidence* and *justice*, and extends this to an understanding of the judgment form as a record only of evidence acquired in a particular case, and not that of justice delivered. Justice, in other words, was cast not as the end of evidence. That end, as we have seen all the judgments mention repeatedly, was *truth*. And in the understanding of the sessions court judgment, truth is not measured by standards of justness. This distinction between *justice* and *evidence* made by the Vadodara Sessions Court judgment acknowledge the legacy of *legalism*, which worked as a rationality that was at the foundations of the passage of the Indian Evidence Act, 1855. Ranabir Samaddar writes on the colonial history of the Evidence Act:

> This was how judicial power took shape, it was rational; hence it could reinforce domination with power. This was judicial power at the behest of the State and its governmental task of maintaining the daily order of the society; at the heart of this particular form of power was the essence of law, legality and objectivity.... The Evidence Act was one of the earliest instances in the country of what Foucault was later famously to call 'governmentality'.[225]

Samaddar points out that this rationality, which was at the heart of colonial judicial power, was responsible for shaping 'the justice-seeking subject ... [who was fashioned to] appeal to justice not only on the grounds of fairness, but also with reason'.[226] Endowing the justice-seeking subject with reason was a means of awakening 'self-interest' to speak the truth in court.[227] This was operationalised through a circular logic where '[e]vidence was above all a matter of procedure—the procedure for arriving at truth ... [where] truth was nothing if there was a lack of procedure, and procedure had to be marked by evidence, because evidence signalled fairness [in legal proceedings]'.[228]

The Vadodara Sessions Court, thus, by performing its *role* as a 'court of evidence', was demonstrating a rationality of *legalism* in its conduct, in both acquitting the accused, and declaring Zahira to be a hostile witness. In other words, *truth* for the court lay in its conduct of procedure—which it believed was in adherence to the Indian Evidence Act and the Code of Criminal Procedure—and not in probing the political content, contexts and conditions of depositions by eyewitnesses, be it Zahira or Lalmohmad. 'Indeed', as Samaddar notes, 'that procedure of working through—the procedural activity—was the truth' for the court.[229]

When the case went to appeal, we see the Gujarat High Court extending the work of this rationality of *legalism*, where instead of asking why Zahira might have recanted her statement at trial, the judgment was more concerned about why she had declared in public that she had been threatened into lying in court. The Gujarat High Court, as I have described in the previous section, wondered why, if Zahira could have spoken the truth outside of court—which is not the realm of legal procedure—she could not have done so in court when the trial was on, when legal procedure was in full, robust operation. In effect, the Gujarat High Court considered what Zahira said outside of court—that she was threatened—to be a lie, and what she had said during trial—that she could not identify the accused—to be the truth. Such a line of thinking by the Gujarat High Court judges, thus, strengthened the rationality of *legalism* that considers 'judicial truth' to carry more weight than other contested versions.[230] Samaddar writes, appositely:

> [J]udicial truth telling is an activity with a specific nature, which problematizes the issue of evidence (of truth) by agreeing to take into consideration all that can spoil truth, that is the untruths, and is prepared to engage in confrontation with these possible untruths. The problematization of truth thus happens through staging an encounter between possible truths and various impurities and untruths present in the world of truth. This kind of problematization is that mark of modern rationality, which prides itself on practical reason.[231]

The multiplicity of narratives in the judicial recordings in the Best Bakery case is furthered when the truth record espoused by the sessions and high court judgments encounters the Supreme Court judgments. The first Supreme Court judgment strongly admonishes the sessions court's characterisation of its *role* as that of a court of evidence by emphasising that courts are expected to 'take a participatory role' in a trial and 'are not expected to be tape recorders to record whatever is being stated by the witness'.[232] It further added that courts 'have to monitor the proceedings in aid of justice in manner that something, which is not relevant, is not unnecessarily brought into record. Even if the prosecutor is remiss in some ways, it can control the proceedings effectively so that ultimate objective i.e. *truth* is arrived at.'[233] By saying this, the Supreme Court recasts the relationship between the tropes of *evidence, justice* and *truth* that the sessions court had inaugurated, and the high court had confirmed, yet holds on to the rationality of *legalism*.

In this recasting, the Supreme Court judgment—*in strict accordance with the law*—was directed by Section 165 of the Indian Evidence Act (judges' power to put questions or order production),[234] and Section 311 of the Code of Criminal Procedure (power to summon material witness or any person present),[235] to foreground its own version of legalism: that courts need to play an active role in the procedure of *truth* finding, and an adherence to such procedure is what will ensure *justice*. This procedure, the Supreme Court notes, demands that courts do more than being 'tape recorders', thus making a direct reference to what form of memorial record judgments are expected be. This other form of record, which the Supreme Court advances, is not a device like the tape recorder that can only capture image-less voices of the proceedings, or testimonies of witnesses to be more exact. As I read it, the Supreme Court expects the judgment to be a record of its procedural commitment to truth seeking 'with an iron hand within the framework of law', and that fidelity to such procedure would enable the court to 'render justice'.[236]

The *legalism* at the foundation of this rationality of the Supreme Court is not different from Samaddar's observations in the quotes cited earlier. The figure of Zahira Sheikh as the hostile witness upsets this rationality of legalism at every stage of the Best Bakery case. She follows self-interest, but does not speak the truth in court. This happens again at the Mumbai retrial, after it was recognised by the Supreme Court that she had been threatened during the trial in Vadodara. This is why, by convicting her for perjury, the Supreme Court through its second judgment was in effect restoring and rehabilitating this rationality. The 'iron hand' that the Supreme Court said that judges should use to 'render justice', thus, included convicting the victim of the Best Bakery case, along with its perpetrators. Both are made culpable for the violation of what the judges referred to as the 'majesty of the law'.

As the highest court of the country, the Supreme Court played a corrective role by identifying two reasons that compromised the Gujarat judgments due to which Zahira and many other eyewitnesses turning hostile: first, the courts' inability to ensure witness protection, and second, faulty police investigation. Despite this recognition, the Supreme Court, while ordering a retrial of the Best Bakery case in Mumbai, continued to rely on the Gujarat administration to provide protection to the witnesses, including Zahira, and to conduct reinvestigation as required. The rule-bound rationality of legalism that explains this is that in the Indian Constitution, law and order and the police are in the state list, and the Supreme Court followed that posited authority.[237] The retrial was then a change of location for where the judicial proceedings would be conducted and judgment delivered, but the structural causes that had led to the inefficient police investigation, and to Zahira turning hostile, were left unquestioned by the Supreme Court.

The J-A reading of the judgments as record has allowed me to string together the tropes of role, evidence, justice and truth to understand how the texts have written the narrative of the law's triumph into the collective memory of the pogrom. In this narrative, *majesty of the law* is rehabilitated despite the violence that the law facilitated. The triumph of judicial process involved a record of the evidence of convictions of whoever threatened or violated its rationality of legalism to reinstate the primacy of 'judicial truth'. This narrative of triumph is further rationalised through the use of tropes in the judgment that frame it as an image for the making and ordering of collective memory.

Judgment as Image

All the judgments in the Best Bakery case that I have read in this chapter are texts that are composed of words, not images. These are texts that are invested in legal interpretation that can lend meaning to the procedure of adjudication they are recording. Yet, when read using the J-A lens, the visual and aural metaphors and allusions in the texts, and the role they play in the meaning-making activity of legal interpretation, become apparent. The first Supreme Court judgment, commenting on the failure of the

Gujarat administration to offer protection to Zahira, characterised the *witness*—drawing on Bentham[238]—as 'the eyes and ears of justice'.[239] That the entire Best Bakery case was built around Zahira Sheikh's eyewitness account points at how fundamentally dependent the law's record is on image-as-evidence transmitted through the figure of the eyewitness.[240] The changing versions of Zahira's testimony acted as what Ronald Barthes has call the 'punctum': an image with the capacity to 'prick' and 'bruise', and one that 'shoots out … like an arrow and pierces' the viewer/reader, in this case the judge or the judiciary.[241] This profoundly disturbed the rationality underlying the 'ultimate objective' that the process of legal interpretation was meant to achieve: 'truth',[242] as the Supreme Court judgment repeated 'ad nauseam'.[243]

The judgments, thus, projected an image of Zahira as a 'split subject':[244] simultaneously a victim of violence, and a perjurer. While the Gujarat High Court interpreted Zahira's conduct as having been adversely influenced by those like Teesta Setalvad, who were allegedly taking advantage of her victimhood, the Supreme Court–appointed inquiry committee cast her as a 'self-condemned liar'.[245] The second Supreme Court judgment, even while being very critical of the sessions and high court judgments, evaluated Zahira's conduct by citing verses from the ancient Hindu text of the Manusmriti.[246] As Kalpana Kannabiran writes:

> [B]y drawing justification from the Manusmriti to negate the liberty of a Muslim survivor of Hindu fundamentalist assault—the Supreme Court demonstrated by its own example the way in which discrimination interlocks with the loss of liberty in the case of persons belonging to religious minority communities, especially the women of these communities … the normativization by constitutional courts of conservative Hindu legal traditions embodied in the Manusmriti, and the situated reading of the constitution within the ideological frameworks of orthodox Hinduism, sharpens the crisis of constitutional disarticulation on the critical issue of non-discrimination.[247]

The first Supreme Court judgment had already ordered the retrial of the Best Bakery case outside of Gujarat, a move that was hailed by the media and human rights activists as a victory against the communalised judiciary of Gujarat which was heavily weighed against the Muslim victim-survivors of the pogrom. In the second judgment, the Supreme Court displays its own *secular* rationality—of not siding with any particular religion, but with law— in the aftermath of violence against a particular religion. It does so, however, by citing from a religious scripture that has been the historical foundation of the ideology of Hindu racial supremacy,[248] and of contemporary Hindutva politics,[249] to declare criminal a Muslim woman whose fear (legally interpreted as hostility) in the space of the courtroom pricked and bruised the judiciary's failure to make meaning of the many changing versions of her witness accounts.

The second Supreme Court judgment constructed its ideal image of the *witness* drawing on Hindu scriptures to uphold *the majesty of secular law*. That the judgment's quest for truth was not meant to be a 'bout over technicalities',[250] as the same court had previously mentioned, provided the justification to use a religious source and not one from secular law. The fact that the Supreme Court was convicting a Muslim victim of an anti-Muslim pogrom with the ultimate objective of rehabilitating the judiciary and the justice delivery system because 'eyebrows' had been 'raised about their *roles*'[251] was in furtherance of the court's own belief that the judges 'must approach the facts of the present case without excitement, exaggeration or eclipse a sense of proportion'.[252] The image of the ideal witness that this judgment records in judicial memory is historic, because 'no one ever had got [a] one year prison sentence on contempt since Independence' and 'Zahira Sheikh was the first to be convicted in the aftermath of the Gujarat violence'.[253] By doing this, the Supreme Court rationalised the use of a religious source as *secular*, because it was meant to serve a secular end—that of convicting a perjurer who had undermined the *majesty of the law*. Zahira as a Muslim victim of the pogrom was, thus, written out of judicial memory.

The trope of the *witness* deployed by the Supreme Court judgment was connected to the framing of another imagistic trope—that of the *atmosphere* of a courtroom. The connection lies in the image of the place that is to be inhabited by the figure of the witness. Just as the Gujarat High Court had wondered why Zahira could not speak the truth in what it considered was the safe *atmosphere* of the courtroom during the trial, the Supreme Court seems to have made the same imagistic assumptions about the safe *atmosphere* of the Mumbai retrial. In imagining the *atmosphere* of the courtroom as safe, both the Gujarat High Court and the Supreme Court judgments effectively carried out an act of purification to externalise the locations of pain and death outside of the physical site of the court.

The repeated references by all the judgments to the *atmosphere* of violence and mayhem that had prevailed on the streets of Vadodara were aimed at demarcating the jurisdictions of violence and law. The city was the site of violence, and law the site of rationality. Such a distinction reflects, curiously, the images of Christian law in the 'City of Man' (the lawless location of violence) versus the 'City of God' (courts as the location of justice).[254] Such an understanding also does not consider both the city and the court as part of a 'lawscape': 'It becomes an *atmosphere*—there but not there, imperceptible yet all-determining.'[255] That lawlessness on the streets is not the outside of law, but constitutive of it, has been integral to the way in which the marginalisation of Muslims has worked in Gujarat, both, during the pogrom and during times of apparent peace. This is particularly the case with the operation of the Disturbed Areas Act, 1991, in Gujarat, which has disproportionately impacted Muslims in certain areas to stop them from distress selling their property to move to locations with mixed religious populations. Over the years, this legislation has organised many cities in Gujarat in a way where Muslim ghettos have emerged, and it was these areas that were specifically targeted during the pogrom.[256]

A related concern expressed by the first Supreme Court judgment regarding the *atmosphere* that prevailed in the Vadodara Sessions Court was about keeping the criminal justice system 'clean beyond the reach of whimsical political wills or agendas and properly insulated from the discriminatory standards or yardsticks of the type prohibited by the mandate of the Constitution'.[257] While this sanitary objective might have been rightly recommended for the highly compromised nature of the conduct of both the Best Bakery case as well as other pogrom-related trials in Gujarat, it was also a push towards rehabilitating the judiciary from the stain on its cultivated reputation of being free and fair. In keeping with this objective, the Supreme Court convicted for perjury the witness who had contaminated the atmosphere of the courtroom, but only asked for the bank accounts of Madhu Srivastava— the local politician who had been accused of threatening Zahira in Vadodara—to be investigated by the Income Tax Department. Srivastava's role in turning Zahira hostile was not of further concern for the judgment because he did not identifiably contaminate the atmosphere of the courtroom.[258]

The Supreme Court's concern with cleanliness can be connected to Urdu writer Saadat Hasan Manto's parable 'Tidiness', written in the context of the Partition of 1947. In the story, when a train transporting people from one side of the partitioned border to the other came to a stop at a station, a group of gunmen from one community came in looking for people from the other community hiding in a compartment. One of the passengers revealed to them that there was one hiding in the lavatory. When the gunmen 'broke down the lavatory door' and were about to 'slash his throat', another suggested: 'No, no, not here! ... It'll mess up the carriage. Take him out.'[259] The Supreme Court's rationality of tidiness was about relegating violence to the outside of the courtroom, and convicting Zahira for the mess she had created.

The court thus recorded Zahira's image as that of a messy *witness*, and it is this image that mobilised its publics and got embedded in collective memory. The media, consequently, referred to her as the witness who went 'flip, flop, flip'.[260] It was this mess that the Supreme Court cleansed by convicting her for perjury, to restore the *atmosphere* of the court so that the *majesty of the law* was upheld. It was her hostility towards the rationality of legal procedure that the conviction sought to discipline. Without an acknowledgment that the courtroom could be and was a memorial site of 'pain and death',[261] a change of location for a retrial could do little for the subjectivity of the witness. That the act of witnessing and its transmission as evidence were practices saturated with vulnerability and trauma escaped the *legalism* of achieving conviction and rehabilitating the *majesty of the law*, singularly pursued by the Supreme Court in its second judgment. To return to Barthes, Zahira's witnessing, its recollection and its transmission as testimony, both in its utterance and recantation, were the punctum that pricked and bruised law's own image of rationality and order, which the judiciary had to protect.

Along with the tropes of the *witness* and *atmosphere*, there is a third imagistic trope in the Best Bakery case, particularly in the text of the Vadodara Sessions Court judgment. This is the deployment of the trope of *crowd*. A key instance of this imagistic framing of the crowd can be found in the Sessions Court judgment, where Judge Mahida wrote: 'The psychology of fanatic mob is dangerous and senseless. Any person associated in crowd [*sic*] may lose his temper and anger and fanaticism of group mind stops the process of mind of individual. The anger is the biggest enemy of the mankind.'[262] At the level of procedure, such a legal interpretation is aided by what has been referred to an 'omnibus FIR' that records the crime without naming the accused or hearing the witnesses[263] and 'then ascribes the *failure* of law in the face of collective violence to the very *nature* of "mob" violence'.[264] To rehabilitate this failure, the judgment's framing undertakes the double move of rationalising the killings even while expressing, as the tone of the text suggests, disappointment at the fact of the violence: 'Four children and three women are burnt absolutely in fire as a result of fanatic anger of crowd as Hindu crowd itself has killed three Hindu youths considering them Muslims. This is very shameful, thoughtless incident.'[265]

In the naming of the *crowd* as Hindu, the judgment re-emphasises the demented and delirious nature of those who composed such a crowd; if it were not so, the court reasoned, would the crowd have killed the three Hindus mistaking them for Muslims? For the court, this counters the possibility of considering the Gujarat violence as a pre-planned pogrom specifically targeting Muslims. The Hinduised image of the crowd also serves to enable its framing as *secular*—to cast the rage as a genuine response to the feelings of Hindu victimisation in Godhra, leading to such an indiscriminate killing that it did not differentiate Hindus from Muslims. The judgment, thus, advanced a reason to counter any claims of the violence being directed at the minority religious community by the majority.

This scenario, coupled with the pitiful picture of the death of innocents that the judgment painted, carries out what Upendra Baxi has called the 'second Gujarat catastrophe' in which 'there is not *much* that constitutional governance [especially in the conduct of the judiciary] can achieve, except to *normalise violence*, almost as a social cost of doing democratic politics'.[266] I would call this rationality, drawing on Baxi, the workings of a death culture. We see in the records of judicial memory images of the killings of Muslims as 'unfortunate', not 'unjust'.[267]

The rationality that enables this second catastrophe—the death culture—in the realm of legal interpretation is mobilised by the tropes in the texts of the judgments, through a coming together of the *record* and the *image* in the making of the mnemohistorical collective memory of the pogrom.

Judgment as Mnemohistory

In the preceding discussion, I considered the text of the judgments as a *record* of *images* that uses tropes to narratively reconstruct the collective memory of the pogrom. This record is a site of memory not only because of the judicial archive it constitutes but also because of the aesthetic expressions through which it mobilises a public to engender collective memory. This way of thinking about memory is not so much about 'the fact that we remember history, but the *way* in which we remember it'.[268] The importance of focusing on the way of remembering is trenchantly captured in the expression 'mnemohistory', which 'is concerned not with the past as such, but only with the past as it is remembered'.[269]

The narrative of the Best Bakery case that I have re-described pays attention to the tropes deployed in the writing of the judgments. These tropes come together as record and image to offer a way of remembering the pogrom through aesthetic and legal invocations, which are set in a linear chronological order. It is this order that lends rationality to the memorial narrative of the law. Reading the judgments from a mnemohistorical approach can disrupt— like a punctum—this linear chronology of the way of remembering the pogrom that the judgments produce.

The question of legal time operates at two levels in the judgments. The first, as has already been demonstrated in this chapter, is the way in which the pogrom in general, and the Best Bakery incident in particular, is acknowledged by all the courts as having come after Godhra, which is recognised in law's chronological memory as what has been called the 'original sin'.[270] In the law's reconstructive imagination, thus, the narrative of the 2002 Gujarat violence begins with the killing of Hindus allegedly by Muslims in Godhra. This outrages the Hindus, who feel victimised.[271] The outrage is so severe that 'delirious' *crowds* of people start their killing spree indiscriminately across Gujarat.[272] These 'amorphous' *crowds* are so driven by rage that they even kill three Hindus at Best Bakery,[273] thus attesting to the fact that the outrage was *secular* in conduct and not singularly directed at Muslims.

The Vadodara Sessions Court and the Gujarat High Court judgments are unambiguous in their condemnation of the Best Bakery killings, but they use non-compliance with procedure—the rationality of *legalism*—as an alibi to acquit the 21 accused. The sessions court expressed anguish about how the incident left a 'black stigma' on the cultural city of Vadodara, while also saying that it was a court of evidence and not of justice.[274] The high court confirmed the sessions court's judgment, and discredited any of the concerns that were raised by the prosecution about Zahira being intimidated into turning hostile. Legal time continues its linear chronological journey through the two

Supreme Court judgments in which the law's commitment to procedure (particularly the judiciary's responsibility to actively pursue truth through the provisions of the Indian Evidence Act and the Code of Criminal Procedure) was strongly affirmed by a return to the question of procedure and the lack of its application in the Gujarat court judgments.

The rationality that marked the *legalism* of procedure in the judicial system was upset by the conduct of the Gujarat courts on the one hand, and by Zahira Sheikh's double instance of hostility on the other. Thus, the second Supreme Court judgment corrected this by convicting Zahira, and ordering a retrial in Mumbai in which some of the accused were also convicted. Conviction served as the rational end to the Best Bakery case—bringing it to a *closure*—a trope that was invoked both in the high court and Supreme Court judgments. This rationality, embedded in the chronological recollection of legal time, offers a way of remembering the pogrom as a crime-event that moves through the standard hierarchy of the legal process of appeals, and ends in convictions. The only aberration is that here the victim and the perpetrators are both convicted, and even that is rationalised in the emphasis through the Supreme Court judgments on the judiciary's *role* in singularly searching for *truth* and upholding the *majesty of the law*.

The judicial memory of the Gujarat pogrom records a story of the triumph of secular law against all odds. Such a way of remembering, which is directed singularly at individual criminalisation of perpetrators (including Zahira as the perjurer), does very little to challenge the discursive workings of law and a *secular* and *developmental* rationality that has historically aided and maintained the structural disenfranchisement of India's Muslim citizens.[275] Convictions can, in fact, create an illusion of the restoration of the rule of law, the state's commitment to liberal rights, which demands that we repose faith in the New India's state-making and state-preserving practices.[276]

The second level at which the question of legal time operates is the linear historical narrative in which the sessions and high court judgments locate the pogrom. Judge Mahida in the sessions court judgment elaborated on three causes of what he called 'riots' in India, the first being British colonialism; the second, the failure of India's industrial policy; and third, policies of affirmative action. This elaboration by him was inaugurated in the judgment under the broad rubric of the concern that riots are the reason that 'cease' the 'development of the country' and bring 'disrepute' to it.[277] He held the British responsible for making 'both the communities ... fight each other and separat[ing] the country' through the divide-and-rule policy.[278] This displacement of responsibility for present-day violence to a colonial past[279] is contrasted with the invocation of the mythological. The judge refers to how, even in the Hindu epic Mahabharata, there was a war, but because of the wisdom of Lord Krishna, 'Bharat' remained intact. The *secular* tone in which the Mahabharata reference appears in the judgment alongside colonialism blurs the line between history and myth, and establishes India's ancient past as singularly Hindu—in line with Hindutva ideology[280]—when there was 'sweet harmony' between the two communities, and 'mutual friendship was common'.[281]

On India's postcolonial industrial policy, Judge Mahida blames—through his references to the Soviet influence on the postcolonial Indian economy—Nehruvian socialism which he considered to have led to a widening of the gap between urban and rural India, which was also why riots happened.[282] Targeting Jawaharlal Nehru and his socialist policies as the first prime minister of India and a leader of the Indian National Congress has been a key feature of Hindutva rhetoric in contemporary times.[283] The judge also considered the policy of affirmative action in favour of disadvantaged groups, like Muslims, to have created resentment among Hindus, thus fuelling the outrage that caused riots. This argument was in keeping with the rise of a Hindu entrepreneurial and aspirational middle class in Gujarat that has historically been opposed to affirmative action policies for lower castes.[284]

Before ordering that all 21 accused be acquitted, the judge said that the only way to attain peace and harmony was *development* and the 'enkindling [*sic*] of patriotic feelings', and that if that was not achieved, the country would turn into a 'jungle raj'.[285] The connection between jungle raj—a postcolonial version of Thomas Hobbes's metaphor for the 'state of nature'[286] and a resistant imagination of a 'sacral polity'[287]—and peace, as the judgment suggests, is *development*. Mahida's secular social contract of transition is explained through the trope of *development*, in which Muslim minorities need to give up on claims to affirmative action,[288] and India needs to follow a different industrial policy (emulating the Gujarat model of development) and learn lessons of secularism from its glorious Hindu past.

The high court judgment repeated Judge Mahida's concerns with more aggression. Where Mahida displaced the causes of 'riots' onto colonialism, and so on, the high court displaced it onto the NHRC and human rights activists like Teesta Setalvad and Mihir Desai—calling them 'certain elements'[289]—who, by supporting Zahira and filing an SLP praying for a retrial outside of Gujarat, the court noted, 'obstruct[ed] the development and progress of the state'.[290] The high court linked the conduct of these 'elements' to previous attempts by human rights activists to resist the construction of the World Bank–funded Sardar Sarovar Dam in Gujarat that has been displacing millions of landless peasants and indigenous peoples.[291] The high court suggested that their attempt to 'misuse poor persons like Zahira' was part of a larger conspiracy to discredit the independence of the judiciary in Gujarat and cause enormous financial damage to the state.[292] The judgment stated, in ominous-sounding prose that the 'Nation will suffer if Gujarat is made to suffer'.[293] Suffering here—using the rationality of *developmentalism*—is measured as the loss of economic growth, and not that of human life.

Given that the high court judgment was delivered close to two years after the Best Bakery incident, the judges were of the opinion that 'normalcy' had been in Gujarat, where Hindus and Muslims had returned to living peacefully and in harmony.[294] The Gujarat High Court considered the attempts by the NHRC and the activists as a means by which 'some persons, for their petty benefits [were] trying to add fuel to fire, which is [*sic*] already extinguished, and keep the situation tense'.[295] Forgetting was what the court was suggesting as a means of *closure*. The court considered it 'unfortunate' that attempts to forget 'the painful past' were being resisted by a 'handful of people [who were] indulging in dirty tactics and wrongly defaming the State and its people for ulterior motives and reasons'.[296] In agreement with the sessions court, the high court judgment stated that the 'honour and dignity' of Gujarat was being challenged by this handful of people with ulterior motives.[297]

Thus, along with displacing the focus from the killings at Best Bakery to the conduct of the NHRC and the activists, the high court judgment effectively also turned the state of Gujarat, and its *developmentalist* vision, into a victim whose honour and dignity were under threat. This reasoning seems to be completely in line, in fact scripted, by the concerns about Gujarati *asmita*, or pride, that Narendra Modi had raised in his letter (discussed earlier in this chapter) to the president of India when the NHRC SLP was filed in the Supreme Court after the Vadodara Sessions Court acquitted the 21 accused.

Upendra Baxi in his reading of the state of Gujarat's responses to the pogrom defines *asmita* as 'collective self-recognition and pride', and argues that its deployment by Modi, and consequently by the high court, provided 'a discourse of transcendence in the worst ever days of shame and sorrow for the entire state and the nation'.[298] This appeal to transcendence by Modi and the high court judgment was meant to operationalise a way of remembering that consolidated the workings of a state-making and state-preserving rationality. Thus, the pogrom is recast as a *secular* misfortune befalling the state of Gujarat (not a state-supported injustice targeted at Muslims). Consequently, questions of state responsibility are replaced by those of *development* ('*asmita* … presents rapid economic development as a final solution to problems of social violence'[299]) and *legalism* takes 'its own course, indifferent to any protected religious identity of perpetrators of violence'.[300] While the first Supreme Court judgment rehabilitates the law from within the captivity of Gujarati *asmita*, the second Supreme Court judgment in convicting Zahira, and framing her conduct as a failed witness by drawing on verses from the Manusmriti, attests to the law's *asmita*, which is an appeal to transcendence in which the law takes its course, indifferent to the vulnerable religious identity of the victim of violence.

* * *

In writing the four judgments described previously, the judges organised the texts around the two broad heads of *judgment* and *reasons*. The judgment part of the text introduces the cast of characters, the events that gave rise to the legal action, and the legal questions that required resolution. In the reasons section, we have seen the judges weighing in on specific provisions of legislations, as well as offering meditative excurses on the causes and consequences of 'riots' by drawing on their versions of history, politics and economics.

The judgment and reasons sections, as organising heads of the texts, reconstruct both the story of the Best Bakery incident and the Best Bakery case by deploying a set of aesthetic tropes. These tropes hold in them the narrative compact of law and aesthetics that the J-A reading identified and analysed. In this chapter, I first re-described what the judges wrote, and then drew out from my re-description the aesthetic tropes that were used in these records of judicial memory.

I categorised these tropes under the rubrics of record, image and mnemohistory, to bring to relief the manner in which they generate a way of remembering the pogrom that simultaneously condemns and normalises it.

The working of this simultaneity, as I have shown, is made possible through a state-making and state preserving rationality comprising the triad of legalism, secularism and developmentalism.

By analysing what the tropes are doing in the texts of the judgments, I have shown that despite the fact that the Vadodara Sessions Court, the Gujarat High Court and the Supreme Court of India framed their responses to the event differently, they were all advancing narratives ordered by the workings of this triad. The rationalities of legalism, secularism and developmentalism were rehearsed and repeated by all the four judgments through the deployment of the tropes. When the judgments are read using the J-A approach, what becomes visible is a convergence in the rationalities that, even while condemning the Best Bakery incident, serves to reify the very foundations of the same New India that provided the ideological justifications for the pogrom.

In the next chapter, we will 'descend the courthouse steps',[301] to enter the cinema as another public site of collective memory making, to carry out a J-A reading of the three Bollywood films whose plots centrally feature the Gujarat pogrom. These films were released through the post-pogrom decade, coinciding with the period during which the Best Bakery case ran.

4 Bollywood's Law

Cinematic Justice and Collective Memory

[T]he cinematic image is written in time, in the body, in sound, tactility and memory.[1]

The film positions us to judge with our entire bodies ... the techniques of image and sound ... press the viewer towards a more open space of judgment, one in which new meanings must be constructed, one in which the viewer will have to actively participate.[2]

[T]o see what law is go to the cinema.[3]

This chapter uses the J-A approach to read (see and hear) three Bollywood feature films that make the Gujarat pogrom central to their plots. The films are *Dev*, *Parzania* and *Kai Po Che*, whose release dates span the period 2004–13, overlapping with the Best Bakery case. Attention to this shared memorial journey of the judicial and the cinematic will further reveal their narrative compact in the making and ordering of collective memories of the pogrom.

I show how narrative tropes and cinematic techniques are used and repeated in the films to reconstruct the memory of the pogrom and project imaginations of justice. The J-A lens examines how the films mobilise spectatorial publics, by bestowing on them the authority to pass judgment on both the cinema and the pogrom. The films severally and collectively train their publics in ways of remembering the pogrom as a story of the triumph of secular law over religious violence. In this way of remembering, the lineaments of the New India—the work of the state-making and state-preserving rationalities in legalism, secularism and developmentalism—become visible in the texts of the films.[4]

In my J-A reading of the texts of judgments in the previous chapter, the *judgment* form was considered to be a record of *images*, by way of the aesthetic tropes embedded in their language. In my J-A reading of the films in this chapter, I will pay attention to how the cinematic form brings together word, image and sound to mobilise *judgment*.

The chapter opens with a brief explanation of how each of these films inaugurates a relationship between cinema and the spectator through the use of a specifically Indian practice of state-sanctioned legal certification and a standard disclaimer. Establishing this relationship is part of a film's declared fictional spectatorial address, and enables a state-authorised mobilisation of its publics. I then proceed to read (see and hear) the three Bollywood feature films using the J-A approach. I will show how Bollywood cinema's aesthetic form lends itself to the making of a memorial *record*; the cinema as the memorial record of an event, through its address, mobilises publics with the authority to pass *judgment*; this combination of address and judgment lends cinema the *mnemohistorical* quality of producing active imaginations of justice that can engender and order ways of remembering the pogrom. I pay particular attention to how they use narrative tropes and cinematic techniques to: reconstruct the pogrom; project imaginations of justice; bestow authority on audiences to pass judgment; and produce a way of remembering in which the reason of secular law protects the New India from the irrationality of religious violence.

'Obiter Depicta'

The pogrom is central to *Dev's* and *Parzania's* stories, and in *Kai Po Che*, it is a parallel plot.[5] In all three films, the pogrom is part of the narrative crisis and resolution. The fictional story in each film is framed using factual details from some of the major massacres that took place during the Gujarat pogrom, including the Best Bakery massacre.

Like all Indian films approved for public exhibition, these three films inaugurate a relationship between themselves and prospective viewers by displaying a certificate from the CBFC.[6] The certificate declares the film's images and sounds as legitimate speech, a legal *record* of state-sanctioned memory, and its audiences are made the rightful recipients of its memorial narrative. The CBFC is mandated by the Indian Cinematograph Act, 1952 (read with the Cinematograph [Certification] Rules, 1983), to classify films for public exhibition under the heads of 'U' (universal), 'U/A' (parental guidance), 'A' (adults only) and 'S' (particular profession or class or persons).[7] These classifications are noted on the certificates issued by the CFBC that appear at the beginning of every Indian film, irrespective of whether it is being screened publicly in a theatre or being watched privately on a DVD.[8]

If we compare the filmic text's appearance to the form of a judicial decision, we will see that it assembles a narrative through images and sounds (statement of facts); the narrative introduces a cast of characters and constructs a conflict between the protagonists (identification of the parties involved and the crime that brings them into a legal relationship) and then offers reasons through cinematic devices like camera positioning, dream sequences, climaxes or flashbacks to help arrive at a judgment through resolution or a moral stalemate (application of rules to the facts to declare one party's victory over another).

A judgment as precedent in the common law tradition is constituted by two key elements: the *ratio decidendi* ('the binding rule') and the *obiter dictum* ('observations made along the way').[9] All films certified for public exhibition in India can also be seen as constituted by two elements, the story framed in the sounds and images that use the Bollywood aesthetic to advance the plot, and the image of the CBFC certificate as state imprimatur that inaugurates the film-watching experience. The 'logic of visual authority' in Bollywood cinema can be said to be constituted by these two elements, as what Peter Goodrich's neologisms characterise as '*imago decidendi* and *obiter depicta*, respectively the image determining decision, and things shown and seen along the way to judgment'.[10]

I would, thus, like to consider the censor certificate as the *obiter depicta* of the Bollywood film form: as an assemblage of words and images that can be seen along the way to the *imago decidendi* in the film's story, as well as an iconic and ubiquitous legal emblem carrying the secular insignia of the Indian state.[11] As is shown in the images of the censor certificates here (Figures 4.1, 4.2 and 4.3), *Dev* and *Parzania* were classified for viewing by adults only, and *Kai Po Che* was granted approval for unrestricted public exhibition. The certificates, then, even before the films begin, mobilise their imagined cinematic publics and inform them about whether they are permitted to consider themselves as legal viewers.

The authority of the visual display of certification works in two ways. First, the state plays the role of deciding and declaring whether a film is meant for mature or universal viewing, thus pre-empting what impact the film might have on its age-restricted viewership. Second, viewers watching the film with the knowledge that they fall outside the age limit set by the

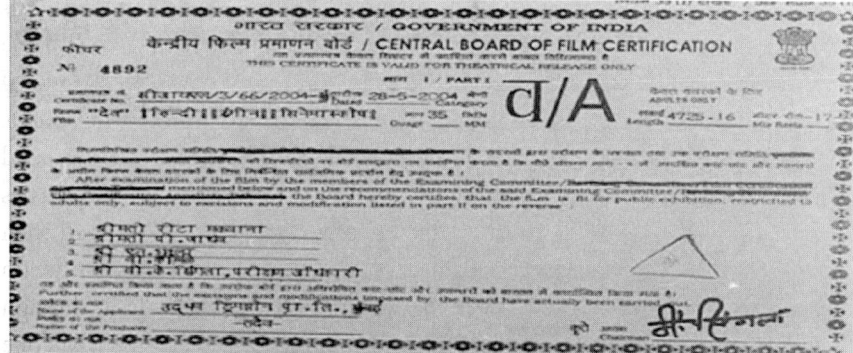

Figure 4.1 CBFC certificate for *Dev*
Source: Screenshot from DVD.

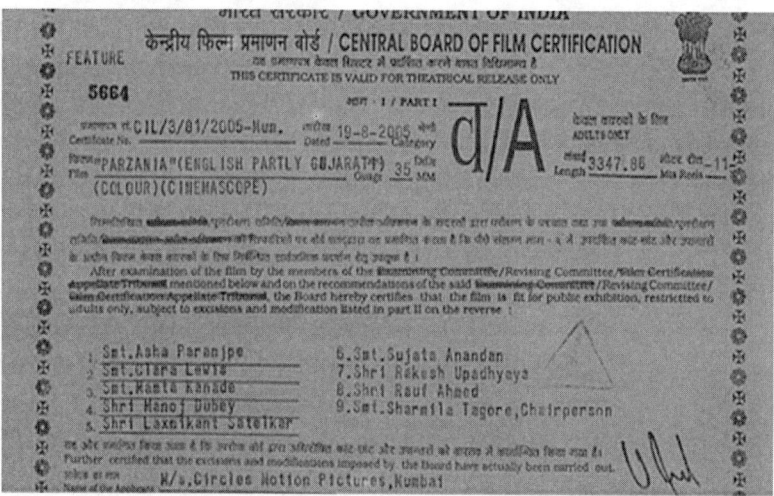

Figure 4.2 CBFC certificate for *Parzania*
Source: Screenshot from DVD.

certification bear the responsibility of not continuing to watch, or bear both the legal and moral consequences.

The other thing of note here is that as the films temporally move away from 2002, the CBFC seems more lenient towards their classification. This happens, as I will show, because of the memorial distance between the

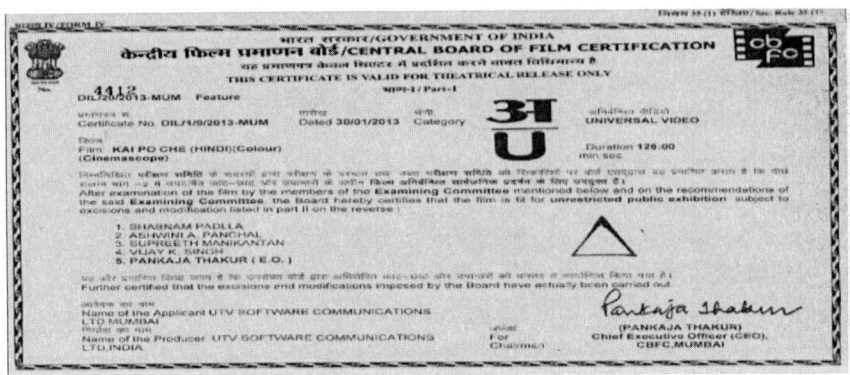

Figure 4.3   CBFC certificate for *Kai Po Che*
Source: Screenshot from DVD.

pogrom and the release of the film, and because the later films tell the story of the pogrom in ways that can be watched by an unrestricted audience.

A second kind of *obiter depicta* appears in a message that comes immediately after the CBFC certificate in the first two films; this is what is referred to as a 'standard disclaimer' that has historically established the feature film genre as works of fiction, thus maintaining a tenuous relationship with authenticity.[12] *Dev*'s standard disclaimer states: 'All characters and incidents in this film are fictitious and bear no resemblance to any person living or dead or to any incident whatsoever. Any similarity so perceived is purely coincidental.' *Parzania*'s declares: 'Inspired by a true story' (Figures 4.4 and 4.5).

Dev's disclaimer completely severs the film's plot from the real, yet, as we will see in the next section, that quarantine does not stop the audience from establishing that the film is about the Gujarat pogrom. *Parzania*'s disclaimer alludes to an idea of the fictional being founded on the factual. It holds on to a claim of authenticity, to establish some legitimacy for the film's content. *Kai Po Che* offers no disclaimer with regard to its claims to truth, the story being adapted from a novel. Its disclaimer, following CBFC guidelines,[13] notifies the audience that during the making of the film, animals were treated with care (Figure 4.6). In this way, the CBFC certificate and the standard disclaimer collectively activate a state-making and state-preserving rationality that attests to Bollywood's 'cinematic apparatus and its pedagogic role as the disseminator of modernity'.[14] Their 'persuasive authority'[15] trains audiences to

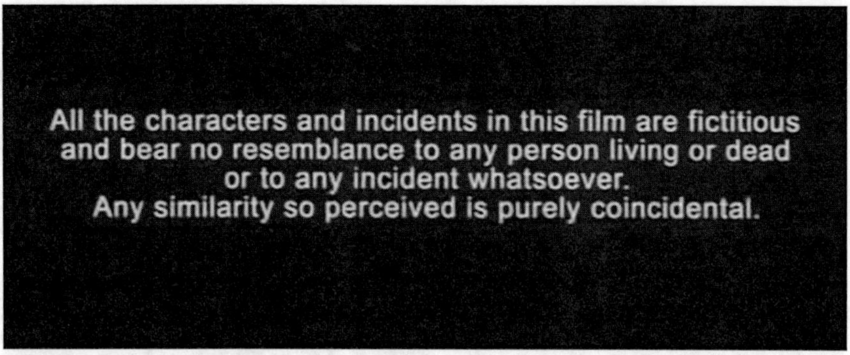

Figure 4.4   *Dev*: Standard disclaimer
Source: Screenshot from DVD.

Figure 4.5   *Parzania*: Standard disclaimer
Source: Screenshot from DVD.

conduct themselves with the responsibility befitting of the good cinematic citizen.[16] As *obiter depicta*, visual declarations in a Bollywood film can be understood to lend life and form to the relations between law, cinema, memory, the nation-state and the citizen.

Despite being fictitious reconstructions, or referents, of 'real' events, all the films, barring *Dev*, are historically accurate about the location of their stories in the city of Ahmedabad and about 27 February 2002 as the date when the train-burning incident happened in Godhra. The violence against Muslims and the train burning are represented as causally connected events,

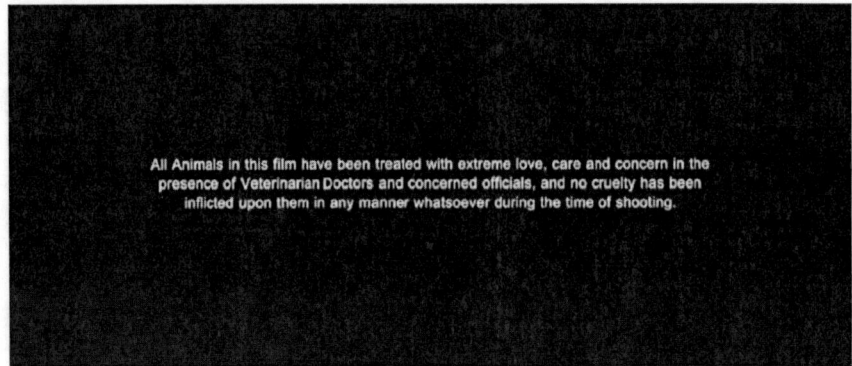

All Animals in this film have been treated with extreme love, care and concern in the presence of Veterinarian Doctors and concerned officials, and no cruelty has been inflicted upon them in any manner whatsoever during the time of shooting.

Figure 4.6   *Kai Po Che*: Standard disclaimer
Source: Screenshot from DVD.

in the way this was recorded in the Best Bakery judgments. The three films offer a clear representation of police participation and political manipulation in aiding and abetting the violence against Muslims. *Parzania*, in particular, is unambiguous about the fact that the pogrom was a pre-planned act of mass atrocity, made possible only through state complicity.

Litigation was initiated against *Dev* and *Kai Po Che* by private petitioners who asked the court to ban their screening, arguing that the films could invoke sectarian violence, or were biased in their representation of the event.[17] *Parzania* faced a lot of trouble releasing in Gujarat because theatre owners refused to screen it fearing backlash from the Hindu Right.[18] *Dev* released in theatres on 11 June 2004, just about two months after the Supreme Court of India ordered the retrial of the Best Bakery case outside Gujarat. The release date for *Parzania* (26 January 2007) coincided with India's Republic Day (when the Constitution was adopted in 1950), and *Kai Po Che*'s (22 February 2013) was just a week prior to the day that would have marked 11 years since the pogrom.

Dev: A Hindu Constitution

Dev, released in 2004, was the first Bollywood film that wove its plot around some key incidents related to the Gujarat pogrom. The film released a few months ahead of India's general elections that year (in which the BJP was voted out at the centre but not in Gujarat) and soon after the Best Bakery case was shifted out of Gujarat to Mumbai (to ensure a fair trial and guard against the intimidation of witnesses).[19]

Despite the fact that *Dev*'s story is located in Mumbai,[20] and makes no mention of the Gujarat pogrom, the 'pure coincidence' that the standard disclaimer might be referring to is the key components in its plot and narrative that borrow from events that took place in 2002 in Gujarat. The violence against Muslims in the film is preceded by a 'precipitating event'[21] like that of the Godhra train-burning incident. *Dev*, interestingly, even in its non-naming and non-identification with the Gujarat pogrom, frames its narrative in the same chronology as the 2002 pogrom: the death of Hindus in the train compartment is replaced by a bomb blast at a Hindu temple that becomes the trigger for the killing of Muslims. The female protagonist in the film is a Muslim woman, who like Zahira Sheikh was witness to the killing of her family members and then is called on to testify. In fact, it was because of these striking similarities with actual events from 2002 that legal action was initiated against *Dev* by private petitioners, who demanded a ban, claiming that the film could instigate sectarian tensions because audiences would identify the connection between the plot and the pogrom.[22]

As journalist Ayesha Khan reports, when *Dev* released in Vadodara, cinema theatre owners put out advertisements in local dailies calling on both Hindus and Muslims to come and watch the film. They did this to get as much business as possible, fearing that it might be banned by a court order. The fact that *Dev*'s story was similar to events related to the pogrom, especially the Best Bakery massacre that took place in Vadodara, was apparent from the text of a film poster, which read: 'Watch Vadodara's Zaheera Sheikh–inspired Kareena Kapoor's role. Naked portrayal of riots, inactive police force and non-performance at the behest of the chief minister.' In fact, as Khan notes, the audiences would shout out 'Zaheera Sheikh' when the actress Kareena Kapoor appeared on the screen.[23] In another reported incident, during the screening of the film in Jamnagar, a city in Gujarat, Hindu and Muslim audiences engaged in a heated argument on the film. In consequence, the theatre authorities had to stop the screening and also refund the price of the tickets to the audience.[24] Martha Nussbaum, commenting on her experience of watching the film in an Ahmedabad theatre, wrote: 'the mood of the audience was staunchly anti-Muslim'.[25] *Dev*, thus, brought into being, through its surrogate address about sectarian violence, cinematic publics that identified the film with the Gujarat pogrom, despite its disclaimer of being fictitious.[26]

Figure 4.7 'Structural bilingualism'
Source: Screenshot from DVD.

The English and Hindi titles of *Dev* are digitally stylised to emerge out of flames, suggesting a trial by fire (Figure 4.7). The titling is accompanied by an intense background score in which a chorus of deep male voices recites a Sanskrit *shloka* (chant) from chapter 2, verse 27, of the Bhagavad Gita: 'karmanye vadhikaraste ma phaleshu kadachana, ma karmaphalaheturbhurma te sangostvakarmani'. The English translation would mean: 'You have a right to perform your prescribed duty, but you are not entitled to the fruits of action. Never consider yourself the cause of the results of your activities, and never be attached to not doing your duty.'[27] It is this message from the Gita—'of action without consequence'[28]—that frames the ethico-juridical universe that the film conjures.

The invocation of the Hindu holy book and the use of language in the title sequence offer a telling instance of how Hindutva ideology subliminally informs *Dev*'s affects of audience initiation and spectatorial address. The use of English and Hindi in the titling suggests the practice of what Prasad has called the 'structural bilingualism of the Indian nation-state': 'a state of affairs where the multitude of Indian languages (here counted as one) function under the direction of a meta-language in which alone the national ideology can be properly articulated'.[29] It is through Bollywood cinema that the meta-languages of English and Hindi have thus emerged as 'defining the linguistic order of new India',[30] in which English works as the language of secular neoliberal aspiration and Hindi as that of secular nationalist unity. This has advanced the logic of 'Hindi nationalism'[31] that wipes out the Islamicate presence of Urdu as a language that used to appear on film posters[32] and the opening title sequences of Bollywood cinema 'as a matter of routine'.[33]

The use of English has strongly aided the processes and practices of Bollywood becoming a transnational and developmentalist export for consumption by the Indian diaspora.[34] Hindi has come to displace Urdu, it can be argued, to advance a mandate enshrined in Articles 343 and 351 of the Constitution of India that make Hindi the official language of India[35] and direct the state to be duty bound to promote and spread it 'relying *primarily* on *Sanskrit*'.[36] Pritam Singh traces the contestations in the Constituent Assembly debates to show how these provisions were aimed at imposing a 'unified Indian nationalism' that, through 'Hindi imperialism', worked 'as a vehicle of "national" aspiration for a regional upper-caste elite'.[37] In other words, constitutional recognition for Hindi as the national language was pushed through by Hindutva ideologues in the Constituent Assembly, ignoring the other regional languages. The primacy given to Sanskrit was also based on a demand by supporters of Hindutva who wanted to keep intact the myth that Sanskrit was 'indigenous to India',[38] that it was the language of the (Hindu) gods, and Hindi its modern and most legitimate and secular offspring.[39] The seamless blending of the Sanskrit *shloka*s (verses) from the Bhagavad Gita, and the English-Hindi titling of *Dev*, initiates the pedagogical project of Bollywood cinema in naturalising Hindutva's secular narrative that reduces anti-Muslim violence to tragedy and politics, and celebrates the mythical Hindu foundations of modernity in India that the Constitution is popularly believed to enshrine.

Bollywood's memorial *record* in *Dev*, thus, produces and mobilises *judgment* that contributes to the active (or *mnemohistorical*) commemoration of the pogrom in a particular way of remembering. This way of remembering, as I will discuss now, even while acknowledging the horror of the pogrom's violence, rationalises it.[40]

Figure 4.8 'He chose to walk the razor's edge....'
Source: 'Dev (2004)', IMDb, https://www.imdb.com/title/tt0364303/ (accessed 18 December 2022).

Dev's story is set at a time in India—taking its cue from the Gujarat pogrom—that is rife with sectarian tension. The main character in the film is Dev Pratap Singh, a joint commissioner of police in Mumbai. The film's second title—'He chose to walk the razor's edge....' (Figure 4.8)—is a comment on Dev's personality: a police officer who does not fear to stand by his convictions and takes the responsibility as a policeman of upholding the rule of law and protecting the nation-state from 'terrorists' with such commitment that he is known for carrying out and defending extra-judicial killings.[41] The film portrays Dev's belief in the supremacy of law as a virtue, especially in the way he repeatedly declares in the film that he does not discriminate between terrorists based on their religion. Dev's righteous commitment to the rule of law is borne out in the opening sequence of the film that introduces him as its titular protagonist. In this scene, Dev is shown confronting a group of agitating student activists on a university campus. Dev asks them to not disrupt law and order through their protests. In response, a student leader mocks Dev. The student unzips his pants and says that he keeps the lowly law safely ordered where his genitalia is. Dev shoots and kills the student immediately. When questioned during an inquiry at the police department as to why he took such a drastic step, Dev emphasises that he had to take a decisive call in the face of such blatant disregard for the police's authority. When the inquiry team asks Dev whether he was aware that the student he shot was from the 'minority community', Dev says that when confronting someone that person is either innocent or guilty in his judgment, and their religion has no influence on his decision. Such a portrayal is, by extension, a comment on his obedience towards the rule of law as a value-neutral idea that is purely committed to maintaining national security by killing anyone, irrespective of identity, who poses a threat to the nation-state and the authority of the police.[42]

The other important character in the film is Dev's very good friend and colleague Tejinder Khosla, whose ideology, as the film progresses, turns him into Dev's antagonist. Tejinder identifies Muslims as Outsiders who are the reason for India's ills. His mission, in the fight against terrorism, is to root out all Muslims, to annihilate them. The Outsider metaphor has been repeatedly used in Bollywood cinema in its representations of Muslim characters; and despite continuing to narrativise the Muslim as exoticised, marginalised and, increasingly, demonised,[43] *Dev*, in Bollywood's tradition of combining technological modernity with the ethos of tradition,[44] rehabilitates the fractured nation through the tropes of familiality, diversity, nationalism and a belief in and obedience towards the rule of law.

A parallel narrative in the film portrays the lives of a young Muslim man called Farhaan Ali, who has just returned to Mumbai after completing his law degree from another city, and his girlfriend Aaliya, a college student in Mumbai. They live in a densely populated Muslim community housing complex called Noor Manzil, located in a working-class area. Farhaan's father, Ali Khan, is a respected local Muslim leader, who has enormous faith in Indian democracy and pluralism, and believes in the ideologies of non-violence and pacifism of anti-colonial leaders like Mohandas Karamchand Gandhi and Khan Abdul Gaffar Khan. The trope that Ali Khan's character follows is that of a *good* Muslim who believes in the constitutional vision of 'unity in diversity'[45] and who is an exception to the rule of the *bad* Muslim as terrorist.[46] Farhaan, however, feels that he has wasted his time studying for a law degree because the lofty ideals of constitutional equality have turned into a sham in current-day India where innocent Muslims are being persecuted by the state and its police in the name of fighting terrorism. It is here that an invocation of law sets up the crisis in the film, which unfolds as an ideological conflict. This conflict is narrated as one between Farhaan—a young Muslim man and a law graduate, whose lived experience leads him to consider the Constitution a document worthy of suspicion—and Dev, a Hindu police officer whose lived experience suggests that even extra-constitutional violence by the state is justified if the end is to uphold the rule of the Constitution.

Soon after Farhaan's return to Mumbai after graduation, at a peaceful protest demonstration on police brutality against Muslims, Ali Khan is killed in police firing. This happens on Dev's orders, when his cadres open fire after the crowd at the protest turns violent. Farhaan decides to avenge his father's death against Dev. Taking advantage of Farhaan's rage, a fundamentalist Muslim politician offers to train Farhaan as a militant. The politician's character, of course, is created using the tropes of the *bad* Muslim, in contrast to Ali Khan's.

Farhaan fails in an assassination attempt against Dev but is then made to plant a bomb outside a Hindu temple. The bomb blast—akin to the Godhra incident, but in this case represented as having been carried out at the behest of the Muslim politician[47]—kills several Hindus, provoking retaliation against Muslims. This *pratikriya* (retributive reaction) in the film—of the kind that followed the Godhra train burning—is openly led by a right-wing Hindu politician, pointing at the connivance of political leaders in fomenting the pogrom. The violence is represented as reactionary and spontaneous outrage, like a riot, and not as a sophisticatedly pre-planned pogrom.

Farhaan survives the blast and realises that he was being used as a foot soldier by the Muslim politician to serve his sectarian agenda. Aaliya also survives the retaliatory violence, though she witnesses the killing and rape of her family members. In the middle of the violence, Dev helps Farhaan take Aaliya to the hospital, and this effects a change of heart in Farhaan, and his hatred for Dev subsides.

While the Hindu mobs are on the rampage killing Muslims, Dev, as part of the anti-terrorism team led by his friend and colleague Tejinder, is ordered not to take action to stop the mobs. This order came from the Hindu chief minister (CM), who had asked Tejinder to ensure that Hindus got to freely vent their anger against Muslims for the blast. Dev arrives at the scene to find Tejinder waiting with the police squad as onlookers allowing the militant Hindu mobs a free rein in killing Muslims. Dev ignores Tejinder's orders and goes ahead with his team of policemen to stop the killings, but his efforts are in vain and several people die.

Dev is deeply distraught about not being able to uphold the rule of law to save the victims, in spite of having the opportunity and authority to do so.

He realises the ideological differences between him and Tejinder. Despite political pressure, Dev organises a public meeting at the site of Noor Manzil, where he urges people to come forward to lodge their FIRs and also identify any police officers or politicians who were involved in carrying out the violence. Despite threats to her life and possible expulsion from her community, Aaliya comes forward to testify.

The mise en scène (Figure 4.9) comprises a large makeshift tent, which has been erected right outside Noor Manzil. Inside the tent there is a table with the necessary files in which FIRs will be recorded. There are local leaders sitting on chairs behind the table. Dev speaks through a loudspeaker that carries his voice to the residents of Noor Manzil who have gathered on their balconies to hear him speak and to be spectators of what is on offer, lending a theatrical feel to the space. This space of the public meeting can be read as an allegory for what has been called a 'jurisdiction of conscience',[48] in which it is not the victims who have to go to the law—that is, to police stations to file their FIRs to put the criminal justice system in motion—but the law that ceremonially travels to them.

The jurisdictional boundaries between the private space of Noor Manzil and the public space of the police station merge, with Dev embodying the force of secular state law and carrying it to Aaliya and other Muslim victim-survivors. The theatrical arrangement of the space also lends to it the form of a public court handing out popular justice outside of the architectural confines of a courtroom. However, here Dev performs the *role* of the *judge*. As shown in Figure 4.9, the camera is placed behind the group of women who have gathered on the balcony to listen to Dev speak. In Dev's authoritative and amplified address as the sole judge in the situation, the spectator in the film watcher is also interpellated as a recipient of that *judgment*. The point of view accorded to the spectatorial public, thus, allows them legitimate entry into this jurisdiction of conscience. Here Dev appears as the human embodiment of the *majesty of the law* and its enforcement, a trope repeatedly used in the Best Bakery judgments and one that the courts considered the police to have failed in upholding. We see this ably demonstrated by Dev, when on Aaliya's identification of the erring policemen, he uses his moral authority to suspend them in summary style, without a hearing, and orders that a charge sheet be filed against them.[49]

Meanwhile, Farhaan and Aaliya take refuge at Dev's home, where it is decided that Dev will present his eyewitness account of police and political

Figure 4.9   Noor Manzil's 'jurisdiction of conscience'
Source: Screenshot from DVD.

inaction and collusion in carrying out violence against Muslims. He submits his report to the CM, but also decides to depose in the court, since he is aware of the CM's anti-Muslim ideology. Farhaan expresses his fear that Dev's life would be under threat if he went ahead with his decision to expose police and political complicity. Dev invokes the morality of the Sanskrit verse from the Bhagavad Gita with which the film opened, to emphasise that life or death does not matter as long as he continues to fight for the truth and uphold the rule of law until his last breath. On hearing about Dev's decision to testify, Tejinder tries to dissuade him. But Dev stands by his convictions.

In the climactic scene, set right outside a symbolically imposing court building, Dev is shot dead by Tejinder. In a show of secular solidarity, Farhaan, a Muslim, lights the Hindu Dev's funeral pyre, a duty that in Hinduism is supposed to be the privilege of the son.[50] Later, unable to deal with the trauma of having murdered his friend, Tejinder kills himself. The film ends with Aaliya, now Dev's wife, handing over a file—a *record* with all the necessary evidence that Dev had collected and a document memorialising Dev himself—to Farhaan, who finally dons the lawyer's attire and walks up the stairs of the courthouse, following Dev's instructions that he must keep faith in the law and begin litigation for the rights of the dead and violated.

Dev, in all-black attire, seated against a black background, in his transcendental post-death avatar fades in (Figure 4.10). In this frontal shot, he repeats with singular intensity, in Amitabh Bachchan's 'inimitable throaty baritone',[51] the Bhagavad Gita's juridico-ethical morality of relentlessly

Figure 4.10 In death, Dev is deified
Source: Screenshot from DVD.

fighting for truth irrespective of consequences. The scene invokes *darsana*—a technique particular to Indian cinema's aesthetic—that demonstrates 'the power exercised by the authoritative image in Hindu religious culture'.[52] The imagistic and acoustic intensity in this ostensibly secular scene accords Dev the power of divine authority. In death, he is deified.[53] Farhaan looks up at the courthouse in hope, but it is Dev's spectral presence that guides him.

The symbolic message, with which the film ends, is that Farhaan, having given up on the path of violence to seek justice, will now follow the path of the secular law to seek justice for the violence against his community and as a tribute to Dev's courage and sacrifice.

The *mnemohistory* of Gujarat 2002 that *Dev's* images and sounds *record* reduces religious strife in India to an 'amorphous politics'[54] of equivalence and linearity. In such a way of remembering, first, the violence is *judged* to be an outcome of a cause-and-effect logic that begins with one community casting 'the first stone'[55] and the other justifying it through retaliation; second, a precipitating event is identified and made foundational to the narrative of violence; and, third, the violence is seen as a consequence of the sectarian agendas of individual fundamentalist politicians who spread hate to gain political mileage. This way of remembering conceals the ideological and structural foundations that lend legitimacy to anti-Muslim hatred in the New India. The film's assessment of religious violence is that ordinary Hindus and Muslims are the victims, first, as pawns in the hands of politicians who brainwash them to propagate their violent agendas; and second, as the innocents who get killed because of this violence. The idea that both Hindus and Muslims bear the brunt of this equally lends a democratic logic to religious violence and equalises its consequences for majority and minority communities. The film emphasises that both sides suffer, that sectarian violence does not choose its victims based on religion, much like Dev's secularism tells him not to kill terrorists based on their faith, but to, nevertheless, extra-judicially execute them. The chronology of events in both the factual *record* of judicial memory of the Best Bakery case, and cinema's fictitious *record*, follows a linear narrative where the cycle of violence is always initiated by the unruly and anti-national Muslims, which is the reason why the tolerant Hindus are forced to retaliate.[56] As Sunera Thobani writes:

> In the cinematic Gujarat—and India … [t]he deeply institutionalized inequities and imbalance of power between Hindus and Muslims is rarely allowed to enter the frame, and if it is, the good intentions of the secular Hindu hero/heroine becomes a mitigating factor—his/her ideals and values, his/her personal acceptance of Muslims will set everything right. The Muslims who do not abide by these ideals and values are hopelessly naïve, and the proof of Muslim loyalty is, without exception, subservience to the values and embrace of enlightened Hindu characters, most of whom are secularists.[57]

As mentioned in Chapter 1, this ordering of collective memory has been a standard refrain of the Hindu Right to justify violence against Muslims, citing inter alia the 'invasion' of India by the Mughals and the Partition in 1947 as the original reasons.[58] In an opening scene, Farhaan is questioned by a police officer on a train. When he learns that Farhaan is Muslim, he conspiratorially asks whether he has relatives in Pakistan. Later, expressing anguish, Farhaan tells his father: 'How does it feel to be a Muslim in India? To be repeatedly reminded that you belong to Pakistan?' *Dev*'s narrative acknowledges this prejudice against Muslims in India and simultaneously normalises it by valorising the way in which Dev repeatedly and unquestioningly connects 'terrorism' to the work of infiltrators and brainwashed Muslim youth who have become anti-nationals.

The roles of law in the film are both metaphorical and material. Its appearances are metaphorically embodied in the character of the film's protagonist Dev. Dev embodies the characteristics of the ideal nationalist: Hindu, secular, liberal and having an unshakeable belief in the rule of law—he is the good secular Hindu hero. Dev's convictions are so powerful that they can on the one hand justify extra-judicial killings and on the other inspire a young Muslim gone astray to repose faith in the secular law in his quest for justice. In the tradition of the psychoanalytic reading of the law of the father, the good secular Hindu in Dev, and his unwavering belief in the rule of law, turns him into a father figure for the fatherless Farhaan, and in the film's affective address to its cinematic publics. In the 'world of danger' that the film conjures, Dev with his Bhagavad Gita–inspired juridico-moral universe offers succour in the form of 'certainty and security' and embodies the role of the 'father substitute'.[59] '[T]he father is the Maker of definite rules of conduct,' writes Jerome Frank. 'He knows precisely what is wrong and … sits in judgment and punishes misdeeds. The Law … inevitably becomes a partial substitute for the Father-as-Infallible-Judge.'[60]

In material form, secular law comes in to resolve the 'acute crisis'[61] or 'ethical dilemmas'[62]—the ways in which narrative crisis features in the Bollywood aesthetic, as discussed in Chapter 2—that *Dev*'s protagonists confront. For Dev, the primary dilemma was, on the one hand, to uphold the rule of law to end terrorism and sectarian violence, and on the other to stay loyal in his friendship with Tejinder. Dev's decision to stand firm on his conviction in the rule of law comes from a certain belief in constitutionalism, which becomes apparent in a very didactic scene in the film where Dev and Tejinder are discussing over a drink what the foundations of their conscience are (Figure 4.11). This discussion takes place in Dev's elite living room over a drink.

> *Dev*: One thing is clear, Mr. Tejinder Khosla, your and my Gitas are different. My Gita is the Constitution of India, and the rule of law. What is your Gita?
>
> *Tejinder*: It is like this dear Dev. If there is a nation, only then will there be a Constitution. Without the nation, the Constitution and rule of law have no basis. My Gita is power. The power to completely annihilate the enemies of this nation.
>
> *Dev*: Oh dear Tejinder! Power, you see, is not in the police, the army, or weapons. A nation's power lies in its political organization, its economy,

Figure 4.11 Living room constitutionalism: Gita as conscience
Source: Screenshot from DVD.

in its justice system, in social equality, and religious harmony. And all of this is given to us by our Constitution.[63]

Also present in the living room is Dev's wife, Bharti, who has been listening in silence. The conversation briefly turns to her when Tejinder apologises for not including her in the conversation and requests her to share what her Gita is.

> *Bharti*: I have no Gita, only a dream. An ordinary person's dream: who wants a nation that doesn't just provide food, clothing and shelter, but also respect and justice; the freedom to think and choose. What happened? Have I asked for too much?
>
> *Tejinder*: You have asked for the whole of Ramrajya, Bharti!
>
> *Bharti*: And Ramrajya isn't possible in Kaliyug, right?[64]

The Bhagavad Gita, it is apparent, is a metaphor with a shared meaning for all the three characters in this scene. It is being invoked as a reference to a foundation of their conscience and imagination as citizens of the Indian nation. The conversation is set up primarily to demonstrate the ideological differences between two friends and inaugurates the 'ethical dilemma' that will serve as the 'acute crisis' that demands resolution in the film's climax. Tejinder's Gita is power, which, in line with John Austin, considers postcolonial state sovereignty to be illimitable by a document like the Constitution.[65] For Tejinder, the power to protect the sovereignty of India from its enemies (who for him are Muslims) must override constitutional restrictions on the use of force. This has historically been the case with special security legislations in India that have always been upheld by the Supreme Court despite their provisions being draconian and in contravention of guaranteed rights in the Constitution of India.[66] Tejinder, though, can be said to be drawing inspiration for his Gita from the Constitution of India itself, which carries within it a clause that produces the exceptional conditions for using preventive detention laws to legitimise custodial violence on both suspect citizens and 'enemy aliens'.[67]

Dev's rival Gita, the guiding source of his conscience, is the 'material' Constitution of India, which can be 'grasped only by properly grappling with the deeper societal context in which formal constitutional development is embedded'.[68] This societal context is the story of the New India and of religious violence that the film tells. However, the depth of Dev's living room constitutionalism is much like Kelsen's 'basic norm'.[69] He 'presupposes' the Constitution as the normative basis of sovereignty and human flourishing for India's postcolonial social context,[70] which for him is founded on the secular religious ideas of Hinduism enshrined in the Gita. Dev's assertions about the Constitution point to his passionate investments in the triad of secularism (religious harmony), legalism (justice system) and developmentalism (economy). It is this belief in the Constitution that convinces Dev to depose in court against the misdeeds of the police and politicians who supported the pogrom, the court for him being the highest institutional authority that upholds the Constitution.

Bharti's intervention in this conversation offers yet another rival imagination. While on the one hand she does not consider the Gita to be the foundation of her conscience, on the other, she dreams of a future India of prosperity and rights for all, only possible in Ramrajya, the rule of the mythological Aryan-raced Hindu warrior-god Ram. That imagination for her has become an impossibility in Kaliyug—'the dark age',[71] 'the era of greatest spiritual decline in Hindu cosmic time'.[72] As mentioned in Chapter 1, Hindutva politics in modern India continues to be mobilised most powerfully around the figure of Ram and in the campaign to build a temple in Ayodhya at the exact location where he was claimed to have been born. It was at this location that the Babri Mosque was demolished in 1992 by cadres of

Hindutva activists to make way for the building of the temple.[73] The vision of achieving Ramrajya, or what has been called 'pure Hindu rule',[74] has also been an articulated promise of Hindutva political parties to rescue India from its Kaliyug.[75] Kaliyug here could also be understood as an equivalent to the expression 'jungle raj' that the Vadodara Sessions Court judgment (discussed in Chapter 3) used, while acquitting all the 21 accused, to warn against the tragedy that will befall India if patriotism and *development* are not pursued by the people in response to the violence.[76]

Thus, all the three characters offer rival visions of their attachment to and imagination of the Indian nation-state. While each of these visions is presented as secular, the foundational ethos remains Hindu. In particular, to strengthen the integrity of Dev as the film's hero, this narrative equates the Constitution of India to the Bhagavad Gita.[77] Dev's conscience—captured in the affective force of the Sanskrit *shloka*s that opened the film—considers the idea and imagination of the Constitution to be sacred, as is borne out by Dev's own invocation of the Gita. By doing this, Dev Hinduises not only his own conscience, but also the conscience and legal foundations of the nation, in keeping with an Indian Supreme Court judgment from 1994 that did not find any reason for Hindutva ideology to be considered antithetical to secularism.[78]

The location of this conversation is also pertinent to my J-A reading. The art direction of the living room makes the space look agnostic to the religion of the Hindu characters present. Their clothing also provides no indicator of their religion or religiosity.[79] These particularities are of significance for two reasons. First, they produce a sense of seamless cohabitation of the secular and the religious when it comes to Hinduism. Second, they provide a contrast, in art and costume direction, to the representations of the domestic spaces inside Noor Manzil, where specific kinds of clothing—the skullcap, the veil and the *lungi* (Indian sarong)—and identifiable Islamic symbols, greetings, rituals and gestures make the space and its inhabitants look overtly Muslim. The affect of secularity that the living room scene and its screenplay generate, despite the exchange between the characters being imbued with Hindu metaphors, in effect secularises Hinduism and Hinduises secularism as 'cultural common sense'.[80]

Dev is the hero of the film—he is characterised as progressive, secular and liberal (the unmarked Hindu in secular police uniform). He does not hate Muslims, but at the same time likens the secular Constitution to the Hindu holy book. The film, though, draws a distinction between Dev's good

Hinduism and Tejinder's bad version. The good version rationalises, modernises and secularises the imagined Hindu foundations of postcolonial India by using the Constitution as an alibi, whereas the bad version offers extra-constitutional justifications for the annihilation of Muslims. Both these versions ultimately celebrate two versions of Hindutva ideology. Dev's version speaks more to Hindutva's neoliberal avatar that speaks of developmentalism and legalism as a means of assimilating the Muslim as a 'reluctant citizen'[81] into the Hindu nation's fold. If Muslims resist this tactic, it will be 'read in jurisprudential terms as a self-imposed injury of an ethnic group caught in a time-warp and reluctant to embrace citizenship and development'.[82] Farhaan's lawyerly transformation into the good Muslim citizen, as a seeker of justice using constitutional means, rehabilitates him as a Muslim and champions the promise of Dev's Bhagavad Gita as the Constitution.

This script of equivalence has also been the secular rhetoric on the basis of which Narendra Modi had appealed for votes during his prime ministerial campaigns. Time and again, Modi referred to the Constitution as the 'holy book' that should drive his 'India First' mission.[83] This secular rhetoric of constitutionalism has been a part of Indian juridical governance techniques since 1976, when the word 'secular' was inserted into the text of the Constitution for the first time through the Constitution (42nd Amendment) Act.[84] This secular rhetoric, thus, works as a mask to cover the actual Hindu foundations of the Constitution that the film incorporates into its narrative, even as it condemns the violence against Muslims.

Pointing out the 'Hindu bias' in the Constitution of India, Pritam Singh writes: 'The progressive and genuinely secular forces in India need to recognise a bitter truth, namely that uncritically claiming a secular heritage from … the Constitution of India is to play a potentially losing game from the very beginning against their *Hindutva* opponents.'[85] The appeal to the Constitution, like in *Dev*, as the panacea for all injustices against Muslims, and the contradictory projection of it as a sacred text that is secular, is in fact institutionalised within India's legal and cultural imagination.[86]

As I have discussed in my reading of the Best Bakery judgments in Chapter 3, the Supreme Court ordered that the case be shifted out of Gujarat for fear of political manipulation by the state and to uphold constitutional standards of fair trial. Alongside, the Supreme Court also tried Zahira Sheikh—the key witness who turned hostile due to political threats against her and her family—and held her guilty for perjury. In sentencing Zahira, the same court that expressed anguish over how the justice process in Gujarat was weighted against its Muslim minority population, and how that was an affront to our constitutional principles of secularism, began the judgment by quoting from the Manusmriti—a classical Hindu religious scripture that also forms the basis of Hindu law—on the duties of a witness.[87] In upholding the secular Constitution, the Supreme Court, much like Dev, Hinduised it.

For Farhaan, the dilemma is between subscribing to his father's belief in the non-violence and pacifism of freedom fighters like Gandhi and Khan as the way to respond to the discrimination faced by Muslims in India and taking the path of violence. After his brush with violence, and seeing Dev's firm conviction in siding with his constitutional beliefs, Farhaan also reposes faith in the justice system—the courts—by donning the lawyer's attire to take up litigation to fight for Dev's cause and for the Muslims of India, and, in turn, to resolve his own dilemma. Aaliya too—in resolving her dilemma of whether to speak up as an eyewitness in front of the same police force that aided and abetted the violence—reposes trust in Dev's promise at the hearing organised at Noor Manzil. He promised that if people lodged FIRs, the police would ensure justice by arresting and charging the individual wrongdoers—a gesture towards individual criminalisation as a way of ending impunity.

The film, thus, represents the criminal justice system in the aftermath of mass violence as a trustworthy venue for justice seeking. Like the protagonists of the film, the audience is called on to repose faith in the law to pass its *judgment.* This is the performance of a particular kind of state-making and state-preserving rationality that displaces structural concerns about state accountability through the promise of punishment. Legal culpability is individualised, and is singularly focused on specific politicians or a police officer like Tejinder. Responding to the Gujarat pogrom by directing all investments at the individual criminalisation of perpetrators does very little to challenge the historical, structural and ideological foundations that resulted in the pogrom in the first place. Convictions can, in fact, create an illusion of the restoration of rule of law, and the state's commitment to liberal rights, which demands that we repose faith in the New India's state-making and state-preserving practices. As Ratna Kapur has argued in her assessment of the justice-seeking mechanisms in the wake of the Gujarat violence:

The story of the Gujarat riots and subsequent efforts to address the harms and injuries through prosecution and apology does not pay attention to the institutional discursive mechanisms within a democratic polity that can produce moments of extreme violence, moments that cannot be written off as aberrational and deviant.... 2002 cannot be addressed exclusively within a prosecutorial, or reparations framework that seeks to prosecute individual wrongdoers who carried out such atrocities and provide compensation to those who suffered.... [T]he riots were a logical product or outcome of a discursive strategy partly in and through liberal rights discourse and not in opposition to such rights.[88]

By extension, the film exhorts its cinematic publics to repose faith and trust in the Constitution and the courts. The Constitution and the judiciary are represented as incorruptible foundations of the nation-state which can weather all crises and can in consequence unshakeably guard the nation. The courthouse outside which Dev is murdered, and the steps of which Farhaan climbs in his advocate's attire, is an imposing building, painted white, and its environs look sanitised (Figures 4.12 and 4.13). The only traces of memory of the violence are in the fading stain of Dev's blood on the steps leading to the court (immediately to the left of where Farhaan is standing) and the file in Farhaan's hand that contains all the evidence that Dev had gathered.

This material location of law's institutional presence and the location of the elite drawing room where Dev and Tejinder pontificated on

Figure 4.12 Farhaan meets the court: No more 'reluctant citizen'
Source: Screenshot from DVD.

Figure 4.13 Memory's traces on the pedestals of law
Source: Screenshot from DVD.

constitutionalism[89] are set up in contradistinction to the squalid and lawless Muslim ghetto of Noor Manzil—which, when introduced early on in the film, is shown to be a hideout for a Muslim militant. Those like Farhaan and Aaliya, who are victim-survivors of the pogrom, have to exit that lawless location, find refuge in Dev's secular home and then enter the ostensibly secular space of the court in search of justice. The jurisdictional organisation of the city and that of law and legalism are, thus, clearly identified in the film's aesthetic representations.

The way of remembering that *Dev's* reconstruction of the pogrom engenders sees religious strife as the doing of individual evil politicians; it suggests that violence begets violence (and Muslims generally tend to start it), so trust the Constitution and courts, they are secular and will ultimately deliver justice. More importantly, it is trust in the Constitution and the conviction to stand by the rule of law that also resolve the enmity between the Muslim Farhaan and Hindu Dev. The intensity of the constitutional resolution is so powerful that Farhaan is able to overlook the fact that it was because of Dev's extra-judicial orders that his father and many other Muslims were killed in police firing. Despite developing an endearing feeling towards Farhaan, Dev, in fact, never expresses any remorse about his orders that killed Farhaan's father. Dev is placed above the audience's moral judgment because that was in the realm of his Bhagavad Gita–inspired *dharma* (divinely ordained duty) to protect the nation.[90] Farhaan, similarly, never demands justice for Dev's act of ordering the killing of his father.

My J-A reading has shown that through its images and sounds, *Dev's* story *records* a memory of the pogrom where, while the phantasmagoric violence is recognised—in alignment with the Best Bakery judgments—the structural othering of Muslims in India is rationalised. It is the appeal to such a rationalisation that produces and mobilises *judgment* by calling on the film's spectatorial publics. It is the possibility of such judgment that frames the *mnemohistory* of the pogrom in the film, where secular Hindus like Dev, despite their belief in the Hindu foundations of the nation and its Constitution, are rehabilitated in the eyes of the Muslim citizen as being fair to Muslims as long as they stand by the Constitution and the rule of law. The Muslim victim-survivors of the violence in the film ultimately repose faith in Dev's Hindu Constitution and in the secular courts as the ultimate arbiters of justice. It is the rationalities of *legalism* and *secularism* that elide the Hindu foundations of the Indian nation-state, its Constitution and courts, which order and lend meaning to law's institutions and imaginaries of justice. The memorialisation of the pogrom in *Dev*, thus, happens through the projection of the performance of state *legalism*, which is designed to restore faith in the capacity of secular law to deliver justice in response to an event of religious violence. *Dev* ends outside the courtroom, and the audience does not yet know whether the promise of secular law that the film has celebrated will be fulfilled.

Parzania: The Promise of Secular Law

Parzania's second title is 'Heaven and Hell on Earth', which underscores the moral investments of the film's memorial reconstructions of the Gujarat pogrom and its imaginations of justice (Figure 4.14). In place of the standard disclaimer, the film announces that it is 'inspired by a true story' (see Figure 4.5 earlier). This fidelity to *truth* will work as both a narrative and cinematic trope through the film.

As we saw earlier, the CBFC certification for *Parzania*, like *Dev*, was for viewing by 'adults only' (see Figure 4.2 earlier). The film had its theatrical release on 26 January 2007, coinciding with India's Republic Day which commemorates the date in 1950 when the Indian Constitution was adopted. At the time of the release, the retrial of the Best Bakery case had already concluded in Mumbai, and a few days after the release of the film, Zahira Sheikh was released after serving time for perjury.

Figure 4.14   'Heaven and Hell on Earth'

Source: *Parzania* (2005), IMDb, https://www.imdb.com/title/tt0433425/?ref_=nv_sr_2 (accessed 18 December 2022).

The key plot of the film is drawn from the travails of a Parsi family in the city of Ahmedabad, who lived in Gulberg Society—a Muslim-majority housing colony which was the site of a major massacre and another key criminal trial.[91] It also draws on several other events from the Gujarat pogrom, including the Best Bakery case, to aid the film's truth-inspired narrative reconstructions. *Parzania* released at the time when the Congress government was in power at the centre, but the BJP continued to be in power in Gujarat. The film had already received critical appreciation at international festivals and had won some awards before its theatrical release in India.

While it received a CBFC clearance—which means it had legal sanction for public exhibition across India—the film could not be released in theatres across Gujarat. There was no state-level ban imposed on the film, or any litigation filed against it like with *Dev* or *Kai Po Che*. Media reports suggested that it might get a late release in February 2007, but that did not happen.[92]

In fact, it was the Gujarat Multiplex Owners Association—a collective of film exhibitors—who decided to not screen the film, fearing backlash from the Hindutva groups. This fear, as has been reported, was fuelled by a BJP leader called Babu Bajrangi—convicted for leading a massacre during 2002—who had said that theatres could only screen *Parzania* if he approved of it.[93]

Manubhai Patel, the chairman of the Gujarat Multiplex Owners Association, had informed Rahul Dholakia, the film's director, that multiplex owners were concerned that the depictions of the 2002 violence in the film could provoke fresh violence. Patel was quoted as having said: 'By now the public has settled down and is living peacefully and engaged in their regular work. We fear that after watching the movie, their sentiments might get hurt, and there might be an uprising again.'[94] The comment indicates that the film as a *record* of the past had the *mnemohistorical* potential to revive 'forgotten' memories of the violence in the present. The extra-legal decision to not screen the film was, thus, considered legitimate. The filmmaker did not contest this in court.[95]

Although the film's story is located in Ahmedabad, *Parzania*'s characters primarily speak English, with some bits of Gujarati and Hindi. This is unlike Bollywood films whose language of address is Hindi. As an expatriate Gujarati filmmaker who was based out of Los Angeles at that time, using English as the language of the film might have been Dholakia's attempt to reach an international audience to inform them about what had happened in Gujarat in 2002.[96] It is also possible that, along with the depiction of the violence, it was the choice of English as the film's language of spectatorial address that might have contributed to the exhibitors' decision to not screen it.

As I have discussed in my reading of the Gujarat High Court judgment in the Best Bakery case in Chapter 3, the discourse around the pogrom that has emerged through the English-language media has always been considered by local Gujarati media and its publics as a conspiracy to tarnish the *asmita*, or pride, of Gujarat. The same has been the case with the larger Hindu populace of Gujarat, which received the English-language reporting of the pogrom with 'hate'.[97] English here does not merely stand for a language, but also a political and moral orientation. In that sense, *Parzania* further complicates the 'structural bilingualism' that I spoke of in regard to the titling of *Dev*. In this case, English displaces Hindi and emerges as a further secularised language of cinematic address meant for a specific public, and for mobilising a particular kind of *judgment*.

Figure 4.15 The real and the fantastic
Source: Screenshot from DVD.

The title of the film is stylised to emerge and dissolve with rays of light and a glow (Figure 4.15). It appears in ornate lettering, over the images of ordinary scenes from the streets of Ahmedabad city. These shots are not random, but a montage to show people and structures that testify to the city's long-standing claim to a quotidian syncretism (including hand-painted images of Bollywood's Muslim superstars that adorn the insides and outsides of auto-rickshaws).[98] An attentive viewer might indentify a couple of shots that subtly disturb this syncretism—particularly one of a Muslim shop owner with a concerned face hurriedly pulling his shutters down fearing ensuing violence, and a wall carrying posters of the Akhil Bharatiya Vidyarthi Parishad, the youth wing of the BJP.[99]

The title draws on one of the film's central characters—the 10-year-old boy Parzaan Pithawala—who conjures up this land of fantasy called Parzania. The heaven in the film's second title refers to this fantasy, and the hell is the violence that wreaks havoc in the lives of the ordinary Muslims of Ahmedabad, and particularly the Pithawala family, when Parzaan goes missing during the pogrom. That both the fantasy of Parzania and the horror of the pogrom can emanate from the same human location is a key framing of the film's narrative reconstructions of the pogrom.

Many imaginations of law and justice are embedded within the worlds of the real and the fantastic assembled by the film's plot and cinematic form. One such imagination that accompanies the opening credits is invoked through a Gujarati folk song, sung by Karsan Sagathiya, which is a paean to

Gujarat as the land of Gandhi. The song is followed by a voice-over in the American-accented male voice of Alan, one of the film's protagonists who is also the non-diegetic narrator:

> Ahmedabad, a city founded by a Muslim king, later becoming the home of Gandhi, as he broke barriers between the Hindus and the Muslims. There is warmth in the eyes of the people here that you won't find anywhere else. You would have no idea what was brewing beneath that.

There is a level of universal intelligibility that this opening address aims to mobilise. The accented English, despite its international appeal, pronounces the name of the city as Amdavad, as a means of inflecting a local sensibility. This sensibility might lend the film's audience the sound of an imagined authenticity. However, the move to rename Ahmedabad to Amdavad has been a sustained project of Hinduisation aimed at erasing the Islamic roots of the name, and the Muslim heritage that the city has been built on.[100]

Gandhi looms large in the film's narrative and cinematic imaginations of justice in the face of violence. The character of Dr Jayaraman—a man whose life is marked by a visible austerity in pastoral environs—is the Gandhian prototype who makes occasional appearances to offer lessons in Gandhian thought to Alan. These lessons, delivered every time with a melodramatic intensity, are addressed at resolving the 'acute crisis' or 'ethical dilemma' that the film's characters, and in effect its publics, would confront. The ability to resolve these dilemmas is the authority of judgment that the film repeatedly bestows on its audience. During one conversation, Jayaraman comments on Alan's habit of drinking bootlegged alcohol, which is prohibited by law in Gujarat.[101]

> *Jayaraman*: If you are going to break the law, it should not be for selfish reasons.
>
> *Alan*: Everyone here seems to....
>
> *Jayaraman*: Alan, you are here to study Gandhi, not India. You need purity, not reactions made of anger.
>
> *Alan*: A healthy dose of anger is good from time to time....
>
> *Jayaraman*: An eye for an eye makes the whole world blind.

It is this Gandhian juridico-moral universe that is held up in order to characterise the pogrom as a perverse aberration with regard to what the film portrayed in the opening sequence as the secular ethos of Gujarat. The ideas of law that animate concerns of justice in the film are arranged in ways that hold up this Gandhian imagination of syncretism, secularism and reconciliation. This is deployed in narrative and cinematic forms that play a pedagogical role through the medium of cinema. We see this in the scene that introduces Parzaan's character.

Parzaan is in his classroom at school, attending a history lesson. The scene is shot from the point of view of the students; the camera is placed accordingly, constructing the pedagogical address in a way that interpellates the audience as students as well (Figure 4.16). The teacher is discussing the 1947 Partition, and mentions how thousands of Hindus were persecuted in Pakistan and had to flee, but most Muslims in India decided to stay back in this 'great secular democracy'. She says this with a self-congratulatory smile on her face. Clearly, the events that follow in the film are meant to interrogate both the Hindu Right's attempts at rewriting history to glorify India's Hindu past (with school textbooks as the key site of this intervention by the BJP),[102] and whether secularism as India's democratic ethos holds any traction after 2002.

The film's plot is built around Parzaan, the son of Cyrus and Shernaz Pithawala, who 'disappears' during the violence of 2002, never to be found. While escaping a murderous mob of Hindu militants with Parzaan and his

Figure 4.16   History lesson: 'Great secular democracy'
Source: Screenshot from DVD.

sister Dilshad, Shernaz loses her son. Cyrus—who works as a film projectionist—is away at work at that time. The rest of the film follows the story of Cyrus and Shernaz trying frantically to find their son. They console their daughter, Dilshad, that her brother will return and then she can tie him a *rakhi*.[103] Their search results in humiliating encounters with the callous and corrupt police system. While the film shows that the violence unfolds after the Godhra train-burning incident, it does not hold this up as the precipitating event. Rather, right from the beginning, the film offers a *record* of how activists of the Hindu Right were involved in planning the pogrom, using maps to target specific Muslim-majority areas. Although in a particular scene Muslims are shown bursting crackers to celebrate Pakistan's win in a cricket match, and a later scene connects Muslim anger to jihad, the film overall does not stereotype Muslims.

The Pithawalas live in a multi-religious housing complex called Mohmadi Mansion, inhabited mostly by working-class and lower-middle-class families. Muslims, Parsis and Hindus live as friends, chatting and laughing with each other. *Parzania's* Mohmadi Mansion is not a ghetto, unlike *Dev's* Noor Manzil. A cinematic tableau holds it up as an allegory for Indian secularism. To establish the syncretism of secular living, the audience is taken inside Hindu, Muslim and Parsi households, each of which is marked by religious signifiers—images or symbols specific to a particular religion. It is a space also marked by exchanges that signify secular modernity. For example, an elderly Muslim man, sharing the news about his niece getting married to a 'nice Hindu boy' who she met on the internet, says, 'Gone are the days of satis and burqa'. The Muslim-sounding name of the complex, however, gives the audience a sense of why it was targeted by Hindu militant mobs.

The majority–minority dynamics vis-à-vis Parsis and Hindus (and by extension Muslims), and in the larger context of national identity, are made clear in several sequences of the film. For example, in one scene Alan looks at an image of Zarathustra pasted on the wall in Cyrus's projection room at the cinema theatre and asks: 'Is this Allah?' Cyrus replies with a smile: 'I'm a Parsi, not a Muslim.... We are like the Jews of India.'[104] In another scene, Shernaz, while putting Parzaan and Dilshad to bed, tells them a story about who the Parsis are and how they arrived in India. She says that when the Parsis arrived in Gujarat a thousand years back in a ship from Persia, the king of Gujarat told them that there was not enough place to accommodate them. The king demonstrated this by filling a bowl with milk till the brim. In response, a Parsi priest took a spoonful of sugar and mixed it with the milk and told the king that, like the sugar which blended with the milk, Parsis would blend with Indians and make their culture sweeter. Shernaz ends her story by saying: 'Since then Parsis and Indians have lived in peace and harmony.'

On both these counts, the relationship between Parsis and Indians within the film's narrative offers two interrelated addresses. First, it says that although Parsis were outsiders, they assimilated so well into Indian (read: Hindu) culture that their community had never been a reason for any acrimony (unlike the Muslims). This story in many ways sets up the film's condemnation of the tragedy to follow, that despite the fact that Parsis are a peaceful community, only because they also have Islamic names (like Muslims), the Pithawalas were targeted by Hindu mobs. Secondly, even thousand years ago the core of the Indian nation was Hindu, and not only Parsis but also Muslims even today remain on the margins of this core.

However, as Gyanendra Pandey has argued, while the Hindu nation thought of both Parsis and Muslims as outsiders, the former were accepted as Indians because they were thought to be refugees fleeing persecution, while the latter were looked at as aggressors. Moreover, as a 'microscopic minority', Parsis were never thought of as having the capacity to threaten the Hindu core of the Indian nation.[105] Pandey explains the Hindu logic behind the Indian nation's construction of itself:

> The Parsis remained different in religion, culture, and 'language' ... but they had contributed significantly to 'our' political, economic, intellectual, and social development. The Muslims had, on the other hand, put forward their own, separatist demands, and had stood in the way of the united struggle against the British. They had not accepted 'our' conception of India: they were therefore not Indians.[106]

Through Cyrus's and Shernaz's accounts, the film offers a historical *record* of the construction of the Indian nation, to distinguish Parsis from Muslims, and to foreground their harmonious relationship with the Hindu nation. Either way, it establishes and holds on to the idea that India was historically (and thus naturally) Hindu.

The Gujarat High Court's judgment in the Best Bakery case made a reference to Parsis by using an almost identical logic to that analysed by Pandey. The court invoked the identity of the Indian Parsi to state how there was a need to 'learn the patriotic feeling to be Indian along with personal religious observations from Parsis'.[107] The judgment recommended that Parsis be considered a test case for demonstrating how this could be achieved without 'obstruction'.[108] Clearly then, the judgment singles out Muslims, without naming them, as the 'anti-national ... who does not adhere to the essential nature, culture and religion of India'.[109] This essential nature, culture and religion, by default, is thus considered Hindu by the court.

The plot in *Parzania* unfolds through the narrations of Alan, the white, American man who has come to live in Ahmedabad, researching on Gandhi for his PhD thesis. Alan is coming to terms with his own complicated Christian past, and drinks bootlegged liquor incessantly from his hip flask in a state where alcohol is banned by law. His voice-over provides the historical and political context to the pogrom, particularly with regard to the rise of the Hindu Right. This narration grounds the event of the pogrom in evidence that is presented not just as commentary but also as factual *record* keeping.

Alan's non-diegetic voice-over accompanies scenes where he is writing his thesis on an old Lexikon 80 typewriter. These are dramatically charged scenes, where he is writing in a stream-of-consciousness fashion after getting drunk on bootlegged liquor to tide over the violence that he has witnessed outside. It is 'a scene of writing and its subsequent erasure, literally',[110] where Alan *records* his memories of witnessing and burns the papers he has typed on (Figures 4.17 and 4.18). The use of the typewriter as the technology of recording memory and the material destruction of what has been

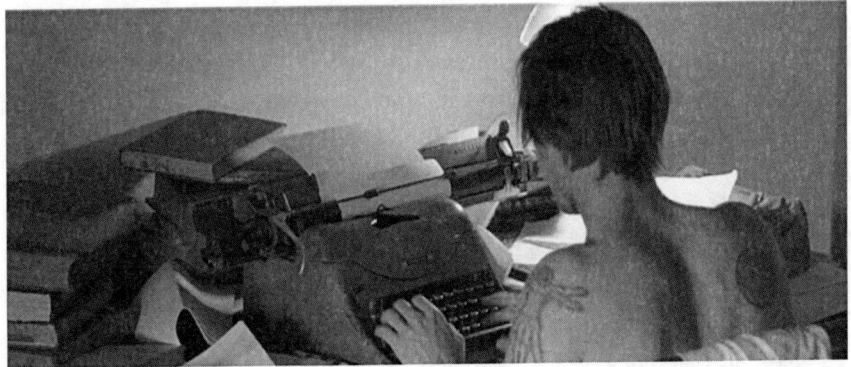

Figure 4.17 'A scene of writing ...'
Source: Screenshot from DVD.

Figure 4.18 '... and its subsequent erasure'
Source: Screenshot from DVD.

recorded—unlike the use of computers to virtually record and delete written text—lends an affective intensity to the impossibility of recording (and thus remembering) the enormity of the violence.

The figuration of the typewriter as the memory-recording device in the film is also curious. Given that the story is set in 2002, it is highly unlikely that a typewriter would be used—that too by an American researcher visiting India—to write his thesis. Interestingly, though, the typewriter continues to remain the most ubiquitous recording device in lower courts in India:[111] 'typists ... seen outside courts in almost any city ... are, in many ways, the last foot soldiers fighting a losing battle in the fight for the survival of the typewriter'.[112] I am reading its use as a narrative prop in the film,[113] one that alludes to it as a faithful yet fallible fact recorder of Alan's eyewitness accounts of the pogrom that are being presented to the audience for their *judgment*. That this *record* carries a legal charge becomes apparent in one scene where Alan's voice-over tells the audience why the violence needs to be named:

> This was no backlash, and people are starting to figure it out. They act as if this was just a natural reaction to Godhra, but you tell me how you can mobilise a hundred thousand citizens with swords and trishuls [tridents] and pipe-bombs within twenty-four hours? How did the men have all the voters lists so that they knew exactly where the Muslims lived? Why was the name of every Muslim business in the area run in the newspapers with their addresses not long before? Why were flags

systematically distributed to all Hindu owned businesses long before Godhra had even occurred? I'll tell you why. This riot isn't a riot. It was a planned act of genocide.

Parzania is the only film that characterises the Gujarat violence as genocide, in opposition to riot, which has been the popular refrain. Both of these are legally defined descriptions, and particularly in the case of Gujarat, they are in contestation with each other. The Indian Penal Code, 1860, identifies collective violence by defining it as 'rioting', which is characterised as the crime of 'unlawful assembly' for achieving a 'common object'.[114] Although India ratified the Convention on the Prevention and Punishment of the Crime of Genocide in 1959, the term 'genocide' does not carry any valence in Indian municipal law.[115] The invocation of the international legal category of genocide to characterise the Gujarat violence emerged primarily out of human rights reports on the event.[116] It might be the case that *Parzania*'s choice of the term can be attributed to the fact that its associate producer was Mihir Desai, a well-known human rights lawyer, who also appeared as counsel in the Best Bakery and many other pogrom-related cases.[117] Desai, along with Teesta Setalvad, was reprimanded by the Vadodara Sessions Court and Gujarat High Court judgments of the Best Bakery case for sullying the prestige of Gujarat by raising questions about the absence of fair trial and witness intimidation.

Parzania, thus, plays its pedagogic role of training its audiences both by providing an explanation for the violence that does not use the logic of equivalence (as was the case with *Dev*)—Muslims attacked Hindus, so Hindus attacked Muslims—and also by calling attention to the legal inadequacies of describing the violence as a riot. This is further made clear when Alan's voice-over compares the Parishad, the Hindu militant political party in the film that organised and perpetrated the violence,[118] to the fascist and xenophobic politics of the Ku Klux Klan. This comparison mobilises an internationalised spectatorial public to make the event intelligible to a Western audience. The use of genocide as the descriptor does the same work by making the Holocaust its most identifiable referent to attest to the enormity of the event.[119]

Alan's typewritten memorial *record* is accompanied by the diegetic and non-diegetic sounds of radio and television reporting (using original media footage) to further ground the depiction of the events in the film as inspired by truth. The cinematic form of *Parzania* uses this method as a way to mobilise collective memory. One particular scene foregrounds the way the character of the CM in the film responds to the violence. The shot captures a whole array of televisions broadcasting the CM's speech, in the wake of the Godhra incident, to the people of Gujarat, in which he says: 'It is our resolve to punish the culprits. No one will be spared.' The CM speaks in a stern and ominous voice. This scene immediately follows Alan's typewriting and voice-over described earlier, thus suggesting what the outcome of the resolve was. What the CM says in the film has been drawn from the actual address of Narendra Modi that was broadcast on state television.[120] Modi was the CM of Gujarat in 2002, and also at the time when *Parzania* was released.

In the original address broadcast via the state television network Doordarshan on 28 February 2002, Modi's response was imbued with *legalism*. Delivering the speech in Gujarati, Modi said that he understood the anger of the Gujarati people, but assured them that 'no one will escape the law'; that instead of taking to violence, people should help 'strengthen the hands of the law'; that his government promised to punish the culprits 'through a legal route'; that he was committed to 'get the highest possible punishment for the culprits'.[121] According to a blog post written by Modi himself, he claimed: 'I had appealed publicly through Doordarshan to maintain peace.'[122] As Manoj Mitta has noted: 'The speech threatened action against Muslims involved in the Godhra crime but issued no such warning to Hindus, although they had by then caused greater havoc.'[123] Modi's commitment to legal action was borne out by the process and outcome of the Best Bakery case, among others, in Gujarat.

In the previous chapter, I provided an elaborate account of the way in which the Gujarat judiciary remained committed to *legalism* even as all the 21 accused were acquitted by the Vadodara Sessions and Gujarat High Courts in the Best Bakery case. *Parzania* aims to cinematically counter this by projecting imaginations of justice that hold out hope in the face of adversity. The film offers three contesting imaginations of justice, one of which triumphs over the other two. In the aftermath of the violence, Alan regains some control over his life by returning to reading Gandhi. He searches for the Pithawalas at a refugee camp, and, on finding them, brings them to his residence. By this time, Cyrus and Shernaz have tried various ways to find Parzaan, to no avail.

The first imagination of justice is presented as one of revenge. At the refugee camp, Asif, a Muslim neighbour of the Pithawalas who also lived in

Mohmadi Mansion, has been mobilising other Muslims to plot an attack on Hindus. Asif, who was earlier shown in the film as one who had expressed secular thoughts, was now invoking Islam as a way to provoke other Muslim men in the refugee camp. He starts gathering arms to plan an attack. Cyrus is a witness to this, but he is too immersed in grief over Parzaan's disappearance to think of revenge as a response. More importantly, he is not Muslim. He instead follows the path of piety, which is the second imagination of justice that the film offers. Cyrus meets with a Zoroastrian priest who advises that he should completely seclude himself for nine days and purify himself, and then Ahura Mazda will answer his prayers. Cyrus tells Dilshad that when he is back, she will get to meet Parzaan.

The third imagination of justice in *Parzania* is the path of state accountability that Shernaz follows through secular law. She decides to depose at a hearing organised by the NHRC to collect testimonies of victim-survivors and law enforcement officials. A significant part of the second half of *Parzania* is dedicated to the public hearings. The space of the hearing architecturally looks like that of a courtroom. In the scene introducing the commission's hearing, the camera is placed inside this room, and Shernaz, Alan (with Dilshad in his lap) and Nikhat, a close Muslim friend of Shernaz's who also lived at Mohmadi Mansion, are shown entering. A big portrait of Gandhi—as an icon of secularism—is seen watching over them on the wall facing, as it were, the gate of law (Figure 4.19). The room is crowded, and there is a palpable police presence. The scene then cuts to a shot that is taken

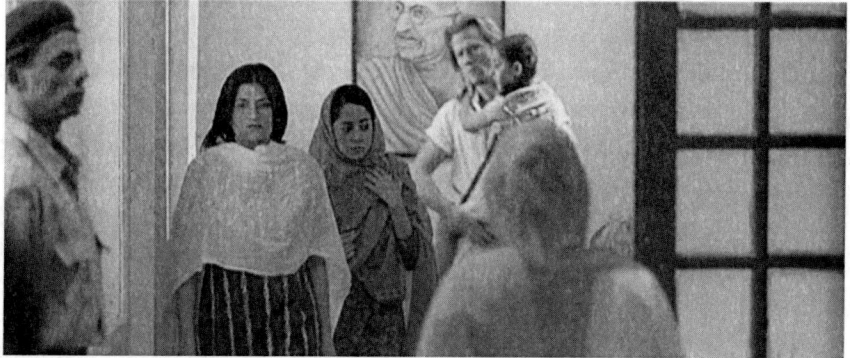

Figure 4.19 Gandhi at the gate of law
Source: Screenshot from DVD.

Figure 4.20   A non-adversarial and secular space of quasi-legalism
Source: Screenshot from DVD.

from the point of view of the cinema's audience, and thus the public gathered in the commission's room, that shows the four-member team of the commission (Figure 4.20).

All the four members speak English in an accent that is remarkably refined in comparison to most of the victim-survivors who testify. Three men and one woman are seated at the head of the room, below what looks like a judge's raised bench. Thus, while the commission members are seated at a bench, a location similar to the judge's, they are shown not occupying the raised platform of the judge. The significance of this becomes apparent when one of the male members lays out the mandate of the commission: 'It should be noted that this is not a criminal proceeding. However, the findings of this board will be presented to the government, and recommendations about how to proceed with criminal prosecution will be made.'

I infer three reasons for the filmmaker's decision to not make a court proceeding part of the film's narrative. First, the two major trials—Gulberg Society and Naroda Patiya—that the film's narrative reconstruction of the pogrom draws on were, at the time of its release, still sub judice. Second, as discussed in Chapter 3, in the aftermath of the pogrom, the actual NHRC was the only state-authorised body which conducted an impartial inquiry and produced reports that powerfully condemned the Gujarat administration. Third, using a trial in the film's plot would have turned the testimonial space into an adversarial one.

In the framing of this space as a commission hearing, the victim-survivors as witnesses are accorded the opportunity to speak in a space of safety without their memorial accounts being challenged or cross-examined. Unlike an adversarial criminal trial, in this ostensibly secular space, witnesses are not required to take an oath by swearing to tell the truth by touching a religious text.

In the next shot, the camera occupies a place behind the commission members, and thus the spectatorial publics are interpellated to take the place of the absent judge (Figure 4.21). This shot provides a wide-view framing of the entire room. The walls of the room are empty. On the right of the frame we see the typewriter return as the technology of recording memory as evidence. On the left, facing the typewriter, we see an empty chair. This is the chair that each of the victim-survivors will occupy to deliver their testimony. The chair is located at a spot akin to that of the witness box or stand in a standard courtroom. From the attire of most of the people in the room, we can identify them as Muslim victim-survivors who have come to testify. There are police officers in khaki uniform. And also visible are members of Hindutva groups with saffron scarves around their necks.

The mise en scène is organised in a way that renders a powerful secular feel to this quasi-legal and state-organised space. The secular affect is addressed through a narrative and a cinematic device. The four members of the commission who will hear and record the testimonies are all dressed in religion-neutral attire—the men in shirts and trousers, and the woman in a salwar kameez. The woman has no markers on her body, like a *bindi* or *sindoor*, to indicate her religion. This neutrality becomes especially apparent when the attire of the rest of the people in the room comes into view.

Figure 4.21   Audience interpellated to take the place of the absent judge
Source: Screenshot from DVD.

The camera pans the room slowly in a stable fashion. When the victim-survivors are testifying, the camera takes close-up frontal shots that accentuate their facial expressions as they remember and narrate incidents of horror. They speak almost directly to the audience. The camera is always located at the position of the commission members' bench when it captures the testimonies, again interpellating the audience as the recipient of this memorial *record* and thus endowed with the capacity to pass *judgment*. This sense of slow stability is palpable in contradistinction to the shaky jump-cuts that were used earlier in the film to represent the lawlessness of the attack by armed Hindu mobs on Mohmadi Mansion.

It is in this secular space of state-organised quasi-legalism, along with many other victim-survivors, that Shernaz Pithawala speaks with dramatic conviction and demands that her son be returned to her, and that she will wait forever if she has to. She says, in no ambiguous terms, that the government was responsible for taking care of her son and that the police had failed to provide any protection. The police are indicted by several of those testifying. Responding to a question by one of the commission members about the role of the police, in a montage, victim-survivors utter an answer that was identically worded as the title of the Human Rights Watch report on the pogrom: 'We have no orders to save you.'[124]

The sense of safety that this secular space affords Shernaz and the others testifying is borne out by the fact that, braving the presence of several members of Hindutva groups in the room, many overcome the threats and intimidation directed at them. Some, of course, succumb. The projection of this space can be read as a sharp criticism and corrective that the film directs at the fearful space at the Vadodara Sessions Court where, during the Best Bakery trial, Zahira Sheikh was intimidated into lying under oath. In one conversation during the hearing, this becomes apparent:

Commission member: And what happened during the criminal pre-trial?

Testifier: All seven men were acquitted.

Commission member: And how did the acquittals come about?

Testifier: The prosecutor was the member of the ruling party, and also had been charged with eight accounts of murder himself.

In the narrative and cinematic framing of this commission's space, the film's plot credits the same state that organised and executed the pogrom, with making this space available for Shernaz's voice to be heard through the organisation of this quasi-legal forum. In this space, making particular use of the placement of the camera, the film makes the audience take up the role of judging repeatedly. The parameters of *judgment* are, however, tied to the generation of the audience's trust for the putatively secular nation-state, in its performance of an impartial and victim-centric *legalism*.

The audience is called on to judge the violent events to which the testimonies of Shernaz and the other victim-survivors have borne witness; but in this act of judgment the audience will have to work within the framework of the secular nation-state, which, despite the breakdown of law and order, is projected as remaining committed to lending an ear to the victims, to listening to their stories. Shernaz's emphatic articulation that she will wait forever is representative of not only a mother's courage to continue the search for Parzaan but also her faith in the secularism and legalism of the process, despite its failures. In doing this, the film, despite its powerful critique of the violence, and of the individual and institutional actors that carried it out, renders the nation-state form beyond critique. In reposing trust in the *legalism* of the state-established justice-seeking procedure, the violence of the nation-state is simultaneously condemned and rationalised.

Thus, the spectatorial address of the film offers the audience three rival imaginations of justice—revenge, piety and secular law—embodied in the conduct of three characters. These imaginations are presented in a cinematic form that enables the audience to acquire the position of passing judgment on which of the three they invest most faith in. These rival imaginations generate an 'acute crisis' or 'ethical dilemma' for the characters that has to be resolved through judgment. The narrative and cinematic organisation of the secular space of the NHRC's hearings offers a closure by making the imagination of justice through secular law triumph over the other two imaginations.

This resolution as closure is sealed when we see the faith in secular law demonstrated by Asif, the Muslim neighbour of the Pithawalas who was planning armed revenge. Earlier in the film, Nikhat (another Muslim resident of Mohmadi Mansion and Shernaz's close friend) had confronted Asif about his plans at the refugee camp.

Nikhat: You know this isn't right.

Asif: Why, what they did was right? Why are you defending the Hindus?

Nikhat: It was a Hindu man who saved my life Asif.

Asif: And it was Hindus who killed my father. They butchered him Nikhat. They tore him up. Why? For no reason. He was 75 years old. What harm could he have possibly done? Nikhat they took him from me for no fucking reason. I think they deserve this, and you don't tell me that they don't deserve it.

Nikhat: How can you pretend that the Hindus you are going to kill are the same ones who killed him?

Asif: I don't care!

Nikhat: You don't care? Okay. What if you do it? Do it. What happens after that you tell me? Have you thought about that? Nothing will have changed Asif, nothing! If you want to hurt them, fine. But go after the ones who did it. But not with a sword, not with a sword Asif.

The close-up shot of Asif's face after this conversation shows how he has been left distraught by Nikhat's rival imagination of justice. The next time we see Asif is at the commission's hearing. He has undergone a change of heart. He gives up on the idea of violent revenge and goes to depose at the commission. Asif's entry into the commission's room coincides with the deposition by a Hindu bootlegger who also lived at Mohmadi Mansion; fearing that the mobs would kill him, he had pointed out to them which of the houses belonged to Muslims. While testifying, he comes clean about this and breaks down. This reconciliatory moment between the vengeful Muslim and the repentant Hindu attests to the power of the secular space of (quasi-)*legalism*.

Similarly, Cyrus after having completed his seclusion and purification rituals arrives at the commission's hearings to join Shernaz and Dilshad. His path through piety might have yielded him answers, but in joining his family at the commission, it is the space of secular law that enables and sustains their collective faith in justice. In fact, faith in religion is replaced by faith in law. We see this cinematically addressed when, at the end of the hearing, a striking top shot captures Shernaz, Cyrus and Dilshad sitting together, holding each other, in the commission's empty room (Figure 4.22). The top shot engenders a transcendental vision of the space—the sacredness of secular law, despite the horrors that they have experienced, will keep them together, safe. This secure space has not come at the cost of forgetting the past. In fact, the familiar typewriter—'the circulating representation of trauma'[125]—as the recorder of memory, with a paper rolled in, can be seen in a corner of the frame.

Figure 4.22 The sacredness of secular law
Source: Screenshot from DVD.

The film ends with Alan's voice-over telling the audience two things. First, that two years after the hearings of the human rights commission, the government of the ruling party was voted out at the centre. This is factually correct information, but presented in a way that connects the electoral outcome to the hearings. Second, he says that he has decided to turn his thesis into a book titled *Parzania*, in which he will write about a world without violence, a world that Parzaan had conjured in his imaginations of Parzania. With the fading out of Alan's voice-over, we see Dilshad looking directly into the camera.

With a measured mix of sentiment, compassion and fact, the film successfully offers a strong condemnation of Hindutva violence, representations of state complicity and sensitive portrayals of how despite not being Muslim, the Pithawalas were affected by the mindlessness of the violence. Not surprisingly, the film's reference point for making sense of the violence is Gandhi, the so-called 'saint' of non-violence.[126] And it is here that the film succumbs to the idea of the Hindu nation. Instead of offering a critique of nationalism as the ideology of the Hindu *rashtra* which was at the root of the pogrom and continues to be a justification for it, the film instead posits Hindu militant nationalism as opposed to Gandhi's secular nationalist religiosity of *sarva dharma sambhava* (equal respect for all religions),[127] thus drawing a fragile distinction between good Hindu nationalism and a bad one, and in effect letting the Hindu foundations of the Indian nation escape scrutiny.[128]

Figure 4.23   A 'weighty mythology'?
Source: Screenshot from DVD.

Rahul Dholakia, the director of the film, has said that he drew inspiration for the story from the real-life incident of the disappearance of Azhar Mody during the Gulberg Society massacre on 28 February 2002.[129] *Parzania* ends with a message asking the audience to write in if they find any information on Azhar (who is still missing). The message has an accompanying photograph showing Azhar holding up the Indian flag in his school uniform (Figure 4.23). It is an address exhorting the viewers to act on their *judgment* of what has preceded in the film and to take a step outside of the sentimentalities attached to watching the tribulations of the Pithawalas. In bringing the audience back to the 'true story' that has 'inspired' the film, the choice of this as the closing image works as a secular and nationalist call to keep intact, despite the fractures, the 'weighty mythology' of what Sudipta Kaviraj has called 'the imaginary institution of India'.[130]

In my reading of *Parzania*, the J-A lens has paid attention to the narrative form and cinematic techniques used in the film for two purposes: first, to examine law's aesthetic role in reconstructing collective memory; and second, to identify how the film's record of the pogrom activates *mnemohistories* through the reification of an imagination of justice where secular law trumps all other rival imaginations. The way of remembering that *Parzania* subscribes to is a projection of the performance and impossible promise of secular state legalism and the quasi-legal process as designed to restore faith in the mythical capacity of law to deliver justice. In comparison to *Dev*—where the actual working of the legal system is not shown—in *Parzania*, the initiation of the process marks a progress in cinematic imaginations of justice. To mobilise *judgment*, audiences are taken inside the architectural confines of a state-organised secular quasi-legal process. It is not yet known where the process will lead. *Kai Po Che*, the third and final film, takes us there.

Kai Po Che: The Developmentalist Road to Justice

Kai Po Che released on 22 February 2013, one day short of a week before the 13th anniversary of the Gujarat pogrom. By this time, the judicial proceedings in the Best Bakery case had come to a close with the final set of acquittals ordered by the Bombay High Court in July 2012. Two other trials had resulted in convictions, including those of two BJP politicians for having played active roles in carrying out massacres at Naroda Patiya and Ode.[131] One of those convicted in the Naroda Patiya case was Babu Bajrangi, whose extra-judicial approval had to be sought to release *Parzania* in Gujarat. The convictions in the Bilkis Bano gang rape case—a paradigmatic incident of sexual violence targeted at Muslim women during the pogrom—also received widespread attention, and were considered as a successful outcome of the relentless efforts of human rights defenders who persisted with the cases and learnt from prior strategic mistakes.[132]

On the one hand, while the criminal justice system's response to the pogrom had a compromised start in 2003 with the Best Bakery acquittals in Vadodara and Ahmedabad, by the time of *Kai Po Che*'s release, it seemed to have regained some lost faith. On the other hand, in 2013, Narendra Modi was poised to win the next general elections scheduled for early 2014.

Since 2002, Modi had not lost a single state election in Gujarat, and his sophisticated media campaigns had propelled him to the national political stage as a strong and decisive leader of a new model of aggressive masculinity.[133] Modi's rise was also connected to the way in which he and his party, the BJP, had marketed the 'Gujarat Model' of development and 'Modi-nomics'—his own neoliberal economic vision—as the ways to launch India into a global club of industrialised countries and establish Gujarat as India's most economically powerful state.[134]

If the 2002 pogrom marked the success of Gujarat as the 'Hindutva laboratory',[135] the 'Gujarat Model' marked the success of the experiment of seamlessly merging neoliberalism to Hindutva.[136] At the time of the release of *Kai Po Che*, Modi was being hailed by Indian and foreign industrialists alike as a visionary leader for the land he was offering them to set up large manufacturing units in Gujarat.[137] In this period Modi was also exonerated for his involvement in enabling the violence of 2002, as the CM and home minister. As discussed in Chapter 3, the Supreme Court–appointed SIT, set up in the wake of the failure of the Gujarat judiciary to impartially prosecute cases related to the pogrom, had given Modi a 'clean chit'.[138] Strong critiques of the SIT's conduct have pointed at the procedural and administrative lapses that led to this eventuality.[139]

Based on a 2008 novel by Chetan Bhagat (who also co-wrote the screenplay),[140] *Kai Po Che*'s story and its reconstructions of the Gujarat pogrom resonate strongly with the mood of the time. This mood is one of the combined triumph of the rationalities of legalism and developmentalism that, even while recognising and condemning the violence against Muslims, valorises the economic arrangements and political institutions that structurally exacerbate the marginalisation of Muslims in the New India. The film adaptation, while retaining the core of the story, makes substantive changes to both the form of telling as well as the plot. For the purposes of my J-A reading, I do not intend to compare the novel and the film. I treat the film as a cultural and jurisprudential text independent of the novel. However, the fact of having been written by Chetan Bhagat—whose moral vision as represented in the novel seems closely aligned with Modi's—has contributed to the controversies that accompanied the film's release.[141]

The event of the pogrom is not central to the film's story, yet it became what the film has been most noticed for. *Kai Po Che* received both popular and critical attention from audiences and commentators alike.[142] The retelling of the pogrom, part of the film's fictional plot and cathartic closure, was one of the major reasons for this attention. While on the one hand it was praised for taking a sensitive look at the pogrom and speaking of friendship, hope and forgiveness in the midst of mindless religious hatred, on the other hand, there was a lot of criticism about the cunning ways in which the film avoided questions of accountability and downplayed the enormity of the pogrom, even as it acknowledged trauma.[143]

A few months after the film's release, a public interest litigation (PIL) was filed in the Gujarat High Court in Ahmedabad, demanding that its clearance by the CBFC be cancelled. The CBFC rated the film 'U' (see Figure 4.3 earlier), making it universally eligible for viewing without any age restriction. A news headline on the petition read: 'PIL against *Kai Po Che* for "Biased"

Portrayal of Gujarat Riots'.[144] The petitioners, a lawyer named Bhautik Bhatt and another applicant, took issue with the representation of the 2002 violence in the film. As the judgment noted, the two reasons for which the petitioners approached the court were: first, 'the film defames group of a certain community, in the guise that the members of the minority community were victimised'; and second, 'the film does not approach the topic even-handedly and projects one community being more responsible than the other'.[145]

The 3 Mistakes of My Life, Bhagat's novel on which the film was based, the film's publicity and trailers, and even the theatrical release did not attract any attention from the Hindu Right—including the ruling BJP in Gujarat at that time—as has been the case with *Dev* and *Parzania*. It was primarily secular critics of Hindutva who found the film problematic for its bias in favour of Hindus, for not depicting the atrocity in all its nuances, and for explaining the causes of the violence through realpolitik framings that displaced its deep ideological foundations.[146] However, the petitioners felt that even in the film's soft-pedalling of the violence carried out by Hindus, it depicted the majority community in a bad light.

The film could not have been challenged on its reconstruction of facts, because it did not make any claims regarding historical accuracy. It was, after all, a work of fiction, adapted from a novel. The filmmakers did not even feel the need to offer a standard disclaimer regarding the story's relation to the pogrom, as was the case with the previous two films. The court in its 2014 judgment rejected the petition by stating why the freedom of speech and expression of the filmmakers could not be curtailed, especially because it was 'made on an imaginatory [*sic*] topic'.[147] It might have been possible to restrain exhibition if the film had provoked sectarian violence because of the reasons that the petitioners had stated. However, as the judges noted: 'Nothing untoward has happened or reported. The viewers across the country, with due maturity, have absorbed the theme.'[148] Both the secular and pro-Hindu critics of *Kai Po Che* were, thus, offering rival *judgments* on the same 'imaginatory' *record* of the pogrom that produced an active way of remembering particular to its time, or its *mnemohistory*.

Kai Po Che is the story of friendship between three young Hindu middle-class men—Ishaan, Omi and Govind—from Ahmedabad. The trials and tribulations of this affective relationship are what animate the juridico-moral universe of the film, which carries the second title *Brothers ... for Life* (Figure 4.24). The ellipsis can be read as hinting at the disruptions that give

Figure 4.24 'Brothers ... for life'
Source: *Kai Po Che* (2013), IMDb, https://www.imdb.com/title/tt2213054/?ref_=fn_al_
tt_1 (accessed 18 December 2022).

rise to the 'acute crisis' or 'ethical dilemmas' that they confront and the faith
in the developmentalist promise of private enterprise that enables them to
overcome these, despite a huge personal loss. This developmentalist promise
in the face of tragedy is captured in the buoyant imagery on the film's poster,
clearly distinctive from the intense and traumatised faces of the protagonists
that were on the posters for *Dev* and *Parzania* respectively (see Figures 4.8
and 4.14 earlier).

The three friends have grown up and live, as the film suggests, in an
almost exclusively Hindu locality in the old city area called Belrampur that
is very different in its sights and sounds from the globalising Ahmedabad of
malls and highways across the Sabarmati River.[149] Ishaan is a passionate
cricket lover and obsessively watches matches on television whenever India
is playing. His cricket nationalism, however, is secular, that is, he does not
differentiate the worth of Indian cricketers on the basis of their religion.

This dimension is significant to the way in which Ishaan's character is developed in the film. He is also very hot-headed, and overly protective of his sister Vidya. The volatility of his character is attributed to the fact that he failed to make it to the state-level cricket team, and carries a sore memory of it.

Omi is the son of the chief priest at the local Hindu temple. He follows Ishaan to the tee, both in his love for cricket as well as in his public conduct. He is the only one among the three friends who carries an identifiable Hindu marker—a streak of saffron on this forehead. His maternal uncle, Bittoo, is the trustee of the temple, and is also the leader of the local Hindu right-wing political party called the Bharatiya Janhith Sangh. Bittoo has been insistent on Omi joining the party's youth wing as an activist.

Govind's character is the most level-headed of the group. The sense of propriety and rationality that he carries is attributed to his love of numbers and enterprise. Govind offers math tuitions to schoolchildren, and pursues his interest in setting up a business of his own with single-minded determination. Given the love of cricket that all three friends share, Govind includes Ishaan and Omi in his plan to set up a sports equipment store right outside Omi's father's temple premises. Bittoo rents out the place to them on Omi's request. The enterprise also doubles as a place to provide math tuition and cricket coaching.

The location and milieu of the major part of the film—Ahmedabad's old city area—and the ordinariness of the middle-class lives of Ishaan, Govind and Omi are germane to the aspirational journeys they make in the film.[150] The film draws on the historical arrangement of the old city that is both sharply segregated on religious lines, as well as syncretic in terms of the proximity between the *pol*s (religion, caste and occupation based residential areas) in which different communities live.[151] In contemporary Ahmedabad, this is an outcome not only of the history of religious sectarianism in the city that has contributed to the making of its urbanity, but also of a modern legislation like the Disturbed Areas Act, 1991. This law has organised the urban demography of Ahmedabad by restricting Muslims and Hindus from selling property to each other in what it deems 'sensitive' areas, 'to avert an exodus or distress sales in neighbourhoods hit by inter-religious unrest'.[152] This law has actively enabled the creation of Muslim ghettos, which contributed to the planning of the pogrom in targeting Muslim businesses and households.[153] The film offers a normalised sense of this segregation, but not with any historical traction.

Within a few months of setting up the shop, and once their business had picked up pace; in one scene Govind is shown trying to convince Ishaan and Omi that they need to move out of the old city, and find a place across the Sabarmati River in an upcoming shopping mall. The Sabarmati, and the bridges that have been built over it, materially and metaphorically divide Ahmedabad city into zones that separate Hindus and Muslims, and the rich and poor. The bridges—one of which the protagonists ride over on a two-wheeler in search of a prospective site for their shop (Figure 4.25)—are 'urban structures, intended to ... represent the modern promise of connectivity, [but have] become, instead, embodiments of division'.[154] When Ishaan responds with indifference to the proposal and Omi resists the idea—because they had rented the shop from his uncle Bittoo—Govind says: 'Malls are the future. Mark my words, in a few years everything will be sold in malls. Malls are the game changer.'[155] While *Kai Po Che* represents this transition over the bridge to the other side of the city as the *developmentalist* desire of the urban Hindu youth in Gujarat,[156] it remains silent about the how the spatial organisation of the city along the lines of such desire had a relationship with the planning and execution of the pogrom.[157]

The characters of the three protagonists hold out three distinct yet related ideas of developmentalism in the new India. Ishaan is a secular nationalist, Omi, with some reluctance, joins the Hindu right-wing party and starts

Figure 4.25   Developmentalist desires
Source: Screenshot from DVD.

campaigning for Bittoo, and Govind believes in the power of private enterprise. While these ideas might, on the face of it, be in contestation with each other, they fuse together into a singular and forceful imagination of justice that marks the cathartic closure of the film's story. This fusion of nationalism, Hindutva and entrepreneurialism constitutes the imagination of justice that is at the core of the film's spectatorial address, through which it mobilises its publics and engenders a particular way of collectively remembering the pogrom.

The film opens with Govind doing a corporate presentation for his company—a sports academy and consultancy called Sabarmati Sports—to an audience of school principals. It is apparent from the presentation that the company is hugely successful, having selected and trained several national-level sports champions. Of these, Govind emphasises the name of a cricketing prodigy, Ali Hashmi, who is now debuting his international cricket career as part of the Indian cricket team.

The scene cuts to cars on a wide highway inside a tunnel, and the film's title appears (Figure 4.26). Highways, a marker of development in the New India, and one that has been used by the Gujarat government to project itself as India's most developed state, work as a narrative trope in the film and bookend a flashback.[158] The flashback as a narrative device makes *Kai Po Che* an identifiable 'memory film':[159] here, not only is the film's narrative a record of the *pogrom*, but the film itself uses a technique of storytelling that invokes memory. In terms of their organisation of time, in *Dev* and *Parzania*, the

Figure 4.26　Highways of development
Source: Screenshot from DVD.

pogrom is located in the real time of the film's narration. In *Kai Po Che*, the pogrom is narrated from a time well past the pogrom. In representing this time, the film does not hold out any visible remnants of the violence for its viewers.

Govind drives a sedan on Gujarat's wide highways to reach a prison. It is the day on which Omi is being released. The audience is unaware of who they are. Omi emerges from the gates of the prison. There are two establishing shots that mark his moment of exit—a top angle and the low-angle long shot of Omi with the prison as the background (Figures 4.27 and 4.28).

Figure 4.27   Outside the gate of law
Source: Screenshot from DVD.

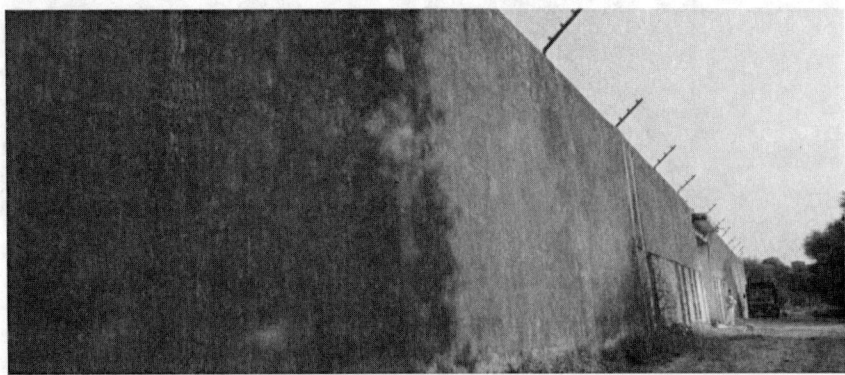

Figure 4.28   The wall as state law's carceral authority
Source: Screenshot from DVD.

The prison is the only institution directly related to state law that is shown in the film. It is only in this scene where the audience sees the prison.

The long highway rides that Govind takes to get there, and get back, suggests that the facility is located outside the limits of urbanity. The convicted seem to have been banished from the civility of the city—a city that looks vastly different from the one where the pogrom was carried out. Both shots accentuate the carceral authority of state law. The gate of the prison through which Omi walks out after having served his time for a crime that is still unknown to the audience, works as a cue for memorial recollection to begin, through a flashback. If Omi is now outside the gate of law, what had come before he had stepped inside through the gate? As the story of the film unfolds, the audience will be taken back in time to reveal what had kept Omi behind the gates. While Govind offers Omi a restrained smile, Omi's face portrays an intense sadness, conveying to the audience a sense of mournfulness that freedom from legal incarceration has not been able to overcome.

Govind drives on more highways through picturesque locales after receiving Omi, and they reach a coffee shop of a well-known chain. Highways and coffee shops are in the continuum of developmentalism that the detour to the prison had momentarily interrupted. It is in the coffee shop that the flashback begins. Omi looks up at the television broadcasting a cricket match, and that takes the audience back to the year 2000, two years prior to the pogrom.

If the present in the film is 2013 (the year of its release), the flashback covers a period of approximately 10 years starting from 2000. The flashback tells the story of the friendship between the three protagonists, and Govind's efforts to set up the sports equipment shop, which, as the beginning of the film suggested, has turned into a massively successful sports academy. During the time of their modest entrepreneurial beginnings in Belrampur, the setting up of the shop is followed by the introduction of a new character that fundamentally determines the story of the rest of the film. This is Ali Hashmi, who Govind had already introduced by name to the audience as a prodigal cricketer trained by his sports academy.

Ali is a young working-class Muslim boy from a Muslim-dominated area close to Belrampur called Juhapura. Juhapura is one of Ahmedabad's least developed localities, and since the 2002 pogrom has become a destination that has accommodated the exodus of fearful Muslims from other parts of the city. Today it is a ghetto, and even pejoratively referred to by many of Ahmedabad's

Hindus as 'mini-Pakistan', reifying the sectarian inheritances of the 1947 Partition (although Gujarat never experienced violence in the aftermath of the Partition).[160] Roads that divide similar Muslim ghettos in Ahmedabad from Hindu localities are, in everyday parlance, called 'the border'.[161] Increasingly, this nomenclature—of mini-Pakistan and the border—is becoming a part of official legal documents like police complaints.[162] Although the film names Juhapura, it steers clear of both the historical and current dynamics that shape the antagonistic relationship between Hindu and Muslim localities in Ahmedabad city.

Ali is shown as the sole Muslim boy—easily identifiable because of his attire (salwar kameez and skullcap)—who comes to play cricket at the park in Belrampur. He has gained quite a reputation for being a fierce batsman among the local youth. Ishaan meets him, and is immediately impressed by his talent, and decides to coach him in their cricket training centre. Ali is very shy and introverted, and hardly speaks in the film.

All the three friends go to Ali's father—who runs a zari-making workshop from home in Juhapura, and is also a member of a secular political party—to seek his permission to train Ali. He reluctantly agrees because of Ishaan's insistence. Ali's encounter with other Hindu boys at the sports academy reveals their prejudice against Muslims. Ishaan puts in committed efforts to train Ali and to get him to play in the upcoming club-level tournament. He provides Ali with a cricketing uniform because he would come to play, stereotypically, in salwar kameez and a skullcap.[163] Ali is a fast learner and performs exceptionally well at the tournament. By this time the three friends also move their store from Belrampur to a big shopping mall across the Sabarmati.

The happy progressive narrative of entrepreneurial, pedagogical and sporting success now confronts two crises, for both of which the film offers a factual *record*—these are events that indeed happened. In the framework of the film's fictional narrative, these events then snowball into a rift between the three friends, and then an irreversible tragedy strikes. The first of these crises is the 2001 Bhuj earthquake that caused enormous damage to life, livelihoods and property.[164]

Ishaan has over time become very close to Ali and his family. After the earthquake, he brings a large group of displaced Muslims from Ali's community to the relief camp for Hindus run by Bittoo's political party. This clearly indicates—as was the case—the discrimination Muslims faced in accessing relief after the earthquake. Omi along with other party members say they cannot provide for them because they are not 'our people'.[165] This results in a scuffle between Omi and Ishaan, and they stop speaking to each other.

The earthquake also affects their business badly. The building in which they had acquired the new store had broken down, and this psychologically devastates Govind. However, they return to the old store in their locality and start working hard to rebuild the business. What passes off as hard work is not just that but also the social capital they possess because of their religion, caste and class, and the political patronage network they benefit from. At this time, Govind finds out that whatever money they were left with has gone. Ishaan, in another act of charity, has given it away to Ali's family to rehabilitate them. The relations between all three friends are on tenterhooks now. Vidya comes in to convince Ishaan to make up with Omi. He tries, but fails. But what brings them together again is nationalist pride in India's triumph in a cricket match against Australia that also becomes the reason for the success of their entrepreneurial endeavour.

The second crisis is the 2002 pogrom. Bittoo, after losing the local elections, is campaigning hard for the upcoming state elections. Omi reluctantly joins the party and is active in campaigning. As part of these efforts, Bittoo decides to send a group of Hindus to Ayodhya for *kar seva* (religious service) to build the Ram temple, and asks Omi to convince his parents to go as well. It is the train in which his parents return from Ayodhya that is burnt at Godhra.

Kai Po Che's memorial *record* identifies the Godhra train-burning incident as the reason for retaliatory attacks on Muslims, repeating the action–reaction story of equivalence that was present in the Best Bakery judgments and in *Dev*. The occurrence of the Godhra incident is announced to the audience through the diegetic sounds of radio commentary and TV news reporting, showing original footage of the burnt train compartments, the number of dead and a journalist's voice-over calling the incident 'barbaric'. This is a cinematic technique of memorial recall that has been called 'referentiality', which 'breaks the film's illusionistic flow' and demands that the audience pass *judgment* (now that they have factual details) rather than remaining passive recipients.[166] This referentiality is authenticated and affirmed through dialogue that confirms the name of the train as Sabarmati Express and the burnt compartment as S-6, and through the date of the incident— 27 February 2002—appearing on the screen (Figures 4.29 and 4.30).

Figure 4.29   'Referentiality' I
Source: Screenshot from DVD.

Figure 4.30   'Referentiality' II
Source: Screenshot from DVD.

The auditory and documentary signposting of the incident through *images* works as a *mnemohistorical* marker to offer a sense of evidential grounding for the film's narrative *record* of the pogrom.

The narrative offers a dense detailing of the Godhra incident and holds it up as the primary reason for what follows after it. That the sophisticated attack on Muslims was not provoked by Godhra, but that it was politically mobilised to justify Hindu victimhood and vengeance, which was planned meticulously through several years, is not part of the film's narrative. The story prior to the pogrom in the film does not detail the historical continuum of

Hindutva hatred for Muslims in Gujarat. Collective memory of the pogrom is thus mobilised by presenting Godhra as a 'flashpoint'—'a centripetal turbulence of illumination so powerful that it may blind the past even as it spotlights the present and lights up the future'.[167] The detailing of this singular incident and its aftermath is presented as tragedy—one that equally affects both communities, but was started by Muslims—and is, thus, stripped of any historicity.

After the burning of the train compartment, the right-wing political party is shown organising for *pratikriya* (retributive action). Bittoo gives a speech to his party members to avenge the killing of Hindus, which is an amalgamation of a whole range of Hindutva invectives against Muslims. However, in this, the words Hindu and Muslim are seldom used. Instead the references are framed as our community and their community—innocuously injecting a sense of vagueness into the intensity of identification that was part of the planning and organisation of the pogrom, particularly in the way census data was used to target Muslim homes and businesses.[168]

In the representation of mob violence on the streets, the police are conspicuously absent. This is unlike *Dev* and *Parzania*, where the complicity of the police is shown quite extensively. The only reference to the police in *Kai Po Che* is when Ali's father is unable to get through to them to ask for protection. The absence of the police can be read in two ways. First, that the film might be offering a radical representation of police inaction, by evacuating their presence completely. Second, this could represent the film's narrative commitment to a vision of privatisation, where the violence—both the Godhra incident as well as the attack on Muslims—is characterised as carried out by private actors, with the state having nothing to do with it.

While Hindu militant mobs armed with *trishul*s (tridents) are roaming through city streets, Ishaan reaches Ali's place in the hope of convincing Ali's father to move out of their residence and come to his house. Ali's father declines the offer because he has to be there for the other Muslim families who have taken refuge in his house. Ali's father's character in this situation is drawn on Ehsan Jafri, in whose house several Muslims had taken shelter in the Gulberg Society in Ahmedabad; he was eventually brutally killed.[169] Ishaan asks Govind to come over as well.[170] In the meantime, Omi reaches Ali's house with a huge mob of Hindus wielding arms, led by Bittoo, chanting 'Jai Shri Ram' (Glory to Lord Ram). The mob breaks into their house and starts killing the many other Muslims who had sought refuge there.

Bittoo attacks Ali's father. The fight results in Bittoo being badly injured. Omi chases Ali's father into the house, Ishaan intervenes, and when Omi shoots, the bullet hits Ishaan.

It is at this moment that the flashback ends and the film returns viewers to the present with Govind driving on wide highways in his sedan with Omi. The highway—as the narrative trope that strings the present and past in the film—now takes them to a huge, lit-up cricket stadium, where Ali, part of the Indian cricket team, is making his international debut. Inside a plush private room at the stadium, which, it seems, is owned by Govind, Omi is introduced to Govind's son, whom he has named Ishaan. Govind had married Ishaan's sister Vidya. He is now a very successful businessman. The small boy hands Omi the Indian flag (Figure 4.31). Later, in the stadium, Omi meets Vidya and breaks down. The closing scene shows Ali hitting a perfect cover drive boundary, the exact shot that Ishaan had trained him in. The scene fades in and out with Ishaan's smiling face against a setting sun, with the background score hitting a soul-stirring crescendo.

Kai Po Che's memorial reconstruction of the pogrom and its imagination of justice bring together the state-making and state-preserving rationalities of *secularism*, *legalism* and *developmentalism* in a seamless fashion. This consolidation had remained only partly complete in *Dev* and *Parzania*. In *Dev*, the rationality of legalism framed the way of remembering, while in *Parzania*, legalism was combined with the rationality of secularism. *Kai Po Che* gives the triad full shape by adding developmentalism to the

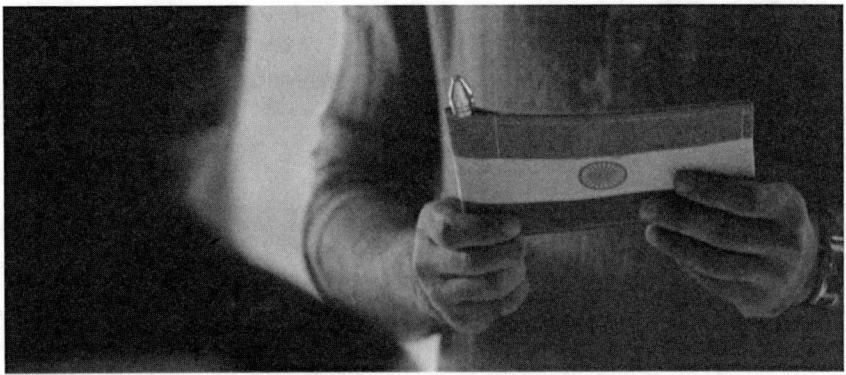

Figure 4.31   The flag of aspiration
Source: Screenshot from DVD.

state-making and state-preserving rationality that condemns the violence of the pogrom and simultaneously normalises the structural disenfranchisement of Indian Muslims.

Dev ended outside the courtroom, *Parzania* took us inside a quasi-legal procedural space and *Kai Po Che* shows us that the adjudicatory mechanism of the law has played its role. Omi has been recognised as having committed a crime and was convicted for it. This crime-act, however, is framed as an accident that works as a rehabilitative gesture in the film. With his mother and father killed in the Godhra train fire, Omi's character is portrayed as one possessed by irrational rage, and that provides a sympathetic justification for why he ends up killing Ishaan, his best friend. That he was part of a Hindu right-wing political party, that he led a Hindu militant mob which was systematically attacking Muslims and killing them, is rendered inconsequential. This narrative logic seems to echo the Best Bakery judgment of the Gujarat High Court where the judges wondered how a Hindu mob could have killed Hindus, thus deducing that the mob was responding with irrational rage which was not specifically directed at Muslims—in consequence, the nature of the violence itself becomes secular.

The narrative address of the film uses the post-conviction location outside the gates of the prison—quite literally after the law—as the place from which to begin the work of memorial recollection. Such an address mobilises a public faith in the criminal justice system, which, unlike the Best Bakery case's beginnings, has played the role it was expected to, that is, to convict. The faith in secular law is left intact despite the thousands killed, and despite the legal organising of the city that enabled the targeting of Muslim homes and businesses. This work of the rationality triad displaces concerns about state accountability in the conduct of remembering. Legal culpability is privatised and is singularly focused on Omi. This rationality has been in actual operation as well, through the Naroda Patiya and Ode convictions that came shortly before the release of *Kai Po Che*. Modi's decision to seek the death penalty for ministers in his party, including Maya Kodnani, Babu Bajrangi and other Hindu right-wing leaders convicted by the court, might have riled up other Hindutva political parties like the Shiv Sena, and it might have also alerted human rights activists to how this strategy might deflect attention from Modi's own culpability.[171] But it strengthened public faith in Modi's commitment not only to governance and development but also to the rule of law.[172]

In *Kai Po Che*, the rationality of legalism is powerfully buttressed by developmentalism. The memorial recollection is located within the larger frame of wide highways, coffee shops, huge stadiums, private entrepreneurial success and cricket. The state is present in articulate form only in the figure of the prison, attesting to Modi's much-publicised slogan: 'Minimum Government, Maximum Governance'.[173] Everything else is private enterprise. The developmentalist metaphor of the road takes the audience on a progressive narrative journey that privatises not only entrepreneurship, violence and culpability, but also reconciliation, mourning and trauma.

The space of the stadium is where Omi confronts his past. Whose death does the film mourn? It is Ishaan's: a Hindu who was killed (by another Hindu) trying to help Muslims and keep Indian secularism alive. Ali is offered no screen time to deal with any trauma. He is shown to have emerged unscathed, without a trace of memory of what happened. The plot offers no insight into where his family is, or what happened to them. The last we had seen, Ali's father was alive. He is, however, not present at the stadium cheering Ali. The secular credentials of the Indian cricket team—popularly considered a microcosm of India's religious diversity[174]—and the fact that a talented Muslim now plays for India, despite having lived through the pogrom, is presented to the audience with buoyant affect.

Govind is married, has a son and because of his business acumen has kept alive the company that the three friends started despite an earthquake, a pogrom and the death of his closest friend. It is this story of success, of how the developmentalist vision of private enterprise can triumph all odds, that is the cathartic message of the film. The workings of the rationality triad regularise any tragedy and emphasise how following the scripts of private enterprise, responsibilisation and the rule of law can ultimately triumph over such interruptions and make the nation-state unshakeable. The death and destruction is ordinary damage and should only remain as sympathetic markers of the New India's path to progress.

It is only Omi as the upper-caste Hindu, whose trauma is cinematically accentuated. And who comes to soothe Omi's soul? The aspirational figure of Govind's child, the new Ishaan, handing him an Indian flag. The innocent gesture of the child is the seductive address for the spectatorial publics to feel buoyant about the jubilant nation. The figure of the child has for long been a symbol for representing both nationalist desire and consumptive reason.[175]

Figure 4.32 Individualised remorse, developmental reconciliation and secular celebration
Source: Screenshot from DVD.

In the reconciliatory space of the stadium, while huge crowds flying the Indian flag cheer for Ali Hashmi, Omi is seen crying uncontrollably when he meets Vidya, Ishaan's sister (Figure 4.32). She offers him consolation. Beside them, Govind is shown clapping excitedly. This scene of reconciliation indicates that despite having served his sentence for killing Ishaan, Omi is still remorseful. The public show of remorse rehabilitates him in the eyes of the audience, and the secular nationalist intensity of the stadium space adds to the affective power of this cathartic moment of cinematic justice. The film trains its audience in a particular way of remembering for which the film's narrative *record* seems to have borrowed a leaf from the Best Bakery case's Vadodara and Gujarat High Court judgments: the pogrom is over, it might have left us scarred, some might have 'disappeared' from the narrative frame of recollection, but let us not forget, the law did play its role, secular India is still together cheering for a Muslim cricketer, we will all continue to ride on the developmentalist road to justice if we maintain our faith in private enterprise.

* * *

In this chapter I have read (seen and listened to) three Bollywood feature films through the J-A lens. My reading has paid particular attention to the narrative compact between law and aesthetics in the films' narratives tropes and cinematic techniques of reconstructing a *record* of the Gujarat pogrom. This reading has shown how collective memory of the pogrom is mobilised by these films through their spectatorial addresses to produce an active way of remembering the pogrom—a *mnemohistory*. Audiences are authorised through that address to pass *judgment* sutured by the rationality triad of legalism, secularism and developmentalism. The collective memory thus produced and ordered through the films condemns the violence of the pogrom and simultaneously normalises the structural marginalisation of Indian Muslims.

In the stories of the three films, the protagonists encounter—following a trope unique to the Bollywood aesthetic—moments of acute crisis or ethical dilemma. Imaginations of cinematic justice emerge in these moments to offer resolution. *Dev* reposes all its trust in the Constitution and the rule of law to enable closure; *Parzania* recognises that it is only secular law that opens up the space for victim-survivors to speak and be heard; *Kai Po Che* privatises criminal responsibility and considers developmentalism as the most effective antidote to trauma. Despite not being conventional courtroom dramas, the ways of remembering that *Dev*, *Parzania* and *Kai Po Che* collectively engender are framed by an imagination/imagery of law and its relationship with justice.

While the films unanimously condemn the violence, and mourn the dead, at the same time they also reify constitutional secularism, legalism and developmentalism as part of the New India's state-making and state-preserving practices, the embrace of which will provide the most effective closure to the trauma of the pogrom. The foundational Hindu-ness of the nation-state, and its buttressing by secularism and legalism, are left unattended by the memorial reconstructions of the pogrom in the films. The landscape of cinematic justice that is painted rationalises the pogrom as aberrant—something that does not fit the way the Indian nation-state conducts its governance—and offers visions of reconciliation and resolution that are deeply invested in the very structures that deepen the disenfranchisement of Muslims.

Thus, the judicial narrative in the Best Bakery judgments and the cinematic narrative in the three films co-constitute collective ways of remembering despite being distinct in form (text and image) and substance (factual and fictional).

5 'As They Ought'

Really to forget something, you have to forget that you have forgotten. You have to be 'forgetful of forgetfulness'.[1]

Ways of Remembering has examined the role secular law plays in the ways in which the Gujarat pogrom is collectively remembered in the New India. In this regard, I worked with two interrelated aims. The first was to offer a critical reading of two memorial narratives of Gujarat 2002 from the disciplinary vantage point of law in/as aesthetics scholarship. The second was to expand the understanding of what constitutes secular law by considering how law and justice are imagined in a broader cultural context, both inside and outside of conventional sources. The book has pursued these aims by developing a methodological orientation that enables the reading of the narrative compact of law and cinema in the making and ordering of collective memory. What has my reading shown, and what is the significance of what has thus emerged? This concluding chapter is organised around these two questions.

I have offered an account of the Gujarat pogrom by unpacking the shared narrative in the texts of the judgments of the Best Bakery case that ran from 2003 to 2012, and in three Bollywood films whose release coincided with this period (2004–13). I have read these texts by developing a novel methodological orientation which I have called the jurisprudential-aesthetic (J-A) approach. This reading has shown that law and cinema, together, are key elements shaping the collective memory of the pogrom. This shared narrative participates in the production, circulation and maintenance of ways of remembering which both condemn the violence and simultaneously facilitate a particular kind of state-making and state-preserving rationality that masks secular law's complicities with religious violence. This rationality is composed by the triad of secularism, legalism and developmentalism.

I locate this inquiry within a temporal and ideological frame called the New India. The first post-pogrom decade is surveyed as a concentrated period of collective memory making. It is in this decade, buoyed by the success of the Hindutva project in Gujarat, that Narendra Modi became India's prime minister in 2014. This period has seen an unprecedented consolidation of the Hindu Right in independent India's history, giving rise to a strong alliance between Hindu right-wing politics and neoliberal development.

Instead of reading the judgments and the films as parallel but separate narratives, I have read them as a shared one, to demonstrate how law and cinema symbiotically participate in the making and ordering of national collective memory. My J-A approach led to the construction of an archive for the book—judgments and films. This approach enabled me to pay attention to the aesthetic dimensions of formal legal texts in the judgments, and the jurisprudential dimensions of traditionally aesthetic texts of the films, in order to consider the representative and affective work that these are doing together in shaping collective memories of the pogrom. My reading has shown how the shared narrative of law and cinema produces imaginations of justice that simultaneously recognise the violence and rationalise the pogrom.

As records of memory, the judgments and the films mobilised an imagined community of national publics through their address. It is these publics that constitute collective memory. The form of the record stored in the texts and images engenders particular ways of remembering that give shape to this memory. This collective memory is not fixed or singular, and might change based on the location and circumstances from which one is reading the judgments or watching the films. However, what brings these two memorial records together, and more importantly, how this shared narrative generates a certain way of remembering the Gujarat pogrom, is contained in the literary and cinematic tropes deployed across the two genres. As the J-A reading shows, in the writing of the judgments and the making of the films, certain images, symbols and metaphors recur. These recurrences generate affective intensities which perform a pedagogic role in training their publics in particular ways of remembering.

By way of an illustrative recapitulation, the reading of the judgments and the films in Chapters 3 and 4 shows distinct and connected ways of remembering the pogrom. These emerge from the modes and positions of address of the texts (in the courts and the cinema), and the literary and cinematic tropes deployed in the narrative reconstruction of the pogrom's stories. As shown in Chapter 3, the voices of the judges in the Best Bakery trials in Gujarat and at the Supreme Court are at sharp variance in their determinations, but the aesthetic tropes deployed show their ideological alignment. When the case comes to a close, some of the Hindu perpetrators have been convicted of murder, and Zahira Sheikh, the Muslim victim-survivor, has been convicted of perjury. The judgments thus offer a way of remembering in which the rationality of secular law equalises murder by Hindus with perjury by a Muslim—in effect, secularising both the law and the event of violence as one in which both parties are culpable.

To convict Zahira, the Supreme Court grounds the moral reasoning contained within the judgment in Hindu scriptures. In the Vadodara Sessions Court, the judge's primary concern is not that people have been killed but that the pogrom will tarnish the pride of Gujarat as India's most developed state. Further, the sessions and high court judgments use the iconography of the delirious crowd as an explanation for undercutting Hindu culpability. The figuration by the sessions court of the idea of the court as a 'court of evidence' and not a 'court of justice' is used to justify the acquittals by asserting the judgment's strict adherence to rule following. Symbolism that portrays the court as something more than a mere tape recorder is used in the Supreme Court judgment, conversely, to speak of the court's responsibility to go beyond rule following to achieve the end of justice. By reading the judgments through the J-A approach, we are able to see that judicial reasoning is projected as an extension of secular law's rationality, which is in effect secular law's alignment with Hindu nationalism and neoliberalism.

In Chapter 4, each of the three films analysed foregrounds the voice of a particular character whose experience frames the juridico-moral universe of justice. These characters occupy dramatically diverse positions—a policeman (*Dev*), a victim-survivor (*Parzania*) and a perpetrator (*Kai Po Che*). It is from these different narrative points of view that the films respectively mount their condemnation of the violence and experiences of trauma. Yet the cinematic narratives—in terms of both content and form—even while acknowledging the horror of the event, rationalise the pogrom by conjuring imaginations of justice that are only achievable because each of these characters pledges loyalty to the practices and performances of secular state law, ensconced in the triad of secularism, legalism and developmentalism.

The ways of remembering that emerge through a J-A reading of the films include the conscientious policeman who rehabilitates the complicit state by equating the secular Constitution to the Hindu holy book, the Bhagavad Gita; the secular space of legalism as represented by a state-organised human rights commission hearing which fosters reconciliation between the Muslim victim and the Hindu perpetrator; and the road to development (entrepreneurial success) and rule of law (individualising culpability) which become the paths to justice in the aftermath of the pogrom.

When the three films are read as a cumulative narrative spanning the post-pogrom decade, we see the pedagogic function of the cinematic medium in training its spectatorial publics. The films provide a window onto the progressive triumph of the reason of secular law over the irrational violence of religion. *Dev* ends outside a court building where a trial related to the pogrom will begin. The audience does not yet know whether secular law is able to perform the promise of its powers that the film has celebrated. In *Parzania*, the audience is taken inside the quasi-legal space of a statutory human rights commission that hears the testimonies of victims. Finally, in *Kai Po Che*, secular law played its role by convicting a Hindu perpetrator, and in flashback mode, the film tells a story of how, when entrepreneurial success combines with the rule of law, forgetting becomes easy.

There are four ways of remembering the pogrom that have emerged from my J-A reading of the judgments and the films. The first can be identified as the way of remembering which celebrates what had happened and considers the violence as a befitting lesson taught to the Muslims. In this way of remembering, Hindus are projected as a historically victimised community whose tolerance reached a tipping point with the Godhra train incident that immediately preceded the pogrom.

The second way of remembering denies that the violence was targeted singularly at Muslims and frames it as a communal conflagration in which both religious communities suffered equally. In this way of remembering, the violence is condemned, its majoritarian nature is ignored and culpability is secularised and equally distributed between Hindus and Muslims. The event is remembered as a cause-and-effect scenario: Hindus were attacked by Muslims, so they retaliated. This way of remembering calls for reconciliation through forgetting and offers the promise of developmentalism as the most effective way to move on.

The third way strongly criticises the Hindu Right and its role in both planning and executing the pogrom. This way of remembering considers Gujarat 2002 and the ensuing travails of justice seeking as an assault on

India's secular ethos and advocates for a restoration of constitutional standards and the rule of law as the most powerful way of defeating Hindutva forces.

It is fairly easy to argue with the first way of remembering. The judgments and the films analysed in this book are also very critical of remembering in a way that explicitly extols the Hindutva vision of establishing a Hindu *rashtra* through the annihilation of the Muslim Other. The narrative compact of the judgments and the films align more closely with the second and third ways of remembering. The second invests faith in a developmentalist vision as the way to end captivity to the memory of the violence. The third valorises secularism and legalism, particularly in terms of upholding constitutional values and achieving criminal convictions, as the most potent form of resistance to attempts that force forgetting.

It is in the second and third ways of remembering that the lineaments of the New India emerge most strikingly. These two ways of remembering condemn the violence in no uncertain terms but simultaneously valorise the very rationalities of secularism, legalism and developmentalism that normalise anti-Muslim ideology. These ways of remembering reconstruct the pogrom and its aftermath as the story of secular law's normative triumph over religious violence. My J-A reading of the judgments and films has brought to the fore the workings of this triad, thus enabling me to demonstrate secular law's complicities with religious violence.

I now come to the fourth way of remembering. The book has interpreted the shared narrative in the texts of the judgments and the films to identify how, in their reconstructions of the pogrom, the rationalities of secularism, legalism and developmentalism are collectively projected by the Indian state as governmental practices directed towards securing the welfare of its population in the aftermath of religious violence. The J-A approach has thus enabled us to see the emergence of a collective memory, in which both victims and perpetrators are responsibilised to internalise this rationality triad, and hence to conduct themselves '*as they ought*'.[2] Such conduct involves the pursuance of self-interest for welfare, health, wealth and longevity,[3] which is attainable by pledging allegiance to the rationality of secular law as the means to overcome and forget the irrationality of religious violence. Secular law in this practice of governmental rationality is cast as equivalent to the Hindu Right's vision of the New India, in which non-Hindus must conduct themselves *as they ought* to be assimilated into the Hindu *rashtra*. If they do not behave in this way, the implication is that their sacrifice will be rationalised as being for the welfare of (Hindu) populations.[4]

It is this fourth way of remembering that is unique to secular law's role in state-making and state-preserving practices in the New India. It is widely accepted that the conduct of government in modernity arrived, through a series of shifts, from control over the body to control over souls.[5] In the New India—which combines majoritarian religious nationalism with neoliberalism—the operation of governmental rationality combines control over minds with brutal violence over bodies: 'killing rather than simply allowing to die or exposing to death'.[6]

As I have shown in the judgments and the films, there is a particular kind of governmental tactic at work that valorises accelerated legalism and developmentalism as primary markers of secular constitutionalism. This is simultaneously accompanied by violence against minority groups that remains implicitly tied to the Indian state's rational performances and enactments of legalism. In this fourth way of remembering, it is not just the state entity that is working to preserve itself, but the responsibilised selves of citizens and would-be citizens that perform the rationality triad, drawing authority from the secular law's promises of welfare.[7]

Ways of Remembering makes a contribution to both a study of the role of secular law in the making and ordering of collective memories of the Gujarat pogrom, as well as to the field of law and cinema. Through its lines of inquiry, I offer an understanding of putatively secular law that combines the legal and the aesthetic. It posits that the collusion between secular law and religious violence will not be visible if we locate the force of secular law only in 'state-formative' practices and institutions like the Constitution, the judiciary and court judgments.[8]

If we do not attend to the aesthetic dimensions of law, we will not be able to see the discursive ways in which secular law organises violence, while presenting itself as a means to overcome that very violence. In the context of India, Bollywood cinema is a key producer of law's aesthetic imaginations that ought to be treated as a jurisprudential source, not only in relation to the way law is represented in film, but more importantly in relation to the affective imaginations about justice that cinema generates through its sights and sounds.

When read as such, using the J-A approach, we are able to see that by reconstructing the story of the Gujarat pogrom as secular law's triumph over the irrationality of religious violence, the judgments and films leave unquestioned the foundational Hindu-ness of the Indian nation-state. The collective memory of the violence, thus ordered, offers imaginations of justice that are deeply invested in the very structures that enabled the pogrom in the first place and that remain on standby to again authorise religious violence in defence of secular justice.

The New India has got the 'fascism that it deserves'.[9]

Notes

If you have come to this page of the book, I would like to believe that, like me, you too take book endnotes seriously. We consider notes to be important in an academic work—especially within the discipline of law—as they offer authoritative references that substantiate the arguments and claims made in the main text of the work. In the organisation of an academic work, book endnotes are usually rendered structurally and symbolically lesser. Despite the conventional location of the endnotes in this book, I would urge you to consider them as deserving of the same attention and care with which you might have read the rest of the book. These notes are at once detailed references that substantiate my claims and arguments and curate a reading list for those who might want to follow up on these, or perhaps even teach a course in the areas that this book speaks to. In this sense, the endnotes carry both evidential and pedagogical value. But these endnotes cannot be reduced to their mere instrumentality as an adjunct to the main text. As you will see, my endnotes are in a relationship of 'narrative compact' with the main text. Through asides and additions, the endnotes enrich the discussions and descriptions underwritten by caste in the story that I am telling. Just because some of these discussions appear in the endnotes does not mean that they are inferior in value to the so-called main text. Further, through my citational gestures, these endnotes acknowledge my political and scholarly inheritances (not that they are fully separable). This story of inheritances is important because it is a demonstration of how the ethics of scholarship (which I believe ought to be an extension of the ethics of life practices) constantly negotiate with paradoxes and contradictions without necessarily trying to transcend them. The endnotes, thus, are a generative space for 'minor' ideas and insights that the 'major' text has failed to consider adequately. Through these endnotes, drawing on the inspiring work of Max Liboiron, I 'contextualize, expand, and emplace' this book and try to do 'good relations within a text, through a text' (Max Liboiron, *Pollution Is Colonialism*, Durham: Duke University Press [2021], 1).

Chapter 1

1. Amitav Ghosh, 'The Ghosts of Mrs. Gandhi', *New Yorker*, 17 July 1995, 41.

2. See Siddharth Varadarajan (ed.), *Gujarat: The Making of a Tragedy* (New Delhi: Penguin, 2002); Megha Kumar, *Communalism and Sexual Violence: Ahmedabad since 1969* (New Delhi: Tulika, 2017), 130–89; Sanjeevini Badigar Lokhande, *Communal Violence, Forced Migration and the State: Gujarat since 2002* (New Delhi: Cambridge University Press, 2015).

3. See Britta Ohm, 'Forgetting to Remember: The Privatisation of the Public, the Economisation of Hindutva, and the Medialisation of Genocide', in *South Asian Media Cultures: Audiences, Representations, Contexts*, ed. Shakuntala Banaji (London: Anthem Press, 2011), 123–44; Anuja Jain, '"Beaming It Live": 24-Hour Television News, the Spectator and the Spectacle of the 2002 Gujarat Carnage', *South Asian Popular Culture* 8, no. 2 (2010): 163; Nalin Mehta, 'Modi and the Camera: The Politics of Television in the 2002 Gujarat Riots', *South Asia: Journal of South Asian Studies* 29, no. 3 (2006): 395; Darshan Desai, 'Massacres and the Media: A Field Reporter Looks Back on Gujarat 2002', in *Sarai Reader 04: Crisis/ Media* (Sarai, CSDS, 2004), 228–34.

4. I use the expression 'event' to characterise the Gujarat pogrom's memorial reconstructions in law and cinema as polysemic rather than singular, exceptional and self-contained. On such an understanding of the term, see Robin Wagner-Pacifici, *What Is an Event?* (Chicago: University of Chicago Press, 2017). The word 'atrocity' conveys a particular form of violence, one whose incidence stands justified by the perpetrator (and the networks they are a part of) due to an alleged transgression of norms by the harmed person or community. In the context of law's complicity with (caste) violence in India, as Anupama Roy has written: 'The jurisprudence of atrocity draws attention to how judicial knowledge is structured by political negotiations outside the framework of law, and to how judicial discourse is embedded in policing practices.' Anupama Rao, *The Caste Question: Dalits and the Politics of Modern India* (Berkeley: University of California Press, 2009), 253.

5. Jeffrey K. Olick, Vered Vinitzky-Seroussi and Daniel Levy (eds.), *The Collective Memory Reader* (New York: Oxford University Press, 2011), 21.

6. Stuart Hall, 'Introduction', in *Representation: Cultural Representations and Signifying Practices*, ed. Stuart Hall (London: Sage, 2009), 1.

7. Stuart Hall, 'The Work of Representation', in *Cultural Representations and Signifying Practices*, ed. Stuart Hall (London: Sage, 2009), 15.

8. For a representative sense of how the memory of the Gujarat pogrom is consistently invoked in the media, see Sandeep Phukan, 'Why Everyone Tiptoes around Memories of 2002 Gujarat Riots', *The Hindu*, 28 November 2017, https://www.thehindu.com/elections/gujarat-2017/why-everyone-tiptoes-around-memories-of-2002/article21040625.ece (accessed 18 December 2022); Ajaz Ashraf, 'Why Memories of Gujarat 2002 Stay', *The Hindu*, 2 April 2013, http://www.thehindu.com/opinion/op-ed/why-memories-of-gujarat-2002-stay/article4570587.ece (accessed 18 December 2022); Sabrang India, 'Lockdown of Memory of Gujarat 2002 Must Be Resisted: Sidharth Bhatia in Conversation with Teesta Setalvad', *Newsclick*, 27 February 2017, https://newsclick.in/lockdown-memory-gujarat-2002-must-be-resisted-sidharth-bhatia-conversation-teesta-setalvad (accessed 18 December 2022); Pallavi Rebbapragada, 'Gujarat Elections: Godhra Muslims Say Godhra Is a Distant Memory, Want Their Daily Needs Addressed', *Firstpost*, 2 December 2017, http://www.firstpost.com/india/gujarat-assembly-election-2017-godhra-residents-wish-to-forget-2002-want-focus-on-development-4238093.html (accessed 18 December 2022); *Indian Express*, 'Patiyawalas Move On but Ghastly Memory Still Lingers', 30 August 2012, http://indianexpress.com/article/cities/gujarat/patiyawalas-move-on-but-ghastly-memory-still-lingers/ (accessed 18 December 2022). To mark two decades of the pogrom a news outlet initiated a project called 'Memories of a Riot'. Himanshi Dahiya, 'Gujarat 2002: Memories of a Riot', *The Quint*, 7 March 2022, https://www.thequint.com/videos/documentaries/20-years-of-2002-gujarat-riots-documentary#read-more (accessed 18 December 2022).

9. See Rachel Dwyer, *Bollywood's India: Hindi Cinema as a Guide to Contemporary India* (London: Reaktion Books, 2014); Akbar S. Ahmed, 'Bombay Films: The Cinema as Metaphor for Indian Society and Politics', *Modern Asian Studies* 26, no. 2 (1992): 289; Brenda Cossman and Ratna Kapur, *Secularism's Last Sigh? Hindutva and the (Mis)rule of Law* (New Delhi: Oxford University Press, 2001).

10. 'Hindutva ("Hindu-ness", shorthand for Hindu nationalism) in India is a chauvinist and majoritarian nationalism that conjures up the image of a Hindu Self vis-à-vis the threatening minority Other.' Dibyesh Anand,

Hindu Nationalism in India and the Politics of Fear (New York: Palgrave Macmillan, 2011), 1. The word 'Hindutva' was used in the title of V. D. Savarkar's 1923 book *Hindutva: Who Is a Hindu?*, which is a foundational text for the Hindu nationalist movement in India. As Jaffrelot writes:

> This work perfectly illustrates the mechanisms of Hindu nationalist identity-building through the stigmatisation and emulation of 'threatening others'.... Savarkar's main argument in *Hindutva* is that the Aryans who settled in India at the dawn of history already formed a nation now embodied in the Hindus. Their *Hindutva*, according to him, rests on three pillars: geographical unity, racial features and a common culture. (Christophe Jaffrelot, *The Hindu Nationalist Movement and Indian Politics: 1925 to the 1990s* [New Delhi: Penguin, 1999]; emphasis in original)

See also V. D. Savarkar, *Hindutva: Who Is a Hindu?* (New Delhi: Hindi Sahitya Sadan, 2012); Jyotirmaya Sharma, *Hindutva: Exploring the Idea of Hindu Nationalism* (New Delhi: Penguin, 2011).

11. See Subhash Gatade, *The Saffron Condition: Politics of Repression and Exclusion in Neoliberal India* (New Delhi: Three Essays Collective, 2011); Achin Vanaik, *Hindutva Rising: Secular Claims, Communal Realities* (New Delhi: Tulika, 2017).

12. Akhil Gupta, *Red Tape: Bureaucracy, Structural Violence, and Poverty in India* (Durham: Duke University Press, 2012), 18.

13. Allan Rodway, 'Form', in *A Dictionary of Modern Critical Terms*, ed. Roger Fowler (London: Routledge, 1999), 99 (emphasis in original).

14. I understand law and cinema as sites of collective memory, and judgments and films as the corresponding intertextual forms that they take. As intertextual forms, they travel outside of their conventional sites and thus become polysemic. On 'intertextuality', see Julia Kristeva, 'Word, Dialogue and Novel', in *The Kristeva Reader*, ed. Toril Moi (New York: Columbia University Press, 1986), 34–61; María Jesús Martínez Alfaro, 'Intertextuality: Origins and Development of the Concept', *Atlantis* 18, nos. 1–2 (1996): 268. On the idea of the 'text', see Roland Barthes, 'From Work to Text', in *The Rustle of Language*, trans. Richard Howard (New York: Hill and Wang, 1986), 58–60.

15. David A. Black, *Law in Film: Resonance and Representation* (Champaign: University of Illinois Press, 1999), 1.

16. See Adam Gearey, *Law and Aesthetics* (Oxford: Hart Publishing, 2001); Susan A. Bandes (ed.), *The Passions of Law* (New York: New York University Press, 2000); Robin West, 'Law's Emotions', in *Law, Reason and Emotion*, ed. M. N. S. Sellers (Cambridge: Cambridge University Press, 2017), 32–54; Gerry Simpson, 'The Sentimental Life of International Law', *London Review of International Law* 3, no. 1 (March 2015): 3; Sheryl N. Hamilton, Diana Majury, Dawn Moore, Neil Sargent and Christiane Wilke (eds.), *Sensing Law* (London: Routledge, 2017).

17. For instantiations of how legalism, secularism and developmentalism are endorsed by the Supreme Court of India, see, respectively, Sudhir Krishnaswamy, *Democracy and Constitutionalism in India: A Study of the Basic Structure Doctrine* (New Delhi: Oxford University Press, 2011); Ronojoy Sen, *Articles of Faith: Religion, Secularism and the Indian Supreme Court* (New Delhi: Oxford University Press, 2010); Mayur Suresh and Siddharth Narrain (eds.), *The Shifting Scales of Justice: The Supreme Court in Neo-liberal India* (Hyderabad: Orient BlackSwan, 2014).

18. See generally Madhav Godbole, *Secularism: India at a Crossroads* (New Delhi: Rupa, 2016); Mani Shankar Iyer, *Confessions of a Secular Fundamentalist* (New Delhi: Penguin, 2004); D. Raja, 'A Nation's Conscience', *Indian Express*, 28 November 2017, https://indianexpress.com/article/opinion/columns/a-nations-conscience-india-constitution-day-hindutva-forces-narendra-modi-4957562/ (accessed 18 December 2022).

19. For a similar line of argument, see Ratna Kapur, 'Normalizing Violence: Transitional Justice and the Gujarat Riots', *Columbia Journal of Gender and Law* 15, no. 3 (2006): 885; Ratna Kapur, 'A Leap of Faith: The Construction of Hindu Majoritarianism through Secular Law', *South Atlantic Quarterly* 113, no. 3 (2014): 109.

20. See Gyanendra Pandey, 'Can a Muslim Be an Indian?', *Comparative Studies in Society and History* 41, no. 4 (1999): 608.

21. See generally Subrata K. Mitra, 'Level Playing Fields: The Post-colonial State, Democracy, Courts and Citizenship in India', *German Law Journal* 9, no. 3 (2008): 343.

22. This justification in recent times has seen the enactment of a new regime of citizenship laws that consider India to be the holy land of Hindus facing religious persecution in any other South Asian country. Furthermore, to advance such a historical narrative, in 2021, Prime Minister Narendra Modi declared 14 August as the Partition Horrors Remembrance Day. Shoaib

Daniyal, 'Partition Horrors Day to CAA: BJP Has Tried to Weaponise 1947 for Electoral Politics', *Scroll.in*, 20 August 2021, https://scroll.in/article/1003098/partition-horrors-day-to-caa-bjp-has-tried-to-weaponise-1947-for-electoral-politics (accessed 18 December 2022). See Pradip Datta, 'Historic Trauma and the Politics of the Present in India', *Interventions* 7, no. 3 (2005): 316; Urvashi Butalia, 'How Should We Remember the Violence and Suffering of Partition?', *India Forum*, 15 October 2021, https://www.theindiaforum.in/article/how-should-we-remember-violence-and-suffering-partition (accessed 18 December 2022).

23. Establishing India as the holy land of the Hindus has been a demand of the Hindu Right in India. This demand is at the foundation of Hindu right-wing ideology (Hindutva) that aims to achieve this through violence, if required, against Muslims and Christians, whose holy lands are considered to be outside of India. Anxieties about caste also motivate this violence because Indian Muslims and Christians are considered by the Hindu Right as betrayers of the caste system because they converted out of Hinduism. The demand for a Hindu *rashtra* gets masked in a secular language of tradition and antiquity when articulated by Hindutva political parties like the Bharatiya Janata Party, which is currently in power and under whose rule the Gujarat pogrom was executed. See Ram Puniyani, *Contours of Hindu Rashtra: Hindutva, Sangh Parivar and Contemporary Politics* (New Delhi: Kalpaz, 2006); Hartosh Singh Bal, 'The Instigator', *The Caravan*, 1 July 2017, http://www.caravanmagazine.in/reportage/golwalkar-ideology-underpins-modi-india (accessed 18 December 2022); Sitaram Yechury, 'What Is a Hindu Rashtra?', *Frontline*, 21 July 2017, https://www.frontline.in/cover-story/what-is-hindu-rashtra/article9748316.ece (accessed 18 December 2022); Samar Halarnkar, 'Inside the Hindu Mind, the Battle for a Hindu Nation', *Scroll.in*, 11 June 2017, https://scroll.in/article/840275/the-battle-for-hindu-rashtra-is-raging-inside-the-hindu-mind-and-it-is-no-longer-a-fringe-fantasy (accessed 18 December 2022).

24. Harsh Mander, 'From Godhra to Una: The Face of the Gujarat Riots Has Attached His Name to the Dalit Cause', *Scroll.in*, 28 August 2016, https://scroll.in/article/813919/from-godhra-to-una-the-face-of-the-gujarat-riots-has-attached-his-name-to-the-dalit-cause (accessed 18 December 2022); Indrajit Hazra, 'The Forgotten Man', *Hindustan Times*, 4 Match 2012, https://www.hindustantimes.com/columns/the-forgotten-man/story-4ho43qxpcuiWRsJSx5EbcL.html (accessed 18 December 2022); Diksha

Sahni, 'Picture Focus: Ansari and the Anatomy of Fear', *Wall Street Journal*, 28 February 2012, https://blogs.wsj.com/indiarealtime/2012/02/28/picture-focus-ansari-and-the-anatomy-of-fear/ (accessed 18 December 2022).

25. Rajeev Dhavan, 'Justice, Justice and the Best Bakery Case', *India International Centre Quarterly* 30, no. 2 (2003): 1; Anupama Katakam, 'A Decade of Shame', *Frontline* 29, no. 4 (February–March 2012), https://www.frontline.in/static/html/fl2904/stories/20120309290400400.htm (accessed 18 December 2022).

26. See Oishik Sircar, 'Bollywood's Law: Collective Memory and Cinematic Justice in the New India', *No Foundations: An Interdisciplinary Journal of Law and Justice* 12 (2015): 94; Oishik Sircar, 'Seductions of the Neoliberal Nation', *Himal Southasian* 26, no. 4 (2013): 80; Alka Kurian, 'The Politics of Hindutva in Nandita Das' *Firaaq*, Rahul Dholakia's *Parzania*, and Rakesh Sharma's *Final Solution*', in *Narratives of Gendered Dissent in South Asian Cinemas* (New York: Routledge, 2012), 63.

27. See Githa Hariharan, *Fugitive Histories* (Delhi: Penguin, 2009); Raj Kamal Jha, *Fireproof* (New Delhi: Picador, 2009); M. G. Vassanji, *The Assassin's Song* (Edinburgh: Canongate, 2007).

28. See Mani Shekhar Singh, 'Religious Iconography, Violence and Making of a Series', in 'Riot Discourses', ed. Deepak Mehta and Roma Chatterji, special issue, *Domains* 3 (2007): 38; Sanjukta Sharma, 'Scars in Vadodara', *LiveMint*, 26 July 2013, https://www.livemint.com/Leisure/NS8gvUYS89gfLf1xLEoq9L/Scars-in-Vadodra.html (accessed 18 December 2022); Tejal Shah, *I Love My India* (documentary), http://www.womanifesto.com/project/tejal-shah-i-love-my-india/ (accessed 18 December 2022).

29. See generally Nicola Lacey, 'Feminist Legal Theory beyond Neutrality', *Current Legal Problems* 48, part 2 (1995): 1; Teju Cole, 'Against Neutrality', in *Known and Strange Things* (New York: Random House, 2016), 212–17.

30. Nivedita Menon, 'Citizenship and the Passive Revolution: Interpreting the First Amendment', in *Politics and Ethics of the Indian Constitution*, ed. Rajeev Bhargava (New Delhi: Oxford University Press, 2010), 189–90.

31. See Michael Warner, 'Uncritical Reading', in *Polemic: Critical or Uncritical*, ed. Jane Gallop (New York: Routledge, 2004), 13–38.

32. Margaret Davies, 'Ethics and Methodology in Legal Theory: A (Personal) Research "Anti-Manifesto"', *Law Text Culture* 6 (2006): 7.

33. My inheritance of this tradition has been acquired through my legal education across common law countries including India, Canada and

Australia. Thus, critical legal thought for me is not just the 'critical legal studies movement', particularly in its American variant. See generally Matthew Stone, Illan rua Wall and Costas Douzinas (eds.), *New Critical Legal Thinking* (London: Birkbeck Law Press, 2012); Costas Douzinas and Adam Gearey, *Critical Jurisprudence: The Political Philosophy of Justice* (Oxford: Hart Publishing, 2005).

34. Duncan Kennedy, 'Legal Education and the Reproduction of Hierarchy', *Journal of Legal Education* 32, no. 4 (1982): 591, 600.

35. Margaret Davies, *Asking the Law Question*, 3rd ed. (Sydney: Thomson Reuters, 2008), 199.

36. Upendra Baxi, 'Taking Suffering Seriously: Social Action Litigation in the Supreme Court of India', *Third World Legal Studies* 4 (1985): 107–32; Arthur Klienman and Joan Klienman, 'The Appeal of Experience; The Dismay of Images: Cultural Appropriations of Suffering in Our Times', *Daedalus* 125, no. 1 (1996): 2.

37. Ranajit Guha, 'The Small Voice of History', in *Subaltern Studies IX: Writings on South Asian History and Society*, ed. Shahid Amin and Dipesh Chakrabarty (New Delhi: Oxford University Press, 1996), 1–12.

38. Ibid., 3.

39. For a timeline of how the pogrom unfolded, see *New York Times*, 'Timeline of the Riots in Modi's Gujarat', 19 August 2015, https://www.nytimes.com/interactive/2014/04/06/world/asia/modi-gujarat-riots-timeline.html#/#time287_8514 (accessed 18 December 2022).

40. See Gyanendra Pandey, *Remembering Partition: Violence, Nationalism and History in India* (Cambridge: Cambridge University Press, 2002).

41. See Mohamad Junaid, 'Death and Life under Occupation: Space, Violence, and Memory in Kashmir', in *Everyday Occupations: Experiencing Militarism in South Asia and the Middle East*, ed. Kamala Visveswaran (Philadelphia: University of Pennsylvania Press, 2013).

42. See Makiko Kimura, *The Nellie Massacre of 1983: Agency of Rioters* (New Delhi: Sage, 2013).

43. See Manoj Mitta and H. M. Phoolka, *When a Tree Shook: The 1984 Carnage and Its Aftermath* (New Delhi: Roli Books, 2008).

44. See Meena Menon, *Riots and after in Mumbai: Chronicles of Truth and Reconciliation* (New Delhi: Sage, 2011).

45. See Angana P. Chatterji, *Violent Gods: Hindu Nationalism in India's Present—Narratives from Orissa* (Gurgaon: Three Essays Collective, 2009).

46. See Hilal Ahmed, 'Muzaffarnagar 2013: Meanings of Violence', *Economic and Political Weekly* 48, no. 40 (2013): 10–13.

47. See Brinda Karat and Vijay Prashad (eds.), *Delhi's Agony: Essays on the February 2022 Communal Violence* (New Delhi: LeftWord Books, 2021).

48. See Paul R. Brass, *The Production of Hindu–Muslim Violence in Contemporary India* (New Delhi: Oxford University Press, 2003); Paul R. Brass, *Forms of Collective Violence: Riots, Pogroms, and Genocide in Modern India* (Gurgaon: Three Essays Collective, 2006). Since the focus of this book is on anti-minority religious violence, the list shared does not mention the structural and symbolic violence carried out by upper castes against lower castes in India since thousands of years prior to British colonisation and that continues with utter impunity even today. See Parthasarathi Muthukkaruppan, 'Critique of Caste Violence: Explorations in Theory', *Social Scientist* 45, nos. 1/2 (2017): 49–71. However, in the context of anti-Muslim and anti-Christian violence carried out by Hindutva forces in contemporary India, there has been the emergence of a kind of political mobilisation by the Hindu Right where young Dalit men have been recruited by upper-caste Hindutva leaders to be the foot soldiers of this violence where Muslims and Christians have been projected through perverse forms of propaganda as the common enemy of all Hindus. This is particularly ironical because the same upper-caste leaders would continue to treat Dalits as inferior in caste status. In the context of the Gujarat pogrom, see Rubina Jasani, 'Violence, Urban Anxieties, and Masculinities: The "Foot Soldiers" of 2002, Ahmedabad', *South Asia: Journal of South Asian Studies* 43, no. 4 (2020): 675–90. See also Tarushi Aswani, 'Gujarat: Why a Sizeable Number of Dalits Are Joining Hindutva Outfits', *The Wire*, 20 March 2023, https://thewire.in/communalism/hindutva-leaders-dharma-sansad-muslim-genocide (accessed 18 December 2022).

49. See Mushirul Hasan, *Legacy of a Divided Nation: Indian Muslims since Independence* (New York: Routledge, 2018).

50. This normalisation is evident in the recent public declaration for a 'Muslim genocide' at a congregation of Hindu religious leaders, with connections to the Bharatiya Janata Party (BJP), that did not attract state condemnation or immediate arrests for hate speech. See *The Wire*, 'Hindutva Leaders at Haridwar Event Call for Muslim Genocide', 22 December 2021, https://thewire.in/communalism/hindutva-leaders-dharma-sansad-muslim-genocide (accessed 18 December 2022).

51. Howard Spodek, 'In the Hindutva Laboratory: Pogroms and Politics in Gujarat, 2002', *Modern Asian Studies* 44, no. 2 (2010): 349; Amrita Basu, *Violent Conjunctures in Democratic India* (New York: Cambridge University Press, 2015); Ghanshyam Shah and Jan Breman, *Gujarat, Cradle and Harbinger of Identity Politics: India's Injurious Frame of Communalism* (New Delhi: Tulika, 2022).

52. Surabhi Chopra and Prita Jha (eds.), *On Their Watch: Mass Violence and State Apathy in India—Examining the Record* (Gurgaon: Three Essays Collective, 2014).

53. Parvis Ghassem-Fachandi, *Pogrom in Gujarat: Hindu Nationalism and Anti-Muslim Violence in India* (New Jersey: Princeton University Press, 2012), 1.

54. This was evident in the way the then BJP prime minister, Atal Bihari Vajpayee, at a speech delivered in Goa in April 2002, justified the pogrom by citing Muslim separatism as its foundational cause and rationalising such alleged Muslim behaviour as an affront to Indian secularism. He had said on record: 'Wherever Muslims live, they don't like to live in co-existence with others, they don't like to mingle with others; and instead of propagating their ideas in a peaceful manner, they want to spread their faith by resorting to terror and threats.' Quoted in Varadarajan, *Gujarat*, 450–51.

55. The imposition of emergency, or president's rule, has been a practice of considerable debate in Indian constitutional jurisprudence, especially given the history of the widespread abuse of power and violent throttling of dissent during the Emergency rule experienced between 1975 and 1977 under Prime Minister Indira Gandhi's leadership. I draw attention to the non-imposition of an emergency during Gujarat 2002 as an attempt by the state to treat the event as an ordinary occurrence, not recognising the complete breakdown of law and order deserving special intervention from the central government to stop the violence. On the constitutional imposition of the Emergency and its narrative memories, see generally Christophe Jaffrelot and Pratinav Anil, *India's First Dictatorship: The Emergency, 1975–77* (New Delhi: HarperCollins, 2021); Emma Tarlo, *Unsettling Memories: Narratives of the Emergency in Delhi* (Berkeley: University of California Press, 2003). For an account of what has been called India's 'undeclared emergency' through the period of Narendra Modi's prime ministership that has seen a form of totalitarian state violence under ostensibly 'normal' circumstances through the rampant use of draconian laws to stifle dissident speech and incarcerate activists critical of the government,

see Arvind Narrain, *India's Undeclared Emergency: Constitutionalism and the Politics of Resistance* (Bengaluru: Context, 2022).

56. Human Rights Watch, *We Have No Orders to Save You* (Human Rights Watch, 2002), http://www.hrw.org/reports/2002/india/ (accessed 18 December 2022); Chopra and Jha, *On Their Watch.*

57. International Initiative for Justice in Gujarat (IIJG), *Threatened Existence: A Feminist Analysis of the Genocide in Gujarat* (Mumbai: IIJG, 2003); Tanika Sarkar, 'Semiotics of Terror', *Economic and Political Weekly* 37, no. 28 (2002); Kumar, *Communalism and Sexual Violence.*

58. Achyut Yagnik and Suchitra Sheth, 'Whither Gujarat?', *Economic and Political Weekly* 37, no. 11 (2002): 1009.

59. Asghar Ali Engineer (ed.), *The Gujarat Carnage* (New Delhi: Orient Longman, 2003).

60. Teesta Setalvad, *Foot Soldier of the Constitution: A Memoir* (New Delhi: LeftWord, 2017), 213.

61. Christophe Jaffrelot and Charlotte Thomas, 'Facing Ghettoisation in Riot City', in *Muslims in Indian Cities: Trajectories of Marginalisation*, ed. Laurent Gayer and Christophe Jaffrelot (Noida: HarperCollins, 2012), 43–81; Arvind Rajagopal, 'Urban Segregation and the Special Political Zone in Ahmedabad: An Emerging Paradigm for Religio-political Violence', *South Asia Multidisciplinary Academic Journal* 5 (2011), https://journals. openedition.org/samaj/3285; Rupal Oza, 'The Geography of Hindu Right Wing Violence in India', in *Violent Geographies: Fear, Terror, and Political Violence*, ed. Derek Gregory and Allan Pred (New York: Routledge, 2007).

62. Teesta Setalvad, 'The Importance of Zakia Jafri's Protest Petition', *Economic and Political Weekly* 48, no. 21 (2013): 10.

63. Amnesty International, 'A Decade on from the Gujarat Riots, an Overwhelming Majority of Victims Await Justice in India', April 2012, http://www.coalitionagainstgenocide.org/reports/2012/Amnesty-International-A-decade-on-from-the-Gujarat%20riots.pdf (accessed 18 December 2022); Mansi Choksi, 'Narendra Modi's Shame: Muslim Survivors of the Gujarat Riots Are Still Suffering', *Vice News*, 7 May 2014, https://news.vice.com/article/narendra-modis-shame-muslim-survivors-of-the-gujarat-riots-are-still-suffering (accessed 18 December 2022); Rina Chandran, 'Fifteen Years after Bloody Riots, Indian Muslims Struggling to Escape Gujarat Ghettos', *Reuters*, 24 July 2017, https://www.reuters.com/article/us-india-property-religion/fifteen-years-after-bloody-riots-indian-

muslims-struggling-to-escape-gujarat-ghettos-idUSKBN1A91OA (accessed 18 December 2022).

64. Amnesty International, 'A Decade on from the Gujarat Riots'; *New Indian Express*, '2002 Bilkis Bano Gangrape: Supreme Court for Gujarat's Reply on Compensation', 10 January 2018, http://www.newindianexpress.com/nation/2018/jan/10/2002-bilkis-bano-gangrape-supreme-court-for-gujarats-reply-on-compensation-1749794.html (accessed 18 December 2022). http://www.newindianexpress.com/nation/2018/jan/10/2002-bilkis-bano-gangrape-supreme-court-for-gujarats-reply-on-compensation-1749794.html.

65. Christophe Jaffrelot, 'Gujarat 2002: What Justice for the Victims?', *Economic and Political Weekly* 47, no. 8 (2012): 77.

66. R. K. Misra, 'Judge Who Convicted Modi's Minister in Riots Case Now Fears for Her Family', *The Wire*, 23 July 2015, https://thewire.in/law/judge-who-convicted-modis-minister-in-riots-case-now-fears-for-her-family (accessed 18 December 2022); Aarefa Johri, 'I Was Sick of the Hateful Climate in Gujarat: Judge Explains Why He Quit after the Riots', *Scroll.in*, 7 August 2015, https://scroll.in/article/746832/i-was-sick-of-the-hateful-climate-in-gujarat-judge-explains-why-he-quit-after-the-riots (accessed 18 December 2022); Human Rights Watch, 'Discouraging Dissent: Intimidation and Harassment of Witnesses, Human Rights Activists, and Lawyers Pursuing Accountability for the 2002 Communal Violence in Gujarat', https://www.hrw.org/legacy/backgrounder/asia/india/gujarat/gujarat0904.pdf (accessed 18 December 2022).

67. See Manoj Mitta, *The Fiction of Fact Finding: Modi and Godhra* (New Delhi: HarperCollins, 2014); Rana Ayyub, *Gujarat Files: Anatomy of a Cover Up* (New Delhi: Rana Ayyub, 2016); Warisha Farasat and Prita Jha, *Splintered Justice: Living the Horror of Mass Communal Violence in Bhagalpur and Gujarat* (Gurgaon: Three Essays Collective, 2016); Ashish Khetan, *Undercover: My Journey into the Darkness of Hindutva* (Bengaluru: Context, 2021).

68. Chopra and Jha, *On Their Watch*, 174.

69. See generally Patrick Hoenig and Navsharan Singh (eds.), *Landscapes of Fear: Understanding Impunity in India* (New Delhi: Zubaan, 2015); Ward Berenschot, *Riot Politics: India's Communal Violence and the Everyday Mediation of the State* (London: Hurst, 2012); Vrinda Grover, 'The Elusive Quest for Justice: Delhi 1984 to Gujarat 2002', in *Gujarat*, Varadarajan,

355–88; Vahida Nainar and Saumya Uma (eds.), *Pursuing Elusive Justice: Mass Crimes in India and Relevance of International Standards* (New Delhi: Oxford University Press, 2013).

70. International Human Rights and Conflict Resolution Clinic (IHRCRC), *When Justice Becomes the Victim: The Quest for Justice after the 2002 Violence in Gujarat* (Stanford: Stanford Law School, 2014), ii. Two decades after the Gujarat pogrom, there is an ongoing trend of key functionaries who were accused and convicted of grave crimes like gang rape and mass killings in 2002, being acquitted *en masse* by lower courts in Gujarat, and some being released on recommendation of the central government in Delhi. See Karan Deep Singh, Suhasini Raj and Mujib Mashal, 'In India, New Wave of Trauma as 11 Convicted of Rape and Murder Walk Free', *New York Times*, 20 August 2022, https://www.nytimes.com/2022/08/20/world/asia/india-rape-muslim-hindu.html (accessed 18 December 2022); Parimal A. Dabhi, 'Newsmaker: Maya Kodnani Cleared in Second 2002 Gujarat Riots Case, BJP Says No Bar on Return to Politics', *Indian Express*, 21 April 2023, https://indianexpress.com/article/political-pulse/maya-kodnani-cleared-in-second-2002-gujarat-riots-case-8567706/ (accessed 21 April 2023).

71. Moyukh Chatterjee, 'The Impunity Effect: Majoritarian Rule, Everyday Legality, and State Formation in India', *American Ethnologist* 44, no. 4 (2017): 118, 120.

72. Kalpana Kannabiran, *Tools of Justice: Non-discrimination and the Indian Constitution* (New Delhi: Routledge, 2012); N. Jayaram, 'Narendra Modi, British Invitation and Universal Jurisdiction', *openIndia*, OpenDemocracy, 16 August 2013, https://www.opendemocracy.net/openindia/n-jayaram/narendra-modi-british-invitation-and-universal-jurisdiction (accessed 18 December 2022); IHRCRC, *When Justice Becomes the Victim*.

73. IIJG, *Threatened Existence.*

74. Mihir Desai, 'The Communal and Targeted Violence Bill', *Economic and Political Weekly* 46, no. 31 (2011): 12.

75. *Outlook*, 'Naroda Patiya: Kodnani Bajrangi among 32 Convicted', 29 August 2012, https://www.outlookindia.com/newswire/story/naroda-patiya-kodnani-bajrangi-among-32-convicted/773493 (accessed 18 December 2022).

76. News18, 'Truth Always Prevails, Says Maya Kodnani on Acquittal in 2002 Gujarat Riots Case', 21 April 2018, https://www.news18.com/news/politics/truth-always-prevails-says-maya-kodnani-on-acquittal-in-2002-

gujarat-riots-case-1725409.html (accessed 18 December 2022); *LiveMint*, 'SIT Gives Clean Chit to Modi, 57 Others', 10 April 2012, https://www. livemint.com/Politics/hJNWc0iH34a25I9E6Tpr1K/SIT-gives-clean-chit-to-Modi-57-others.html (accessed 18 December 2022).

77. *Indian Express*, 'Truth Alone Triumphs, Tweets Modi after SC Relief in Gujarat Riots Case', 9 January 2014, https://indianexpress.com/article/india/india-others/truth-alone-triumphs-tweets-modi-after-sc-relief-in-gujarat-riots-case/ (accessed 18 December 2022); *Indian Express*, 'Gujarat Riots: "Hang Me If I Am Guilty", Says Narendra Modi', 26 July 2012, https://indianexpress.com/article/news-archive/politics/gujarat-riots-hang-me-if-i-am-guilty-says-narendra-modi/ (accessed 18 December 2022).

78. *The Hindu*, '"India First" Only Religion of Government, Constitution Its Only Scripture: Modi', 27 November 2015, https://www.thehindu.com/news/national/india-first-only-religion-of-government-and-constitution-its-only-scripture-says-modi/article7923917.ece (accessed 18 December 2022); *India Today*, 'Modi Asserts India's Secularism, Says Religion a Personal Choice', 17 February 2015, https://www.indiatoday.in/india/story/modi-secularism-communal-violence-church-attacks-religion-240660-2015-02-17 (accessed 18 December 2022); *Deccan Herald*, 'Hindutva Is Reflected in Indian Constitution, Says Mohan Bhagwat', 7 February 2022, https://www.deccanherald.com/national/west/hindutva-is-reflected-in-indian-constitution-says-mohan-bhagwat-1078825.html (accessed 18 December 2022). Historically, though, a certain faction of the Hindu Right in the RSS had bemoaned the Indian Constitution in 1949 to not incorporate the ancient legal wisdom in Hindu scriptures. See Hilal Ahmed, 'Making Sense of India's Citizenship Amendment Act 2019: Process, Politics, Protests', *Asie.Visions* 114 (2020): 9–10.

79. Arundhati Roy, 'Modi's Model Is At Last Revealed for What It Is: Violent Hindu Nationalism Underwritten by Big Business', *Guardian*, 18 February 2023, https://www.theguardian.com/commentisfree/2023/feb/18/narendra-modi-hindu-nationalism-india-gautam-adani (accessed 22 April 2023); Jairus Banaji, 'Indian Big Business', *Phenomenal World*, 20 December 2022, https://www.phenomenalworld.org/analysis/family-business/ (accessed 22 April 2023); Pankaj Mishra, 'The Big Con', *London Review of Books*, 4 May 2023, https://www.lrb.co.uk/the-paper/v45/n09/pankaj-mishra/the-big-con (accessed 19 May 2023); Vinod K. Jose, 'The Emperor Uncrowned: The Rise of Narendra Modi', *The Caravan*, 1 March 2012, https://

caravanmagazine.in/reportage/emperor-uncrowned-narendra-modi-profile (accessed 18 December 2022).

80. See generally Atul Sud (ed.), *Poverty amidst Prosperity: Essays on the Trajectory of Development in Gujarat* (New Delhi: Aakar Books, 2012); Neera Chandoke, 'Modi's Gujarat and Its Little Illusions', *Economic and Political Weekly* 47, no. 49 (2012): 10; Christophe Jaffrelot, 'What "Gujarat Model"? Growth without Development—And with Socio-political Polarisation', *South Asia: Journal of South Asian Studies* 38, no. 4 (2015): 820; Indira Hirway, Amita Shah and Ghanshyam Shah (eds.), *Growth or Development: Which Way Is Gujarat Going?* (New Delhi: Oxford University Press, 2014).

81. See Ornit Shani, *Communalism, Caste and Hindu Nationalism: The Violence in Gujarat* (Cambridge: Cambridge University Press, 2007); K. Balagopal, 'Reflections on Gujarat Pradesh of Hindu Rashtra', *Economic and Political Weekly* 37, no. 22 (2002): 2117.

82. A fusion of Fascism and Zionism might appear contradictory at first; however, the uniqueness of the Hindutva project lies in its ability to sophisticatedly draw on seemingly opposed ideologies to further its own ends, giving rise to a form of right-wing imagination that is a hybrid rather than a direct inheritor of one or another genealogy of hate. In this hybrid, a key homegrown element of Hindutva ideology is caste supremacy that produces what has been called 'spiritual fascism'. Suryapratim Roy and Rahul Sambaraju, 'Hindu Zion: The Politics of Constitutional Accommodation', *SSRN*, 22 March 2023, https://ssrn.com/abstract=4397260 (accessed 22 April 2023); Azad Essa, *Hostile Homelands: The New Alliance Between India and Israel* (London: Pluto Press, 2023); Kancha Ilaiah Shepherd, *Buffalo Nationalism: A Critique of Spiritual Fascism* (New Delhi: SageSamya, 2019). See also A. G. Noorani, 'Modi and Zionism', *Frontline*, 4 August 2017, https://www.frontline.in/the-nation/modi-amp-zionism/article9774462.ece (accessed 18 December 2022); Satadru Sen, 'Fascism without Fascists? A Comparative Look at Hindutva and Zionism', *South Asia: Journal of South Asian Studies* 38, no. 4 (2015): 690.

83. Many scholarly works have traced the origins of Hindutva ideology to that of European fascism. See Aijaz Ahmad, *Lineages of the Present: Ideology and Politics in Contemporary South Asia* (London: Verso, 2002), 129; Tapan Basu, Pradip Datta, Sumit Sarkar, Tanika Sarkar and Sambuddha Sen, *Khaki Shorts, Saffron Flags* (London: Orient Longman, 1993); Sumit Sarkar, 'The

Fascism of the Sangh Parivar', *Economic and Political Weekly* 27, no. 5 (1993): 163; Marzia Casolari, 'Hindutva's Foreign Tie-Up in 1930s: Archival Evidence', *Economic and Political Weekly* 35, no. 4 (2000): 218; Marzia Casolari, *In the Shade of the Swastika: The Relationships between Indian Radical Nationalism, Italian Fascism and Nazism* (Oxford: Routledge, 2020); Jairus Banaji (ed.), *Fascism: Essays on Europe and India* (London: Three Essays Collective, 2016).

84. Anustup Basu, *Hindutva as Political Monotheism* (Durham: Duke University Press, 2020). See also Dorothy M. Figueira, *Aryans, Jews, Brahmins: Theorizing Authority through Myths of Identity* (Albany: SUNY Press, 2002); Tufail Ahmad, 'Abrahamic Hindutva: The Religious Fundamentalism That Is a Threat to India's Tolerant and Pluralist Civilisational Order', *Firstpost*, 18 July 2017, https://www.firstpost.com/india/abrahamic-hindutva-the-religious-fundamentalism-that-is-a-threat-to-indias-tolerant-and-pluralist-civilisational-order-2-3825669.html (accessed 18 December 2022); S. P. Udayakumar, 'Historicizing Myth and Mythologizing History: The "Ram Temple" Drama', *Social Scientist* 25, nos. 7–8 (1997): 11; Bharat Wariavwalla, 'Religion and Nationalism in India: Ram the God of the Hindu Nation', *Round Table: Commonwealth Journal of International Affairs* 89, no. 357 (2000): 593; Christophe Jaffrelot, 'Hindu Nationalism and the (Not So Easy) Art of Being Outraged: The *Ram Setu* Controversy', *South Asia Multidisciplinary Academic Journal* 2 (2008), https://journals.openedition.org/samaj/1372; Hartosh Singh Bal, 'Spare Me the Good Hindu: The Hindu vs Hindutva Battle Is Meaningless in Shaping Our Politics', *The Caravan*, 6 July 2018, http://www.caravanmagazine.in/politics/hindu-vs-hindutva-battle-meaningless-in-shaping-our-politics.

85. See Sumit Sarkar, 'Intimations of Hindutva: Ideologies, Caste, and Class in Post-Swadeshi Bengal', *Proceedings of the Indian History Congress* 60 (1999): 665–66; Meera Nanda, 'Hindu Triumphalism and the Clash of Civilisations', *Economic and Political Weekly* 44, no. 28 (2009): 106–14. In this mythologisation of India's history, Hindutva ideology conveniently bypasses how Hinduism emerged as a modern religious formation propagated by brahmins to impose uniformity over a whole diversity of castes to project the *mlechha*, or outsider, as anti-Hindu on the one hand, and on the other, to forcibly bring non-Hindu castes within the Hindu fold to 'invent' a Hindu majority in the name of resisting British colonisation and maintaining the caste purity of brahmins. See Divya Dwivedi, Shaj Mohan and J. Reghu,

'The Hindu Hoax: How Upper Castes Invented a Hindu Majority', *The Caravan*, 31 December 2020, https://caravanmagazine.in/religion/how-upper-castes-invented-hindu-majority (accessed 18 December 2022).

86. Spodek, 'In the Hindutva Laboratory'.

87. Concerned Citizens Tribunal, *Crime against Humanity*, 3 vols. (Mumbai: Sabrang, 2002), http://www.sabrang.com/tribunal/index.html (accessed 18 December 2022).

88. Syeda Hameed, Ruth Manorama, Malini Ghose, Sheba George, Farah Naqvi and Mari Thekaekara, 'The Survivors Speak: How Has the Gujarat Massacre Affected Minority Women', *Outlook*, 2 May 2002, http://www.outlookindia.com/article.aspx?215433 (accessed 18 December 2022).

89. *The Hindu*, 'I Was Warned against Deposing: Sreekumar', 20 August 2009, http://www.thehindu.com/news/national/article5896.ece (accessed 18 December 2022); *Times of India*, 'Gujarat IPS Officer Sanjeev Bhatt Who Took On Narendra Modi Arrested', 1 October 2012, http://timesofindia.indiatimes.com/india/Gujarat-IPS-officer-Sanjeev-Bhatt-who-took-on-Narendra-Modi-arrested/articleshow/10191519.cms (accessed 18 December 2022).

90. *Tehelka*, 'The Truth: Gujarat 2002', 2 November 2007, http://archive.tehelka.com/story_main35.asp?filename%3DNe031107gujrat_sec.asp (accessed 18 December 2022); Ayyub, *Gujarat Files*; Khetan, *Undercover*.

91. Setalvad, *Foot Soldier of the Constitution*.

92. *Zahira Habibulla Sheikh and Another v. State of Gujarat and Others*, Appeal (crl.) 446–449 of 2004 (12 April 2004), https://indiankanoon.org/doc/105430/ (accessed 18 December 2022).

93. Rakesh Sharma's 2002 documentary film *Final Solution* carries footage of several such hate speeches by Narendra Modi and many others.

94. Ayodhya is a city in the state of Uttar Pradesh. On 6 December 1992, militant Hindu mobs, led by key leaders of the BJP, demolished the Babri Masjid (built in 1527 by Babur, the first Mughal emperor of India) because they claimed that the mythological Aryan-raced Hindu warrior-god Ram was born exactly where the mosque stood. The demolition led to widespread anti-Muslim violence and erupted in the Bombay riots of 1992. Both the demolition and the Bombay riots catapulted the BJP as a party of national significance, leading to their winning the general elections in 1998 and installing Atal Bihari Vajpayee as India's first BJP prime minister. See A. G. Noorani, *Destruction of the Babri Masjid: A National Dishonour* (New Delhi:

Tulika, 2017); Ashis Nandy, Shikha Trivedy, Shail Mayaram and Achyut Yagnik, *Creating a Nationality: The Ramjanmabhumi Movement and Fear of the Self* (New Delhi: Oxford University Press, 1998).

95. Martha Nussbaum, *The Clash Within: Democracy, Religious Violence and India's Future* (Cambridge: Harvard University Press, 2007), 2.

96. Quoted in Mitta, *The Fiction of Fact Finding*, 237.

97. Setalvad, *Foot Soldier of the Constitution*, 78.

98. The idea of the tolerant Hindu has been a long-used trope in Hindutva politics which tells a story about India's past as one where because of the so-called passive nature of the pure and pious (non-meat eating) Hindus, virile Christians and Muslims invaded and conquered India and could rule over the Hindus by emasculating their personhood. Hindutva politics aims to awaken the Hindu-ness among victimised Bharatiyas (the authentic inhabitants of Bhatatvarsha) by training them in militant conduct, weaponising and hypermasculinising Hindu gods like Ram, to defend India against the 'infiltration' by those whose holy lands are elsewhere. The death of Hindu *kar sevak*s in Godhra was explained through this very trope of the Hindu victim–Muslim aggressor that made the anti-Muslim violence that followed stand justified. See John R. McLane, 'Hindu Victimhood and India's Muslim Minority', in *The Fundamentalist Mindset: Psychological Perspectives on Religion, Violence, and History*, ed. Charles B. Strozier, David M. Terman, James W. Jones and Katharine A. Boyd (New York: Oxford University Press, 2010), 195–215. The tolerant Hindu rhetoric has now metamorphosed into a public interest litigation in the Supreme Court demanding that Hindus be declared a minority in certain states in India. See Satya Prakash, 'Hindus Can Be Declared "Minority" in States Where They're Numerically Lower Strength: Centre Tells Supreme Court', *The Tribune*, 27 March 2023, https://www.tribuneindia.com/news/nation/hindus-can-be-declared-minority-in-states-where-theyre-numerically-lower-strength-centre-tells-supreme-court-381292 (accessed 18 May 2023).

99. Atal Bihari Vajpayee, the BJP prime minister in 2002, buttressed this logic to justify the pogrom when he said during a speech in Goa:

> What happened in Gujarat? If a conspiracy had not been hatched to burn alive the innocent passengers of the Sabarmati Express, then the subsequent tragedy in Gujarat could have been averted. But this did not happen. People were torched alive. Who were those culprits? ...

The subsequent developments were no doubt condemnable, but who lit the fire? How did the fire spread? (Quoted in Varadarajan, *Gujarat*, 450–51)

100. Setalvad, *Foot Soldier of the Constitution*, 78.

101. Jasbir Puar, citing David Kazanjian, understands a 'flashpoint' as 'a centripetal turbulence of illumination so powerful that it may blind the past even as it spotlights the present and lights up the future'. Jasbir K. Puar, *Terrorist Assemblages: Homonationalism in Queer Times* (Durham: Duke University Press, 2007), xviii.

102. Harsh Mander, 'Where Are India's Dissenting Hindus?', *The Wire*, 12 April 2017, https://thewire.in/123008/india-hindutva-narendra-modi-rss-muslims/.

103. Teesta Setalvad, 'Contours of a Conspiracy', *Frontline*, 17 May 2013, https://www.frontline.in/cover-story/contours-of-a-conspiracy/article4660251.ece (accessed 18 December 2022).

104. Achyut Yagnik and Suchitra Sheth, *The Shaping of Modern Gujarat: Plurality, Hindutva, and Beyond* (New York: Penguin, 2005); Howard Spodek, *Ahmedabad: Shock City of Twentieth-Century India* (Bloomington: Indiana University Press, 2011).

105. Studies have established that riots that precede elections result in an 'increase [in] the vote share of the Hindu nationalist Bharatiya Janata Party by at least 5 percentage points'. Sriya Iyer and Anand Shrivastava, 'Religious Riots and Electoral Politics in India', *Journal of Development Economics* 131 (2018): 104. See also Sanjay Kumar, 'Gujarat Assembly Elections 2002: Analysing the Verdict', *Economic and Political Weekly* 38, no. 4 (2002): 270; Paul D. Kenny, *Populism and Patronage: Why Populists Win Elections in India, Asia, and Beyond* (Oxford: Oxford University Press, 2017).

106. See Paula Chakravartty and Srirupa Roy, 'Mr Modi Goes to Delhi: Mediated Populism and the 2014 Indian Elections', *Television and New Media* 16, no. 4 (2015): 311; Ronojoy Sen, 'Narendra Modi's Makeover and the Politics of Symbolism', *Journal of Asian Public Policy* 9, no. 2 (2016): 98; Tommaso Bobbio, 'Never-Ending Modi *Hindutva* and Gujarati Neoliberalism as Prelude to All-India Premiership?', *Focaal: Journal of Global and Historical Anthropology* 67 (2013): 123.

107. See Priya Chacko and Peter Mayer, 'The Modi Lahar (Wave) in the 2014 Indian National Election: A Critical Realignment?', *Australian Journal of Political Science* 49, no. 3 (2014): 518; Edward Simpson, 'The State of

Gujarat and the Men without Souls', *Critique of Anthropology* 26, no. 3 (2006): 331.

108. *Times of India*, 'Narendra Modi Gets Clean Chit in SIT Report on Gujarat Riots', 10 April 2012, https://timesofindia.indiatimes.com/india/Narendra-Modi-gets-clean-chit-in-SIT-report-on-Gujarat-riots-Zakia-Jafri-vows-to-continue-her-fight/articleshow/12612345.cms (accessed 18 December 2022).

109. Mitta, *The Fiction of Fact Finding*; Setalvad, 'The Importance of Zakia Jafri's Protest Petition'; Arshu John, 'The Professional Fortunes of Cops, Bureaucrats and SIT Members Associated with the 2002 Godhra Investigation', *The Caravan*, 22 September 2017, http://www.caravanmagazine.in/vantage/postings-cops-bureaucrats-sit-members-godhra-2002-investigation.

110. *Indian Express*, '2002 Riots Case: Gujarat High Court Rejects Zakia Jafri's Plea, Upholds Clean Chit to Narendra Modi, Others', 6 October 2017, https://indianexpress.com/article/india/2002-post-godhra-riots-case-gulbarg-riots-case-zakia-jafri-petition-rejected-by-narendra-modi-gujarat-high-court-4875374/ (accessed 18 December 2022); Vinod K. Jose, '"There Was No Question of Help": Zakia Jafri on the Gulburg Society Massacre', *The Caravan*, 5 October 2017, http://www.caravanmagazine.in/vantage/zakia-jafri-gulburg-society-massacre-modi-2002 (accessed 18 December 2022). In late 2021, the Supreme Court of India started hearing the Zakia Jafri petition challenging the SIT's report. See Ziya Us Salam, 'Explained: Understanding the Supreme Court Verdict on the Zakia Jafri Protest Petition', *The Hindu*, 26 June 2022, https://www.thehindu.com/news/national/explained-understanding-supreme-court-verdict-zakia-jafri-protest-petition-ziya-us-salam/article65567152.ece (accessed 24 April 2023).

111. *Indian Express*, 'Truth Alone Triumphs'.

112. The State Emblem of India (Prohibition of Improper Use) Act, 2005, https://legislative.gov.in/sites/default/files/A2005-50.pdf (accessed 18 December 2022); for a culturally revisionist account of how and why the motto was selected as a secular expression by Jawaharlal Nehru (India's first prime minister), though originating in a Hindu scripture, see Ananya Vajpayee, *Righteous Republic: The Political Foundations of Modern India* (Cambridge: Harvard University Press, 2012), 170–203. Historian Upinder Singh notes that 'these combinations of images and words [in the Sarnath

pillar] created a highly charged political iconography that connected the new Indian nation with its ancient past'. Upinder Singh, *Political Violence in Ancient India* (Cambridge: Harvard University Press, 2017), 3.

113. Ross Colvin and Sruthi Gottipati, 'Interview with BJP Leader Narendra Modi', *Reuters*, 12 July 2013, http://blogs.reuters.com/india/2013/07/12/ interview-with-bjp-leader-narendra-modi/.

114. Narendra Modi, 'Should We Run Relief Camps? Open Child Producing Centres?', *Outlook*, 30 September 2002, http://www.outlookindia.com/ article/should-we-run-relief-camps-open-child-producing-centres/217398 (accessed 18 December 2022).

115. *Firstpost*, 'Here It Comes: An Apology from Modi for Gujarat Riots', *Firstpost*, 1 April 2013, http://www.firstpost.com/politics/here-it-comes-an-apology-from-modi-for-gujarat-riots-680400.html (accessed 18 December 2022).

116. Quoted in William Dalrymple, 'Narendra Modi: Man of the Masses', *New Statesman*, 12 May 2014, http://www.newstatesman.com/politics/2014/05/ narendra-modi-man-masses (accessed 18 December 2022).

117. This rhetoric is now being deployed even by Modi's strong detractors among so-called liberal Hindus. A case in point is the Congress party member of parliament Shashi Tharoor's response to a recent BBC documentary on the Gujarat pogrom that strongly indicts Modi for failure as the chief minister in 2002 to stop the violence. In an interview Tharoor said, 'If India has moved on from this tragedy, why should a foreign channel open old wounds? … This is an event that happened 21 years ago, which people, including Muslims, feel we should put behind and move on'. Mojo Story, 'Shashi Tharoor on BBC Documentary on PM Modi', *Youtube*, 24 January 2023, https://www.youtube.com/watch?v=uf8yol0erMU (accessed 19 May 2023). For a powerfully worded critique of Tharoor's position, see Zahir Janmohamed, 'Why Shashi Tharoor's "Move On" Comment on 2002 Riots Is Particularly Disappointing', *The Wire*, 31 January 2023, https:// thewire.in/communalism/shashi-tharoor-bbc-documentary-gujarat-riots-2002 (accessed 19 May 2023).

118. Ghassem-Fachandi, *Pogrom in Gujarat*, 2. Such an invocation of an amorphous politics was on demonstration in a speech by Amit Shah, the BJP home minister and Modi's long term close aide. During a Gujarat state assembly election campaign rally in November 2022, Shah said that 'anti-social elements' in 2002 were 'taught a lesson' by the BJP to ensure that

Gujarat experienced 'permanent peace' thereafter. The Hindu Bureau, 'Gujarat Assembly Elections: BJP Evokes 2002 Riots to Gain Vote Favour', *The Hindu*, 25 November 2022, https://www.thehindu.com/elections/ gujarat-assembly/bjps-gujarat-campaign-evokes-2002-post-godhra-riots/ article66183228.ece (accessed 24 April 2023). The reference to an amorphous group called anti-social elements, without naming Muslims and the BJP's capacity to teach them lessons, would escape legal scrutiny for hate speech because of the 'strategic silences and metaphoric insults' that are regularly used to propagate and normalise anti-minority rhetoric in India. S. F., 'The Silence and Symbolism of Hate', *India Forum*, 4 August 2022, https:// www.theindiaforum.in/article/silence-and-symbolism-hate (accessed 18 December 2022).

119. Ghassem-Fachandi, *Pogrom in Gujarat*, 2–3.

120. Ibid., 3.

121. See Costas Douzinas, Shaun McVeigh and Ronnie Warrington, 'The Alta(e)rs of Law: The Judgement of Legal Aesthetics', *Theory, Culture and Society* 9, no. 4 (1992): 93; Desmond Manderson, *Songs without Music: Aesthetic Dimensions of Law and Justice* (Berkeley: University of California Press, 2000); Gearey, *Law and Aesthetics*; Peter D. Rush and Andrew T. Kenyon (eds.), *An Aesthetics of Law and Culture: Texts, Images, Screens*, vol. 34, Studies in Law, Politics and Society, (Bingley: Emerald Group Publishing, 2004).

122. See Cassandra Sharp and Marett Leiboff (eds.), *Cultural Legal Studies: Law's Popular Cultures and the Metamorphosis of Law* (New York: Routledge, 2016); Rosemary Coombe, 'Critical Cultural Legal Studies', *Yale Journal of Law and the Humanities* 10, no. 2 (2013): 463; Cristyn Davies and Sara L. Knox (eds.), *Cultural Studies of Law* (New York: Routledge, 2015); Austin D. Sarat and Jonathan Simon (eds.), *Cultural Analysis, Cultural Studies, and the Law: Moving beyond Legal Realism* (Durham: Duke University Press, 2003).

123. See Pierre Schlag, 'The Aesthetics of American Law', *Harvard Law Review* 115, no. 4 (2002): 1047.

124. See generally James Boyd White, *Heracles' Bow: Essays on the Rhetoric and Poetics of the Law* (Madison: University of Wisconsin Press, 1989); Robin West, 'Jurisprudence as Narrative: An Aesthetic Analysis of Modern Legal Theory', *New York Law Review* 60, no. 2 (1985): 145; Ian Ward, *Law and Literature: Possibilities and Perspectives* (New York: Cambridge University

Press, 1995); Desmond Manderson, *Kangaroo Courts and the Rule of Law: The Legacy of Modernism* (New York: Routledge, 2012); Christian Hiebaum, Susan Knaller and Doris Pichler (eds.), *Law and Literature In-Between* (Bielefeld: Transcript Verlag, 2015); Michael Hanne and Robert Weisberg (eds.), *Narrative and Metaphor in the Law* (Cambridge: Cambridge University Press, 2018).

125. See Sharp and Leiboff, *Cultural Legal Studies*.

126. See Robert Cover, 'Violence and the Word', *Yale Law Review* 95 (1986): 1601; Austin Sarat (ed.), *Law, Violence and the Possibility of Justice* (Princeton: Princeton University Press, 2001); Costas Douzinas, Ronnie Warrington and Shaun McVeigh, *Postmodern Jurisprudence: The Law of Text in the Texts of Law* (London: Routledge, 1991).

127. See Greta Olson, 'The Turn to Passion: Has Law and Literature Become Law and Affect?', *Law and Literature* 28, no. 3 (2016): 335; Daniel Hourigan, 'Spectres and Psychoanalysis in the Turn to Law and Affect', *Law and Literature* 31, no. 1 (2017): 129–45.

128. See Mark Antaki, 'Making Sense of Minor Jurisprudence', *Law Text Culture* 21 (2017): 74.

129. Douzinas and Gearey, *Critical Jurisprudence*, 10; Margaret Davies, *Law Unlimited: Materialism, Pluralism, and Legal Theory* (New York: Routledge, 2017), 22. There is a minor disagreement between the authors of the two books regarding the philosophical worth of a question like 'what is law?'. While Douzinas and Gearey feel that the question is an impediment to their imagination of a critical jurisprudence, for Davies, the question carries contingent valence.

130. Davies, *Law Unlimited*, viii.

131. See Peter Fitzpatrick, *The Mythology of Modern Law* (London: Routledge, 1992); Richard K. Sherwin, *Visualizing Law in the Age of the Digital Baroque: Arabesques and Entanglements* (New York: Routledge, 2011); Linda Mulcahy, *Legal Architecture: Justice, Due Process and the Place of Law* (New York: Routledge, 2010); James E. K. Parker, *Acoustic Jurisprudence: Listening to the Trial of Simon Bikindi* (Oxford: Oxford University Press, 2015); Kieran Tranter, *Living in Technical Legality: Science Fiction and Law as Technology* (Edinburgh: Edinburgh University Press, 2018); Kjell Å. Modéer and Martin Sunnqvist (eds.), *Legal Stagings: The Visualization, Medialization and Ritualization of Law in Language, Literature, Media, Art and Architecture* (Copenhagen: Museum Tusculanum Press, 2012).

132. See Costas Douzinas and Lynda Nead (eds.), *Law and the Image: The Authority of Art and the Aesthetics of Law* (Chicago: University of Chicago Press, 1999); Peter Goodrich, *Legal Emblems and the Art of Law: Obiter Depicta as the Vision of Governance* (Cambridge: Cambridge University Press, 2014); Desmond Manderson and Cristina S. Martinez, 'Justice and Art, Face to Face', *Yale Journal of Law and the Humanities* 28, no.2 (2016); Thomas Giddens (ed.), *Graphic Justice: Intersections of Comics and Law* (New York: Routledge, 2015); Desmond Manderson, *Danse Macabre: Temporalities of Law in the Visual Arts* (Cambridge: Cambridge University Press, 2019).

133. See Ian Ward, *Law and Literature: Possibilities and Perspectives* (Cambridge: Cambridge University Press, 2008); Kieran Dolin, *A Critical Introduction to Law and Literature* (Cambridge: Cambridge University Press, 2012); Desmond Manderson, *Kangaroo Courts and the Rule of Law: The Legacy of Modernism* (New York: Routledge, 2012).

134. See Black, *Law in Film*; Orit Kamir, *Framed: Women in Law and Film* (Durham: Duke University Press, 2006); Steve Greenfield, Guy Osborn and Peter Robson, *Film and the Law: The Cinema of Justice* (Oxford: Hart Publishing, 2010).

135. See Peter Robson and Jessica Silbey (eds.), *Law and Justice on the Small Screen* (Oxford: Hart Publishing, 2012); Michael Asimow (ed.), *Lawyers in Your Living Room! Law on Television* (Chicago: American Bar Association, 2009); Peter Robson and Jennifer L. Schulz (eds.), *A Transnational Study of Law and Justice on TV* (Oxford: Hart Publishing, 2016); Elayne Rapping, *Law and Justice as Seen on TV* (New York: New York University Press, 2003).

136. See Nina Philadelphoff-Puren and Peter Rush, 'Fatal (F)laws: Law, Literature and Writing', *Law and Critique* 14, no. 2 (2003): 191; Marco Wan, *Masculinity and the Trials of Modern Fiction* (New York: Routledge, 2016); Mark Sanders, *Ambiguities of Witnessing: Law and Literature in the Time of a Truth Commission* (Stanford: Stanford University Press, 2007).

137. See Jonathan Simon, Nicholas Temple and Renée Tobe (eds.), *Architecture and Justice: Judicial Meanings in the Public Realm* (London: Routledge, 2013); Piyel Haldar, 'In and Out of Court: On Topographies of Law and the Architecture of Court Buildings', *Revue internationale de semiotique juridique* 7, no. 2 (1994): 185; Rahela Khorakiwala, *From the Colonial to the Contemporary: Images, Iconography, Memories, and Performances of Law in India's High Courts* (New Delhi: Bloomsbury, 2020).

138. See Austin Sarat, Lawrence Douglas and Martha Merrill Umphrey (eds.), *Law and Performance* (Amherst: University of Massachusetts Press, 2018); Catharine M. Cole, *Performing South Africa's Truth Commission: Stages of Transition* (Bloomington: Indiana University Press, 2009); Alan Read, *Theatre and Law* (London: Methuen Drama, 2022).

139. See Rob McQueen, 'Of Wigs and Gowns: A Short History of Legal and Judicial Dress in Australia', *Law in Context* 16, no. 1 (1999): 31; Ruthann Robson, *Dressing Constitutionally: Hierarchy, Sexuality, and Democracy from Our Hairstyles to Our Shoes* (New York: Cambridge University Press, 2013).

140. See Sara Ramshaw, 'Deconstructin(g) Jazz Improvisation: Derrida and the Law of the Singular Event', *Critical Studies in Improvisation* 2, no. 1 (2006), https://www.criticalimprov.com/index.php/csieci/article/download/81/188/ (accessed 18 December 2022); Parker, *Acoustic Jurisprudence*.

141. See Alison Young, *The Scene of Violence: Cinema, Crime, Affect* (New York: Routledge, 2009); Ruth Buchanan and Rebecca Johnson, 'Strange Encounters: Exploring Law and Film in the Affective Register', in vol. 46, *Studies in Law, Politics and Society*, ed. Austin Sarat, Studies in Law, Politics and Society (Bingley: Emerald Group Publishing, 2008), 33–60; Austin Sarat (ed.), *Imagining Legality: Where Law Meets Popular Culture* (Tuscaloosa: University of Alabama Press, 2011); Timothy Peters and Karen Crawley (eds.), *Envisioning Legality: Law, Culture and Representation* (New York: Routledge, 2017).

142. See Neal Feigenson and Christina Spiesel, *Law on Display: The Digital Transformation of Legal Persuasion and Judgment* (New York: New York University Press, 2009); Jacqueline Horan and Shelley Maine, 'Criminal Jury Trials in 2030: A Law Odyssey', *Journal of Law and Society* 41, no. 4 (2014): 551; Katherine Biber, *Captive Images: Race, Crime, Photography* (London: Routledge, 2014); Katherine Biber, *In Crime's Archive: The Cultural Afterlife of Evidence* (London: Routledge, 2017); Marit Paasche and Judy Radul (eds.), *A Thousand Eyes: Media Technology, Law, and Aesthetics* (Berlin: Sternberg, 2011).

143. As notable exceptions, see Lawrence Liang, 'Cinematic Citizenship and the Illegal City', *Inter-Asia Cultural Studies* 6, no. 3 (2005): 366; Lawrence Liang, 'Media's Law: From Representation to Affect', *Bioscope: South Asian Screen Studies* 2, no. 1 (2011): 23.

144. See Lawrence Liang, Mayur Suresh and Namita Avriti Malhotra, *The Public Is Watching: Sex, Laws and Videotapes* (New Delhi: Public Service Broadcasting Trust, 2007).

145. See Arul George Scaria, *Piracy in the Indian Film Industry: Copyright and Cultural Consonance* (New Delhi: Cambridge University Press, 2014).

146. See Danish Sheikh, 'The Students vs Larry Flynt: Bringing Popular Culture into the Law School', *Asian Journal of Legal Education* 1, no. 1 (2014): 45.

147. See Yasmeen Arif, 'The Audacity of Method', *Economic and Political Weekly* 50, no. 1 (2015): 53.

148. See Upendra Baxi, 'Postcolonial Legality: A Postscript from India', *Law and Politics in Africa, Asia and Latin America* 45, no. 2 (2012): 178; Ratna Kapur, '"A Love Song to Our Mongrel Selves": Hybridity, Sexuality and the Law', *Social and Legal Studies* 8, no. 3 (1999): 353; Arvind Rajagopal, 'Notes on Postcolonial Visual Culture', *BioScope* 2, no. 1 (2011): 11; Bill Ashcroft, 'Towards a Postcolonial Aesthetics', *Journal of Postcolonial Writing* 51, no. 4 (2015): 410.

149. See Ann Genovese, 'Inheriting and Inhabiting the Pleasures and Duties of Our Own Existence: *The Second Sex* and Feminist Jurisprudence', *Australian Feminist Law Journal* 38, no. 1 (2013): 41.

150. See generally Oishik Sircar, *Violent Modernities: Cultural Lives of Law in the New India* (New Delhi: Oxford University Press, 2021); Kanishka Chowdhury, *The New India: Citizenship, Subjectivity, and Economic Liberalization* (London: Palgrave Macmillan, 2011); Atul Kohli, *Poverty amid Plenty in the New India* (New York: Cambridge University Press, 2012); Siddhartha Deb, *The Beautiful and Damned: A Portrait of the New India* (New York: Farrar, Straus and Giroux, 2011); Harsh Mander, *Looking Away: Inequality, Prejudice and Indifference in New India* (New Delhi: Speaking Tiger Books, 2015); Ravinder Kaur and Nayanika Mathur (eds.), *The People of India: New Indian Politics in the 21st Century* (Gurugram: Penguin Random House, 2022).

151. See Shankar Gopalakrishnan, 'Defining, Constructing and Policing a "New India": Relationship between Neoliberalism and Hindutva', *Economic and Political Weekly* 41, no. 26 (2006): 2803; Meera Nanda, *The God Market: How Globalization Is Making India More Hindu* (Gurugram: Random House India, 2009).

152. Ahmad, *Lineages of the Present*, 189.

153. Priya Chacko, 'Marketizing Hindutva: The State, Society, and Markets in Hindu Nationalism', *Modern Asian Studies* (2008): 1, first view, https://www. cambridge.org/core/journals/modern-asian-studies/article/marketizing-hindutva-the-state-society-and-markets-in-hindu-nationalism/92243742 C585CD73910BA63030F6A655 (accessed 8 December 2022).

154. See Rowena Robinson, 'Indian Muslims: The Varied Dimensions of Marginality', *Economic and Political Weekly* 42, no. 10 (2007): 839; Amir Ali, 'The Sachar Committee Report and Multiculturalism in India: Questions of Group Equality and the Public Sphere', in *Religion, Communities and Development: Changing Contours of Politics and Policy in India*, ed. Gurpreet Mahajan and Surinder S. Jodhka (New Delhi: Routledge, 2010), 65; Tanweer Fazal, *Millennium Development Goals and Muslims of India* (New Delhi: Oxfam India, 2013).

155. Muslims in India are not a homogeneous community, and they experience marginalisation on the basis of a whole range of class, caste, demographic and political factors that cannot be flattened. A secularised and liberal narrative of the history of sectarian violence in India tends to project Muslim marginalisation through the binarisation of Hindu majorities and Muslim minorities. Such a binarisation, for example, overlooks the ways in which the fusion of Hindutva ideology and caste supremacy intensifies violence against oppressed caste Pasmanda Muslims while dominant caste and elite Ashraf Muslims tend to gain from upper caste Hindu patronage. Under the rule of the BJP since 2014, India has seen a blatant intensification of structural and symbolic forms of violence and domination against poor and oppressed caste Muslims, which is now increasingly being carried out by Hindu vigilante groups with active police backing on the one hand, and on the other through state policies and legislation to deny citizenship status to Muslims. The concerted nature of this violence, which includes the bulldozing of homes and mosques and calls for mass annihilation, has led to some commentators calling it 'genocidal'. See Khalid Anis Ansari, 'Revisiting the Minority Imagination: An Inquiry into the Anticaste Pasmanda-Muslim Discourse in India', *Critical Philosophy of Race* 11, no. 1 (2023): 120–47; Imtiaz Ahmad (ed.), *Caste and Social Stratification among Muslims in India* (New Delhi: Aakar Books, 2018); Hilal Ahmed, *Siyasi Muslims: A Story of Political Islams in India* (New Delhi: India Viking, 2019); Ghazala Wahab, *Born a Muslim: Some Truths about Islam in India* (New Delhi: Aleph Book Company, 2021); Ali Khan Mahmudabad, 'Indian Muslims and the

Anti-CAA Protests: From Marginalisation towards Exclusion', *South Asia Multidisciplinary Academic Journal* 24/25 (2020), https://journals. openedition.org/samaj/6701; Mujib Mashal, Suhasini Raj and Hari Kumar, 'As Officials Look Away, Hate Speech in India Nears Dangerous Levels', *New York Times*, 8 February 2022, https://www.nytimes.com/2022/02/08/ world/asia/india-hate-speech-muslims.html (accessed 18 December 2022); Sara Ather, 'India's Bulldozer War on Muslim Neighbourhoods', *Middle East Eye,* 6 February 2023, https://www.middleeasteye.net/opinion/india-muslims-undeclared-war-neighbourhoods (accessed 17 May 2023).

156. Piyush Rai, 'Hate Crimes Highest in UP, Gujarat Second: Amnesty Report', *Times of India*, 17 July 2018, https://timesofindia.indiatimes.com/india/ hate-crimes-highest-in-up-guj-second-says-amnesty-report/articleshow/ 65014822.cms (accessed 18 December 2022); Alison Saldanha and Karthik Madhavapeddi, 'Our New Hate-Crime Database: 76% of Victims over Ten Years Minorities; 90% of Attacks Reported since 2014', *Fact Checker*, 30 October 2018, https://factchecker.in/our-new-hate-crime-database-76-of-victims-over-10-years-minorities-90-attacks-reported-since-2014/.

157. See Pralay Kanungo, 'Hindutva's Discourse on Development', in *Religion, Communities and Development: Changing Contours of Politics and Policy in India*, ed. Gurpreet Mahajan and Surinder S. Jodhka (New Delhi: Routledge, 2010), 83; Tereza Kuldova, 'Designing an Illusion of India's Future Superpowerdom: Of the Rise of Neo-aristocracy, Hindutva and Philanthrocapitalism', *Unfamiliar: An Anthropological Journal* 4, no. 1 (2014): 15; Nidhi Jacob, 'Status Update: Will Centre Achieve or Miss "New India" Targets 2022', *Fact Checker*, 8 January 2022, https://www.factchecker.in/ explained/status-update-will-centre-achieve-or-miss-new-india-targets-for-2022-796561 (accessed 18 December 2022).

158. See Radhika Desai, 'Gujarat's Hindutva of Capitalist Development', *South Asia: Journal of South Asian Studies* 34, no. 3 (2011): 354; Nikita Sood, *Liberalization, Hindu Nationalism and the State: A Biography of Gujarat* (New Delhi: Oxford University Press, 2012).

159. See Saba Mahmood, 'Religious Reason and Secular Affect: An Incommensurable Divide?', *Critical Inquiry* 35, no. 4 (Summer 2009): 858–59:

> As much recent scholarship suggests, contrary to the ideological self-understanding of secularism (as the doctrinal separation of religion and state), secularism has historically entailed the regulation and re-formation of religious beliefs, doctrines, and practices to yield a

particular normative conception of religion.... Historically speaking, the secular state has not simply cordoned off religion from its regulatory ambitions but sought to remake it through the agency of the law.

160. 'Legalism' is understood in this book both as a governmental obsession with 'rule following' and an over-reliance on law reform as forms of governance practice. Judith N. Shklar, *Legalism: Law, Morals and Political Trials* (Cambridge: Harvard University Press, 1964); see also Wendy Brown and Janet Halley (eds.), *Left Legalism/Left Critique* (Durham: Duke University Press, 2002).

161. See Arif Dirlik, 'Developmentalism: A Critique', *Interventions: International Journal of Postcolonial Studies* 16, no. 1 (2014): 30–31:

By developmentalism—to be distinguished from development—I mean an ideological orientation characterised by the fetishisation of development, or the attribution to development of the power of a natural (or even, divine) force which humans can resist or question only at the risk of being condemned to stagnation and poverty. The ideology renders opaque the historical forces that have shaped the idea of development. It also disguises the social and political forces that have played, and continue to play, a crucial part in endowing it with the power to dominate human consciousness.

162. 'Common sense is a vitally important social institution because it supplies the cement that holds up the social structure.... Common sense is pre-judice in the strict sense—it is "always already" in place and hard at work long before we make any conscious judgments.' Satish Deshpande, *Contemporary India: A Sociological View* (New Delhi: Penguin, 2003), 2.

163. I approach the writing of this book from what Paul Cilliers would call a 'modest position'—one that acknowledges the 'limitations of our understanding of this world'. This is not a position of relativism, but a 'counter-position' to 'arrogant self-assurance' that engages with complexity without any predetermined technocratic objective of problem-solving. Paul Cilliers, 'Complexity, Deconstruction and Relativism', *Theory, Culture and Society* 22, no. 5 (2005): 256, 260; Karin Van Marle, 'Liminal Landscape: Law, Literature and Landscape in Post-apartheid South Africa', in *Genres of Critique: Law, Aesthetics and Liminality*, ed. Karin Van Marle and Stewart Motha (Stellenbosch: African Sun Media, 2013) 109, 122.

164. See Ghassem-Fachandi, *Pogrom in Gujarat*; Moyukh Chatterjee, *Composing Violence: The Limits of Exposure and the Making of Minorities* (Durham: Duke University Press, 2023).

165. See generally Berenschot, *Riot Politics*; Yasmeen Arif, *Life, Emergent: The Social in the Afterlives of Violence* (Minneapolis: University of Minnesota Press, 2016); T. K. Oommen, *Reconciliation in Post-Godhra Gujarat: The Role of Civil Society* (New Delhi: Pearson Longman, 2008); Dipankar Gupta, *Justice before Reconciliation: Negotiating a 'New Normal' in Post-riot Mumbai and Ahmedabad* (New Delhi: Routledge, 2011); Raheel Dhattiwala, *Keeping the Peace: Spatial Differences in Hindu–Muslim Violence in Gujarat in 2002* (Cambridge: Cambridge University Press, 2019).

166. See Shani, *Communalism, Caste and Hindu Nationalism*; Lokhande, *Communal Violence, Forced Migration and the State*.

167. See Spodek, 'In the Hindutva Laboratory'; Kumar, *Communalism and Sexual Violence*; Tommaso Bobbio, *Urbanisation, Citizenship and Conflict in India: Ahmedabad 1900–2000* (London: Routledge, 2015).

168. See Subarno Chattarji, 'Some Comments on Media Representations of the Gujarat Riots and the Kargil War', in *Tracking the Media: Interpretations of Mass Media Discourses in India and Pakistan* (New York: Routledge, 2008), 36–59; Ohm, 'Forgetting to Remember'; Jain, 'Beaming It Live'; Mehta, 'Modi and the Camera'.

169. See Rustom Bharucha, *Terror and Performance* (London: Routledge, 2014).

170. See Upendra Baxi, 'The Second Gujarat Catastrophe', *Economic and Political Weekly* 37, no. 34 (2002): 3519; Nussbaum, *The Clash Within*; Kapur, 'Normalizing Violence'.

171. See Setalvad, *Foot Soldier of the Constitution*; Mitta, *The Fiction of Fact Finding*; Ayyub, *Gujarat Files*; Farasat and Jha, *Splintered Justice*; Varadarajan, *Gujarat*; Engineer, *The Gujarat Carnage*; Amrita Kumar and Prashun Bhaumik (eds.), *Lest We Forget: Gujarat 2002* (New Delhi: World Report in association with Rupa, 2002); Valson Thampu, *Harvest of Hate: Gujarat under Siege* (New Delhi: Rupa, 2002); IIJG, *Threatened Existence*; K. Lalita and Deepa Dhanraj, *Rupture, Loss and Living: Minority Women Speak about Post-conflict Life* (Hyderabad: Orient BlackSwan, 2016); Dionne Bunsha, *Scarred: Experiments with Violence in Gujarat* (New Delhi: Penguin, 2007); Revati Laul, *The Anatomy of Hate* (New Delhi: Context, 2018); Ashish Khetan, *Undercover: My Journey into the Darkness of Hindutva* (New Delhi: Context, 2021).

172. See Wendy Doniger and Martha Nussbaum (eds.), *Pluralism and Democracy in India: Debating the Hindu Right* (New Delhi: Oxford University Press, 2015).

173. Farasat and Jha, *Splintered Justice*.

174. Jaffrelot, 'Gujarat 2002'.

175. See Arvind Narrain, 'Truth Telling, Gujarat and the Law', in *Sarai Reader 04: Crisis/Media* (New Dlehi: Sarai, 2004), http://archive.sarai.net/files/orig inal/4ac595f03bc91168e27c97719a12cadc.pdf (accessed 18 December 2022); Anita Abraham, 'Mass Crimes Committed in Gujarat in 2002: Immediate Need for a Mass Crimes Law', Working Paper Series CSLG/WP/15, Centre for the Study of Law and Governance, Jawaharlal Nehru University, New Delhi, November 2012, https://www.jnu.ac.in/sites/default/files/u63/15-Mass%20%28Anita%29.pdf (accessed 18 December 2022).

176. See Christophe Jaffrelot and Gilles Verniers, 'Absence on the Bench', *Indian Express*, 10 September 2018, https://indianexpress.com/article/opinion/columns/muslims-in-prison-india-judiciary-supreme-court-5347728/ (accessed 18 December 2022).

177. See Teesta Setalvad, 'When Guardians Betray: The Role of the Police', in *Gujarat*, ed. Varadarajan, 177–211; Vibhuti Narain Rai, 'An Open Letter to My Fellow Police Officers', in *Gujarat*, ed. Varadarajan, 212–13.

178. See Rajeev Bhargava (ed.), *Secularism and Its Critics* (New Delhi: Oxford University Press, 2000); T. N. Srinivasan (ed.), *The Future of Secularism* (New Delhi: Oxford University Press, 2007).

179. See Anuradha Dingwaney Needham and Rajeswari Sunder Rajan (eds.), *The Crisis of Secularism in India* (Durham: Duke University Press, 2007); Ashis Nandy, 'An Anti-Secularist Manifesto', *India International Centre Quarterly* 22, no. 1 (1995): 35–64; Cossman and Kapur, *Secularism's Last Sigh*.

180. Rajeev Bhargava, 'What Is Indian Secularism and What Is It For?', *India Review* 1, no. 1 (2002): 1; Rajeev Bhargava, 'The Distinctiveness of Indian Secularism', in *The Future of Secularism*, Srinivasan, 20–53; Rajeev Bhargava, *The Promise of India's Secular Democracy* (New Delhi: Oxford University Press, 2010).

181. See Gyanendra Pandey, 'Which of Us Are Hindus?', in *Hindus and Others: The Question of Identity in India Today*, ed. Gyanendra Pandey (New Delhi: Viking, 1993), 238–72.

182. See Thomas Blom Hansen, *The Saffron Wave: Democracy and Hindu Nationalism in Modern India* (Princeton: Princeton University Press, 1999);

Dibyesh Anand, 'The Violence of Security: Hindu Nationalism and the Politics of Representing "the Muslim" as a Danger', *Round Table: Commonwealth Journal of International Affairs* 94, no. 379 (2005): 203.

183. Naresh Kamath, '150 Hindu Outfits to Meet in Goa to Discuss "Hindu Rashtra" by 2023, BJP, RSS to Stay Away', *Hindustan Times*, 11 June 2017, https://www.hindustantimes.com/mumbai-news/150-hindu-outfits-to-meet-in-goa-to-discuss-possibility-of-hindu-rashtra-by-2023/story-R8HWIzIvoUdHytWeZZguRI.html (accessed 18 December 2022); *India Today*, 'India is a Hindu Rashtra, It is Non-negotiable: RSS Chief Mohan Bhagwat', 2 October 2019, https://www.indiatoday.in/india/story/india-is-a-hindu-rashtra-it-is-non-negotiable-rss-chief-mohan-bhagwat-1605313-2019-10-01 (accessed 18 December 2022); Sanjay Pandey, 'Now, Uttar Pradesh "Dharm Sansad" Calls for "Hindu Rashtra", Seers Say Gandhi Not Father of the Nation, Nehru Not "First" PM', *Deccan Herald*, 30 January 2022, https://www.deccanherald.com/national/now-uttar-pradesh-dharm-sansad-calls-for-hindu-rashtra-seers-say-gandhi-not-father-of-the-nation-nehru-not-first-pm-1076216.html (accessed 18 December 2022).

184. Banaji, *Fascism*.

185. See A. G. Noorani, *The RSS and the BJP: A Division of Labour* (New Delhi: LeftWord, 2000).

186. See Suhas Palshikar, Sanjay Kumar and Sanjay Lodha (eds.), *Electoral Politics in India: The Resurgence of the Bharatiya Janata Party* (New Delhi: Routledge, 2017); Saba Naqvi, *Shades of Saffron: From Vajpayee to Modi* (Chennai: Westland, 2018).

187. See Bhagwan Josh, 'Partition and the Rise of Hindutva Movement in Contemporary India', *Revista Canaria de Estudios Ingleses* 76 (2018): 175; Pranav Kohli, *Memories in the Service of the Hindu Nation: The Afterlife of the Partition of India* (Cambridge: Cambridge University Press, 2023).

188. See Faisal Devji, *Muslim Zion: Pakistan as a Political Idea* (London: Harvard University Press, 2013).

189. See Teesta Setalvad, *Beyond Doubt: A Dossier on Gandhi's Assassination* (New Delhi: Tulika, 2015); A. G. Noorani, *Savarkar and Hindutva: The Godse Connection* (New Delhi: LeftWord, 2004); Dhirendra K. Jha, *Gandhi's Assassin: The Making of Nathuram Godse and His Idea of India* (New Delhi: Vintage, 2022); Appu Esthose Suresh and Priyanka Kotamraju, *The Murderer, The Monarch and the Fakir: A New Investigation of Mahatma Gandhi's Assassination* (New Delhi: HarperCollins, 2021).

190. See Mushirul Hasan (ed.), *India's Partition: Process, Strategy and Mobilization* (New Delhi: Oxford University Press, 1997).

191. See Kuldip Nayar, *Emergency Retold* (New Delhi: Konark, 2013); Vishwajyoti Ghosh, *Delhi Calm* (Noida: HarperCollins, 2010); Gyan Prakash, *Emergency Chronicles: Indira Gandhi and Democracy's Turning Point* (New Delhi: Penguin Viking, 2018).

192. See Coomi Kapoor, *The Emergency: A Personal History* (Gurgaon: Viking, 2015).

193. See Katharine Adeney and Lawrence Sáez (eds.), *Coalition Politics and Hindu Nationalism* (New York: Routledge, 2005).

194. See Dhirendra Jha, *Shadow Armies: Fringe Organizations and Foot Soldiers of Hindutva* (New Delhi: Juggernaut, 2017).

195. See Christophe Jaffrelot (ed.), *Sangh Parivar: A Reader* (New Delhi: Oxford University Press, 2005).

196. See generally Achin Vanaik, 'Making India Strong: The BJP-Led Government's Foreign Policy Perspectives', *South Asia: Journal of South Asian Studies* 25, no. 3 (2002): 321; Sumantra Bose, *Kashmir: Roots of Conflict, Paths to Peace* (Cambridge: Harvard University Press, 2005); Pankaj Mishra, 'Kashmir: The Unending War', *New York Review of Books*, 19 October 2000, https://www.nybooks.com/articles/2000/10/19/kashmir-the-unending-war/ (accessed 18 December 2022); Aman, '"Tuhindi Article" ("The Articles Were Yours")', *Verfassungsblog: On Matters Constitutional*, 29 December 2022, https://verfassungsblog.de/tuhindi-article-the-articles-were-yours/ (accessed 17 May 2023); Itty Abraham, *The Making of the Indian Atomic Bomb: Science, Secrecy and the Postcolonial State* (New Delhi: Orient Longman, 1999).

197. S. Anand, 'Hindutva Has More Legitimacy than the Constitution', *Outlook*, 23 September 2002, https://www.outlookindia.com/website/story/hindutva-has-more-legitimacy-than-the-constitution/217199 (accessed 18 December 2022); *Huffington Post*, 'At the "Hindu Rashtra" Conclave in Goa, an Open Call for Violence against Beef Eaters and "Seculars"', 15 June 2017, https://www.huffingtonpost.in/2017/06/15/at-the-hindu-rashtra-conclave-an-open-call-for-violence-again_a_22266930/ (accessed 18 December 2022); NDTV, '"We Are Here to Change the Constitution", Says Union Minister in New Controversy', 26 December 2017, https://www.ndtv.com/india-news/we-are-here-to-change-the-constitution-says-union-minister-anant-kumar-hegde-in-new-controversy-1792197 (accessed 18

December 2022); *Business Standard*, 'BJP, RSS against the Constitution of India, Want to Impose Hindutva: Mayawati', 6 December 2016, https://www.business-standard.com/article/politics/bjp-rss-against-the-constitution-of-india-want-to-impose-hindutva-mayawati-116120600 554_1.html (accessed 18 December 2022).

198. See Subramanian Swamy, *The Ideology of India's Modern Right* (New Delhi: Har-Anand, 2018).

199. See Omar Khalidi, 'Hinduising India: Secularism in Practice', *Third World Quarterly* 29, no. 8 (2008): 1545; Manjari Katju, *Hinduising Democracy* (New Delhi: New Text, 2017).

200. For some instances of the Hindu liberal position, see Hindol Sengupta, *Being Hindu* (New Delhi: Penguin, 2015); Vamsee Juluri, *Rearming Hinduism* (Chennai: Westland, 2016). For an instance of how this Hindu liberal articulation appropriates left radical positions like 'decoloniality' to offer a revisionist account of India's pasts as Hindu, see J. Sai Deepak, *India, That Is Bharat: Coloniality, Civilisation, Constitution* (New Delhi: Bloomsbury, 2021). The position espoused by the Hindu Right uses the same decolonisation argument as the Hindu liberals do. See Shalini Sharma, 'India: How Some Hindu Nationalists Are Rewriting Caste History in the Name of Decolonisation', *Conversation*, 9 May 2019, https://theconversation.com/india-how-some-hindu-nationalists-are-rewriting-caste-history-in-the-name-of-decolonisation-114133 (accessed 18 December 2022).

201. See Flavia Agnes, 'The Supreme Court, the Media, and the Uniform Civil Code Debate in India', in *The Crisis of Secularism in India*, ed. Needham and Rajan, 295–315; Flavia Agnes, 'Has the Codified Hindu Law Changed Gender Relationships?', *Social Change* 46, no. 4 (2016): 611. A recent manifestation of such a liberal Hindu position, ironically mimicking French secularism, has been the demand by Hindutva outfits for banning Muslim students from wearing the hijab in the state of Karnataka. See Rajeev Kadambi, 'Hijab Row: Why Is the BJP Echoing Liberal Playbook by Seeking to Ban Religious Symbols in Public?' *Scroll.in*, 10 February 2022, https://scroll.in/article/1016862/one-nation-one-uniform-hijab-row-shows-hindutvas-utter-failure-to-accept-cultural-difference (accessed 18 December 2022).

202. See generally Ashwini Deshpande, *Affirmative Action in India* (New Delhi: Oxford University Press, 2013).

203. See K. Balagopal, 'This Anti-Mandal Mania', *Economic and Political Weekly* 25, no. 40 (1990): 2231–34; Ajantha Subramanian, *The Caste of Merit: Engineering Education in India* (Cambridge: Harvard University Press, 2019). The upper-caste anti-reservation position evokes merit as a bogey because in the logic of the caste system merit is existentially related to birth and not human effort. So, when arguments against reservations are made to emphasise how they will compromise on merit, it is a reflection of a brahminical angst about losing their naturalised worth in being better than non-brahmins.

204. See generally Jayabrata Sarkar, *Politics as Social Text in India: The Bahujan Samaj Party in Uttar Pradesh* (New Delhi: Routledge, 2021).

205. Jayati Ghosh, 'Hindutva, Economic Neoliberalism, and the Abuse of Economic Statistics in India', *South Asia Multidisciplinary Academic Journal* 24, no. 25 (2020), https://journals.openedition.org/samaj/6882; Deonnie Moodie, 'Retail Religion: Hinduism for a Neoliberal Age', *Journal of the American Academy of Religion* 89, no. 3 (2021): 863–84.

206. Cossman and Kapur, *Secularism's Last Sigh*; Saumya Saxena, '"Court"ing Hindu Nationalism: Law and the Rise of Modern Hindutva', *Contemporary South Asia* 26, no. 4 (2018): 378–99.

207. Such an inquiry is interested in 'how secularism, with its own more sober and distinguished truth claims, could have allowed this alternative form of [Hindu national] realism to grow with so little resistance'. Arvind Rajagopal, 'The Gujarat Experiment and Hindu National Realism', in *The Crisis of Secularism in India*, ed. Anuradha Dingwaney Needham and Rajeshwari Sunder Rajan (Ranikhet: Permanent Black, 2007), 210. Hindutva's secular turn has also had its liberal Hindu secular detractors, who contend that Hinduism as a religion and Hindutva as a political ideology cannot be equated and that Hindu religion needs to be defended against Hindutva's incursions. See Shashi Tharoor, *Why I Am a Hindu* (New Delhi: Aleph Book Company, 2018). Such a rehabilitative move in favour of Hinduism is deeply problematic because it elides how Hindu scriptures lay the foundations for the caste system and the role that caste plays in both the production and sustenance of Hindutva ideology. See Dilip M. Menon, *The Blindness of Insight: Essays on Caste in Modern India* (Pondicherry: Navayana, 2005); Anand Teltumbde (ed.), *Hindutva and Dalits: Perspectives for Understanding Communal Praxis* (New Delhi: Sage, 2020).

208. *The Hindu*, '"India First" Only Religion of Government'; *Financial Express*, 'Narendra Modi Government for Gita as National Scripture', *Financial*

Express, 8 December 2014, https://www.financialexpress.com/india-news/
bhagwad-gita-only-an-announcement-away-from-national-scripture-
sushma-swaraj/16757/ (accessed 18 December 2022).

209. See generally Amit Bhaduri and Deepak Nayyar, *The Intelligent Person's
Guide to Liberalization* (New Delhi: Penguin, 1996); Arundhati Roy,
Capitalism: A Ghost Story (London: Verso, 2015); Montek S. Ahluwalia,
Deepak Nayyar and Prabhat Patnaik, *Quarter Century of Liberalisation in
India* (New Delhi: Oxford University Press, 2018).

210. There is a contradiction that emerges here in the narratives of the past that
the Hindu Right propagate. While on the one hand the Hindu Right claim
that Hindus are indigenous to India and casts Muslims and Christians as
outsiders, on the other hand, brahmins are portrayed as inheritors of the
Aryan race. To make this latter argument, the Hindu Right has produced a
whole gamut of mythical arguments—'mythistory' and 'pseudoarcheology'—
that are passed off as historical and scientific claims against what has been
called the Aryan invasion theory that considers Aryans to be outsiders to
the South Asian region (thus, Hindus not being indigenous) who
manufactured the fiction of caste to oppress and colonise the Dravidians
who were the original inhabitants of the landmass that has later come to be
called India. Thus, as many like B. R. Ambedkar have argued, caste is at the
foundation of the idea of the Hindu *rashtra*. This dynamic has immense
bearing on the ways in which Hindutva politics consolidated its cultural
might through the demolition of the Babri Mosque in the name of Ram.
Cynthia Ann Humes, 'Hindutva, Mythistory, and Pseudoarcheology',
Numen 59, nos. 2–3 (2012): 178–201; Arvind Sharma, 'Dr B. R. Ambedkar
on the Aryan Invasion and the Emergence of the Caste System in India',
Journal of the American Academy of Religion 73, no. 3 (2005): 843–70; Ashish
Kumar, 'Aryans versus Non-Aryans: A Study of Dalit Narratives of India's
Ancient Past', *Contemporary Voice of Dalit* 10, no. 2 (2018): 127–37.

211. See Dhirendra K. Jha and Krishna Jha, *Ayodhya: The Dark Night* (New
Delhi: HarperCollins, 2016); Noorani, *Destruction of the Babri Masjid*. The
mosque was demolished on 6 December 1992, which tragically coincided
with the 36th death anniversary of B. R. Ambedkar, chairperson of the
drafting committee of the Constitution of India and a revolutionary leader
of the anti-caste movement. In a tract titled *Pakistan or the Partition of India*
published in 1940, Ambedkar offered a searing critique of Hindutva
ideology: 'If Hindu Raj does become a fact, it will, no doubt, be the greatest

calamity for this country. No matter what the Hindus say, Hinduism is a menace to liberty, equality and fraternity. On that account it is incompatible with democracy. Hindu Raj must be prevented at any cost.' It is necessary to note here that at the time that Ambedkar wrote this, he considered the INC to be as much a vehicle for establishing Hindu Raj as the BJP is today. For Ambedkar, the distinction between the progressive Hindu as secular and the conservative Hindu as communal was a false one because both contributed to the strengthening of brahminism. In other words, Hindu Raj is equivalent to Brahmin Raj, irrespective of the ideological proclivities of the political party in question. B. R. Ambedkar, *Pakistan or the Partition of India* (Bombay: Thackers Publishers, 1940), http://www.columbia.edu/itc/mealac/pritchett/00ambedkar/ambedkar_partition/index.html (accessed 18 December 2022). For an analysis of how the story of the Ramayana has been politicised by the Hindu Right to lay its claim to Ram's birthplace in Ayodhya, by arguing without any historical veracity that 'Rama is an immemorial object for worship basic to Hinduism, and this worship was being impeded by the presence of a mosque', see Sheldon Pollock, 'Ramayana and Political Imagination in India', *Journal of Asian Studies* 52, no. 2 (1993): 261.

212. For a detailed analysis of the work of the Archeological Survey of India in a different context that has profound bearings on its excavations at the site of the Babri Mosque in Ayodhya and what evidentiary value it carried in the court proceedings to determine whether 'a monumental Hindu temple complex existed under the medieval mosque', see Ashish Avikunthak, *Bureaucratic Archeology: State, Science and Past in Postcolonial India* (New Delhi: Cambridge University Press, 2021), xiv–xvii.

213. See Ratna Kapur, 'The "Ayodhya" Case: Hindu Majoritarianism and the Right to Religious Liberty', *Maryland Journal of International Law* 29 (2014): 305; Deepak Mehta, 'The Ayodhya Dispute: The Absent Mosque, State of Emergency and the Jural Deity', *Journal of Material Culture* 20, no. 4 (2015): 397; Amit Bindal, '"Complete Justice"? Silences and Erasures in the Ayodhya Judgment', *Journal of Indian Law and Society* 11, no. 1 (2020): 48. The judgment of the Supreme Court of India that is of relevance here is *M. Siddiq v. Mahant Suresh Das and others*, Civil Appeal Nos. 10866–0867 of 2010, Supreme Court of India (2019), https://indiankanoon.org/doc/107745042/ (accessed 18 December 2022). In the context of this judgment, Peter Goodrich offers a way to consider its implication from a law and literature perspective:

Can the earth bring a law suit, can dirt, *humus*, be recognized as a legal person? … In the case of Lord Ram there was only the testimony of the earth and the claim that close to half a millennium ago the site had been home to reliquaries and ceremonies that celebrated the birthplace of the deity. (Peter Goodrich, *Advanced Introduction to Law and Literature* [Cheltenham: Edward Elgar, 2021] 37; emphasis in original)

214. Zeeshan Shaikh, 'Mumbai Riots 1992: Srikrishna Commission Report and Action Taken', *Indian Express*, 6 December 2017, https://indianexpress.com/article/india/babri-masjid-demolition-mumbai-riots-1992-srikrishna-commission-report-and-action-taken-4970003/ (accessed 18 December 2022).

215. See generally Nivedita Menon and Aditya Nigam, *Power and Contestation: India since 1989* (London: Zed Books, 2007); Sukumar Muralidharan, 'Mandal, Mandir aur Masjid: "Hindu" Communalism and the Crisis of the State', *Social Scientist* 18, no. 10 (1990): 27–49.

216. Jaffrelot, 'What "Gujarat Model"?'; Sruthi Muraleedharan, 'Narendra Modi's "Gujarat Model": Re-moulding Development in the Service of Religious Nationalism', *Commonwealth and Comparative Politics*, 14 May 2023, https://www.tandfonline.com/doi/citedby/10.1080/14662043.2023.2203997?scroll=top&needAccess=true&role=tab&aria-labelledby=cit (accessed 17 May 2023).

217. Accompanying this turn has been a demonstration of legalism, where the state is always in a mode of legislative overdrive in response to demands from activists and social movements, where rights are doled out as a way to show how people friendly the state is. See Oishik Sircar, 'Spectacles of Emancipation: Reading Rights Differently in India's Legal Discourse', *Osgoode Hall Law Journal* 49, no. 3 (2012): 527; Suresh and Narrain, *The Shifting Scales of Justice*; Paul O'Connell, 'The Death of Socio-economic Rights', *Modern Law Review* 74, no. 4 (2011): 532; Ritu Birla, 'Jurisprudence of Emergence: Neo-liberalism and the Public as Market in India', *South Asia: Journal of South Asian Studies* 38, no. 3 (2015): 466; Sanjay Ruparelia, 'India's New Rights Agenda: Genesis, Promises, Risks', *Pacific Affairs* 86, no. 3 (2013): 569–90.

218. See generally Maya Ranganathan and Usha M. Rodrigues (eds.), *Indian Media in a Globalised World* (New Delhi: Sage, 2010); K. Moti Gokulsingh and Wimal Dissanayake (eds.), *Popular Culture in a Globalised India*

(New Delhi: Routledge, 2009); Amir Ullah Khan and Bibek Debroy, 'Indian Economic Transition through Bollywood Eyes', Working Paper, August 2002, http://citeseerx.ist.psu.edu/viewdoc/download?doi=10.1.1.200.8312 &rep=rep1&type=pdf (accessed 18 December 2022).

219. See Christiane Brosius and Melissa Butcher (eds.), *Image Journeys: Audio-Visual Media and Cultural Change in India* (New Delhi: Sage, 1999).

220. See generally Leela Fernandes, *India's New Middle Class: Democratic Politics in an Era of Economic Reform* (Minneapolis: University of Minnesota Press, 2006); Christiane Brosius, *India's Middle Class: New Forms of Urban Leisure, Consumption and Prosperity* (New Delhi: Routledge, 2010); Anustup Basu, *Bollywood in the Age of New Media: The Geo-televisual Aesthetic* (Edinburgh: Edinburgh University Press, 2010); Raminder Kaur and Ajay J. Sinha (eds.), *Bollyworld: Popular Indian Cinema through a Transnational Lens* (New Delhi: Sage, 2005); Amit Rai, *Untimely Bollywood: Globalization and India's New Media Assemblage* (Durham: Duke University Press, 2009); Ingrid Therwath, '"Shining Indians": Diaspora and Exemplarity in Bollywood', *South Asia Multidisciplinary Academic Journal* 4 (2010), http://samaj.revues.org/3000; David J. Schaefer and Kavita Karan (eds.), *Bollywood and Globalization: The Global Power of Popular Hindi Cinema* (London: Routledge, 2013); Rini Bhattacharya Mehta and Rajeshwari V. Pandharipande (eds.), *Bollywood and Globalization: Indian Popular Cinema, Nation, and Diaspora* (Delhi: Anthem, 2011); Robina Mohammad, '*Phir Bhi Dil Hai Hindustani* (Yet the Heart Remains Indian): Bollywood, the "Homeland" Nation-State, and the Diaspora', *Society and Space* 25, no. 6 (2007): 1015.

221. See Arvind Rajagopal, *Politics after Television: Hindu Nationalism and the Reshaping of the Public in India* (Cambridge: Cambridge University Press, 2001); Anirudh Deshpande, *Class, Power and Consciousness in Indian Cinema and Television* (Delhi: Primus, 2009).

222. See Sudeep Dasgupta, 'Gods in the Sacred Marketplace: Hindu Nationalism and the Return of the Aura in the Public Sphere', in *Religion, Media, and the Public Sphere*, ed. Birgit Meyer and Annelies Moors (Bloomington: Indiana University Press, 2005), 251–72.

223. See Sanjeev Kumar H. M., 'Constructing the Nation's Enemy: Hindutva, Popular Culture and the Muslim "Other" in Bollywood Cinema', *Third World Quarterly* 34, no. 3 (2013): 458; Sanjeev Kumar H. M., 'Metonymies of Fear: Islamophobia and the Making of Muslim Identity in Hindi Cinema', *Society and Culture in South Asia* 2, no. 2 (2016): 233; Ananya

Jahanara Kabir, 'The Kashmiri as Muslim in Bollywood's "New Kashmir Films"', *Contemporary South Asia* 18, no. 4 (2010): 373.

224. See Nandini Bhattacharya, 'Romancing Religion: Neoliberal Bollywood's Gendered Visual Repertoire for a Pain-Free Globalisation', in *Tracing an Indian Diaspora: Contexts, Memories, Representations* ed. Parvati Raghuram, Ajaya Kumar Sahoo, Brij Maharaj and Dave Sangha (New Delhi: Sage, 2008); Meheli Sen, '"It's All about Loving Your Parents": Liberalization, Hindutva and Bollywood's New Fathers', in *Bollywood and Globalization*, ed. Mehta and Pandharipande, 145.

225. See Rachel Dwyer, 'The Saffron Screen? Hindu Nationalism and the Hindi Film', in *Religion, Media, and the Public Sphere*, ed. Birgit Meyer and Annelies Moors (Bloomington: Indiana University Press, 2005), 273–89; Narinderjit Kaur Dhillon and Joel Gwynne, 'Saffronizing Bollywood Cinema: The Good Indian and the Muslim Threat', *Film International* 12, no. 2 (2014): 47.

226. See generally Shoba Sharad Rajgopal, 'Bollywood and Neonationalism: The Emergence of Nativism as the Norm in Indian Conventional Cinema', *South Asian Popular Culture* 9, no. 3 (2011): 237; Madhavi Murty, 'Representing Hindutva: Nation, Religion and Masculinity in Indian Popular Cinema, 1990 to 2003', *Popular Communication* 7, no. 4 (2009): 267; Sikata Banerjee, *Gender, Nation and Popular Film in India: Globalizing Muscular Nationalism* (New York: Routledge, 2016).

227. See Bhavya Dore, 'The Player: Akshay Kumar's Role as Hindutva's Poster Boy', *The Caravan*, 31 January 2021, https://caravanmagazine.in/reportage/akshay-kumar-role-hindutva-poster-boy (accessed 18 December 2022); Kamayani Sharma, 'Supporting Role: How Bollywood Acted under the Modi Government', *The Caravan*, 1 April 2019, https://caravanmagazine.in/perspective/how-bollywood-acted-under-modi-government (accessed 18 December 2022); Nivedita Menon, 'Hindu Rashtra and Bollywood: A New Front in the Battle for Cultural Hegemony', *South Asia Multidisciplinary Academic Journal* 24, no 25 (2020), https://journals.openedition.org/samaj/6846; Samanth Subramanian, 'When the Hindu Right Came for Bollywood', *New Yorker*, 10 October 2022, https://www.newyorker.com/magazine/2022/10/17/when-the-hindu-right-came-for-bollywood (accessed 18 May 2023); Aathira Konnikkara, 'The Warrior Queen: Kangana Ranaut's Role in the BJP's Battle for Bollywood', *The Caravan*, 1 June 2022, https://caravanmagazine.in/film/kangana-ranaut-role-in-bjp-

battle-for-bollywood (accessed 18 May 2023); Rana Ayyub, 'Why an Indian Film's Success at the Box Office Should Worry Us All', *Washington Post*, 15 November 2021, https://www.washingtonpost.com/opinions/2021/11/15/why-an-indian-films-success-box-office-should-worry-us-all/ (accessed 18 May 2023).

228. Stefan Machura, Stefan Ulbrich, Francis M. Nevins and Nils Behling, 'Law in Film: Globalizing the Hollywood Courtroom Drama', *Journal of Law and Society* 28, no. 1 (2001): 117.

229. See generally Apar Gupta, 'Tareek par tareek: Indian Lawyers in Popular Hindi Cinema', *Journal of Indian Law and Society* 2 (Winter 2010): 1.

230. See Michael H. Hoffheimer, 'Bollywood Law: Commercial Hindi Films with Legal Themes', *Law Library Journal* 98, no. 1 (2006): 61.

231. See generally Priya Kumar, 'Islamic Terrorism and Visions of Justice', in *Cinema, Law, and the State in Asia*, ed. C. Creekmur and M. Sidel (New York: Palgrave Macmillan, 2007), 63–82; Sujala Singh, 'Terror, Spectacle and the Secular State in Bombay Cinema', in *Terror and the Postcolonial: A Concise Companion*, ed. Elleke Boehmer and Stephen Morton (Chichester: Wiley-Blackwell, 2009), 345–60; Sweta Kaushal, '*Jolly LLB, Damini, Pink, Court* and More: Bollywood's 10 Best Courtroom Dramas', *Hindustan Times*, 27 February 2017, https://www.hindustantimes.com/bollywood/jolly-llb-damini-pink-court-and-more-bollywood-s-10-best-courtroom-drama/story-IYTPwv776wbs64bbNTwreJ.html-state (accessed 18 December 202); Lata Jha, 'Ten Bollywood Courtroom Dramas', *LiveMint*, 19 September 2016, https://www.livemint.com/Leisure/my1ffkZY8BmZVTlZAQi9ML/Ten-Bollywood-courtroom-dramas.html (accessed 18 December 2022).

232. Patrick Olivelle (ed. and trans.), *A Dharma Reader: Classical Indian Law* (New York: Columbia University Press, 2017).

233. See generally Sheila J. Nayar, 'Dreams, Dharma, and *Mrs Doubtfire*: Exploring Hindi Popular Cinema via Its "Chutneyed" Western Scripts', *Journal of Popular Film and Television* 31, no. 2 (2003): 73; Michael H. Hoffheimer, '*Awāra* and the Post-colonial Origins of the Hindi Law Drama', *Historical Journal of Film, Radio and Television* 26, no. 3 (2006): 341; Goldie Osuri, '"Ma" and a Political Theology of Hindi Cinema', *Theory, Culture and Society* 31, nos. 7–8 (2014): 343.

234. See William Mazzarella, *Censorium: Cinema and the Open Edge of Mass Publicity* (Durham: Duke University Press, 2013); Raminder Kaur and

William Mazzarella (eds.), *Censorship in South Asia: Cultural Regulation from Sedition to Seduction* (Bloomington: Indiana University Press, 2009); Someswar Bhowmik, *Cinema and Censorship: The Politics of Control in India* (New Delhi: Orient BlackSwan, 2009); Liang, Suresh and Malhotra, *The Public Is Watching*.

235. See Nandana Bose, 'The Hindu Right and the Politics of Censorship: Three Case Studies of Policing Hindi Cinema, 1992–2002', *Velvet Light Trap* 63 (Spring 2009): 22; Ratna Kapur, 'Too Hot to Handle: The Cultural Politics of Fire', *Feminist Review* 64, no. 1 (2000): 53; Rajeev Dhavan, *Publish and Be Damned: Censorship and Intolerance in India* (New Delhi: Tulika, 2008); Lawrence Liang, 'Censorship and the Politics of Micro-fascism', *Television and New Media* 16, no. 4 (2015): 388; Malvika Maheshwari, *Art Attacks: Violence and Offer-Taking in India* (New Delhi: Oxford University Press, 2018).

236. See generally Lakshmi Srinivas, 'Active Viewing: An Ethnography of the Indian Film Audience', *Visual Anthropology* 11, no. 4 (1998): 323; Lawrence Liang, 'Jana Gana Mana and the Danger of Passing Sentiment as Law', *The Wire*, 1 December 2016, https://thewire.in/83606/jana-gana-mana-dangers-passing-sentiment-law/?fromNewsdog=1 (accessed 18 December 2022); Arun Sagar, 'Law, Honour, Violence: The Supreme Court's Legal and Non-legal Voice', *Indian Law Review* 2, no. 2 (2018): 119–34.

237. Krishnadas Rajagopal, 'National Anthem Must Be Played before Screening of Films: Supreme Court', *The Hindu*, 30 November 2016, https://www.thehindu.com/news/national/National-anthem-must-be-played-before-screening-of-films-Supreme-Court/article16729264.ece (accessed 18 December 2022); Krishnadas Rajagopal, 'SC Modifies Order, Says Playing of National Anthem in Cinema Halls Is Not Mandatory', *The Hindu*, 9 January 2018, https://www.thehindu.com/news/national/sc-modifies-order-says-national-anthem-not-mandatory/article22403095.ece (accessed 18 December 2022).

238. *Indian Express*, 'A "Pakistani" Is Here: Wheelchair-Bound Man Abused for Sitting during National Anthem in Guwahati Theatre', 2 October 2017, https://indianexpress.com/article/india/arman-ali-disabled-man-called-pakistani-on-not-standing-up-for-national-anthem-in-guwahati-4871021/ (accessed 18 December 2022).

239. In the current moment, this statement requires some qualification, given the ways in which the Modi government has been using the cinematic

apparatuses of the Bollywood film industry as a means for its political propaganda. The recent support from the BJP, including the prime minister, to the films *The Kashmir Files* and *The Kerala Story* are cases in point. In fact, a scene in the film *The Kashmir Files* intensified anti-Muslim violence in Khargone in 2022. See Sanjay Kak, 'The Dangerous "Truth" of The Kashmir Files', *Aljazeera*, 13 April 2022, https://www.aljazeera.com/opinions/2022/4/13/the-dangerous-truth-of-the-kashmiri-files (accessed 18 May 2023); Rana Ayyub, 'I Tried Watching "The Kashmir Files." I Left the Theatre to Screams of "Go to Pakistan."', *Washington Post*, 29 March 2022, https://www.washingtonpost.com/opinions/2022/03/29/india-movie-kashmir-files-screams-go-to-pakistan/ (accessed 18 May 2023); Soumya Rajendran, 'The Kerala Story Review: A No-Nuance Propaganda Film That Thrives on Shock Value', *News Minute*, 5 May 2023, https://www.thenewsminute.com/article/kerala-story-review-no-nuance-propaganda-film-thrives-shock-value-176794 (accessed 18 May 2023); Supriya Sharma, 'How "Kashmir Files" Added to Communal Fires in Khargone That Ended with Bulldozer Injustice', *Scroll.in*, 29 April 2022, https://scroll.in/article/1022860/how-kashmir-files-added-to-communal-fires-in-khargone-that-ended-with-bulldozer-injustice (accessed 18 May 2023).

240. See Ashvin Immanuel Devasundaram, *India's New Independent Cinema: Rise of the Hybrid* (New York: Routledge, 2016); K. P. Jayasankar and Anjali Monteiro, *A Fly in the Curry: Independent Documentary Film in India* (New Delhi: Sage, 2016); Kasturi Basu and Dwaipayan Banerjee (eds.), *Towards a People's Cinema: Independent Documentary and Its Audience in India* (Gurgaon: Three Essays Collective, 2018); Ashish Rajadyaksha, *John–Ghatak–Tarkovsky: Citizens, Filmmakers, Hackers* (New Delhi: Tulika, 2023).

241. Vijay Mishra, 'Spectres of Sentimentality: The Bollywood Film', *Textual Practice* 23, no. 3 (2009): 439.

242. Ravi Vasudevan, *The Melodramatic Public: Film Form and Spectatorship in Indian Cinema* (New York: Palgrave Macmillan, 2011); Karen Gabriel, *Melodrama and the Nation: Sexual Economies of Bombay Cinema, 1970–2000* (New Delhi: Women Unlimited, 2010).

243. Sangita Gopal and Sujata Moorti (eds.), *Global Bollywood: Travels of Hindi Song and Dance* (Minneapolis: University of Minnesota Press, 2008); Vijay Mishra, 'The Aching Joys of Bollywood Song and Dance', *Postcolonial Studies* 12, no. 2 (2009): 247.

244. Bhaskar Sarkar, *Mourning the Nation: Indian Cinema in the Wake of Partition* (Durham: Duke University Press, 2009).

245. Daya Kishan Thussu, 'Infotainment Inc.', in *Media Perspectives for the 21st Century* ed. Stylianos Papathanassopoulos (New York: Routledge, 2010), 68–82.

246. Daya Kishan Thussu, *News as Entertainment: The Rise of Global Infotainment* (London: Sage, 2009), 91–112.

247. See Natalie Zemon Davis, '"Any Resemblance to Persons Living or Dead": Film and the Challenge of Authenticity', *Historical Journal of Film, Radio and Television* 8, no. 3 (1988): 269.

248. See Rina Ramdev, Sandhya D. Nambiar and Debaditya Bhattacharya (eds.), *Sentiment, Politics, Censorship: The State of Hurt* (New Delhi: Sage, 2016).

249. Leam Grealy, 'Challenging the Censor: An Interview with Indian Political Documentarian Rakesh Sharma', *Bright Lights Film Journal*, 2 December 2016, https://brightlightsfilm.com/challenging-censor-interview-indian-political-documentarian-rakesh-sharma/#.YgPdjurMLEZ (accessed 18 December 2022).

250. See generally M. Madhava Prasad, *Ideology of the Hindi Film: A Historical Construction* (New Delhi: Oxford University Press, 2008); Ashish Rajadhyaksha, *Indian Cinema in the Time of Celluloid: From Bollywood to the Emergency* (New Delhi: Tulika, 2009); M. K. Raghavendra, *Seduced by the Familiar: Narration and Meaning in Indian Popular Cinema* (New Delhi: Oxford University Press, 2015); Ravi Vasudevan (ed.), *Making Meaning in Indian Cinema* (New Delhi: Oxford University Press, 2001); Ranjani Mazumdar, *Bombay Cinema: An Archive of the City* (Minneapolis: University of Minnesota Press, 2007); Jyotika Virdi, *The Cinematic ImagiNation: Indian Popular Films as Social History* (New Brunswick: Rutgers University Press, 2003); Vinay Lal and Ashis Nandy (eds.), *Fingerprinting Popular Culture: The Mythic and the Iconic in Indian Cinema* (New Delhi: Oxford University Press, 2006); Tejaswini Ganti, *Producing Bollywood: Inside the Contemporary Hindi Film Industry* (Durham: Duke University Press, 2012); William Elison, Christian Lee Novetzke and Andy Rotman, *Amar Akbar Anthony: Bollywood, Brotherhood, and the Nation* (Cambridge: Harvard University Press, 2016); Vijay Mishra, *Bollywood Cinema: Temples of Desire* (New York: Routledge, 2013); Shyam Benegal, 'Secularism and Popular Indian Cinema', in *The Crisis of Secularism in India*, ed. Anuradha Dingwaney Needham and Rajeshwari Sunder Rajan (Ranikhet: Permanent Black, 2007), 225–38.

251. Some gestures in this direction are available in the following works: Alka Kurian, *Narratives of Gendered Dissent in South Asian Cinemas* (New York: Routledge, 2014), 63–97; Sunera Thobani, 'Performing Terror, Mediating

Religion: Indian Cinema and the Politics of National Belonging', *International Journal of Communication* 8 (2014): 483; Sisir Basu, 'The Tragedy of Gujarat 2002 Haunts', in *Experiments in Film Appreciation* ed. Sisir Basu, Alessandro Monti and Carole Rozzonelli (Torino: New Dost Edition, 2012), 5–16; Nirmala Menon and Reema Chowdhary, 'Muslim Identity and Representation in Deepa Mehta's *Earth* and Abhishek Kapur's *Kai Po Che*', *Postcolonial Text* 11, no. 2 (2016), http://postcolonial.univ-paris13.fr/index.php/pct/article/viewArticle/2036.

252. See Joachim J. Savelsberg and Ryan D. King, 'Law and Collective Memory', *Annual Review of Law and Social Science* 3 (December 2007): 189; Susanne Karstedt (ed.), *Legal Institutions and Collective Memories* (London: Bloomsbury, 2009); Mark Osiel, *Mass Atrocity, Collective Memory, and the Law* (New Brunswick: Transaction, 1999).

253. See Urvashi Butalia, *The Other Side of Silence: Voices from the Partition of India* (Durham: Duke University Press, 2000); Ritu Menon and Kamla Bhasin, *Borders and Boundaries: Women in India's Partition* (New Delhi: Kali for Women, 2007); Aanchal Malhotra, *Remnants of a Separation: A History of the Partition through Material Memory* (New Delhi: HarperCollins, 2017); Pippa Virdee, 'Remembering Partition: Women, Oral Histories and the Partition of 1947', *Oral History* 41, no. 2 (2013): 49; Deepti Misri, 'The Violence of Memory: Renarrating Partition Violence in Shauna Singh Baldwin's *What the Body Remembers*', *Meridiens* 11, no. 1 (2011): 1.

254. See Veena Das, *Life and Words: Violence and the Descent into the Ordinary* (Berkeley: University of California Press, 2006); Darshan S. Tatla, 'The Morning After: Trauma, Memory and the Sikh Predicament since 1984', *Sikh Formations: Religion, Culture, Theory* 2, no. 1 (2006): 57; Radhika Chopra, '1984: Disinterred Memories', *Sikh Formations: Religion, Culture, Theory* 11, no. 3 (2015): 306.

255. See Roma Chatterji and Deepak Mehta, *Living with Violence: An Anthropology of Events and Everyday Life* (New Delhi: Routledge, 2007); Sameena Dalwai, Ramu Ramanathan and Irfan Engineer (eds.), *Babri Masjid, 25 Years On* (New Delhi: Kalpaz, 2018).

256. A notable exception is Heba Ahmed, 'The Gulbarg Memorial and the Problem of Memory', in *Partition and the Practice of Memory*, ed. Churnjeet Mahn and Anne Murphy (Cham: Palgrave Macmillan, 2018), 175–210; see also Nida Kirmani, 'History, Memory and Localised Constructions of Insecurity', *Economic and Political Weekly* 43, no. 10 (2008): 57.

257. See generally Kavita Daiya, *Violent Belongings: Partition, Gender, and National Culture in Postcolonial India* (Philadelphia: Temple University Press, 2011); Jayson Beaster-Jones and Natalie Sarrazin (eds.), *Music in Contemporary Indian Film: Memory, Voice, Identity* (New York; London: Routledge, 2016); Jisha Menon, *The Performance of Nationalism: India, Pakistan, and the Memory of Partition* (Cambridge: Cambridge University Press, 2013), 54–85; Rini Bhattacharya Mehta and Debali Mookerjea-Leonard (eds.), *The Indian Partition in Literature and Films: History, Politics, and Aesthetics* (New York: Routledge, 2014); Gurmukh Singh, 'Representations of the 1984 Tragedy in Punjabi Cinema: Ideology and Cultural Politics', *Sikh Formations: Religion, Culture, Theory* 11, no. 3 (2015): 418.

258. For two notable exceptions, see Anuj Bhuwania, 'Black Friday: Mediation and the Impossibility of Justice', Working Paper Series CSLG/WP/17, Centre for the Study of Law and Governance, Jawaharlal Nehru University, New Delhi, November 2012, https://www.jnu.ac.in/sites/default/files/u63/17-Black%20%28Anuj%29.pdf (accessed 18 December 2022); Upendra Baxi, *Memory and Rightlessness* (New Delhi: Centre for Women's Development Studies, 2003).

259. Maurice Halbwachs, *On Collective Memory* (Chicago: University of Chicago Press, 1992), 38.

260. Jeffrey K. Olick, *The Politics of Regret: On Collective Memory and Historical Responsibility* (New York: Routledge, 2007), 20 (emphasis added).

261. Benedict Anderson, *Imagined Communities: Reflections on the Origin and Spread of Nationalism* (London: Verso, 2016), 14; Sumitra S. Chakravarty, *National Identity in Indian Popular Cinema, 1947–1987* (Austin: University of Texas Press, 1993), 11.

262. As Michael Warner writes:

> Each time we address a public ... we draw on what seems like simple common sense. If we did not have a practical sense of what publics are, if we could not oneself-consciously take them for granted as really existing and addressable social entities, we could not produce most of the books or films or broadcasts or journals [or laws] that make up so much of our culture; we could not conduct elections or indeed imagine ourselves as members of nations or movements. Yet, publics exist only by virtue of their imagining. They are a kind of fiction that has taken on life, and very potent life at that. (Michael Warner, *Publics and Counter Publics* [New York: Zone Books, 2005], 8.)

263. 'What is an assemblage? It is a multiplicity which is made up of many heterogeneous terms and which establishes liaisons, relations between them.... Thus, the assemblage's only unity is that of a co-functioning: it is a symbiosis....' Gilles Deleuze and Claire Parnet, *Dialogues II* (New York: Columbia University Press, 2007), 69.

264. See Edward Mussawir, 'The Cinematics of Jurisprudence', *Law and Literature* 17, no. 1 (2005): 131.

265. John Berger, *Ways of Seeing* (London: Penguin, 1972), 8.

Chapter 2

1. Peter Goodrich, 'Law by Other Means', *Cardozo Studies in Law and Literature* 10, no. 2 (1998): 111, 114.

2. For a discussion distinguishing 'approach' from 'method', see Alan Hunt, 'The Critique of Law: What Is "Critical" about Critical Legal Theory', *Journal of Law and Society* 14, no. 1 (1987): 13.

3. Douzinas and Gearey, *Critical Jurisprudence*, 5.

4. Ibid.

5. See Richard Delgado, 'The Inward Turn in Outsider Jurisprudence', *William and Mary Law Review* 34, no. 3 (1993): 741; Francisco Valdes, 'Outsider Jurisprudence, Critical Pedagogy and Social Justice Activism: Marking the Stirrings of Critical Legal Education', *Asian American Law Journal* 10, no. 1 (2003): 65.

6. Franz Kafka, *The Trial*, trans. Breon Mitchell (New York: Schocken, 1998).

7. The parable has been a text widely referred to in critical legal, and law and literature scholarship. See Douglas E. Litowitz, 'Review: Franz Kafka's Outsider Jurisprudence', *Law and Social Inquiry* 27, no. 1 (2002): 103; Edward Mussawir, 'The Trial', in *An Aesthetics of Law and Culture*, ed. Rush and Kenyon, 111–31.

8. Franz Kafka, 'Before the Law', trans. Ian Johnston, *Franz Kafka Online: The Works and Life of Franz Kafka*, http://www.kafka-online.info/before-the-law.html (accessed 18 December 2022).

9. Davies, *Asking the Law Question*, 14, 21 (emphasis in original). Davies, of course, goes on to offer a critique of this position, which is primarily attributed to the work of H. L. A. Hart.

10. Andreas Philippopoulos-Mihalopoulos, 'Atmospheres of Law: Senses, Affects, Lawscapes', *Emotion Space Society* 7 (May 2013): 2 (emphasis in original).

11. See Shaunnagh Dorsett and Shaun McVeigh, *Jurisdiction* (London: Routledge-Cavendish, 2012).

12. Kafka, 'Before the Law'.

13. Sundhya Pahuja, 'Laws of Encounter: A Jurisdictional Account of International Law', *London Review of International Law* 1, no. 1 (2013): 63–98.

14. See generally Douzinas and Gearey, *Critical Jurisprudence*; Davies, *Law Unlimited*.

15. There are multiple ways of theorising and understanding minor jurisprudence. For two surveys, see Antaki, 'Making Sense of Minor Jurisprudence'; Christopher Tomlins, '"Law As …" III—*Glossolalia*: Toward a Minor (Historical) Jurisprudence', *UC Irvine Law Review* 5, no. 2 (2015): 239.

16. Peter Goodrich, *Law in the Courts of Love: Literature and Other Minor Jurisprudences* (London: Routledge, 1996), 2.

17. Ian Christie, 'Heavenly Justice', in *Law's Moving Image*, ed. Leslie J. Moran, Elena Loizidou, Ian Christie and Emma Sandon (New York: Glass House Press, 2004), 3.

18. Hans Kelsen, *Pure Theory of Law* (Berkeley: University of California Press, 1967).

19. H. L. A. Hart, *The Concept of Law* (Oxford: Oxford University Press, 2012).

20. Lon Fuller, *The Morality of Law*, rev. ed. (New Haven: Yale University Press, 1965).

21. The recourse to legal pluralism as the logical outcome of secularism poses particular difficulties. This is in the case of both the origins of legal pluralism in colonial forms of governance and in postcolonial India, especially for Muslim women. See generally Vrinda Narain, 'Law, Gender, Nation: Muslim Women and the Discontents of Legal Pluralism in India', in *Islam, Gender and Democracy in Comparative Perspective*, ed. Jocelyne Cesari and José Casanova (New York: Oxford University Press, 2017), 188–210; Shaunnagh Dorsett and Ian Hunter (eds.), *Law and Politics in British Colonial Thought: Transpositions of Empire* (New York: Palgrave, 2010).

22. Gilles Deleuze and Felix Guattari, 'What Is an Assemblage?', in *Kafka: Toward a Minor Literature* (Minneapolis: University of Minnesota Press, 1986), 81.

23. See Oren Ben-Dor, 'Standing before the Gates of the Law?', in *Law and Art: Ethics, Aesthetics, Justice*, ed. Oren Ben-Dor (London: Routledge-Cavendish, 2011) 1–29.

24. Basu, *Bollywood in the Age of New Media*, 12.

25. Peter Goodrich, *Languages of Law: From Logics of Memory to Nomadic Masks* (London: Weidenfeld, 1990), vii.

26. Cornelia Vismann, *Files: Law and Media Technology* (Stanford: Stanford University Press, 2008).

27. See Barbara A. Misztal, *Theories of Social Remembering* (Maidenhead: McGraw-Hill Education, 2003).

28. See Jothie Rajah, 'Law as Record: The Death of Osama bin Laden', *No Foundations: An Interdisciplinary Journal of Law and Justice* 13 (2016): 45; Fleur Johns, Richard Joyce and Sundhya Pahuja (eds.), *Events: The Force of International Law* (New York: Routledge-Cavendish, 2010).

29. See Espen Ytreberg, 'Towards a Historical Understanding of the Media Event', *Media, Culture and Society* 39, no. 3 (2016): 309.

30. See Mehta, 'Modi and the Camera'; Jain, 'Beaming It Live'.

31. See Richard K. Sherwin, *When Law Goes Pop: The Vanishing Line between Law and Popular Culture* (Chicago: University of Chicago Press, 2000).

32. See Jessica Silbey, 'Persuasive Visions: Film and Memory', *Law, Culture and the Humanities* 10, no. 1 (2014): 24; Michelle Brown and Nicole Rafter, 'Genocide Films, Public Criminology, Collective Memory', *British Journal of Criminology* 53, no. 6 (2013): 1017.

33. Jan Assman, *Moses the Egyptian: The Memory of Egypt in Western Monotheism* (Cambridge: Harvard University Press, 1997), 14.

34. Ibid.

35. For a discussion on conceptual distinctions and similarities between these terms, see Brass, *Forms of Collective Violence*; Paul R. Brass (ed.), *Riots and Pogroms* (London: Macmillan, 1996).

36. Ghassem-Fachandi, *Pogrom in Gujarat*, 1.

37. Ibid., 76–77.

38. Maksymilian Del Mar, 'The Legal Imagination', *Aeon*, 28 March 2017, https://aeon.co/essays/why-judges-and-lawyers-need-imagination-as-much-as-rationality (accessed 18 December 2022). See also James Boyd White, *The Legal Imagination*, 2nd ed. (Chicago: University of Chicago Press, 1987).

39. Cornelia Vismann, 'Image and Law: A Troubled Relationship', *Parallax* 14, no. 4 (2008): 1.

40. Ibid.

41. Peter Goodrich, *Oedipus Lex: Psychoanalysis, History, Law* (Berkeley: University of California Press, 1995), x.

42. Costas Douzinas and Lynda Nead, 'Introduction', in *Law and the Image*, ed. Douzinas and Nead, 1–18, 1.

43. Ibid., 3.

44. Manderson, *Songs without Music*, 201.

45. Costas Douzinas, 'Law and Justice in Postmodernity', in *The Cambridge Companion to Postmodernism*, ed. Steven Connor (Cambridge: Cambridge University Press, 2004), 197.

46. Nicholas Mirzoeff, 'On Visuality', *Journal of Visual Culture* 5, no. 1 (2006): 53.

47. Peter Goodrich, 'Europe in America: Grammatology, Legal Studies, and the Politics of Transmission', *Columbia Law Review* 101, no. 8 (2001): 2033, 2035.

48. West, 'Jurisprudence as Narrative'.

49. Peter D. Rush and Andrew T. Kenyon, 'Alter Egos: The Mise-en-Scene of Law and Aesthetics', in *An Aesthetics of Law and Culture*, ed. Rush and Kenyon, 2–3.

50. Manderson, *Songs without Music*, ix.

51. Ibid.

52. The template for this is borrowed from Robert Weisberg's formulations of 'law-*as*-literature' and 'law-*in*-literature'. Robert Weisberg, 'The Law-Literature Enterprise', *Yale Journal of Law and the Humanities* 1, no. 1 (1989) (emphasis in original).

53. Raymond Williams, 'Structures of Feeling', in *Performance Analysis: An Introductory Coursebook*, ed. Colin Counsell and Laurie Wolf (New York: Psychology Press, 2001), 196.

54. See Simon O'Sullivan, 'The Aesthetics of Affect: Thinking Art beyond Representation', *Angelaki: Journal of the Theoretical Humanities* 6, no. 3 (2001): 125.

55. See Olson, 'The Turn to Passion'.

56. Sherwin, *Visualizing Law in the Age of Digital Baroque*, 3 (emphasis added).

57. Niall McCarthy, 'Bollywood: India's Film Industry by the Numbers', *Forbes*, 3 September 2014, https://www.forbes.com/sites/niallmccarthy/2014/09/03/bollywood-indias-film-industry-by-the-numbers-infographic/#1c4c5d7b2488 (accessed 18 December 2022); Marc Fetscherin, 'The Main Determinants of Bollywood Movie Box Office Sales', *Journal of Global Marketing* 23, no. 5 (2010): 461; Ganti, *Producing Bollywood*; Prasad, *Ideology of the Hindi Film*.

58. David M. Seymour, 'Film and Law: In Search of a Critical Method', in *Law's Moving Image*, ed. Moran, Loizidou, Christie and Sandon, 107.
59. Buchanan and Johnson, 'Strange Encounters'.
60. Gregory Flaxman, 'Once More, with Feeling: Cinema and Cinesthesia', *SubStance* 42, no. 3 (2016): 174.
61. Ibid.; Buchanan and Johnson, 'Strange Encounters', 39.
62. For one of the most authoritative discussions of the relationship between word and image, see W. J. T. Mitchell, *Iconology: Image, Text, Ideology* (Chicago: University of Chicago Press, 1986).
63. William P. MacNeil, *Lex Populi: The Jurisprudence of Popular Culture* (Stanford: Stanford University Press, 2007), 2.
64. William Twining, *General Jurisprudence: Understanding Law from a Global Perspective* (Cambridge: Cambridge University Press, 2009).
65. Austin Sarat, Lawrence Douglas and Martha Merrill Umphrey, 'On Film and Law: Broadening the Focus', in *Law on the Screen*, ed. Austin Sarat, Lawrence Douglas and Martha Merrill Umphrey (Stanford: Stanford University Press, 2005), 1–26, 1.
66. Richard K. Sherwin, 'Imagining Law as Film (Representation without Reference?)', in *Law and Humanities: An Introduction*, ed. Austin Sarat, Matthew Anderson and Cathrine O. Frank (Cambridge: Cambridge University Press, 2010), 241.
67. Silbey, 'Persuasive Visions', 26 (emphasis added).
68. Anthony Chase, *Movies on Trial: The Legal System on the Silver Screen* (New York: The New Press, 2002), xiii.
69. Alison Young, 'Murder in the Eyes of the Law', *Studies in Law, Politics and Society* 17 (1997): 31.
70. Philadelphoff-Puren and Rush, 'Fatal (F)laws', 211.
71. As far as I am aware, there are five other Bollywood films in which the pogrom features either centrally or marginally as part of their plots. These are *Chand Bujh Gaya* (2005), *Road to Sangam* (2009), *Firaaq* (2010), *Mausam* (2011) and *Rajdhani Express* (2013). Of these, *Chand Bujh Gaya* was involved in litigation to fight cuts demanded by the Central Board of Film Certification because the character of a minister in the film allegedly resembled Narendra Modi, and *Rajdhani Express* was taken to court by Qutubuddin Ansari, a pogrom victim-survivor, who alleged that the film used his photograph, which had turned him into the face of the violence, without his consent. *Firaaq* might not be considered an all-out Bollywood

film both with regard to the circulation channels its used as well as the form of its making. It was primarily screened at international film festivals and did modest business at the box office. For a discussion of *Firaaq* in the context of cinematic reconstructions of Gujarat 2002, see Oishik Sircar, 'Seductions of the Neoliberal Nation', *Himal Southasian*, 15 September 2013, https://www.himalmag.com/seductions-of-the-neoliberal-nation/ (accessed 18 December 2022).

72. *Dev*, directed by Govind Nihalani (Udbhav Productions, 2004); *Parzania*, directed by Rahul Dholakia (PVR Pictures, 2007); *Kai Po Che!*, directed by Abhishek Kapoor (UTV Motion Pictures, 2013).

73. 'Bollywood' does not carry a stable meaning. As M. Madhava Prasad writes:

> It is precisely the act of naming that is the most interesting aspect of Bollywood. It is a strange name, a hybrid, that seems to at once mock the thing it names and celebrate its difference.... Today, the term 'Bollywood' has become naturalized not only in the English-language media, which is probably the term's original habitat, but also the Indian-language press, not only among journalists but also film scholars. (M. Madhava Prasad, 'Surviving Bollywood', in *Global Bollywood*, ed. Anandam P. Kavoori and Aswin Punathambekar [New York: New York University Press, 2008], 41–51, 41)

74. Ashish Rajadhyaksha, 'The "Bollywoodization" of the Indian Cinema: Cultural Nationalism in a Global Arena', in *Global Bollywood*, ed. Kavoori and Punathambekar, 17–40, 20.

75. See Mishra, *Bollywood Cinema*; Tejaswini Ganti, *Bollywood: A Guide to Popular Hindi Cinema* (London: Routledge, 2013).

76. Prasad, *Ideology of the Hindi Film*, 9.

77. Rajadhyaksha, 'The "Bollywoodization" of the Indian Cinema', 29 (emphasis in original).

78. Prasad, 'Surviving Bollywood', 46.

79. Rajadhyaksha, 'The "Bollywoodization" of the Indian Cinema', 34.

80. Ibid., 35.

81. Liang, 'Cinematic Citizenship and the Illegal City'.

82. Rajadhyaksha, 'The "Bollywoodization" of the Indian Cinema', 33.

83. Ibid.

84. Ravi S. Vasudevan, 'Neither State nor Faith: The Transcendental Significance of the Cinema', in *The Crisis of Secularism in India*, ed. Anuradha Dingwaney

Needham and Rajeshwari Sunder Rajan (Ranikhet: Permanent Black, 2007), 243 (emphasis in original).

85. Susannah Radstone, 'Cinema and Memory', in *Memory: Histories, Theories, Debates*, ed. Susannah Radstone and Bill Shwarz (New York: Fordham University Press, 2010), 337.

86. One would notice this in the case of the Babri Masjid demolition and the Bombay riots of 1992 as well. I would think that the general public in India remembers the events through Mani Ratnam's feature film *Bombay* (1995) rather than through Anand Patwardhan's documentary films *Ram ke Naam* (1992), or *Father, Son and Holy War* (1995).

87. Aniruddha Dutta, 'Digitizing the National Imaginary: Technology and Hybridization in Hindi Film Songs of the Post-liberalization Period', in *Routledge Handbook of Indian Cinemas*, ed. K. Moti Gokulsingh and Wimal Dissanayake (London: Routledge, 2013), 231–45.

88. Ashis Nandy, 'Introduction: Indian Popular Cinema as a Slum's Eye View of Politics', in *The Secret Politics of Our Desires: Innocence, Culpability and Indian Popular Cinema*, ed. Ashis Nandy (London: Zed Books, 1999), 1 (emphasis in original).

89. Virdi, *The Cinematic ImagiNation*, xi.

90. Mazumdar, *Bombay Cinema*, xvii.

91. See Lloyd I. Rudolph and Susanne Hoeber Rudolph, *In Pursuit of Lakshmi: The Political Economy of the Indian State* (University of Chicago Press, 1987).

92. As mentioned in Chapter 1, the BJP's direct engagement with Bollywood is marking a sharp shift in the ways in which Hindutva ideology through the state apparatus is using Bollywood as its propaganda machine. See Samanth Subramanian, 'When the Hindu Right Came for Bollywood', *New Yorker*, 10 October 2022, https://www.newyorker.com/magazine/2022/10/17/when-the-hindu-right-came-for-bollywood (accessed 18 May 2023). Political intervention in Bollywood cinema, however, is not new and has precedents where the so-called secular Congress party tried to use the law to censor films that were critical of the role of Indira Gandhi and her ministers in the wake of the Emergency. Such censorship also included not permitting radio broadcast of songs by Kishore Kumar, a massively popular playback singer and actor, because he refused to perform at a Youth Congress event that was meant to raise funds for the party's disastrous forced sterilisation programme. An especially controversial film was *Kissa Kursi Kaa* (1978) which critiqued the role of the Congress party in the

context of the Emergency. The reels of the film were destroyed by Congress party politicians. This resulted in a particularly 'inadequate and unconvincing' judgment by the Supreme Court of India in *V. C. Shukla v. State (Delhi Administration)*—that seemed to side with the government in power—by setting aside the convictions of these politicians by a lower court. A.G. Noorani, 'Kissa Kursi Kaa Case', *Economic and Political Weekly* 15, nos. 24–25 (June 1980): 1067–74; Christopher Jaffrelot and Pratinav Anil, *India's First Dictatorship: The Emergency, 1975–1977* (New York: Oxford University Press, 2020), 61; *V. C. Shukla v. State (Delhi Administration)* 1980 AIR 1382, https://indiankanoon.org/doc/220229/ (accessed 27 May 2023). See generally Nandana Bose, '"We Do Not Certify Backwards": Film Censorship in Postcolonial India', in *Silencing Cinema: Film Censorship Around the World*, ed. Daniel Biltereyst and Roel Vande Winkel (New York: Palgrave Macmillan, 2013), 197, 204.

93. Saeed Akhtar Mirza, 'Outlook for the Cinema', *Social Scientist* 8, nos. 5–6 (December 1979–January 1980), 125. Also quoted in Prasad, *Ideology of the Hindi Film*, 1.

94. Ibid., 9.

95. Ibid.

96. Kalyanee Chadha and Anandam P. Kavoori, 'Exoticized, Marginalized, Demonized: The Muslim "Other" in Indian Cinema', in *Global Bollywood*, ed. Kavoori and Punathambekar, 131–45, 131.

97. Virdi, *The Cinematic ImagiNation*, 9.

98. Before the advent of Bollywood in its post-1991 avatar, 'the cinema of the post-independence period exhibited an investment in the capacity of the state to redress social injustice'. As Ravi S. Vasudevan has noted:

> This is observable in a host of films centered on a new engagement with criminality and its roots. The genre of the crime film assigned central significance to the bigoted exclusiveness of social hierarchies in determining attitudes of the marginal and dispossessed. The context was recurrently acknowledged by the police and in courts and law, where the transcendent equalizing imprimatur of the state is staged in film after film. (Vasudevan, 'Neither State nor Faith', 253)

99. Prasad, 'Surviving Bollywood', 47.

100. As Donald R. Davis, Jr, writes: *Dharmaśāstra* are 'a specific genre of text in the Sanskrit language' that 'contain Hindu jurisprudence, a way of thinking about law from a distinctively Hindu perspective'. Hindutva ideology has

historically drawn its inspiration from the *Dharmaśāstra*, among other classical Hindu legal texts. Donald R. Davis, Jr, *The Spirit of Hindu Law* (Oxford University Press, 2010), 12–13.

101. Basu, *Bollywood in the Age of New Media*, 3.
102. Ibid.
103. Sarat, Douglas and Umphrey, 'On Film and Law', 11.
104. Richard K. Sherwin, 'Anti-Oedipus, Lynch: Initiatory Rites and the Ordeal of Justice', in *Law on the Screen*, ed. Sarat, Douglas and Umphrey, 106–52, 106.
105. Silbey, 'Persuasive Visions', 31.
106. Tejaswini Niranjana, quoted in Liang, 'Cinematic Citizenship and the Illegal City', 372.
107. Ibid., 373.

Chapter 3

1. Ann Genovese, 'Critical Decision, 1982: Remembering Koowarta v Bjelke-Petersen', *Griffith Law Review* 23, no. 1 (2014): 1.
2. Philadelphoff-Puren and Rush, 'Fatal (F)laws', 211.
3. Manderson, *Songs without Music*, 42.
4. J. A. Cuddon, 'Trope', in *The Penguin Dictionary Literary Terms and Literary Theory* (London: Penguin Books, 1998), 24.
5. Regarding the work tropes perform in the formation of (legal) language, Goodrich quotes Friedrich Neitzsche: 'Tropes are not something which can be added or subtracted from language at will, they are its truest nature.' Peter Goodrich, *Legal Discourse: Studies in Linguistics, Rhetoric and Legal Analysis* (London: Palgrave Macmillan, 1987), 107, 110.
6. The connection between judicial decisions and memory is foundational to the organisation of the common law. As Peter Goodrich writes:

   Memory in the hands of the legal tradition is not an historical method but rather a technique of faith: through the recollection of previous instances of legal presence, through establishment of precedent, the law continuously rediscovers itself; it is made present to itself as *logos* or the world incarnate. Memory within such an internal history of a discipline is simply the witness of presence, the testimony of authority, the repetition of externally given truths. (Goodrich, *Languages of Law*, 51; emphasis added)

7. Shagufa Kapadia, *Adolescence in Urban India: Cultural Construction in a Society in Transition* (New Delhi: Springer, 2017), 60.

8. 'Vadodara City Census 2011 Data', Census 2011, http://www.census2011. co.in/census/city/338-vadodara.html (accessed 18 December 2022).

9. Ruhi Tewari and Abhishek Mishra, 'Every Second ST, Every Third Dalit and Muslim in India Poor, Not Just Financially: UN Report', *The Print*, 12 July 2019, https://theprint.in/india/every-second-st-every-third-dalit-muslim-in-india-poor-not-just-financially-un-report/262270/ (accessed 18 December 2022).

10. Sourjya Bhowmick, 'Census 2011: India's Muslims Are No Better Today Than a Few Decades Earlier', *Catchnews*, 14 February 2015, http://www. catchnews.com/india-news/census-2011-india-s-largest-minority-muslims-are-no-better-today-than-a-few-decades-earlier-1452283107. html (accessed 18 December 2022).

11. Asghar Ali Engineer, 'Now Vadodara Goes Up in Communal Flames', in *Communal Riots in Post-Independence India*, ed. Asghar Ali Engineer, 2nd ed. (Hyderabad: Sangam Books, 1984), 281.

12. Pratiksha Baxi, '"Mock Trial": Law, Violence and Governance in the Aftermath of Gujarat 2002' (Paper presented at the Just-India Workshop, Paris, 28 October 2010), 2.

13. Baxi, 'Mock Trial', 2.

14. Engineer, *The Gujarat Carnage*.

15. The term 'hostile witness' does not appear in statutory criminal law in India. However, in case law, 'hostile witness' has broadly been understood as 'one who is not desirous of telling the truth at the instance of the party calling him'. Section 154 of the Indian Evidence Act, 1872, permits the prosecution, based on the discretion of the court, to cross-examine such witnesses. *Sat Pal v. Delhi Administration*, 1976 AIR 294 (29 September 1975), https:// indiankanoon.org/doc/916840/ (accessed 18 December 2022); Section 154, Indian Evidence Act, 1872, https://indiankanoon.org/doc/1646837/ (accessed 18 December 2022).

16. When a complaint of a cognisable offence is brought to the notice of the police, they are by law required to record it in written form and convey a copy of the record to the complainant. This record is called the first information report. Section 154 of the Code of Criminal Procedure, 1973, lays down what constitutes the FIR. The Supreme Court of India has made it mandatory for the police to record an FIR if it is convinced that a

cognisable offence has been committed. See Section 154, Code of Criminal Procedure, 1973, https://indiankanoon.org/doc/1980578/ (accessed 18 December 2022); *Lalita Kumari v. Govt. of Uttar Pradesh*, 1 Writ Petition (Criminal) No. 68 of 2008 (12 November 2013), https://indiankanoon.org/doc/10239019/ (accessed 18 December 2022).

17. *State of Gujarat v. Rajubhai Dhamirbhai Baria and Ors*, Fast Track Court No. 1, Vadodara, Sessions Case No. 248/2002 of the Additional Sessions Judge H. U. Mahida (Judgment of 27 June 2003) (hereinafter, 'J1'), 11.

18. Manas Dasgupta, 'NHRC Team Report on Best Bakery Case in a Week', *The Hindu*, 9 July 2003, https://www.thehindu.com/2003/07/09/stories/2003070905651100.htm (accessed 18 December 2022).

19. J1, 6.

20. A. G. Noorani, 'Muslims and Police', *Frontline*, 26 December 2014, https://www.frontline.in/the-nation/muslims-and-police/article6672575.ece (accessed 18 December 2022).

21. J1.

22. S. Muralidhar, 'Access to Criminal Justice: Challenges and Prospects', in *Towards Legal Literacy: An Introduction to Law in India*, ed. Kamala Sankaran and Ujjwal Kumar Singh (New Delhi: Oxford University Press, 2008), 45–60.

23. Fast-track courts (FTCs) were established in India to realise the fundamental right to a speedy trial, which was read into the right to life provision of the Constitution of India (Article 21) by the Supreme Court in 1986. The other reason for the establishment of FTCs was to create a new institutional mechanism for the expedited clearing of the huge backlog of cases in the Indian court system. The central government financed the establishment and running of FTCs from 2000 to 2011, after which the scheme was discontinued. States could continue to finance their own FTCs. Based on data from 2011, FTCs in Gujarat had the highest numbers of pending cases in the whole of India. *Sheela Barse and Ors v. Union of India and Ors*, JT 1986 136 (13 August 1986), http://indiankanoon.org/doc/525548/ (accessed 18 December 2022); Government of India, Department of Justice, 'Fast Track Courts', http://doj.gov.in/other-programmes/fast-track-courts (accessed 18 December 2022); The PRS Blog, 'An Overview of Fast Track Courts', 31 December 2012, http://www.prsindia.org/theprsblog/?p=2388 (accessed 18 December 2022).

24. Ratna Kapur, *Makeshift Migrants and Law: Gender, Belonging, and Postcolonial Anxieties* (London: Routledge, 2010), 177.

25. Code of Criminal Procedure, 1973, Section 354 (1)(b), https://indiankanoon. org/doc/1266667/ (accessed 18 December 2022).

26. J1, 3.

27. Ibid.

28. Ibid., 3.

29. Ibid., 4.

30. Ibid., 5.

31. Ibid., 7.

32. Ibid.

33. Ibid., 8 (emphasis in original). 'Lakh' is a unit followed in the South Asian numbering system, where 1 lac or lakh =100,000.

34. Ibid.

35. Ibid., 9.

36. Ibid.

37. Uday Mahurkar, 'Best Bakery Trial: Zaheera Sheikh Says She Lied under Oath out of Fear for Her Life', *India Today*, 21 July 2003, http://indiatoday. intoday.in/story/best-bakery-trial-zaheera-sheikh-says-she-lied-under-oath-out-of-fear-for-her-life/1/205856.html (accessed 18 December 2022).

38. Annapurna Waughray, 'The "Best Bakery" Case: Zahira Habibullah H. Sheikh and Another vs State of Gujarat and Others', *Journal of Islamic Practices in International Law* 2, no. 1 (2006): 18. As Waughray also notes: 'The balance who did not [recant their statements] were only formal witnesses such as doctors who had treated injuries.'

39. J1, 10.

40. 'Zahira's brother Nafitullah and sister Saira also retracted their statements. On the day that Zahira turned hostile, saying she could not identify the accused, her mother Sherunissa and younger brother Naseebullah also denied their statements given to the police.' J1, 10–11.

41. Ibid., 9.

42. Ibid., 10.

43. Ibid., 10–11.

44. Ibid., 12.

45. Ibid.

46. Ibid., 20.

47. Ibid., 12 (emphasis added).

48. Ibid., 13–16.

49. Ibid., 13. On the history of riots in Gujarat because of affirmative action policies, see Upendra Baxi, 'Reflections on the Reservations Crisis in

Gujarat', in *Mirrors of Violence: Communities, Riots and Survivors in South Asia*, ed. Veena Das (New Delhi: Oxford University Press, 1992), 215–39.

50. J1, 16.
51. Ibid., 15.
52. Ibid., 16.
53. Ibid.
54. Ibid.
55. Ibid., 7.
56. Ibid., 16. Sec. 327 of the Code of Criminal Procedure, 1973, stipulates that all criminal proceedings will be 'deemed to be an open court'. The section provides a mandated exception to this stipulation in proceedings concerning rape trials. Code of Criminal Procedure, 1973, Section 327, https://indiankanoon.org/doc/1134316/ (accessed 18 December 2022).
57. Dhavan, 'Justice, Justice and the Best Bakery Case'.
58. CJP, 'Statement Released by the Citizens for Justice and Peace at a Packed Press Conference in Mumbai on July 7, 2003', SANN, 7 July 2003, http://www.sabrang.com/news/7july03.htm (accessed 18 December 2022) (emphasis added).
59. Ibid.
60. Mahurkar, 'Best Bakery Trial'.
61. Ibid.
62. Article 136 of the Constitution of India allows the Supreme Court to exercise discretion to grant an appeal ('special leave') to an aggrieved party against a judgment, decree, order or sentence by any other court in India. 'Article 136 in the Constitution of India, 1949', https://indiankanoon.org/doc/427855/ (accessed 18 December 2022).
63. CJP, 'Zahira SLP', 8 May 2017, https://cjp.org.in/zahiraslp/ (accessed 18 December 2022).
64. Waughray, 'The "Best Bakery" Case', 19.
65. Ibid., 21.
66. Ibid.
67. Mitta, *The Fiction of Fact Finding*, 49.
68. See Aseem Prakash, 'Re-imagination of the State and Gujarat's Electoral Verdict', *Economic and Political Weekly* 38, no. 16 (2003): 1601; see generally Steven I. Wilkinson, *Votes and Violence: Ethnic Riots in India* (Cambridge: Cambridge University Press, 2004).

69. Rediff.com, 'Modi for "Appeasement of None and Justice to All"', 16 December 2002, http://www.rediff.com/election/2002/dec/16guj4.htm (accessed 18 December 2022).

70. Mitta, *The Fiction of Fact Finding*, 50.

71. Ibid., 50–51.

72. Ibid.

73. Ibid., 54.

74. Ibid.

75. Ibid., 56–57.

76. Ibid., 57.

77. Ibid.

78. See Nivedita Menon, 'Foucault and Indian Scholarship: History, Governmentality, Modernity', in *Trajectory of French Thought* (New Delhi: French Information Resource Centre/Rupa, 2004), 61–82; Ranabir Samaddar, 'Michel Foucault and Our Postcolonial Time', in *The Biopolitics of Development: Reading Michel Foucault in the Postcolonial Present*, ed. Sandro Mezaddra, Julian Reid and Ranabir Samaddar (New York: Springer, 2013), 25–44.

79. Mitta, *The Fiction of Fact Finding*, 57.

80. Ibid., 58.

81. Ibid., 58.

82. Ibid., 59.

83. Ibid.

84. Ibid.

85. *State of Gujarat v. Rajubhai Dhamirbhai Baria and Ors*, 2004 CriLJ 771 (26 December 2003), https://indiankanoon.org/doc/789410/ (accessed 18 December 2022) (hereinafter, 'J2').

86. Mitta, *The Fiction of Fact Finding*, 61.

87. Ibid.

88. Ibid., 62.

89. Ibid., 61.

90. J2.

91. Ibid.

92. Ibid.

93. Ibid.

94. Ibid. This was mentioned by the prosecuting lawyer, Advocate General Shelat, in his submissions to the Gujarat High Court.

95. Ibid.
96. Ibid.
97. Ibid.
98. Ibid.
99. Ibid.
100. Ibid.
101. Ibid.
102. Ibid.
103. Ibid.
104. Ibid.
105. Ibid. (emphasis added).
106. Ibid.
107. Ibid.
108. Ibid.
109. Ibid.
110. Ibid.
111. Ibid.
112. Ibid. (emphasis added).
113. Ibid.
114. Ibid.
115. Ibid. (emphasis added).
116. Ibid.
117. Ibid.
118. Ibid.
119. Ibid.
120. Ibid.
121. Ibid. (emphasis added).
122. Ibid.
123. Ibid.
124. Ibid.
125. Ibid.
126. Ibid.
127. Ibid.
128. Ibid.
129. Ibid.
130. Ibid.
131. Ibid.

132. *Zahira Habibulla Sheikh and Another v. State of Gujarat and Others*, Appeal (crl.) 446–449 of 2004 (12 April 2004), https://indiankanoon.org/doc/105430/ (accessed 18 December 2022) (hereinafter, 'J3').

133. Ibid.

134. Ibid.

135. Neither does the Supreme Court identify the victims as 'Muslim'. Apart from the use of words such as 'communal', it does not directly refer to either 'Hindu' or 'Muslim' by name even once in the judgment. I thank Siddharth Saxena for pointing this out to me.

136. J3.

137. Ibid.

138. Ibid.

139. Ibid.

140. Ibid.

141. Ibid.

142. Ibid.

143. While the lawyers for the appellants argued that the Gujarat High Court did not use its powers under Section 391 of the Code of Criminal Procedure to admit the new affidavits, the lawyers for the respondents submitted that the affidavits were admitted and rejected on merit. Section 391, Code of Criminal Procedure, 1973, https://indiankanoon.org/doc/782148/ (accessed 18 December 2022).

144. J3 (emphasis added).

145. Ibid. (emphasis added).

146. Ibid.

147. See generally S. P. Sathe, *Judicial Activism in India: Transgressing Borders and Enforcing Limits*, 2nd ed. (New Delhi: Oxford University Press, 2003).

148. J3 (emphasis added).

149. Ibid. (emphasis added).

150. Ibid. (emphasis added).

151. Ibid.

152. Ibid.

153. Ibid.

154. Ibid.

155. Ibid. (emphasis added).

156. Ibid. (emphasis added).

157. Ibid.

158. Ibid.

159. Ibid. (emphasis added).

160. Ibid.

161. Ibid.

162. Ibid.

163. Ibid.

164. Ibid. The comparison between 'the fanatics' and the 'alien enemy' and terrorists is an interesting one here. In the Constitution of India, the 'enemy alien' is an exceptional category of persons whose entitlement to civil and political rights stands suspended when arrested under preventive detention laws [Article 22 (3)]. One wonders if the Supreme Court, even if rhetorically, is indicating here that no procedural safeguards should apply in case of those being tried for crimes of religious mass violence. If so, would such treatment be meted out to 'fanatics' irrespective of their religious denomination? This question gains significance in a context where the criminal justice system in India is structurally and culturally heavily prejudiced against Muslims. Article 22 (3), Constitution of India, 1949, https://indiankanoon.org/doc/581566/ (accessed 18 December 2022). Roshan Kishore, 'Do Muslims in India Suffer a Bias When It Comes to Imprisonment, Convictions?', *Mint*, 12 May 2016, https://www.livemint.com/Opinion/93JZlySuxiVURtuqbA61TN/Do-Muslims-in-India-suffer-a-bias-when-it-comes-to-imprisonm.html (accessed 18 December 2022); *Firstpost*, 'NCRB Data Show Muslims, Dalits, Tribal Population in Prisons Disproportionate to Their Numbers Outside', 2 September 2020, https://www.firstpost.com/india/ncrb-data-shows-muslims-dalits-tribal-population-in-prisons-disproportionate-to-their-numbers-outside-8775161.html (accessed 18 December 2022).

165. The surname of the poet is incorrectly reported in the judgment as Cabney.

166. J3.

167. Ibid.

168. Ibid.

169. Ibid. (emphasis added).

170. Section 311, Code of Criminal Procedure, 1973, https://indiankanoon.org/doc/1780550/ (accessed 18 December 2022).

171. Section 165, Indian Evidence Act, 1872, https://indiankanoon.org/doc/302809/ (accessed 18 December 2022).

172. Section 406, Code of Criminal Procedure, 1973, https://indiankanoon.org/doc/664789/ (accessed 18 December 2022).

173. J3.

174. Ibid.

175. Ibid.

176. Ibid.

177. Ibid.

178. *Teesta Setalvad and Anr v. State of Gujarat and Ors*, Appeal (crl.) 443–445 of 2004 (12 April 2004), https://indiankanoon.org/doc/387523/ (accessed 18 December 2022).

179. Ibid.

180. *Outlook*, 'SC Makes the Best Possible History', 12 April 2004, https://www.outlookindia.com/website/story/sc-makes-the-best-possible-history/223541 (accessed 18 December 2022).

181. Mahesh Langa, 'Best Bakery Case: When SC Stepped In for Justice', *Hindustan Times*, 12 February 2012, https://www.hindustantimes.com/india/best-bakery-case-when-sc-stepped-in-for-justice/story-mrksvuqebiynp58bntwntm.html (accessed 18 December 2022).

182. BBC, 'Fresh Trial for Gujarat Riot Case', 12 April 2004, http://news.bbc.co.uk/2/hi/south_asia/3619079.stm (accessed 18 December 2022).

183. Colin Gonsalves, *Kaliyug: The Decline of Human Rights Law in the Period of Globalization* (New Delhi: Human Rights Law Network, 2011), 359–60.

184. Lakshmi Iyer, 'Best Bakery Case: SC Verdict before Gujarat Polls Puts Narendra Modi in a Tight Spot', *India Today*, 26 April 2004, https://www.indiatoday.in/magazine/states/story/20040426-best-bakery-case-sc-verdict-before-gujarat-polls-puts-narendra-modi-in-a-tight-spot-790191-2004-04-26 (accessed 18 December 2022).

185. *Outlook*, 'Guj Bar Council for "Reviewing" SC Order in Best Bakery Case', 14 April 2004, https://www.outlookindia.com/newswire/story/guj-bar-council-for-reviewing-sc-order-in-best-bakery-case/214889 (accessed 18 December 2022).

186. Uday Mahurkar, 'Best Bakery Case: Nine Accused Get Life Imprisonment', *India Today*, 13 March 2006, https://www.indiatoday.in/magazine/indiascope/story/20060313-best-bakery-case-nine-accused-get-life-imprisonment-783565-2006-03-13 (accessed 18 December 2022); Dionne Bunsha, 'Verdict in Best Bakery Case', *Frontline* 23, no. 4 (2006),

https://www.frontline.in/static/html/fl2304/stories/20060310005611700. htm (accessed 18 December 2022).

187. Manas Dasgupta, 'Zahira Retracts Statements', *The Hindu*, 4 November 2004, https://www.thehindu.com/2004/11/04/stories/2004110407510100. htm (accessed 18 December 2022).

188. Mahurkar, 'Best Bakery Trial'.

189. Uday Mahurkar, 'Best Bakery Case Hangs in Balance as Key Players Turn against Each Other', *India Today*, 22 November 2004, https://www. indiatoday.in/magazine/states/story/20041122-zaheera-sheikh-accuses-teesta-setalvad-of-abduction-789216-2004-11-22 (accessed 18 December 2022).

190. Satarupa Bhattacharjya, 'Best Bakery Case: Supreme Court Slams Witness Zahira Sheikh for Flip-Flops', *India Today*, 12 September 2005, https:// www.indiatoday.in/magazine/indiascope/story/20050912-best-bakery-case-supreme-court-slams-witness-zahira-sheikh-for-flip-flops-787015-2005-09-12 (accessed 18 December 2022).

191. *Outlook*, 'Court Allows Zaheera to Depose in Narrative Form', 22 December 2004, https://www.outlookindia.com/newswire/story/court-allows-zaheera-to-depose-in-narrative-form/268910 (accessed 18 December 2022).

192. *Outlook*, 'Zahira a "Self-Condemned Liar": SC Committee', 29 August 2005, http://www.outlookindia.com/news/article/zahira-a-selfcondemned-liar-sc-committee/319677 (accessed 18 December 2022).

193. *Zahira Habibullah Sheikh and Anr v. State of Gujarat and Ors*, Appeal (crl.) 446-449 of 2004 (8 March 2006), https://indiankanoon.org/doc/1067991/ (accessed 18 December 2022) (hereinafter, 'J4').

194. Wendy Doniger and Brian K. Smith (trans.), *The Laws of Manu* (London: Penguin, 1991).

195. J4.

196. Ibid.

197. Ibid.

198. J.J. Spigelman, 'The Principle of Open Justice: A Comparative Perspective', *University of New South Wales Law Journal* 29, no. 2 (2006): 147.

199. *Leeson v. General Medical Council* (1889) LJ 59 Ch NS 233, 241.

200. J4.

201. Section 60, Indian Penal Code, 1860, https://indiankanoon.org/doc/1144631/ (accessed 18 December 2022).

202. The court also ordered the income tax authorities to seek explanation from Madhu Srivastava and Bhattoo Srivastava, BJP members of Parliament, who were alleged to have paid off Zahira to make her recant her statements.

203. *Times of India*, 'Best Bakery Case: Zahira Sheikh Surrenders in Mumbai', 10 March 2006, https://timesofindia.indiatimes.com/india/Best-Bakery-case-Zahira-Sheikh-surrenders-in-Mumbai/articleshow/1445736.cms (accessed 18 December 2022).

204. Rediff.com, 'Zaheera Surrenders before Mumbai Court', 11 March 2006, http://in.rediff.com/news/2006/mar/10godhra.htm (accessed 18 December 2022).

205. Baxi, 'Mock Trial', 18.

206. *Times of India*, 'Zaheera Sheikh Released from Nasik Jail', 14 March 2007, https://timesofindia.indiatimes.com/india/Zaheera-Sheikh-released-from-Nasik-jail/articleshow/1762108.cms (accessed 18 December 2022).

207. Mahesh Langa, 'Best Bakery Case: Too Little, Too Late', *Hindustan Times*, 10 July 2012, https://www.hindustantimes.com/india/best-bakery-case-too-little-too-late/story-2uNz1I3qIM5xC00MU7S29H.html (accessed 18 December 2022).

208. *The Hindu*, 'Best Bakery Case: 5 Acquitted, Life Term for Four Upheld', 9 July 2012, http://www.thehindu.com/news/national/other-states/best-bakery-case-5-acquitted-life-term-for-four-upheld/article3620604.ece (accessed 18 December 2022).

209. Cover, 'Violence and the Word', 1613.

210. Ibid., 1610.

211. J3.

212. Cover, 'Violence and the Word', 1617.

213. Ibid.

214. In this, Cover is building on what has been called 'speech act' theory. See J. L. Austin, *How to Do Things with Words*, 2nd ed. (Cambridge: Harvard University Press, 1975). Speech act theory has 'illuminated the ability of language to do other things than describe reality.' Mitchell Green, 'Speech Acts', *The Stanford Encyclopedia of Philosophy*, 3 July 2007, https://plato.stanford.edu/archives/fall2021/entries/speech-acts/ (accessed 18 December 2022).

215. See generally Mari J. Matsuda, Charles R. Lawrence III, Richard Delgado and Kimberlé Williams Crenshaw, *Words that Wound: Critical Race Theory, Assaultive Speech, and the First Amendment* (New York: Routledge, 1993).

216. Cover, 'Violence and the Word', 1609 (emphasis added).

217. Ibid., 1612 (emphasis added).
218. J3.
219. J1, 1.
220. J2.
221. J3.
222. J1, 16.
223. J3.
224. J1, 12 (emphasis added).
225. Ranabir Samaddar, 'Beyond the Frame of Practical Reason: The Indian Evidence Act and Its Performative Life', *Diogenes* 60, nos. 3–4 (2015): 58, 65, 67.
226. Ibid., 59.
227. Ibid., 63.
228. Ibid., 64, 67.
229. Ibid., 70.
230. Ibid.
231. Ibid.
232. J3.
233. Ibid. (emphasis added).
234. Section 165, Indian Evidence Act, 1872.
235. Section 311, Code of Criminal Procedure, 1973.
236. J3.
237. See David H. Bayley, *The Police and Political Development in India* (Princeton: Princeton University Press, 1969).
238. Cited in T. Honore, 'The Primacy of Oral Evidence', in *Crime, Proof and Punishment: Essays in Memory of Sir Rupert Cross* (London: Butterworths, 1981), 174.
239. J3.
240. Piyel Haldar, 'The Return of the Evidencer's Eye: Rhetoric and the Visual Technologies of Proof', *Griffith Law Review* 8, no. 1 (1999): 86.
241. Roland Barthes, *Camera Lucida: Reflections on Photography*, trans. Richard Howard (New York: Farrar, Straus and Giroux, 1981), 26–27.
242. J3.
243. Ibid.
244. Baxi, 'Mock Trial', 18.
245. *ExpressIndia*, 'Zaheera Sheikh a "Self-Condemned Liar": SC Panel', 20 August 2005, expressindia.indianexpress.com/news/fullstory.php?newsid=53608 (accessed 18 December 2022).

246. J4.

247. Kannabiran, *Tools of Justice*, 298. This judgment's reference to Hindu scripture is in line with the Supreme Court of India's own motto, which is the the Sanskrit verse from the Hindu epic Mahabharata: *Yato Dharmastato Jayaha* (Where there is Dharma, there is victory). This is an instance of how Hindu traditions remain germane to the founding ideals of India's secular institutions. This emboldens the Hindu Right's claim that India is a Hindu *rashtra* and that there is nothing inimical between Hinduism and secularism. For a detailed engagement with how the Hindu Right is not anti-secular, but uses secularism as 'a strategy of rule', see Nivedita Menon, *Secularism as Misdirection: Critical Thought from the Global South* (Ranikhet: Permanent Black, 2023).

248. V. D. Savarkar, one of the key founding figures of Hindutva, had written: 'Today Manusmriti is Hindu Law. That is Fundamental.' Cited in Shamsul Islam, *Religious Dimensions of Indian Nationalism: A Study of RSS* (New Delhi: Media House, 2006), 217. Speaking from an oppositional position, B. R. Ambedkar, a crusader against caste discrimination and the chairperson of India's Constituent Assembly that drafted the Constitution of India, said: 'What does the Manu Smriti show? It shows that the [Hindu] caste system is a legal system maintained at the point of a bayonet.' B. R. Ambedkar, 'The Doom of the Untouchables', in *The Essential Writings of B. R. Ambedkar*, ed. Valerian Rodrigues (New Delhi: Oxford University Press, 2010), 164. See also Sharmila Rege (ed.), *Against the Madness of Manu: B. R. Ambedkar's Writings on Brahminical Patriarchy* (New Delhi: Navayana, 2013).

249. Badri Narayan, *Fascinating Hindutva: Saffron Politics and Dalit Mobilization* (New Delhi: Sage, 2009); Kama Kellie Maclean, 'Embracing the Untouchables: The BJP and Scheduled Caste Votes', *Asian Studies Review* 23, no. 4 (1999): 488.

250. J3.

251. J4 (emphasis added).

252. J3.

253. Baxi, 'Mock Trial', 18.

254. Marianne Constable, 'The Silence of the Law: Justice in Cover's "Field of Pain and Death"', in *Law, Violence and the Possibility of Justice*, ed. Sarat, 91.

255. Philippopoulos-Mihalopoulos, 'Atmospheres of Law', 2 (emphasis in original).

256. See Renu Desai, 'Producing and Contesting the "Communalized City": Hindutva Politics and Urban Space in Ahmedabad', in *The Fundamentalist*

City? Religiosity and the Remaking of Urban Space, ed. Nezar AlSayyad and Mejgan Massoumi (New York: Routledge, 2011), 99–124; John Chalmers, 'In Narendra Modi's Gujarat, a Case of Rule and Divide', *LiveMint*, 14 May 2014, https://www.livemint.com/Politics/xDcv5reXXuzWlCMdDBtstI/In-Narendra-Modis-Gujarat-a-case-of-rule-and-divide.html (accessed 18 December 2022); Damayantee Dhar, 'Disturbed Areas Act in Gujarat: A Tool to Discriminate against Muslims', *The Wire*, 26 June 2018, https://thewire.in/rights/disturbed-areas-act-in-gujarat-a-tool-to-discriminate-against-muslims.

257. J3.
258. Baxi, 'Mock Trial', 17.
259. Saadat Hasan Manto, 'Tidiness', in *Bitter Fruit: The Very Best of Saadat Hasan Manto*, ed. Khalid Hasan (New York: Penguin, 2008), 409.
260. *Times of India*, 'Zahira Goes Flip, Flop, Flip …', 23 December 2004, https://timesofindia.indiatimes.com/india/Zahira-goes-flip-flop-flip-/articleshow/969471.cms (accessed 18 December 2022).
261. Cover, 'Violence and the Word', 1601.
262. J1, 16.
263. Navaz Kotwal, 'An Omnibus FIR', *Frontline* 20, no. 21 (2003), https://www.frontline.in/static/html/fl2021/stories/20031024002204000.htm (accessed 18 December 2022).
264. Baxi, 'Mock Trial', 7 (emphasis in original).
265. J1, 16.
266. Baxi, 'The Second Gujarat Catastrophe', 3520 (emphasis in original).
267. Ibid.
268. K. Asmal, L. Asmal and R. S. Roberts, *Reconciliation through Truth: A Reckoning with Apartheid's Criminal Governance* (Cape Town: David Philip Publishers, with Mayibue, University of the Western Cape), 26.
269. Assman, *Moses the Egyptian*, 14.
270. Mitta, *The Fiction of Fact Finding*, 19.
271. One could also say re-victimised since Godhra is understood in the Hindutva imagination as a repetition of the Hindu victim–Muslim aggressor trope.
272. J1, 16.
273. Baxi, 'Mock Trial', 7.
274. J1, 16.
275. See Abdul Shaban (ed.), *Lives of Muslims in India: Politics, Exclusion and Violence*, 2nd ed. (New Delhi: Routledge, 2018); Taylor C. Sherman, *Muslim*

Belonging in Secular India: Negotiating Citizenship in Postcolonial Hyderabad (Cambridge: Cambridge University Press, 2015).

276. See Kapur, 'Normalizing Violence'.

277. J1, 13.

278. Ibid.

279. On the divide-and-rule policy, see Ajay Verghese, *The Colonial Origins of Ethnic Violence in India* (Stanford: Stanford University Press, 2016).

280. S. P. Udayakumar, *'Presenting' the Past: Anxious History and Ancient Future in Hindutva India* (Westport: Praeger, 2005).

281. J1, 13.

282. See Christophe Jaffrelot, 'Refining the Moderation Thesis: Two Religious Parties and Indian Democracy—the Jana Sangh and the BJP between Hindutva Radicalism and Coalition Politics', *Democratization* 20, no. 5 (2013): 876.

283. See Manisha Basu, *The Rhetoric of Hindu India: Language and Urban Nationalism* (New York: Cambridge University Press, 2017).

284. See Ghanshyam Shah, 'Middle Class Politics: Anti-reservation Agitations in Gujarat', *Economic and Political Weekly* 22, nos. 19–21 (1987): 155.

285. J1, 16.

286. See Julia Wardhaugh, 'The Jungle and the Village: Discourses on Crime and Deviance in Rural North India', *South Asia Research* 25, no. 2 (2005): 129.

287. There is a resistant idea of 'Jungle Raj' that upends the Hobbseian 'state of nature' in the worlds of India's Adivasis (Indigenous peoples) whose lives and livelihoods are in an intimate relationship with the forests that they inhabit. Alpa Shah writes that as a 'traditional system of indigenous governance ... from which a radical politics could emerge to better serve the poor', this 'Jungle Raj' represents 'an alternative political system to the secular postcolonial state ... a scaral polity ... in which the sacred and the secular are intimately connected or are one and the same, and which promotes values of egalitarianism, consensus building, reciprocity, and mutual aid'. It would not be too remote to suggest that the idea of the jungle raj in the Vadodara Sessions Court judgment considers such indigenous governance arrangements to be antithetical to its secularised idea of development. It is no surprise that the idea of development in the New India has devastated Adivasi life worlds through mass displacements in the name of progress and uplift. Alpa Shah, *In the Shadows of the State: Indigenous Politics, Environmentalism, and Insurgency in Jharkhand, India* (Durham: Duke University Press, 2010), 12, 43. In Chapter 4, in my reading

of the Bollywood film *Dev*, we will see an invocation of the idea of Ramrajya—the rule of the Hindu warrior god Ram—as a normative vision of good in the Hindutva imagination that also contrasts with the expression 'jungle raj' used in the Vadodara Sessions Court judgment. The expression used as an equivalent of jungle raj in Dev is 'kaliyug'—the dark times.

288. Seik Rahim Mondal, 'Social Structure, OBCs and Muslims', *Economic and Political Weekly* 32, no. 46 (2003): 4892.

289. J2.

290. Ibid. The harassment and intimidation of Teesta Setalvad is still continuing with regard to another key case that she and CJP has supported and pursued, that of victim-survivor Zakia Jafri. This case is related to another massacre that took place at Gulberg Society in Ahmedabad during the 2002 pogrom. See Anupama Katakam, 'Gulberg Society Case: A Verdict and Three Arrests', *Frontline*, 10 July 2022, https://frontline.thehindu.com/the-nation/gulberg-society-case-a-supreme-court-verdict-and-three-arrests-teesta-setalvad-rb-sreekumar-sanjiv-bhatt/article65615918.ece (accessed 22 May 2023); Oishik Sircar, 'The Silence of Gulberg: Refracted Memories, Inadequate Images', in *Violent Modernities: Cultural Lives of Law in the New India* (New Delhi: Oxford University Press, 2021), 189–209.

291. See Amita Baviskar, *In the Belly of the River: Tribal Conflicts over Development in the Narmada Valley* (New Delhi: Oxford University Press, 2004); Arundhati Roy, *The Greater Common Good* (Bombay: India Book Distributor, 1999).

292. J2.

293. Ibid.

294. Ibid.

295. Ibid.

296. Ibid.

297. Ibid.

298. Baxi, 'The Second Gujarat Catastrophe', 3521.

299. Ibid., 3523.

300. Ibid., 3522.

301. Manderson, *Songs without Music*, 42.

Chapter 4

1. Young, *The Scene of Violence*, 7.

2. Buchanan and Johnson, 'Strange Encounters', 56.

3. Samaddar, 'Beyond the Frame of Practical Reason', 71.

4. I had watched *Dev* when it was released at a theatre in Pune, but have hardly any recollection of what my response to the film was at that time. For the purposes of my J-A reading in this book, I watched all the three films on DVDs in Melbourne. While the affective intensities experienced within a private cinematic space like the drawing room are distinct from those of the movie theatre in India, what might be comparable is the spectatorial identification that is brought into being through the cinematic address of Bollywood cinema.

5. *Dev*, directed by Govind Nihalani (Udbhav Productions, 2004); *Parzania*, directed by Rahul Dholakia (PVR Pictures, 2007); *Kai Po Che*, directed by Abhishek Kapoor (UTV Motion Pictures, 2013).

6. The CBFC in India, also known as the Censor Board, is a statutory body established by the Indian Cinematograph Act of 1952, which makes it mandatory for films to apply for a censor certificate before they can be publicly exhibited. The CBFC also classifies films based on their content for universal or restricted viewing. The CBFC's decisions to censor films considered sexually explicit or communally sensitive tend to reflect the moral and political views of the government in power at the time. The CBFC's decisions have met with resistance from free speech advocates and right-wing conservatives. On the history and politics of film censorship in India, see Bhowmik, *Cinema and Censorship*; Mazzarella, *Censorium*.

7. The Indian Cinematograph Act, 1952, https://indiankanoon.org/doc/980182/ (accessed 18 December 2022). The Cinematograph (Certification) Rules, 1983, https://indiankanoon.org/doc/9685550/ (accessed 18 December 2022). The regulatory regime, particularly that of 'prior restraint' that this law advances, has been the cause for much contestation regarding issues of freedom of speech and expression, leading to the CBFC being considered by filmmakers as a governmental body that censors in the name of certifying. In the 1970 case of *K. A. Abbas v. Union of India*, the petitioner—a filmmaker—challenged the draconian 'prior restraint' provision of the law as an affront to the constitutionally guaranteed freedom of speech and expression. The Supreme Court in its deeply paternalistic judgment exceptionalised films as a particular form of artistic expression (in contradistinction to books) that must be subject to 'prior restraint' by the CBFC because it considered images to have a greater impact on immature audiences. The judgment said:

> The motion picture is able to stir up emotions more deeply than any other product of art. Its effect particularly on children and adolescents is very great since their immaturity makes them more willingly suspend their disbelief than mature men and women. They also remember the action in the picture and try to emulate or imitate what they have seen.

The sentiment expressed in this judgment became the basis for the 1968 Khosla Committee Report on Film Censorship which argued in defence of 'prior restraint' in almost identical fashion:

> The written word is understood by very few people, and spoken word reaches out even fewer, but the film contains a complete and immediate appeal for everyone, men, women, children, whether literate or illiterate, whether intelligent or unintelligent. It makes it impact by simultaneously arousing the visual and aural sense. It is possible for a film to be seen by two million people in a day and if post-production measures are taken then it will be too late. And it will have already have done irreparable damage. This circumstance places film in a class by itself, as it affords an irresistible temptation of filmmakers to exploit the baser senses of the immature and simple-minded people for commercial purposes.

See *K. A. Abbas v. Union of India* (1971 AIR 481), https://indiankanoon.org/doc/1719619/ (accessed 25 May 2023); Ministry of Information and Broadcasting, *Report of the Enquiry Committee on Film Censorship* (Government of India, 1968), https://indianculture.gov.in/reports-proceedings/report-enquiry-committeefilm-censorship (accessed 25 May 2023). See generally Tejaswini Ganti, 'The Limits of Decency and the Decency of Limits: Censorship and the Bombay Film Industry', in *Censorship in South Asia*, ed. Kaur and Mazzarella, 117; Shohini Ghosh, 'Censorship Myths and Imagined Harms', *Sarai Reader 04: Crisis/Media* (New Delhi: SARAI/ CSDS, 2004), 447–54, http://archive.sarai.net/files/original/755257fc6f a5744 ae93c402cd54bc039.pdf (accessed 25 May 2023); Gautam Bhatia, *Offend, Shock or Disturb: Free Speech Under the Indian Constitution* (New Delhi: Oxford University Press, 2016).

8. Proposed amendments to the Indian Cinematograph Act through the Cinematograph (Amendment) Bill, 2021, can, if passed, result in giving the state 'revisionary powers' to deny certification based on 'complaints' after a film has been granted certification for public exhibition. Another proposed amendment requires streaming platforms to seek certification for films even

if those films have previously been certified. Tatsam Mukherjee, 'The Slow Death of Artistic Freedom in India', *Slate*, 20 September 2021, https://slate.com/technology/2021/09/india-censorship-films-freedom-netflix-amazon.html (accessed 18 December 2022).

9. Goodrich, *Advanced Introduction to Law and Literature*, 83.

10. Peter Goodrich, 'Pictures as Precedents: The Visual Turn and the Status of Figures in Judgments', in *New Directions in Law and Literature*, ed. Elizabeth S. Anker and Bernadette Mayler (New York: Oxford University Press, 2017), 179.

11. For Goodrich, *obiter depicta* is 'the study of the visible figures of norm and law, the images internal to the text and also surrounding it in the embodiments and performances that influence advocacy and decision.' Goodrich, *Legal Emblems and the Art of Law*, 23.

12. See Davis, 'Any Resemblance to Persons Living or Dead', 269; Apar Gupta, 'Movie Disclaimers: A Contract with the Offended', *Seminar* 716 (April 2015), https://www.india-seminar.com/2019/716/716_apar_gupta.htm (accessed 25 May 2023).

13. CBFC Guidelines, https://www.cbfcindia.gov.in/main/guidelines.html (accessed 18 December 2022).

14. Prasad, 'Surviving Bollywood', 46.

15. Goodrich, *Legal Emblems and the Art of Law*, 9.

16. Liang, 'Cinematic Citizenship and the Illegal City'.

17. Zee News, 'Gujarat Court to Hear Petition Banning Dev on June 28', 25 June 2004, http://zeenews.india.com/news/nation/gujarat-court-to-hear-petition-banning-dev-on-june-28_165029.html (accessed 18 December 2022); *Indian Express*, 'PIL Puts Kai Po Che in the Dock in HC', 3 May 2013, http://archive.indianexpress.com/news/pil-puts-kai-po-che-in-the-dock-in-hc/1110917/ (accessed 18 December 2022).

18. Urvish Kothari, 'Parzania and the Dictator of Gujarat', *Himal Southasian* 20, no. 3 (2007): 68.

19. Urvi Mahajani, 'Best Bakery: Case Was Shifted for Fair Trial', *Daily News and Analysis*, 10 July 2012, http://www.dnaindia.com/mumbai/report-best-bakery-case-was-shifted-for-fair-trial-1712893 (accessed 18 December 2022).

20. The renaming of Bombay as Mumbai was an outcome of a cultural revisionist campaign led by the Shiv Sena, a Hindutva political party. See Rashmi Varma, 'Provincializing the Global City: From Bombay to Mumbai', *Social Text* 22, no. 4 (2004): 65. I use the name 'Mumbai' because that is the term used to refer to the city in the film.

21. Martha Nussbaum, 'Body of the Nation: Why Women Were Mutilated in Gujarat', *Boston Review*, 1 June 2004, http://bostonreview.net/martha-nussbaum-women-mutilated-gujarat (accessed 18 December 2022).

22. Haresh Pandya, 'Govind Nihalani's Dev in Trouble', Rediff India Abroad, 16 June 2004, http://www.rediff.com/movies/2004/jun/16dev.htm (accessed 18 December 2022).

23. Ayesha Khan, 'In Best Bakery City, They Are Lining Up to Watch Dev's Aaliya', *Indian Express*, 21 June 2004, http://expressindia.indianexpress.com/news/fullstory.php?newsid=32798 (accessed 18 December 2022).

24. Haresh Pandya, 'Hindu, Muslim Join Hands, Defend Dev', Rediff.com, 19 June 2004, http://www.rediff.com/movies/2004/jun/19dev.htm (accessed 18 December 2022).

25. Nussbaum, *The Clash Within*, 10.

26. This particular spectatorial identification also carried strong legal and aesthetic traction, given that Zahira Sheikh in the Best Bakery judgments was repeatedly referred to as the 'star witness'—like a movie star—and was accorded fallen celebrity status by the media, not so much for the violence she witnessed and experienced, but for being the unreliable Muslim who flip-flopped on her testimony, ultimately being convicted for perjury by the Supreme Court of India.

27. Bhaktivedanta Swami A. C. Prabhupada, *Bhagavad-Gita as It Is* (Vaduz: Bhaktivedanta Book Trust, 1983), 69.

28. Shruti Kapila and Faisal Devji, 'The Bhagavad Gita and Modern Thought: Introduction', *Modern Intellectual History* 7, no. (2010): 269, 271.

29. Prasad, 'Surviving Bollywood', 45.

30. Ibid.

31. See Alok Rai, *Hindi Nationalism* (New Delhi: Orient BlackSwan, 2001). The BJP's Amit Shah, home minister of India and chairman of the Parliamentary Official Language Committee, has recently suggested that the unity of the nation will be achieved if Hindi is made the official language. He also went on to say that 'that central universities and institutes of national importance should carry out teaching and exams only in Hindi, rather than English'. This move is part of Hindutva ideology's long-term agenda, inspired by V. D. Savarkar's slogan 'Hindi, Hindu, Hindustan', that conflates 'nationalism with both religion and language'. Hannah-Ellis Petersen, '"A Threat to Unity": Anger over Push to Make Hindi National

Language of India', *Guardian*, 25 December 2022, https://www.theguardian.com/world/2022/dec/25/threat-unity-anger-over-push-make-hindi-national-language-of-india (accessed 25 May 2023); Amrit Dhillon, 'Modi Employs New Tools in India's War against the English Language: Hindi Medical Degrees', *Guardian*, 22 October 2022, https://www.theguardian.com/world/2022/oct/22/modi-employs-new-tool-in-indias-war-against-the-english-language-hindi-medical-degrees (accessed 25 May 2023).

32. Ranjani Mazumdar, 'The Bombay Film Poster', *Seminar* (2003): 525, http://www.india-seminar.com/2003/525/525%20ranjani%20mazumdar.htm (accessed 18 December 2022).

33. Prasad, 'Surviving Bollywood', 46.

34. Therwath, 'Shining Indians'.

35. Article 343, Constitution of India, 1949, https://indiankanoon.org/doc/379861/ (accessed 18 December 2022); Article 351, Constitution of India, 1949, https://indiankanoon.org/doc/1581449/ (accessed 18 December 2022).

36. Pritam Singh, 'Hindu Bias in India's Secular Constitution: Probing Flaws in the Instruments of Government', *Third World Quarterly* 26, no. 6 (2005): 921 (emphasis in original).

37. Ibid., 919. On the contemporary manifestations of the relationship between Hindi hegemony and caste hierarchy in India, see Sagar, 'Biting My Tongue: What Hindi Keeps Hidden', *The Caravan*, 26 June 2019, https://caravanmagazine.in/caste/what-hindi-keeps-hidden (accessed 18 December 202).

38. As 'the dominant culture language of precolonial southern Asia outside the Persianate order', Sanskrit has been central to the revisionist narratives propagated by Hindutva ideology. As Sheldon Pollock writes:

    Hindutva propagandists have sought to show, for example, that Sanskrit was indigenous to India, and they purport to decipher Indus Valley seals to prove its presence two millennia before it actually came into existence. In a farcical repetition of Romantic myths of primevality, Sanskrit is considered—according to the characteristic hyperbole of the VHP [Vishwa Hindu Parishad or the World Hindu Council]—the source and sole preserver of world culture.

    See Sheldon Pollock, 'The Death of Sanskrit', *Comparative Studies in Society and History* 43, no. 2 (2001): 392.

39. Singh, 'Hindu Bias in India's Secular Constitution', 921.

40. Nihalani is reputed as a filmmaker with a committed secular and progressive outlook and is credited for making the 'first film to take up the issue of Hindu–Muslim divide during Partition … based on Bhisham Sahni's novel *Tamas*….' Since it was made for television, the film was presented as a miniseries. As filmmaker Shyam Benegal writes:

> As [*Tamas*] was made for television, the series did not have to be cleared by the Film Censor Board; otherwise the censors would have banned it on grounds that it showed hostility between the communities. While the national television channel, Doordarshan, was considering telecasting it, the RSS and some of its other constituents objected violently to the screening. Nihalani's apartment in Mumbai was attacked and threats were issued against his life. As a result, Doordarshan decided against showing the series, citing a threat to peace as right-wing Hindu organizations had also threatened to burn down the television station. Nihalani went to court and the Bombay High Court, after viewing the series, directed Doordarshan to show it as there was nothing unconstitutional in the film to warrant a ban. It was only then that it was shown in its entirety on prime time to a record audience over three evenings that passed without incident.

   Despite being a filmmaker, whose works have drawn the ire of the Hindu Right and successfully resisted it, in *Dev*, Nihalani's secular imagination meets with a unique crisis as my reading will demonstrate. See Shyam Benegal, 'Secularism and Popular Indian Cinema', in *The Crisis of Secularism in India*, ed. Needham and Rajan, 236.

41. At the time of the making of the film, the Gujarat police establishment was receiving massive media attention for two cases of 'fake encounters' (the phrase used in India to refer to extra-judicial killings). Two Muslims, Ishrat Jahan and Sohrabuddin Sheikh, were killed by the police on the flimsy pretext that they were planning to assassinate Narendra Modi. A judge investigating one of these incidents, who had previously exonerated some key ministers involved in the encounter, died under suspicious circumstances, raising concerns about the role of the state in sabotaging the investigation. I am referring to this as an aside to emphasise the deep collusion between the police, state, investigating agencies and the judiciary in Gujarat that has institutionalised prejudice against Muslims in the name of national security. Niranjan Takle, 'A Family Breaks Its Silence: Shocking Details Emerge in Death of Judge Presiding over Sohrabuddin Trial', *The Caravan*, 20 November 2017, https://caravanmagazine.in/vantage/shocking-details-

emerge-in-death-of-judge-presiding-over-sohrabuddin-trial-family-breaks-silence (accessed 18 December 2022); Nikita Saxena and Atul Dev, 'Death of Judge Loya: Government Letter Concealed from the Supreme Court Detailed Purpose of Loya's Visit to Nagpur and Arrangements for His Stay', *The Caravan*, 12 June 2018, https://caravanmagazine.in/vantage/death-of-judge-loya-government-letter-concealed-supreme-court-detailed-purpose-of-loya-visit-nagpur-arrangements (accessed 18 December 2022).

42. 'A general "obligation to obey the law" is a poor guide at a time when revolutionary changes are needed and we are racing against ominous lines on the social cardiograph.' For a polemic on the way the rule of law maintains and normalises inequalities and prejudice against the powerless, see Howard Zinn, 'The Conspiracy of Law' in *The Rule of Law*, ed. Robert P. Wolff (New York: Simon and Schuster, 1971), 35.

43. Chadha and Kavoori, 'Exoticized, Marginalized, Demonized', 131.

44. As discussed in Chapter 2, this has been referred to as Bollywood's 'techno-folk' form or its 'techno-nationalism'. Mazumdar, *Bombay Cinema*, xvii; Rajadhyaksha, 'The "Bollywoodization" of the Indian Cinema', 29.

45. M. P. Singh and Surya Deva, 'The Constitution of India: Symbol of Unity in Diversity', *Jahrbuch des öffentlichen Rechts der Gegenwart* 53 (2005): 649.

46. Mahmood Mamdani, *Good Muslim, Bad Muslim: America, the Cold War, and the Roots of Terror* (New York: Doubleday, 2004).

47. This direct invocation of a conspiracy by Muslims to provoke Hindus follows the template of how the Godhra killings were represented without any evidence by the Hindu Right as the consequence of an Islamist terrorist conspiracy. See Mitta, *The Fiction of Fact Finding*.

48. Dorsett and McVeigh, *Jurisdiction*, 112.

49. According to Section 173 of the Code of Criminal Procedure, a charge sheet can be filed only after proper investigation has concluded. Section 173, Code of Criminal Procedure, 1973, https://indiankanoon.org/doc/1412034/ (accessed 18 December 2022).

50. See Pittu Laungani, 'Death in a Hindu Family', in *Death and Bereavement across Cultures*, ed. Colin Murray, Pittu Laungani and Bill Young (New York: Routledge, 2000), 52–72. In a scene after Dev's death, Tejinder asks Farhaan what the nature of his relationship with Dev was. Farhan's says that he considers Dev to be his spiritual father and emphasises that Tejinder would not understand that. The scene seems to convey that the secular and syncretic bond of the Dev–Farhaan relationship is beyond the comprehension

of those like Tejinder who essentialise Muslims as terrorists and enemies of the state.

51. Nasreen Munni Kabeer, 'Playback Time', *Film Comment* 38, no. 3 (2002): 42.

52. Ravi Vasudevan, 'Aesthetics and Politics in Popular Cinema', in *The Cambridge Companion to Modern Indian Culture*, ed. Vasudha Dalmia and Rashmi Sadana (Cambridge: Cambridge University Press, 2012), 233. The cinematographic form that *darsana* takes combines 'frontality' and 'direct address'. In Ravi S. Vasudevan's words:

> This is done through a pronounced register of frontality, with the scene shot at a 180-degree angle to the characters or objects, rather than through oblique framing. The latter suggests a look into the world of the fiction, the former a breaking of its cordons, as if addressing a world beyond the fiction. This may be summarized in the notion of direct address, where characters look directly into the camera, as if addressing the audience rather than another character in the fiction. (Vasudevan, 'Neither State nor Faith', 242)

53. In fact, the Sanskrit version of the word Dev is Deva, which means 'divine', most appropriately used to characterise a brahmin, an upper-caste man. Vaman Shivaram Apte, *The Practical Sanskrit-English Dictionary* (Poona: Prasad Prakashan, 1957), 835.

54. Ghassem-Fachandi, *Pogrom in Gujarat*, 2

55. Setalvad, *Foot Soldier of the Constitution*, 78.

56. This rationalising logic of equivalence, in terms of how Hindus and Muslims can be said to collectively suffer the punishment for an originary retaliatory action by one of the comunities, can be compared to the legal principle of *lex talionis*, which in its theological terms would suggest that violence begets violence, or would advance the commonsense rhetoric of "'and eye for an eye, a tooth for a tooth ... a life for a life".' As Jeremy Waldron writes:

> *lex talionis* [LT] ... is a theory that purports to guide us in our choice of appropriate penalties.... But LT is not just a principle about eyes, teeth and murder. What these formulae have in common is the idea of doing to the offender, as punishment, what the offender did to his victim. There are two actions to consider: the act of offending and the act of punishment. LT holds that they should be the same; and since the act

of punishment is the only one over which we have any control, we should choose a punishment that matches the character of the offense.

The logic of equilavence, thus, rationalises violence against Muslims by Hindus based on the originary Hindutva trope of the Muslim aggressor–Hindu victim. Jeremy Waldron, 'Lex Talionis', *Arizona Law Review* 34, no. 1 (1992): 25, 26.

57. Thobani, 'Performing Terror, Mediating Religion', 493.

58. Josh, 'Partition and the Rise of Hindutva Movement', 175; Kohli, *Memories in the Service of the Hindu Nation*.

59. Austin Sarat, 'Imagining the Law of the Father: Loss, Dread, and Mourning in "The Sweet Hereafter"', *Law and Society Review* 34, no. 1 (2000): 13.

60. Quoted in ibid., 14.

61. Basu, *Bollywood in the Age of New Media*, 3.

62. Virdi, *The Cinematic ImagiNation*, 9.

63. My translation from Hindi to English.

64. My translation from Hindi to English.

65. Hoveyda Abbas and Ranajay Kumar, *Political Theory* (New Delhi: Pearson, 2012), 154–55; John Austin, *The Province of Jurisprudence Determined* (Cambridge: Cambridge University Press, 1995).

66. See Ujjwal Kumar Singh, *The State, Democracy and Anti-terror Laws in India* (New Delhi: Sage, 2007).

67. Article 22(3), The Constitution of India, 1949, https://indiankanoon.org/doc/581566/ (accessed 18 December 2022). See generally A. G. Noorani and South Asia Human Rights Documentation Centre, *Challenges to Civil Rights Guarantees in India* (New Delhi: Oxford University Press, 2012). This provision has been called the 'undemocratic heart of the Indian Constitution'. In the Supreme Court's landmark judgment in *ADM Jabalpur v. Shivkant Shukla*, Justice H. R. Khanna famously stated in his dissent:

> To condone or allow relaxation in the matter of compliance with procedural requirements would necessarily have the effect of practically doing away with even the slender safeguards provided by the legislature against the arbitrary use of the provisions relating to preventive detention. The history of personal liberty is largely the history of insistence upon procedure.

The closing sentence of this paragraph is hailed as a bulwark against the constitutional sanction for preventive detention that is increasingly being eroded under conditions of what has been called the BJP's 'autocratic legalism'. Interestingly though, as my discussion in Chapter 3 demonstrated, it was in fact an insistence upon procedure (though not concerning preventive detention laws) in judgment after judgment in the Best Bakery cases that resulted in compromising the personal liberty of Zahira Sheikh, a vulnerable Muslim victim-survivor of the pogrom, leading to her conviction for perjury. An insistence on procedure was also the alibi the courts were resorting to absolve their complicity with that of the police and the ruling party in Gujarat in 2002. It was a means to present the judiciary as secular to mask its tacit and covert relationship with Hindutva ideology. See P. Padmanabhan, 'Undemocratic Heart of the Indian Constitution', in *Violation of Democratic Rights in India*, ed. A. R. Desai (Bombay: Popular Prakashan, 1986), 73–78; John Sebastian and Faiza Rahman, 'Improving Preventive Detention Laws', *India Forum*, 15 May 2023, https://www.theindiaforum.in/law/improving-preventive-detention-laws (accessed 25 May 2023); *ADM Jabalpur v. Shivkant Shukla* (1976 AIR 1207), https://indiankanoon.org/doc/1735815/ (accessed 26 May 2023); Deepa Das Acevedo, 'Autocratic Legalism in India: A Roundtable', *Jindal Global Law Review* 13, no. 1 (June 2022): 117–40.

68. Marco Goldoni and Michael A. Wilkinson, 'The Material Constitution', *Modern Law Review* 81, no. 4 (2018): 569.

69. Joseph Raz, 'Kelsen's Theory of the Basic Norm', *American Journal of Jurisprudence* 19, no. 1 (1974): 94.

70. See generally Rakesh Kumar, 'Structural Analysis of the Indian Legal System through the Normative Theory', *Journal of the Indian Law Institute* 41, nos. 3–4 (1999): 500.

71. Triloki Nath Madan, 'The Householder Tradition in Hindu Society', in *The Blackwell Companion to Hinduism*, ed. Gavin Flood (Oxford: Blackwell, 2003), 298.

72. Pamela Lothspeich, 'The *Kaliyug* of Modernity in Surendra Verma's *Draupadi*', in *Interpreting Homes in South Asian Literature*, ed. Malashri Lal and Suktara Paul Kumar (New Delhi: Pearson, 2007), 159. See also Irfan Ahmad, 'In Conversation with an Ordinary Indian: Kaliyuga, War, End of the Word and Hindutva', *Journal of Religious and Political Practice* 3, nos. 1–2 (2017): 57.

73. See Noorani, *Destruction of the Babri Masjid*.

74. Iftikhar Haider Malik, *Jihad, Hindutva, and the Taliban: South Asia at the Crossroads* (Karachi: Oxford University Press, 2005), 99.

75. Udayakumar, *'Presenting' the Past*. Bharti's aspirational imagination of Ramrajya as utopia reinscribes the four-fold hierarchy, or *chaturvarnya*, of the Hindu caste system. As Ambedkar has commented, the very edifice of Ram's divine rule or 'Ram Raj' in the *Ramayana* is 'based on Chaturvarnya' and 'Chaturvarnya cannot subsist by its own inherent goodness. It must be enforced by law'. Interestingly then, we can see here a convergence between Dev's, Tejinder's and Bharti's imaginations where all three are imbued with a certain kind of legalism aimed at establishing a normative brahminical Hindu order. Also, is it a coincidence that the character in the film who aspires for Ramrajya is called Bharti? B. R. Ambedkar, 'Annihilation of Caste', in *The Essential Writings of B. R. Ambedkar*, ed. Valerian Rodrigues (New Delhi: Oxford University Press, 2010), 280.

76. *State of Gujarat v. Rajubhai Dhamirbhai Baria and Ors*, Fast Track Court No. 1, Vadodara, Sessions Case No. 248/2002 of the Additional Sessions Judge H. U. Mahida (Judgment of 27 June 2003), 16.

77. The Constitution of India has been considered, by Ambedkarite thinkers, to be in an 'oppositional relationship' with the Gita, where the former is committed to the cultivation of the morality of justice and reason and the latter 'defend[s] India's peculiar institution of *chaturvarna* (aka caste) on the ground of its usefulness in maintaining social harmony'. This equation, thus, enables a brahminical re-imagination of the Constitution of India by the good upper-caste liberal in Dev by making use of the malleability of the Gita to produce the illusion of rehabilitating Hinduism from Hindutva. Meera Nanda, 'Ambedkar's Gita', *Economic and Political Weekly* 51, no. 49 (2016): 39 (emphasis in original). On the malleability of the Bhagavad Gita, Ambedkar writes:

> [It] is not a gospel and it can therefore have no message and it is futile to search for one. The question will no doubt be asked: What is the *Bhagvad Gita* if it is not a gospel? My answer is that the *Bhagvad Gita* is neither a book of religion nor a treatise on philosophy. What the *Bhagvad Gita* does is to defend certain dogmas of religion on philosophic grounds. If on that account anybody wants to call it a book of religion or a book of philosophy he may please himself. But essentially it is neither. It uses philosophy to defend religion.

B. R. Ambedkar, 'Krishna and His Gita', in *The Essential Writings of B. R. Ambedkar*, ed. Valerian Rodrigues (New Delhi: Oxford University Press, 2010), 193 (emphasis in original).

78. See generally Cossman and Kapur, *Secularism's Last Sigh?*; Sen, *Articles of Faith*; Saxena, '"Court"ing Hindu Nationalism'.

79. A very short scene from earlier in the film established Dev and Bharti as Hindus when they were shown praying to Hindu deities.

80. Meera Nanda, 'Secularism without Secularisation: Reflections on God and Politics in US and India', *Economic and Political Weekly* 42, no. 1 (2007): 39.

81. Shiv Viswanathan and Teesta Setalvad, 'Narratives of Vulnerability and Violence: Retelling the Gujarat Riots', in *Vulnerability in Technological Cultures: New Directions in Research and Governance*, ed. Anique Hommels, Jessica Mesman and Wiebe E. Bijker (Cambridge: MIT Press, 2014), 109–30, 125.

82. Ibid.

83. *Business Standard*, '"India First" Should Be Govt's Religion and "Constitution" Its Holy Book: Narendra Modi', http://www.business-standard.com/video-gallery/general/india-first-should-be-govt-s-religion-and-constitution-its-holy-book-narendra-modi-3442/india-first-should-be-govt-s-religion-and-constitution-its-holy-book-narendra-modi-6767.htm (accessed 18 December 2022).

84. See The Constitution (42nd Amendment) Act, 1976, https://www.india.gov.in/my-government/constitution-india/amendments/constitution-india-forty-second-amendment-act-1976 (accessed 18 December 2022).

85. Singh, 'Hindu Bias in India's Secular Constitution', 911 (emphasis in original).

86. See Achin Vanaik, 'By the Book: Does the Constitution Keep Its Promises?', *The Caravan*, 1 May 2019, https://caravanmagazine.in/reportage/does-constitution-keep-promises (accessed 18 December 2022). The Hindu dimensions of the Indian Constitution operates not only at the level of judicial interpretation or cultural metaphor but is also present in the material form of the original version of the document. This material form has aesthetic and textual components. For example, the art that adorns the cover and pages of the Constitution carries distinctive forms of Hindu iconography whose presence has led to courts in India to make the argument that Lord Ram is not a mythological but 'constitutional entity'. Likewise, BJP ministers have cited the artwork to argue that the Constitution recognizes 'Vedic life in India', thus establishing the nation's Hindu civilizational origins. There have been counter arguments from a secular standpoint presented against these positions that offer a more complex reading of the art in the Constitution, particularly the syncretized traditions that its illustrator Nandalal Bose and calligrapher Prem Behari Narain

Raizada drew on. Some secular commentators have unhelpfully suggested that the words in the Constitution need to be taken more seriously than its art to resist these Hindutva appropriations. This is a counterproductive argument because some of the words in the Constitution buttress the art's Hindu inheritances. For example, Article 1 opens with the words 'India that is Bharat …' What does the equivalence between India and Bharat signify? As Upendra Baxi has commented:

> Does it contain codes of memory and identity of some vision of pre-British, even millenarian, Hindu empire and civilization? What would the word 'Bharat' mean, for example, to a Konyak Naga, a Bhil, a Santhal, and a Bodo person/woman? What would this mean to India's Islamic peoples, among them the Bohras, Meos, Khojas, the Ahmadiyas, the Shias and the Sunnis? And what may this notion convey to Indian Christians, the Parsees and the microscopic Jewish communities? And how may [we] relate the idea of Bharat to the diasporic Tibetan, Pakistani, and East Bengal (Bangladeshi) migrants to India after the independence? How may be one an *Indian* without at the same time being a *Bharati*? What mix of human rights and rightlessness does this all signify? [emphasis in original]

See Shreyas Narla, 'Indians Should Stop Reading Too Much into the Artwork on the Constitution and Instead Heed Its Words', *Scroll.in*, 26 January 2021, https://scroll.in/article/984978/indians-should-stop-reading-too-much-into-the-artwork-on-the-constitution-and-instead-heed-its-words (accessed 29 May 2023); Naman Ahuja, 'Can the Historic Art of Our Constitution Look into the Future?', *Mint Lounge*, 25 January 2020, https://lifestyle.livemint.com/how-to-lounge/art-culture/can-the-historic-art-of-our-constitution-look-to-the-future-111641402068457.html (accessed 29 May 2023); Janaki Nair, 'Reading the Constitution', *The Hindu*, 26 January 2018, https://www.thehindu.com/opinion/op-ed/reading-the-constitution/article22524714.ece (accessed 29 May 2023); Vandana Kalra, 'The Handcrafter Constitution Is a Work of Art', *Indian Express*, 27 January 2020, https://indianexpress.com/article/express-sunday-eye/handcrafted-constitution-india-6233517/ (accessed 29 May 2023); Baxi, *Memory and Rightlessness*, 11.

87. The Manusmriti forms part of the Dharmasastra texts and serves as an important source of what constitutes Hindu law. Several parts of the Manusmriti are outrightly discriminatory towards women and lower castes. See Doniger, *The Laws of Manu*.

88. Kapur, 'Normalizing Violence', 889. Kapur's piece also offers a reading of *Dev*, and engages particularly in a feminist interpretation of Aaliya's character as not just a victim of mass violence but an agential Muslim woman. However, in her overall assessment, Kapur considers the film to be one that advances a progressive critique of the pogrom. Strangely enough, despite the sophisticated reading of both the film and of Gujarat 2002, Kapur pays little attention to the politics of naming and the inadequacy of the expression 'riots' to characterise the violence.

89. That the concerns of elite (Hindu) citizens provide the foundational legitimacy to the Indian Constitution, despite the text's emancipatory promises, is appositely captured in Upendra Baxi's evocative expression the 'unwritten constitution'. According to Baxi:

> The unwritten constitution signifies series of tacit understandings developed among the wielders of state power in ways which sustain the legitimacy of the totality of the organization of political power in society. In particular, the unwritten constitution must operate to protect the overall interests of the regime or the ruling bloc even when the interpretation of the written Constitution generates the appearance of accountability.

Upendra Baxi, 'Law and State Regulated Capitalism in India: Some Preliminary Remarks', in *Capitalist Development: Critical Essays*, ed. Ghanshyam Shah (Bombay: Popular Prakashan, 1990), 190.

90. This commitment to *dharma* in the Bhagavad Gita is a justification of the caste hierarchy in Hindu society that places the brahmin in a divinely ordained superior position over other castes. Christians and Muslims in India are mostly converts from lower caste demoninations who wanted to escape the violence and humiliation of the caste system. Hinduism, thus, is a brahminical construct that wears the mask of a religion to control non-brahmins from stepping out of its fold. It does this through a combination of 'commands and prohibitions' that scripturally justify violence against the lower castes and politically invoke a narrative of threat to their lives and livelihoods by the imagined outsider in the the Muslim and Christian. It is for this reason that B. R. Ambedkar wrote of Hindu scriptures:

> To put it in plain language, what the Hindus call Religion is really Law, or at best legalized class-ethics. Frankly, I refuse to call this code of ordinances as Religion. The first evil of such a code of ordinances, misrepresented to the people as Religion, is that it tends to deprive

moral life of freedom and spontaneity, and to reduce it (for the conscientious, at any rate) to a more or less anxious and servile conformity to externally imposed rules. Under it, there is no loyalty to ideals; there is only conformity to commands.

Dev's deified transcendental avatar in death seems to convey such a command to both Farhaan and the audience that places him beyond judgment. Ambedkar, 'Annihilation of Caste', 298, 299.

91. Oishik Sircar, 'The Silence of Gulbarg: Some Inadequate Images', *Human Rights Defender* 25, no. 1 (2016): 24.

92. Jumana Shah, '"Parzania" to Open in Gujarat in February', *DNA*, 30 January 2007, http://www.dnaindia.com/india/report-parzania-to-open-in-gujarat-in-february-1077047 (accessed 18 December 2022).

93. J. S. Bandukwala, 'Why Gujarat "Banned" Parzania', *Outlook*, 19 February 2007, http://www.outlookindia.com/magazine/story/why-gujarat-banned-parzania/233909 (accessed 18 December 2022); Urvish Kothari, 'Parzania and the Dictator of Gujarat', *Himal Southasian*, March 2007, https://old.himalmag.com/component/content/article/1193-parzania-and-the-dictator-of-gujarat.html (accessed 18 December 2022). Bajrangi had a template to follow. *Bombay*, a 1995 film on the anti-Muslim violence that spread through Mumbai in the wake of the demolition of the Babri Masjid, was also stalled from being released until it was approved by Bal Thackeray, a Hindutva leader of the Shiv Sena party. See Ravi S. Vasudevan, 'Bombay and Its Public', in *Pleasure and the Nation: The History, Politics and Consumption of Public Culture in India*, ed. Rachel Dwyer and Christopher Pinney (New Delhi: Oxford University Press, 2001), 186–211. In April 2023, Bajrangi was acquitted in the Naroda Gam massacre case where he was accused of killing 11 Muslims. This is in line with an emerging trend in Gujarat where many close to the BJP who were convicted for their role as perpetrators in the 2002 pogrom are now being acquitted by courts *en masse*. Nachiket Deuskar, 'Why Are Gujarat's Courts Increasingly Acquitting 2002 Riots Accused?', *Scroll.in*, 26 April 2023, https://scroll.in/article/1047905/why-are-gujarats-courts-increasingly-acquitting-2002-riots-accused (accessed 25 May 2023).

94. Somini Sengupta, 'In India, Showing Sectarian Pain to Eyes That Are Closed', *New York Times*, 20 February 2007, http://www.nytimes.com/2007/02/20/movies/20parz.html?n=Top/Reference/Times%20Topics/People/S/Sengupta,%20Somini&_r=0 (accessed 18 December 2022).

95. Ibid.

96. Rahul Dholakia, 'In Search of Parzania', CJP, 26 November 2007, https://cjp.org.in/in-search-of-parzania/ (accessed 18 December 2022).

97. Desai, 'Massacres and the Media'.

98. See Amrita Shah, *Ahmedabad: A City in the World* (New Delhi: Bloomsbury, 2015).

99. See Priyanka Dubey, 'Student Days: The Age of ABVP', *The Caravan*, 1 October 2017, https://caravanmagazine.in/reportage/age-of-abvp (accessed 18 December 2022).

100. TwoCircles, 'BJP's Bid to Rename Ahmedabad as "Amdavad"', 16 February 2011, http://twocircles.net/2011feb16/bjp%E2%80%99s_bid_rename_ahmedabad_%E2%80%98amdavad%E2%80%99.html#.VvzczuJ96Uk (accessed 18 December 2022); *Times of India*, 'AMC Officially Changes Logo, Makes Ahmedabad "Amdavad"', 10 February 2011, http://timesofindia.indiatimes.com/city/ahmedabad/AMC-officially-changes-logo-makes-Ahmedabad-Amdavad/articleshow/7463751.cms (accessed 18 December 2022). More recently, there has been a proposal to completely Hinduise the name of the city to Karnavati before the 2019 general elections. *Indian Express*, 'Looking at Legal Aspects to Rename Ahmedabad to Karnavati, Says Gujarat CM', 8 November 2018, https://indianexpress.com/article/india/looking-at-legal-aspects-to-rename-ahmedabad-to-karnavati-says-gujarat-cm-vijay-rupani-5437309/ (accessed 18 December 2022).

101. See Ornit Shani, 'Bootlegging, Politics and Corruption: State Violence and the Routine Practices of Public Power in Gujarat (1985–2002)', *South Asian History and Culture* 1, no. 4 (2010): 494.

102. See Neeladri Bhattacharya, 'Teaching History in Schools: The Politics of Textbooks in India', *History Workshop Journal* 67, no. 1 (2009): 99–110; Sylvie Guichard, *The Construction of History and Nationalism in India: Textbooks, Controversies and Politics* (London: Routledge, 2010). Kumkum Roy, 'Cleansing the Past? Creating the Future? Do (History) Books Matter?', *India Forum*, 3 May 2023, https://www.theindiaforum.in/education/cleansing-past-creating-future-do-history-books-matter (accessed 25 May 2023); Nehal Ahmed, 'Q&A: "The Word Hindu Is Arabic. Why Don't They Throw It Out?"', *Aljazeera*, 10 May 2023, https://www.aljazeera.com/news/2023/5/10/qa-the-word-hindu-is-arabic-why-dont-they-throw-it-out (accessed 25 May 2023); Romila Thapar, 'If NCERT Has Its Way, the Study of Indian History Will Move Entirely Outside of India', *The Wire*, 2 May 2023, https://thewire.in/history/ncert-

history-textbooks-mughals-india (accessed 25 May 2023). As revealed in an investigation carried out by the *Indian Express* newspaper, the re-writing of history textbooks for school students under the BJP has also resulted in references to Gujarat 2002 being taken out. See Ritika Chopra, 'Express Investigation—Part 1: From Emergency to Gujarat Riots, Lessons of Past Deleted from Textbooks of Future', *Indian Express*, 18 June 2022, https://indianexpress.com/article/express-exclusive/express-investigation-part-1-from-emergency-to-gujarat-riots-lessons-of-past-deleted-from-textbooks-of-future-7976207/ (accessed 25 May 2023).

103. A patriarchal Hindu ritual where the sister ties a bracelet on the brother's wrist and the brother promises to protect her from all evil. That a Parsi family can also observe the *rakhi* ceremony is used by the film to project it as a secularised practice.

104. For a history of the Parsis in India, see Jesse S. Palsetia, *The Parsis of India: Preservation of Identity in Bombay City* (Leiden: Brill, 2001). For a historical account of the position of Parsis as a religious minority in Indian law during colonialism, see Mitra Sharafi, *Law and Identity in Colonial South Asia: Parsi Legal Culture, 1772–1947* (Cambridge: Cambridge University Press, 2014).

105. Pandey, 'Can a Muslim be an Indian?', 622.

106. Ibid., 623–24.

107. *State of Gujarat v. Rajubhai Dhamirbhai Baria and Ors*, 2004 CriLJ 771 (26 December 2003), https://indiankanoon.org/doc/789410/ (accessed 18 December 2022).

108. Ibid.

109. Ibid.

110. Peter Rush, 'Dirty War Crimes: Jurisdictions of Memory and International Criminal Law', in *The Hidden Histories of War Crimes Trials*, ed. Kevin Heller and Gerry Simpson (Oxford: Oxford University Press, 2013), 377.

111. Rajagopalan Venkataraman, 'Courts, Last Bastion of the Good Old Typewriter', *Indian Express*, 9 November 2013, http://www.newindianexpress.com/cities/chennai/Courts-last-bastion-of-the-good-old-typewriter/2013/11/09/article1879797.ece (accessed 18 December 2022).

112. Chirodeep Chaudhuri, 'Street Typists of India', in *With Great Truth and Regard: The Story of the Typewriter in India*, ed. Sidharth Bhatia (Mumbai: Roli Books, 2016), 44.

113. For an account of the use of the typewriter as a prop in Hindi cinema, see Madhulika Liddle, 'Writing the Script of Life: The Typewriter in Hindi Cinema', in *With Great Truth and Regard*, ed. Bhatia, 280–92.

114. Section 146, Indian Penal Code, 1860, https://indiankanoon.org/doc/1601950/ (accessed 18 December 2022).

115. Narrain, 'Truth Telling, Gujarat and the Law'.

116. See IIJG, *Threatened Existence*.

117. Megha Chaturvedi and Puneet Nicholas Yadav, 'City Questions "Ban" on Parzania', *DNA*, 30 January 2007, http://www.dnaindia.com/mumbai/report-city-questions-ban-on-parzania-1077095 (accessed 18 December 2022).

118. This is, in all likelihood, a direct reference to the Vishva Hindu Parishad, a militant Hindu political outfit active in perpetrating violence in 2002. See generally Sarkar, 'Semiotics of Terror'.

119. The Nazi connection was also seen in a fleeting moment of a scene in *Dev*. During a conversation between Tejinder and Dev over a drink (a different one from the one discussed earlier), when Tejinder says that all Muslims should be brought out on the streets and shot, Dev in a somewhat jocular tone raises his hand with the glass of whiskey at Tejinder and says, 'Hail Hitler!'

120. Mehta, 'Modi and the Camera', 395.

121. 'Narendra Modi Speech after Godhra Incident 2002', https://www.youtube.com/watch?v=4CiuBBKJ30Q (accessed 18 December 2022).

122. Mitta, *The Fiction of Fact Finding*, 233.

123. Ibid.

124. Human Rights Watch, *We Have No Orders to Save You*.

125. Rush, 'Dirty War Crimes', 378.

126. Arundhati Roy, 'The Doctor and the Saint: Ambedkar, Gandhi and the Battle against Caste', *The Caravan*, 1 March 2014, https://caravanmagazine.in/essay/doctor-and-saint (accessed 18 December 2022). See also Faisal Devji, *The Impossible Indian: Gandhi and the Temptation of Violence* (Cambridge: Harvard University Press, 2012).

127. Vidhu Verma, 'Secularism in India', in *The Oxford Handbook of Secularism*, ed. Phil Zuckerman and John R. Shook (Oxford: Oxford University Press, 2017), 217.

128. See Kancha Ilaiah Shepherd, 'Swami Shashi', *The Caravan*, 1 May 2018, https://caravanmagazine.in/reviews-essays/political-hinduism-shashi-tharoor (accessed 18 December 2022).

129. Dholakia, 'In Search of Parzania'.

130. Sudipta Kaviraj, *The Imaginary Institution of India: Politics and Ideas* (New York: Columbia University Press, 2010), 167.

131. *Outlook*, 'Naroda Patiya: Kodnani, Bajrangi among 32 Convicted', 29 August 2012, https://www.outlookindia.com/newswire/story/naroda-patiya-kodnani-bajrangi-among-32-convicted/773493 (accessed 18 December 2022); Mahesh Langa, '2002 Post-Godhra Riots: Gujarat High Court Upholds Conviction of 19 in Ode Massacre Case', *The Hindu*, 11 May 2018, https://www.thehindu.com/news/national/other-states/2002-post-godhra-riots-gujarat-high-court-upholds-conviction-of-19-in-ode-massacre-case/article23856779.ece (accessed 18 December 2022).

132. *The Hindu*, 'Convictions in Bilkis Bano Case Hailed', 24 January 2008, https://www.thehindu.com/todays-paper/tp-national/tp-newdelhi/Convictions-in-Bilkis-Bano-case-hailed/article15150118.ece (accessed 18 December 2022). Those convicted in this case were released in August 2022 on the basis of the Gujarat government's remission policy. On their release, the accused were fed sweetmeats and garlanded by Hindutva activists. A BJP member of the Legislative Assembly said that since the accused were brahmins, they are cultured people so deserved to be out of jail. Gopi Maniar Ganghar, 'Bilkis Bano Rape Case: Released Convicts Greeted with Garlands at VHP Office', *India Today*, 17 August 2022, https://www.indiatoday.in/india/story/bilkis-bano-rape-case-convicts-greeted-garlands-vhp-office-1988996-2022-08-17 (accessed 26 May 2023); PTI, 'Some Convicts in Bilkis Bano Case Are "Brahmins with Good Sanskaar", Says BJP MLA', *The Hindu*, 19 August 2022, https://www.thehindu.com/news/national/other-states/some-convicts-in-bilkis-bano-case-are-brahmins-with-good-sanskaar-says-gujarat-bjp-mla/article65786447.ece (accessed 26 May 2023); Jyoti Punwani, 'Bilkis Bano Convicts Felicitated: Why Are We Surprised?', *Deccan Herald*, 19 August 2022, https://www.deccanherald.com/opinion/bilkis-bano-convicts-felicitated-why-are-we-surprised-1137467.html (accessed 26 May 2023).

133. Sanjay Srivastava, 'Modi-Masculinity: Media, Manhood, and "Traditions" in a Time of Consumerism', *Television and New Media* 16, no. 4 (2015): 331. Catarina Kinnvall, 'Populism, Ontological Insecurity and Hindutva: Modi and the Masculinization of Indian Politics', *Cambridge Review of International Affairs* 32, no. 3 (2019): 283–302.

134. Jivanta Schöttli and Markus Pauli, 'Modi-nomics and the Politics of Institutional Change in the Indian Economy', *Journal of Asian Public Policy* 9, no. 2 (2016): 154.

135. Spodek, 'In the Hindutva Laboratory'.

136. Priya Chacko, 'The Right Turn in India: Authoritarianism, Populism and Neoliberalisation', *Journal of Contemporary Asia* 48, no. 4 (2018): 541.

137. Vinod K. Jose, 'The Emperor Uncrowned: The Rise of Narendra Modi', *The Caravan*, 1 March 2012, https://caravanmagazine.in/reportage/emperor-uncrowned-narendra-modi-profile (accessed 18 December 2022).

138. Manas Dasgupta, 'SIT Finds No Proof against Modi, Says Court', *The Hindu*, 10 April 2012, http://www.thehindu.com/news/national/sit-finds-no-proof-against-modi-says-court/article3300175.ece (accessed 18 December 2022). This is a curious aside but nonetheless significant in the context of Hindutva's attempts to erase India's syncretic and Islamic pasts. So many expressions that are a regular part of modern Indian legal vocabulary—both inside and outside of posited texts—have pre-modern Islamicate origins. Clean chit can be traced back to the Persian expression *farigh-khatti*, a deed of release or discharge. Adhiraj Parthasarathy and Mohammad Dawood, 'Clean Chit, Taluka, Zilla: How Persian Lingers On in India's Legal and Revenue Language', *Scroll.in*, 31 December 2022, https://scroll.in/article/1040685/clean-chit-taluka-zilla-how-persian-lingers-on-in-indias-legal-and-revenue-language (accessed 26 May 2023); Nandini Chatterjee, 'Translating Obligations: *Tamassuk* and *Fārigh-Khattī* in the Indo-Persian World', *Journal of the Economic and Social History of the Orient* 64, no. 5–6 (2021): 541–82.

139. Mitta, *The Fiction of Fact Finding*.

140. Chetan Bhagat, *3 Mistakes of My Life* (New Delhi: Rupa, 2008).

141. Rakesh Ramamoorthy, 'Cricket and Majoritarian Nationalism in Chetan Bhagat's "The 3 Mistakes of My Life"', *Explicator* 74, no. 4 (2016): 202.

142. Snigdha Poonam, '"Kai Po Che" and the Strange Case of the Vanishing Villain', *New York Times*, 27 February 2013, https://india.blogs.nytimes.com/2013/02/27/did-chetan-bhagat-scrub-whitewash-the-godhra-riots-in-kai-po-che/ (accessed 18 December 2022); Aakar Patel, 'Riot Act', *The Caravan*, 1 April 2013, https://caravanmagazine.in/perspectives/riot-act (accessed 18 December 2022).

143. Zahir Janmohamed, 'Kai Po Che and the Reduction of 2002', *Kafila*, 2 March 2013, https://kafila.online/2013/03/02/kai-po-che-and-the-reduction-of-2002-zahir-janmohamed/ (accessed 18 December 2022); Debashree Mukherjee, 'No Time for Grieving—or Why We Should Talk Some More About Kai Po Che', *Kafila*, 19 March 2013, https://kafila.online/2013/03/19/no-time-for-grieving-or-why-we-should-talk-some-more-about-kai-po-che-debashree-mukherjee/ (18 December 2022).

144. *Times of India*, 'PIL against Kai Po Che for "Biased" Portrayal of Gujarat Riots', 3 May 2013, http://articles.timesofindia.indiatimes.com/2013-05-03/news-interviews/39007874_1_po-che-the-3-mistakes-hindi-film (accessed 18 December 2022).

145. *Bhautik Vijaykumar Bhatt v. Central Board of Film Certification*, C/WPPIL/104/2013 (23 September 2014), https://indiankanoon.org/doc/36425680/ (accessed 18 December 2022).

146. Iram Ghufran, 'Kai Po Che and the Politics of Appeasement and Reconciliation', *Phar'aat*, 13 March 2013, http://pharaat.blogspot.com/2013/03/kai-po-che-and-politics-of-appeasement.html (accessed 18 December 2022); Oishik Sircar, 'Coffee Shops, Cricket and a Pogrom', Infochange India, May 2013, http://infochangeindia.org/human-rights/373-human-rights/rights-and-resistance (accessed 18 December).

147. *Bhautik Vijaykumar Bhatt v. Central Board of Film Certification*.

148. Ibid.

149. See Desai, 'Producing and Contesting the "Communalized City"'.

150. It would not be too remote to suggest that the characters of the three friends symbolically map on to the characteristics attributed to the three topmost castes in the Hindu caste system. Omi is a brahmin (because his father is a priest and only brahmins can be priests). Although Govind and Ishaan are sartorially not marked as Hindu, Govind's entrepreneurial skills is a feature of the Baniya or merchant caste and Ishaan's fighting spirit as a sportsperson as well as his general aggressive temperament is a feature of the Kshatriya or warrior caste. The story of friendship that the film tells, thus, can also be read as one about how the deep bond between upper-caste friends help sustain the supremacy of Hindus in the face of acute trials and tribulations.

151. Madhavi Desai and Miki Desai, 'Ahmedabad: The City as Palimpsest', *Architecture Plus Design* 8, no. 3 (1991): 22.

152. Chalmers, 'In Narendra Modi's Gujarat, a Case of Rule and Divide'.

153. See Jaffrelot and Thomas, 'Facing Ghettoisation in Riot City'; Dhar, 'Disturbed Areas Act in Gujarat'.

154. Parvis Ghassem-Fachandi, 'Bridge over the Sabarmati: An Urban Journey into Violence and Back', *Journeys* 9, no. 1 (2008): 68.

155. My translation from Hindi to English.

156. For a discussion on the relationship between desire and development in the New India, see Aditya Nigam, *Desire Named Development* (New Delhi: Penguin, 2011). For an in-depth study of this relationship in the context of

international law and religion, see Jennifer L. Beard, *The Political Economy of Desire: International Law: Development and the Nation State* (New York: Routledge, 2007).

157. Ghassem-Fachandi, 'Bridge over the Sabarmati', 84–85. See also Raheel Dhattiwala, 'The Ecology of Ethnic Violence: The Attacks on Muslims of Ahmedabad in 2002', *Qualitative Sociology* 39 (2016): 71; Rajagopal, 'Urban Segregation and the Special Political Zone in Ahmedabad'.

158. Simpson, 'The State of Gujarat and the Men without Souls'.

159. Radstone, 'Cinema and Memory'.

160. See Desai, 'Producing and Contesting the "Communalized City"'.

161. Darshini Mahadevia, 'A City with Many Borders: Beyond Ghettoisation in Ahmedabad', in *Indian Cities in Transition*, ed. Annapurna Shaw (Hyderabad: Orient Longman, 2007), 341.

162. Saeed Khan, 'FIR Brands Ahmedabad's Muslim Area as Pakistan', *Times of India*, 19 September 2015, http://timesofindia.indiatimes.com/city/ahmedabad/FIR-brands-Ahmedabads-Muslim-area-as-Pakistan/article show/49019847.cms (accessed 18 December 2022).

163. The Western white man in *Parzania*, the secular Hindu police officer in *Dev* and the secular Hindu youth in *Kai Po Che*, all play the role of saviour. The subjects attracting saving are all religious minorities (Muslims in *Dev* and *Kai Po Che*, and Parsi in *Parzania*). As a critic has asked: 'Would the success of Hashmi be possible without the benevolence of Ishan?' See Ali Khan Mahmudabad, 'The Kai Po Che Question', *Outlook*, 8 March 2013, https://www.outlookindia.com/website/story/the-kai-po-che-question/284287 (accessed 18 December 2022).

164. See Edward Simpson, *The Political Biography of an Earthquake: Aftermath and Amnesia in Gujarat, India* (New Delhi: Oxford University Press, 2013).

165. My translation from Hindi to English.

166. Berenike Jung, *Narrating Violence in Post-9/11 Action Cinema: Terrorist Narratives, Action Cinema and Referentiality* (Wiesbaden: VS Research, 2010), 52. Another expression used in cinema studies literature for this narrative technique has been called 'liveness' that uses televisual referentiality that invokes in the audience of a film a 'sense of synchronicity with the event'. Abhijit Roy, 'Live(li)ness and Network Publics in Post Liberalization Indian Popular Films', *Journal of the Moving Image* 5 (2006), http://jmionline.org/article/liveli_ness_and_network_publics_in_post_liberalization_indian_popular_films (accessed 18 December 2022).

167. David Kazanjian, quoted in Puar, *Terrorist Assemblages*, xviii.

168. See generally Varadarajan, *Gujarat: The Making of a Tragedy*.

169. Satish Jha, 'Gulbarg Society Massacre Verdict: "Mob Dragged Out Ahsan Jafri, Burnt Him Alive"', *Indian Express*, 18 June 2016, https://indianexpress. com/article/india/india-news-india/gulberg-society-massacre-verdict-details-mob-dragged-out-ahsan-jafri-burnt-him-alive-2859757/ (accessed 18 December 2022).

170. In the middle of this tense situation, Ishaan comes to know of Govind's romantic relationship with Vidya, his sister (by reading an SMS on Govind's mobile), and he beats him up when he arrives. Thus, while Ishaan demonstrates secular benevolence towards Ali, his response to his sister is a demonstration of a patriarchal protectiveness.

171. *The Hindu*, 'Gujarat Government to Seek Death Penalty for Kodnani, Bajrangi', 17 April 2013, http://www.thehindu.com/news/national/other-states/gujarat-government-to-seek-death-penalty-for-kodnani-bajrangi/article4626829.ece (accessed 18 December 2022); Press Trust of India, 'Modi's Decision to Seek Death Penalty for Maya Kodnani a Deadly Attack on Hindus: Shiv Sena', *Indian Express*, 20 April 2013, http://www. indianexpress.com/news/modis-decision-to-seek-death-for-maya-kodnani-a-deadly-attack-on-hindus-shiv-sena/1105307/ (accessed 18 December 2022).

172. Modi's later decision to put the death penalty on hold for seeking legal opinion from the advocate general can be read as further attesting to his belief in due process. *The Telegraph*, 'Modi Rethink on Death for Ex-minister', 15 May 2013, https://www.telegraphindia.com/india/modi-rethink-on-death-for-ex-minister/cid/1312328 (accessed 18 December 2022).

173. Sanjay Ruparelia, '"Minimum Government, Maximum Governance": The Restructuring of Power in Modi's India', *South Asia: Journal of South Asian Studies* 38, no. 4 (2015): 755.

174. See generally Sharda Ugra, 'Play Together, Live Apart: Religion, Politics and Markets in Indian Cricket since 1947', in *Cricket and National Identity in the Postcolonial Age: Following On*, ed. Stephen Wagg (Abingdon: Routledge, 2005), 77–93; Satadru Sen, 'History without a Past: Memory and Forgetting in Indian Cricket', in *Cricket and National Identity in the Postcolonial Age*, 94–109.

175. The tragedy faced by the child is the most painful blow to the secular nation, and the popular consumption of hope is also extracted through the child.

See generally Patricia Uberoi, *Freedom and Destiny: Gender, Family and Popular Culture in India* (New Delhi: Oxford University Press, 2006).

Chapter 5

1. Jacqueline Rose, *On Not Being Able to Sleep: Psychoanalysis and the Modern World* (London: Chatto and Windus, 2003), 7.
2. David Scott, 'Colonial Governmentality', *Social Text* 43 (Autumn 1995): 202–03 (emphasis in original).
3. Michel Foucault, 'Governmentality', in *The Foucault Effect: Studies in Governmentality*, ed. Graham Burchell, Colin Gordon and Peter Miller (Chicago: University of Chicago Press, 1991), 87–104, 100.
4. The language of developmentalism that is being deployed by the BJP in making a virtue out of such a rationality is *atmanirbharta*, or self-reliance. In the operationalisation of this rationality Indian Muslims are being responsibilised and disciplined as the 'agents of their own abuse'. This responsibilised version of the Muslim citizen can now be seen in characters in Bollywood blockbusters as one who is secular, patriotic and will go to any lengths to protect the nation from rogue outsiders. See Priya Chacko, 'Disciplining India: Paternalism, Neo-liberalism and *Hindutva* Civilizationalism', *International Affairs* 99, no. 2 (March 2023): 551–65; Jacqueline Rose, 'Agents of Their Own Abuse', *London Review of Books* 41, no. 19 (October 2019), https://www.lrb.co.uk/the-paper/v41/n19/jacqueline-rose/agents-of-their-own-abuse (accessed 24 May 2023); Azad Essa, 'How Shahrukh Khan's Pathaan Will Strengthen Hindu Nationalism', *Middle East Eye*, 3 February 2023, https://www.middleeasteye.net/opinion/india-shah-rukh-khan-pathaan-hindutva-strengthen-how (accessed 23 May 2023).
5. Ibid.
6. Gupta, *Red Tape*, 17. Since 2019, Narendra Modi's second term as prime minister, the intensification of violence against India's Muslim citizens has only gained in strength and impunity. These newer forms of anti-Muslim violence in the New India combine state-supported mass killing, like the 2020 pogrom in Delhi, with everyday forms of 'maiming' through psychic wounds, economic boycotts and legal disenfranchisement. It is not surprising that Bollywood cinema has become a key site for contestations around narratives that advance a justification for Hindutva's hatred of Muslims or for violence directed at films that question or critique such hatred. For a conceptual

understanding of maiming as a new form of violence sanctioned through sovereign power that is distinct yet related to the sovereign's technologies of killing, see Jasbir K. Puar, *The Right to Maim: Debility, Capacity, Disability* (Durham: Duke University Press, 2017). For accounts of these newer forms of anti-Muslim violence that have emerged in India over the last decade, see Mohsin Alam Bhat, 'Stateless and Hyperlegalized', *The Baffler*, 3 January 2020, https://thebaffler.com/logical-revolts/stateless-and-hyperlegalized-alam (accessed 23 May 2023); Shivangi Mariam Raj, 'The Forsaken Ones', *Verso Blog*, 10 May 2022, https://www.versobooks.com/en-gb/blogs/news/5348-the-forsaken-ones?_pos=1&_sid=3e3a5626f&_ss=r (accessed 25 May 2023); Mani Chander, 'The Rising Intimidation of Indian Muslims and the Criminalisation of Eating, Praying, Loving and Doing Business', *Article 14*, 16 September 2022, https://article-14.com/post/the-rising-intimidation-of-india-s-muslims-the-criminalisation-of-eating-praying-loving-doing-business-6323ce1e74c10 (accessed 23 May 2023); Chander Uday Singh (ed.), *Routes of Wrath: Weaponising Religious Processions* (New Delhi: Citizens and Lawyers Initiative, 2023); Bebaak Collective, *Social Suffering in a World Without Support: Report on the Mental Health of Indian Muslims* (New Delhi: Bebaak Collective, 2022), https://kafila.online/2023/05/19/social-suffering-in-a-world-without-support-report-on-the-mental-health-of-indian-muslims-bebaak-collective/#more-45139 (accessed 23 May 2023); Azad Essa, 'For Indian Muslims the End Times Have Arrived', *Middle East Eye*, 14 April 2023, https://www.middleeasteye.net/opinion/india-muslims-end-times-arrived (accessed 23 May 2023). For accounts of how Bollywood cinema is emerging as a vehicle for the Hindu Right's anti-Muslim maiming machine even in case of films with seemingly secular credentials, see Debasish Roy Choudhury, 'How Bollywood Rolled Over to Hindu Supremacists', *Time*, 26 January 2023, https://time.com/6250414/bollywood-hindu-supremacists/ (accessed 23 May 2023); Atish Taseer, 'The War on Bollywood', *The Atlantic*, 10 June 2021, https://www.theatlantic.com/magazine/archive/2021/07/can-bollywood-survive-modi/619008/ (accessed 23 May 2023); Akshat Jain, 'Setting the Scene: How Hindi Film Adaptations Align with the Hindutva Project', *Caravan*, 31 August 2022, https://caravanmagazine.in/film/adaptations-foreign-films-hindi-cinema-hindutva (accessed 23 May 2023); Pooja Biraia Jaiswal, 'How RSS Is Furthering the Idea of Hindutva through Bollywood', *The Week*, 30 April 2023, https://www.theweek.in/theweek/leisure/2023/04/22/rss-hindutva-agenda-in-hindi-films.html (accessed 23 May 2023).

7. See Tania Murray, *The Will to Improve: Governmentality, Development, and the Practice of Politics* (Durham: Duke University Press, 2007).

8. Upendra Baxi, 'Constitutionalism as a Site of State Formative Practices', *Cardozo Law Review* 21 (February 2000): 1183.

9. Aijaz Ahmad, 'Right-Wing Politics, and the Cultures of Cruelty', *Social Scientist* 26, nos. 9–10 (September–October 1998): 5.

Glossary

asmita	pride
atmanirbharta	self-reliance
bindi	a dot of varying sizes that mostly South Asian women adorn in between their eyebrows
chaturvarnya	four-fold hierarchy of the Hindu caste system
darsana	a technique particular to Indian cinema's aesthetic
dharma	a divinely ordained duty as revealed in the scriptures of Hindu law
Dharmaśātra	a specific set of Hindu scriptures that form the foundations and corpus of Hindu jurisprudence
farigh-khatti	a deed of release or discharge
kar seva	religious service
lakhs	a unit followed in the South Asian numbering system, where 1 lakh = 100,000
lungi	Indian sarong
mlechha	outsider
*pol*s	religion, caste and occupation based residential areas
pratikriya	retributive reaction
rakhi	a patriarchal Hindu ritual where the sister ties a bracelet on the brother's wrist and the brother promises to protect her from all evil
rashtra	nation; homeland
salwar kameez	a traditional knee-length shirt and loose pajamas worn both by men and women in many South Asian countries
sanskari nagari	city of culture
shloka	chant; verse
sindoor	a smear of vermilion worn traditionally by Hindu women on the parting of their hair right above the forehead as a mark of being married
*trishul*s	tridents
zari	decorative embroidery on clothing using gold threads

Bibliography

Legislation

Code of Criminal Procedure, 1973.

Constitution of India, 1949.

Disturbed Areas Act, 1991.

Indian Cinematograph Act, 1952.

Indian Evidence Act, 1855.

The State Emblem of India (Prohibition of Improper Use) Act, 2005.

Case Law

ADM Jabalpur v. Shivkant Shukla (1976 AIR 1207). https://indiankanoon.org/doc/1735815/. Accessed 26 May 2023.

Bhautik Vijaykumar Bhatt v. Central Board of Film Certification. C/WPPIL/104/2013, 23 September 2014. https://indiankanoon.org/doc/36425680/. Accessed 18 December 2022.

K. A. Abbas v. Union of India. 1971 AIR 481. https://indiankanoon. org/doc/1719619/. Accessed 25 May 2023.

Lalita Kumari v. Govt of Uttar Pradesh. 1 Writ Petition (Criminal) No. 68 of 2008, 12 November 2013. https://indiankanoon.org/doc/10239019/. Accessed 18 December 2022.

Leeson v. General Medical Council. LJ 59 Ch NS 233, 1889.

M. Siddiq v. Mahant Suresh Das and others. Civil Appeal Nos. 10866–0867 of 2010, Supreme Court of India, 2019. https://indiankanoon.org/doc/107745042/. Accessed 18 December 2022.

Sat Pal v. Delhi Administration. 1976 AIR 294, 29 September 1975. https://indiankanoon.org/doc/916840/. Accessed 18 December 2022.

Sheela Barse and Ors v. Union of India and Ors. JT 1986 136, 13 August 1986. http://indiankanoon.org/doc/525548/. Accessed 18 December 2022.

State of Gujarat v. Rajubhai Dhamirbhai Baria and Ors. Fast Track Court No. 1, Vadodara, Sessions Case No. 248/2002 of the Additional Sessions Judge H. U. Mahida, Judgment of 27 June 2003.

State of Gujarat v. Rajubhai Dhamirbhai Baria and Ors. 2004 CriLJ 771, 26 December 2003. https://indiankanoon.org/doc/789410/. Accessed 18 December 2022.

Teesta Setalvad and Anr v. State of Gujarat and Ors. Appeal (crl.) 443–445 of 2004, 12 April 2004. https://indiankanoon.org/doc/387523/. Accessed 18 December 2022.

V. C. Shukla v. State (Delhi Administration). 1980 AIR 1382.

Zahira Habibullah Sheikh and Another v. State of Gujarat and Others. Appeal (crl.) 446–449 of 2004, 12 April 2004. https://indiankanoon.org/doc/105430/. Accessed 18 December 2022.

Zahira Habibullah Sheikh and Anr v. State of Gujarat and Ors. Appeal (crl.) 446–449 of 2004, 8 March 2006. https://indiankanoon.org/doc/1067991/. Accessed 18 December 2022.

Scholarship, Human Rights Reports and Journalism

Abbas, Hoveyda, and Ranajay Kumar. *Political Theory.* New Delhi: Pearson, 2012, 154–55.

Abraham, Anita. 'Mass Crimes Committed in Gujarat in 2002: Immediate Need for a Mass Crimes Law'. Working Paper Series CSLG/WP/15, Centre for the Study of Law and Governance, Jawaharlal Nehru University, New Delhi, November 2012. https://www.jnu.ac.in/sites/default/files/u63/15-Mass%20%28Anita%29.pdf. Accessed 18 December 2022.

Abraham, Itty. *The Making of the Indian Atomic Bomb: Science, Secrecy and the Postcolonial State.* New Delhi: Orient Longman, 1999.

Acevedo, Deepa Das. 'Autocratic Legalism in India: A Roundtable'. *Jindal Global Law Review* 13, no. 1 (June 2022): 117–40.

Adeney, Katharine, and Lawrence Sáez (eds.). *Coalition Politics and Hindu Nationalism.* New York: Routledge, 2005.

Agnes, Flavia. 'Has the Codified Hindu Law Changed Gender Relationships?' *Social Change* 46, no. 4 (2016): 611–23.

———. 'The Supreme Court, the Media, and the Uniform Civil Code Debate in India'. In *The Crisis of Secularism in India*, edited by Anuradha Dingwaney Needham and Rajeswari Sunder Rajan, 295–315. Durham: Duke University Press, 2007.

Ahluwalia, Montek S., Deepak Nayyar and Prabhat Patnaik. *Quarter Century of Liberalisation in India.* New Delhi: Oxford University Press, 2018.

Ahmad, Aijaz. *Lineages of the Present: Ideology and Politics in Contemporary South Asia.* London: Verso, 2002.

———. 'Right-Wing Politics, and the Cultures of Cruelty'. *Social Scientist* 26, nos. 9–10 (September–October 1998): 3–25.

Ahmad, Irfan. 'In Conversation with an Ordinary Indian: Kaliyuga, War, End of the Word and Hindutva'. *Journal of Religious and Political Practice* 3, nos. 1–2 (2017): 57–74.

Ahmed, Akbar S. 'Bombay Films: The Cinema as Metaphor for Indian Society and Politics'. *Modern Asian Studies* 26, no. 2 (1992): 289–320.

Ahmed, Heba. 'The Gulbarg Memorial and the Problem of Memory'. In *Partition and the Practice of Memory*, edited by Churnjeet Mahn and Anne Murphy, 175–210. Cham, Switzerland: Palgrave Macmillan, 2018.

Ahmed, Hilal. 'Making Sense of India's Citizenship Amendment Act 2019: Process, Politics, Protests'. *Asie.Visions* 114 (June 2020): 9–10.

———. 'Muzaffarnagar 2013: Meanings of Violence'. *Economic and Political Weekly* 48, no. 40 (2013): 10–13.

———. *Siyasi Muslims: A Story of Political Islams in India*. New Delhi: India Viking, 2019.

Ahmad, Imtiaz (ed.). *Caste and Social Stratification among Muslims in India*. New Delhi: Aakar Books, 2018.

Alfaro, María Jesús Martínez. 'Intertextuality: Origins and Development of the Concept'. *Atlantis* 18, nos. 1–2 (1996): 268–85.

Ali, Amir. 'The Sachar Committee Report and Multiculturalism in India: Questions of Group Equality and the Public Sphere'. In *Religion, Communities and Development: Changing Contours of Politics and Policy in India*, edited by Gurpreet Mahajan and Surinder S. Jodhka, 65–82. New Delhi: Routledge, 2010.

Ambedkar, B. R. 'Annihilation of Caste'. In *The Essential Writings of B. R. Ambedkar*, edited by Valerian Rodrigues, 263–305. New Delhi: Oxford University Press, 2010.

———. 'Krishna and His Gita'. In *The Essential Writings of B. R. Ambedkar*, edited by Valerian Rodrigues, 193–204. New Delhi: Oxford University Press, 2010.

———. *Pakistan or the Partition of India*. Bombay: Thackers Publishers, 1940.

———. 'The Doom of the Untouchables'. In *The Essential Writings of B. R. Ambedkar*, edited by Valerian Rodrigues. New Delhi: Oxford University Press, 2010.

Amnesty International. 'A Decade on from the Gujarat Riots, an Overwhelming Majority of Victims Await Justice in India'. April 2012. http://www.coalitionagainstgenocide.org/reports/2012/Amnesty-International-A-decade-on-from-the-Gujarat%20riots.pdf. Accessed 18 December 2022.

Anand, Dibyesh. *Hindu Nationalism in India and the Politics of Fear*. New York: Palgrave Macmillan, 2011.

————. 'The Violence of Security: Hindu Nationalism and the Politics of Representing "the Muslim" as a Danger'. *Round Table: Commonwealth Journal of International Affairs* 94, no. 379 (2005): 203–15.

Anderson, Benedict. *Imagined Communities: Reflections on the Origin and Spread of Nationalism*. London: Verso, 2016.

Ansari, Khalid Anis. 'Revisiting the Minority Imagination: An Inquiry into the Anticaste Pasmanda-Muslim Discourse in India'. *Critical Philosophy of Race* 11, no. 1 (2023): 120–47.

Antaki, Mark. 'Making Sense of Minor Jurisprudence'. *Law Text Culture* 21, nos. 1–4 (2017): 54–75.

Apte, Vaman Shivaram. *The Practical Sanskrit-English Dictionary*. Poona: Prasad Prakashan, 1957, 835.

Arif, Yasmeen. *Life, Emergent: The Social in the Afterlives of Violence*. Minneapolis: University of Minnesota Press, 2016.

————. 'The Audacity of Method'. *Economic and Political Weekly* 50, no. 1 (2015): 53–61.

Ashcroft, Bill. 'Towards a Postcolonial Aesthetics'. *Journal of Postcolonial Writing* 51, no. 4 (2015): 410–21.

Asimow, Michael (ed.). *Lawyers in Your Living Room! Law on Television*. Chicago: American Bar Association, 2009.

Asmal, K., L. Asmal and R. S. Roberts. *Reconciliation through Truth: A Reckoning with Apartheid's Criminal Governance*. Cape Town: David Philip Publishers, with Mayibue, University of the Western Cape, 1996.

Assman, Jan. *Moses the Egyptian: The Memory of Egypt in Western Monotheism*. Cambridge: Harvard University Press, 1997.

Austin, John. *The Province of Jurisprudence Determined*. Cambridge: Cambridge University Press, 1995.

Austin, J. L. *How to Do Things with Words*. 2nd ed. Cambridge: Harvard University Press, 1975.

Avikunthak, Ashish. *Bureaucratic Archeology: State, Science and Past in Postcolonial India*. New Delhi: Cambridge University Press, 2021, xiv-xvii

Ayyub, Rana. *Gujarat Files: Anatomy of a Cover Up*. New Delhi: Rana Ayyub, 2016.

Balagopal, K. 'Reflections on Gujarat Pradesh of Hindu Rashtra'. *Economic and Political Weekly* 37, no. 22 (2002): 2117–19.

————. 'This Anti-Mandal Mania'. *Economic and Political Weekly* 25, no. 40 (1990): 2231–34.

Banaji, Jairus (ed.). *Fascism: Essays on Europe and India*. Gurgaon: Three Essays Collective, 2016.

Bandes, Susan A. (ed.). *The Passions of Law*. New York: NYU Press, 2000.

Banerjee, Sikata. *Gender, Nation and Popular Film in India: Globalizing Muscular Nationalism*. New York: Routledge, 2016.

Barthes, Roland. *Camera Lucida: Reflections on Photography*. Translated by Richard Howard. New York: Farrar, Straus and Giroux, 1981.

———. 'From Work to Text'. In *The Rustle of Language*. Translated by Richard Howard. New York: Hill and Wang, 1986.

Basu, Amrita. *Violent Conjunctures in Democratic India*. New York: Cambridge University Press, 2015.

Basu, Anustup. *Bollywood in the Age of New Media: The Geo-televisual Aesthetic*. Edinburgh: Edinburgh University Press, 2010.

———. *Hindutva as Polilitcal Monotheism*. Durham: Duke University Press, 2020.

Basu, Manisha. *The Rhetoric of Hindu India: Language and Urban Nationalism*. New York: Cambridge University Press, 2017.

Basu, Kasturi, and Dwaipayan Banerjee (eds.). *Towards a People's Cinema: Independent Documentary and Its Audience in India*. Gurgaon: Three Essays Collective, 2018.

Basu, Sisir. 'The Tragedy of Gujarat 2002 Haunts'. In *Experiments in Film Appreciation*, edited by Sisir Basu, Alessandro Monti and Carole Rozzonelli, 5–16. Torino: New Dost Edition, 2012.

Basu, Tapan, Pradip Datta, Sumit Sarkar, Tanika Sarkar and Sambuddha Sen. *Khaki Shorts, Saffron Flags*. New Delhi: Orient Longman, 1993.

Baviskar, Amita. *In the Belly of the River: Tribal Conflicts over Development in the Narmada Valley*. New Delhi: Oxford University Press, 2004.

Bayley, David H. *The Police and Political Development in India*. Princeton: Princeton University Press, 1969.

Baxi, Pratiksha. '"Mock Trial": Law, Violence and Governance in the Aftermath of Gujarat 2002'. Paper presented at the Just-India Workshop, Paris, 28 October 2010.

Baxi, Upendra. 'Constitutionalism as a Site of State Formative Practices'. *Cardozo Law Review* 21 (February 2000): 1183–210.

———. 'Law and State Regulated Capitalism in India: Some Preliminary Remarks'. In *Capitalist Development: Critical Essays*, edited by Ghanshyam Shah, 185–209. Bombay: Popular Prakashan, 1990.

———. *Memory and Rightlessness*. New Delhi: Centre for Women's Development Studies, 2003.

———. 'Postcolonial Legality: A Postscript from India'. *Law and Politics in Africa, Asia and Latin America* 45, no. 2 (2012): 178–94.

————. 'Reflections on the Reservations Crisis in Gujarat'. In *Mirrors of Violence: Communities, Riots and Survivors in South Asia*, edited by Veena Das, 215–39. New Delhi: Oxford University Press, 1992.

————. 'Taking Suffering Seriously: Social Action Litigation in the Supreme Court of India'. *Third World Legal Studies* 4, no. 1 (1985): 107–32.

————. 'The Second Gujarat Catastrophe'. *Economic and Political Weekly* 37, no. 34 (2002): 3519–31.

Beard, Jennifer L. *The Political Economy of Desire: International Law: Development and the Nation State*. New York: Routledge, 2007.

Beaster-Jones, Jayson, and Natalie Sarrazin (eds.). *Music in Contemporary Indian Film: Memory, Voice, Identity*. New York: Routledge, 2016.

Bebaak Collective. *Social Suffering in a World Without Support: Report on the Mental Health of Indian Muslims*. New Delhi: Bebaak Collective, 2022. https://kafila.online/2023/05/19/social-suffering-in-a-world-without-support-report-on-the-mental-health-of-indian-muslims-bebaak-collective/#more-45139. Accessed 23 May 2023.

Ben-Dor, Oren. 'Standing before the Gates of the Law?' In *Law and Art: Ethics, Aesthetics, Justice*, edited by Oren Ben-Dor, 1–29. London: Routledge-Cavendish, 2011.

Benegal, Shyam. 'Secularism and Popular Indian Cinema'. In *The Crisis of Secularism in India*, edited by Anuradha Dingwaney Needham and Rajeshwari Sunder Rajan, 225–38. Ranikhet: Permanent Black, 2007.

Berenschot, Ward. *Riot Politics: India's Communal Violence and the Everyday Mediation of the State*. London: Hurst, 2012.

Berger, John. *Ways of Seeing*. London: Penguin, 1972.

Bhaduri, Amit, and Deepak Nayyar. *The Intelligent Person's Guide to Liberalization*. New Delhi: Penguin, 1996.

Bhargava, Rajeev. 'The Distinctiveness of Indian Secularism'. In *The Future of Secularism*, edited by T. N. Srinivasan, 20–53. Delhi: Oxford University Press, 2007.

————. *The Promise of India's Secular Democracy*. New Delhi: Oxford University Press, 2010.

———— (ed.). *Secularism and Its Critics*. New Delhi: Oxford University Press, 2000.

————. 'What Is Indian Secularism and What Is It For?' *India Review* 1, no. 1 (2002): 1–32.

Bharucha, Rustom. *Terror and Performance*. London: Routledge, 2014.

Bhatia, Gautam. *Offend, Shock or Disturb: Free Speech Under the Indian Constitution*. New Delhi: Oxford University Press, 2016.

Bhattacharya, Nandini. 'Romancing Religion: Neoliberal Bollywood's Gendered Visual Repertoire for a Pain-Free Globalisation'. In *Tracing an Indian Diaspora: Contexts, Memories, Representations*, edited by Parvati Raghuram, Ajaya Kumar Sahoo, Brij Maharaj and Dave Sangha, 346–67. New Delhi: Sage, 2008.

Bhattacharya, Neeladri, 'Teaching History in Schools: The Politics of Textbooks in India'. *History Workshop Journal* 67, no. 1 (2009): 99–110.

Bhowmik, Someswar. *Cinema and Censorship: The Politics of Control in India*. New Delhi: Orient BlackSwan, 2009.

Bhuwania, Anuj. 'Black Friday: Mediation and the Impossibility of Justice'. Working Paper Series CSLG/WP/17, Centre for the Study of Law and Governance, Jawaharlal Nehru University, New Delhi, November 2012. https://www.jnu.ac.in/sites/default/files/u63/17-Black%20%28Anuj%29. pdf. Accessed 18 December 2022.

Biber, Katherine. *Captive Images: Race, Crime, Photography*. London: Routledge, 2014.

———. *In Crime's Archive: The Cultural Afterlife of Evidence*. London: Routledge, 2017.

Bindal Amit, '"Complete Justice"? Silences and Erasures in the Ayodhya Judgment'. *Journal of Indian Law and Society* 11, no. 1 (Monsoon 2020): 48–71.

Birla, Ritu. 'Jurisprudence of Emergence: Neo-liberalism and the Public as Market in India'. *South Asia: Journal of South Asian Studies* 38, no. 3 (2015): 466–80.

Black, David A. *Law in Film: Resonance and Representation*. Champaign: University of Illinois Press, 1999.

Bobbio, Tommaso. 'Never-Ending Modi *Hindutva* and Gujarati Neoliberalism as Prelude to All-India Premiership?' *Focaal: Journal of Global and Historical Anthropology* 67 (December 2013): 123–34.

———. *Urbanisation, Citizenship and Conflict in India: Ahmedabad 1900–2000*. London: Routledge, 2015.

Bose, Nandana. 'The Hindu Right and the Politics of Censorship: Three Case Studies of Policing Hindi Cinema, 1992–2002'. *Velvet Light Trap* 63 (Spring 2009): 22–33.

———. '"We Do Not Certify Backwards": Film Censorship in Postcolonial India'. In *Silencing Cinema: Film Censorship Around the World*, edited by Daniel Biltereyst and Roel Vande Winkel, 191–206. New York: Palgrave Macmillan, 2013.

Bose, Sumantra. *Kashmir: Roots of Conflict, Paths to Peace*. Cambridge: Harvard University Press, 2005.

Brass, Paul R. *Forms of Collective Violence: Riots, Pogroms, and Genocide in Modern India*. Gurgaon: Three Essays Collective, 2006.

——— (ed.). *Riots and Pogroms*. London: Macmillan, 1996.

———. *The Production of Hindu–Muslim Violence in Contemporary India*. New Delhi: Oxford University Press, 2003.

Brosius, Christiane. *India's Middle Class: New Forms of Urban Leisure, Consumption and Prosperity*. New Delhi: Routledge, 2010.

Brosius, Christiane, and Melissa Butcher (eds.). *Image Journeys: Audio-visual Media and Cultural Change in India*. New Delhi: Sage, 1999.

Brown, Michelle, and Nicole Rafter. 'Genocide Films, Public Criminology, Collective Memory'. *British Journal of Criminology* 53, no. 6 (2013): 1017–32.

Brown, Wendy, and Janet Halley (eds.). *Left Legalism/Left Critique*. Durham: Duke University Press, 2002.

Buchanan, Ruth, and Rebecca Johnson. 'Strange Encounters: Exploring Law and Film in the Affective Register'. In *Studies in Law, Politics and Society*, edited by Austin Sarat, 33–60. Studies in Law, Politics and Society, vol. 46. Bingley: Emerald Group Publishing, 2008.

Bunsha, Dionne. *Scarred: Experiments with Violence in Gujarat*. New Delhi: Penguin, 2007.

Butalia, Urvashi. *The Other Side of Silence: Voices from the Partition of India*. Durham: Duke University Press, 2000.

Casolari, Marzia. 'Hindutva's Foreign Tie-Up in 1930s: Archival Evidence'. *Economic and Political Weekly* 35, no. 4 (2000): 218–28.

———. *In the Shade of the Swastika: The Relationships between Indian Radical Nationalism, Italian Fascism and Nazism*. Oxford: Routledge, 2020.

Chacko, Priya. 'Disciplining India: Paternalism, Neo-liberalism and *Hindutva* Civilizationalism'. *International Affairs* 99, no. 2 (March 2023): 551–65.

———. 'Marketizing Hindutva: The State, Society, and Markets in Hindu Nationalism'. *Modern Asian Studies* (First View) (2008): 1. https://www-cambridge-org./core/journals/modern-asian-studies/article/marketizing-hindutva-the-state-society-and-markets-in-hindu-nationalism/. Accessed 18 December 2022.

———. 'The Right Turn in India: Authoritarianism, Populism and Neoliberalisation'. *Journal of Contemporary Asia* 48, no. 4 (2018): 541–64.

Chacko, Priya, and Peter Mayer. 'The Modi Lahar (Wave) in the 2014 Indian National Election: A Critical Realignment?' *Australian Journal of Political Science* 49, no. 3 (2014): 518–28.

Chadha, Kalyanee, and Anandam P. Kavoori. 'Exoticized, Marginalized, Demonized: The Muslim "Other" in Indian Cinema'. In *Global Bollywood*, edited by Anandam P. Kavoori and Aswin Punathambekar, 131–45. New York: New York University Press, 2008.

Chakravartty, Paula, and Srirupa Roy. 'Mr Modi Goes to Delhi: Mediated Populism and the 2014 Indian Elections'. *Television and New Media* 16, no. 4 (2015): 311–22.

Chakravarty, Sumita S. *National Identity in Indian Popular Cinema, 1947–1987*. Austin: University of Texas Press, 1993.

Chandoke, Neera. 'Modi's Gujarat and Its Little Illusions'. *Economic and Political Weekly* 47, no. 49 (2012): 10–11.

Chase, Anthony. *Movies on Trial: The Legal System on the Silver Screen*. New York: The New Press, 2002.

Chattarji, Subarno. 'Some Comments on Media Representations of the Gujarat Riots and the Kargil War'. In *Tracking the Media: Interpretations of Mass Media Discourses in India and Pakistan*, 36–59. New York: Routledge, 2008.

Chatterjee, Moyukh. *Composing Violence: The Limits of Exposure and the Making of Minorities*. Durham: Duke University Press, 2023.

———. 'The Impunity Effect: Majoritarian Rule, Everyday Legality, and State Formation in India'. *American Ethnologist* 44, no. 1 (2017): 118–30.

Chatterjee, Nandini. 'Translating Obligations: *Tamassuk* and *Fārigh-Khaṭṭī* in the Indo-Persian World'. *Journal of the Economic and Social History of the Orient* 64, no. 5–6 (2021): 541–82.

Chatterji, Angana P. *Violent Gods: Hindu Nationalism in India's Present— Narratives from Orissa*. Gurgaon: Three Essays Collective, 2009.

Chatterji, Roma, and Deepak Mehta. *Living with Violence: An Anthropology of Events and Everyday Life*. New Delhi: Routledge, 2007.

Chaudhuri, Chirodeep. 'Street Typists of India'. In *With Great Truth and Regard: The Story of the Typewriter in India*, edited by Sidharth Bhatia, 38–51. Mumbai: Roli Books, 2016.

Chopra, Radhika. '1984: Disinterred Memories'. *Sikh Formations: Religion, Culture, Theory* 11, no. 3 (2015): 306–15.

Chopra, Ritika. 'Express Investigation—Part 1: From Emergency to Gujarat Riots, Lessons of Past Deleted from Textbooks of Future'. *Indian Express*, 18

June 2022. https://indianexpress.com/article/express-exclusive/express-investigation-part-1-from-emergency-to-gujarat-riots-lessons-of-past-deleted-from-textbooks-of-future-7976207/. Accessed 25 May 2023.

Chopra, Surabhi, and Prita Jha (eds.). *On Their Watch: Mass Violence and State Apathy in India—Examining the Record*. Gurgaon: Three Essays Collective, 2014.

Chowdhury, Kanishka. *The New India: Citizenship, Subjectivity, and Economic Liberalization*. London: Palgrave Macmillan, 2011.

Christie, Ian. 'Heavenly Justice'. In *Law's Moving Image*, edited by Leslie J. Moran, Elena Loizidou, Ian Christie and Emma Sandon. New York: Glass House Press, 2004.

Cilliers, Paul. 'Complexity, Deconstruction and Relativism'. *Theory, Culture and Society* 22, no. 5 (2005): 255–67.

Citizens for Justice and Peace (CJP). 'Statement Released by the Citizens for Justice and Peace at a Packed Press Conference in Mumbai on July 7, 2003'. SANN, 7 July 2003. http://www.sabrang.com/news/7july03.htm. Accessed 18 December 2022.

———. 'Zahira SLP'. 8 May 2017. https://cjp.org.in/zahiraslp/. Accessed 18 December 2022.

Coates, Ta-Nehisi. *Between the World and Me*. New York: Spiegel and Grau, 2015.

Cole, Catharine M. *Performing South Africa's Truth Commission: Stages of Transition*. Bloomington: Indiana University Press, 2009.

Cole, Teju. 'Against Neutrality'. In *Known and Strange Things*, 212–15. New York: Random House, 2016.

Concerned Citizens Tribunal. *Crime against Humanity*. 3 vols. Mumbai: Sabrang, 2002. http://www.sabrang.com/tribunal/index.html. Accessed 18 December 2022.

Coombe, Rosemary. 'Critical Cultural Legal Studies'. *Yale Journal of Law and the Humanities* 10, no. 3 (2013): 463–86.

Cossman, Brenda, and Ratna Kapur. *Secularism's Last Sigh? Hindutva and the (Mis)rule of Law*. New Delhi: Oxford University Press, 2001.

Cover, Robert M. 'Violence and the Word'. Faculty Scholarship Series, Paper 2708 (1986). https://digitalcommons.law.yale.edu/cgi/viewcontent.cgi?article=3687&context=fss_paper. Accessed 18 December 2022.

———. 'Violence and the Word'. *Yale Law Review* 95, no. 8 (July 1986): 1601–29.

Cuddon, J. A. 'Trope'. In *The Penguin Dictionary of Literary Terms and Literary Theory*, 948. London: Penguin Books, 1998.

Daiya, Kavita. *Violent Belongings: Partition, Gender, and National Culture in Postcolonial India*. Philadelphia: Temple University Press, 2011.

Dalwai, Sameena, Ramu Ramanathan and Irfan Engineer (eds.). *Babri Masjid, 25 Years On*. New Delhi: Kalpaz, 2018.

Das, Veena. *Life and Words: Violence and the Descent into the Ordinary*. Berkeley: University of California Press, 2006.

Dasgupta, Sudeep. 'Gods in the Sacred Marketplace: Hindu Nationalism and the Return of the Aura in the Public Sphere'. In *Religion, Media, and the Public Sphere*, edited by Birgit Meyer and Annelies Moors, 251–72. Bloomington: Indiana University Press, 2005.

Datta, Pradip. 'Historic Trauma and the Politics of the Present in India'. *Interventions* 7, no. 3 (2005): 316–20.

Davies, Cristyn, and Sara L. Knox (eds.). *Cultural Studies of Law*. New York: Routledge, 2015.

Davies, Margaret. *Asking the Law Question*. 3rd ed. Sydney: Thomson Reuters, 2008.

———. 'Ethics and Methodology in Legal Theory: A (Personal) Research "Anti-Manifesto"'. *Law Text Culture* 6, no. 2 (January 2002): 7–27.

———. *Law Unlimited: Materialism, Pluralism, and Legal Theory*. New York: Routledge, 2017.

Davis, Natalie Zemon. '"Any Resemblance to Persons Living or Dead": Film and the Challenge of Authenticity'. *Historical Journal of Film, Radio and Television* 8, no. 3 (1988): 269–83.

Davis, Jr, Donald R. *The Spirit of Hindu Law*. New Delhi: Oxford University Press, 2010.

Deb, Siddhartha. *The Beautiful and Damned: A Portrait of the New India*. New York: Farrar, Straus and Giroux, 2011.

Deepak, J Sai. *India, That Is Bharat: Coloniality, Civilisation, Constitution*. New Delhi: Bloomsbury, 2021.

Del Mar, Maksymilian. 'The Legal Imagination'. *Aeon*, 28 March 2017. https://aeon.co/essays/why-judges-and-lawyers-need-imagination-as-much-as-rationality. Accessed 18 December 2022.

Deleuze, Gilles, and Felix Guattari. 'What Is an Assemblage?' In *Kafka: Toward a Minor Literature*, 81–90. Minneapolis: University of Minnesota Press, 1986.

Deleuze, Gilles, and Claire Parnet. *Dialogues II*. New York: Columbia University Press, 2007.

Delgado, Richard. 'The Inward Turn in Outsider Jurisprudence'. *William and Mary Law Review* 34, no. 3 (1993): 741–68.

Desai, Darshan. 'Massacres and the Media: A Field Reporter Looks Back on Gujarat 2002'. In *Sarai Reader 04: Crisis/Media*, 228–34. Delhi: Sarai, CSDS, 2004.

Desai, Madhavi, and Miki Desai. 'Ahmedabad: The City as Palimpsest'. *Architecture Plus Design* 8, no. 3 (1991): 22–32.

Desai, Mihir. 'The Communal and Targeted Violence Bill'. *Economic and Political Weekly* 46, no. 31 (2011): 12–16.

Desai, Radhika. 'Gujarat's Hindutva of Capitalist Development'. *South Asia: Journal of South Asian Studies* 34, no. 3 (2011): 354–81.

Desai, Renu. 'Producing and Contesting the "Communalized City": Hindutva Politics and Urban Space in Ahmedabad'. In *The Fundamentalist City? Religiosity and the Remaking of Urban Space*, edited by Nezar AlSayyad and Mejgan Massoumi, 99–124. New York: Routledge, 2011.

Deshpande, Anirudh. *Class, Power and Consciousness in Indian Cinema and Television*. Delhi: Primus, 2009.

Deshpande, Ashwini. *Affirmative Action in India*. New Delhi: Oxford University Press, 2013.

Deshpande, Satish. *Contemporary India: A Sociological View*. New Delhi: Penguin, 2003.

Devasundaram, Ashvin Immanuel. *India's New Independent Cinema: Rise of the Hybrid*. New York: Routledge, 2016.

Devji, Faisal. *Muslim Zion: Pakistan as a Political Idea*. London: Harvard University Press, 2013.

———. *The Impossible Indian: Gandhi and the Temptation of Violence*. Cambridge: Harvard University Press, 2012.

Dhattiwala, Raheel. *Keeping the Peace: Spatial Differences in Hindu–Muslim Violence in Gujarat in 2002*. Cambridge: Cambridge University Press, 2019.

———. 'The Ecology of Ethnic Violence: The Attacks on Muslims of Ahmedabad in 2002'. *Qualitative Sociology* 39, no. 1 (2016): 71–95.

Dhavan, Rajeev. 'Justice, Justice and the Best Bakery Case'. *India International Centre Quarterly* 30, no. 2 (Monsoon 2003): 1–11.

———. *Publish and Be Damned: Censorship and Intolerance in India*. New Delhi: Tulika, 2008.

Dhillon, Narinderjit Kaur, and Joel Gwynne. 'Saffronizing Bollywood Cinema: The Good Indian and the Muslim Threat'. *Film International* 12, no. 2 (2014): 47–57.

Dholakia, Rahul. 'In Search of Parzania'. CJP, 26 November 2007. https://cjp.org.in/in-search-of-parzania/. Accessed 18 December 2022.

Dirlik, Arif. 'Developmentalism: A Critique'. *Interventions: International Journal of Postcolonial Studies* 16, no. 1 (2014): 30–48.

Dolin, Kieran. *A Critical Introduction to Law and Literature*. Cambridge: Cambridge University Press, 2012.

Doniger, Wendy, and Martha Nussbaum (eds.). *Pluralism and Democracy in India: Debating the Hindu Right*. New Delhi: Oxford University Press, 2015.

Doniger, Wendy, and Brian K. Smith, trans. *The Laws of Manu*. London: Penguin, 1991.

Dorsett, Shaunnagh, and Ian Hunter (eds.). *Law and Politics in British Colonial Thought: Transpositions of Empire*. New York: Palgrave, 2010.

Dorsett, Shaunnagh, and Shaun McVeigh. *Jurisdiction*. London: Routledge-Cavendish, 2012.

Douzinas, Costas. 'Law and Justice in Postmodernity'. In *The Cambridge Companion to Postmodernism*, edited by Steven Connor, 196–223. Cambridge: Cambridge University Press, 2004.

Douzinas, Costas, and Adam Gearey. *Critical Jurisprudence: The Political Philosophy of Justice*. Oxford: Hart Publishing, 2005.

Douzinas, Costas, and Lynda Nead (eds.). *Law and the Image: The Authority of Art and the Aesthetics of Law*. Chicago: University of Chicago Press, 1999.

Douzinas, Costas, Shaun McVeigh and Ronnie Warrington. 'The Alta(e)rs of Law: The Judgement of Legal Aesthetics'. *Theory, Culture and Society* 9, no. 4 (1992): 93–117.

Douzinas, Costas, Ronnie Warrington and Shaun McVeigh. *Postmodern Jurisprudence: The Law of Text in the Texts of Law*. London: Routledge, 1991.

Dutta, Aniruddha. 'Digitizing the National Imaginary: Technology and Hybridization in Hindi Film Songs of the Post-liberalization Period'. In *Routledge Handbook of Indian Cinemas*, edited by K. Moti Gokulsingh and Wimal Dissanayake, 231–45. London: Routledge, 2013.

Dwyer, Rachel. *Bollywood's India: Hindi Cinema as a Guide to Contemporary India*. London: Reaktion Books, 2014.

———. 'The Saffron Screen? Hindu Nationalism and the Hindi Film'. In *Religion, Media, and the Public Sphere*, edited by Birgit Meyer and Annelies Moors, 273–89. Bloomington: Indiana University Press, 2005.

Elison, William, Christian Lee Novetzke and Andy Rotman. *Amar Akbar Anthony: Bollywood, Brotherhood, and the Nation*. Cambridge: Harvard University Press, 2016.

Engineer, Asghar Ali. 'Now Vadodara Goes Up in Communal Flames'. In *Communal Riots in Post-Independence India*, edited by Asghar Ali Engineer, 281–87. 2nd ed. Hyderabad: Sangam Books, 1984.

——— (ed.). *The Gujarat Carnage*. New Delhi: Orient Longman, 2003.

Essa, Azad. *Hostile Homelands: The New Alliance Between India and Israel*. London: Pluto Press, 2023.

Farasat, Warisha, and Prita Jha. *Splintered Justice: Living the Horror of Mass Communal Violence in Bhagalpur and Gujarat*. Gurgaon: Three Essays Collective, 2016.

Fazal, Tanweer. *Millennium Development Goals and Muslims of India*. New Delhi: Oxfam India, 2013.

Feigenson, Neal, and Christina Spiesel. *Law on Display: The Digital Transformation of Legal Persuasion and Judgment*. New York: New York University Press, 2009.

Fernandes, Leela. *India's New Middle Class: Democratic Politics in an Era of Economic Reform*. Minneapolis: University of Minnesota Press, 2006.

Fetscherin, Marc. 'The Main Determinants of Bollywood Movie Box Office Sales'. *Journal of Global Marketing* 23, no. 5 (2010): 461–76.

Figueira, Dorothy M. *Aryans, Jews, Brahmins: Theorizing Authority through Myths of Identity*. Albany: SUNY Press, 2002.

Fitzpatrick, Peter. *The Mythology of Modern Law*. London: Routledge, 1992.

Flaxman, Gregory. 'Once More, with Feeling: Cinema and Cinesthesia'. *SubStance* 45, no. 3 (2016): 174–89.

Foucault, Michel. 'Governmentality'. In *The Foucault Effect: Studies in Governmentality*, edited by Graham Burchell, Colin Gordon and Peter Miller, 87–104. Chicago: University of Chicago Press, 1991.

Fuller, Lon. *The Morality of Law*. Revised ed. New Haven: Yale University Press, 1965.

Gabriel, Karen. *Melodrama and the Nation: Sexual Economies of Bombay Cinema, 1970–2000*. New Delhi: Women Unlimited, 2010.

Ganti, Tejaswini. *Bollywood: A Guide to Popular Hindi Cinema*. London: Routledge, 2013.

———. *Producing Bollywood: Inside the Contemporary Hindi Film Industry*. Durham: Duke University Press, 2012.

Gatade, Subhash. *The Saffron Condition: Politics of Repression and Exclusion in Neoliberal India*. Gurgaon: Three Essays Collective, 2011.

Gearey, Adam. *Law and Aesthetics*. Oxford: Hart Publishing, 2001.

Genovese, Ann. 'Critical Decision, 1982: Remembering Koowarta v Bjelke-Petersen'. *Griffith Law Review* 23, no. 1 (2014): 1–15.

———. 'Inheriting and Inhabiting the Pleasures and Duties of Our Own Existence: *The Second Sex* and Feminist Jurisprudence'. *Australian Feminist Law Journal* 38, no. 1 (2013): 41–57.

Ghassem-Fachandi, Parvis. 'Bridge over the Sabarmati: An Urban Journey into Violence and Back'. *Journeys* 9, no. 1 (2008): 68–94.

———. *Pogrom in Gujarat: Hindu Nationalism and Anti-Muslim Violence in India*. New Jersey: Princeton University Press, 2012.

Ghosh, Jayati. 'Hindutva, Economic Neoliberalism, and the Abuse of Economic Statistics in India'. *South Asia Multidisciplinary Academic Journal* 24, no. 25 (2020). https://journals.openedition.org/samaj/6882.

Ghosh, Shohini. 'Censorship Myths and Imagined Harms'. *Sarai Reader 04: Crisis/Media*. New Delhi: SARAI/CSDS, 2004. http://archive.sarai.net/files/original/755257fc6f a5744 ae93c402cd54bc039.pdf. Accessed 25 May 2023.

Ghosh, Vishwajyoti. *Delhi Calm*. Noida: HarperCollins, 2010.

Ghufran, Iram. 'Kai Po Che and the Politics of Appeasement and Reconciliation'. *Phar'aat*, 13 March 2013. http://pharaat.blogspot.com/2013/03/kai-po-che-and-politics-of-appeasement.html. Accessed 18 December 2022.

Giddens, Thomas (ed.). *Graphic Justice: Intersections of Comics and Law*. New York: Routledge, 2015.

Godbole, Madhav. *Secularism: India at a Crossroads*. New Delhi: Rupa, 2016.

Gokulsingh, K. Moti, and Wimal Dissanayake (eds.). *Popular Culture in a Globalised India*. New Delhi: Routledge, 2009.

Goldoni, Marco, and Michael A. Wilkinson. 'The Material Constitution'. *Modern Law Review* 81, no. 4 (2018): 567–97.

Gonsalves, Colin. *Kaliyug: The Decline of Human Rights Law in the Period of Globalization*. New Delhi: Human Rights Law Network, 2011.

Goodrich, Peter. *Advanced Introduction to Law and Literature*. Cheltenham: Edward Elgar, 2021, 37.

———. 'Europe in America: Grammatology, Legal Studies, and the Politics of Transmission'. *Columbia Law Review* 101, no. 8 (2001): 2033–84.

———. *Languages of Law: From Logics of Memory to Nomadic Masks*. London: Weidenfeld, 1990.

———. 'Law by Other Means'. *Cardozo Studies in Law and Literature* 10, no. 2 (1998): 111–16.

———. *Law in the Courts of Love: Literature and Other Minor Jurisprudences.* London: Routledge, 1996.

———. *Legal Discourse: Studies in Linguistics, Rhetoric and Legal Analysis.* London: Palgrave Macmillan, 1987.

———. *Legal Emblems and the Art of Law: Obiter Depicta as the Vision of Governance.* Cambridge: Cambridge University Press, 2014.

———. *Oedipus Lex: Psychoanalysis, History, Law.* Berkeley: University of California Press, 1995.

———. 'Pictures as Precedents: The Visual Turn and the Status of Figures in Judgments'. In *New Directions in Law and Literature*, edited by Elizabeth S. Anker and Bernadette Mayler, 176–92. New York: Oxford University Press, 2017.

Gopal, Sangita, and Sujata Moorti (eds.). *Global Bollywood: Travels of Hindi Song and Dance.* Minneapolis: University of Minnesota Press, 2008.

Gopalakrishnan, Shankar. 'Defining, Constructing and Policing a "New India": Relationship between Neoliberalism and Hindutva'. *Economic and Political Weekly* 41, no. 26 (2006): 2803+2805–13.

Green, Mitchell. 'Speech Acts'. *The Stanford Encyclopedia of Philosophy*, 3 July 2007. https://plato.stanford.edu/archives/fall2021/entries/speech-acts/. Accessed 18 December 2022.

Greenfield, Steve, Guy Osborn and Peter Robson. *Film and the Law: The Cinema of Justice.* Oxford: Hart Publishing, 2010.

Grover, Vrinda. 'The Elusive Quest for Justice: Delhi 1984 to Gujarat 2002'. In *Gujarat: The Making of a Tragedy*, edited by Siddharth Varadarajan, 355–88. New Delhi: Penguin, 2002.

Guha, Ranajit. 'The Small Voice of History'. In *Subaltern Studies IX: Writings on South Asian History and Society*, edited by Shahid Amin and Dipesh Chakrabarty, 1–12. New Delhi: Oxford University Press, 1996.

Guichard, Sylvie. *The Construction of History and Nationalism in India: Textbooks, Controversies and Politics.* London: Routledge, 2010.

Gupta, Akhil. *Red Tape: Bureaucracy, Structural Violence, and Poverty in India.* Durham: Duke University Press, 2012.

Gupta, Apar. 'Movie Disclaimers: A Contract with the Offended'. *Seminar* 716 (April 2015). https://www.india-seminar.com/2019/716/716_apar_gupta.htm. Accessed 25 May 2023.

———. 'Tareek par tareek: Indian Lawyers in Popular Hindi Cinema'. *Journal of Indian Law and Society* 2 (Winter 2010): 1–27.

Gupta, Dipankar. *Justice before Reconciliation: Negotiating a 'New Normal' in Post-riot Mumbai and Ahmedabad*. New York: Routledge, 2011.

Halbwachs, Maurice. *On Collective Memory*. Chicago: University of Chicago Press, 1992.

Haldar, Piyel. 'In and Out of Court: On Topographies of Law and the Architecture of Court Buildings'. *Revue internationale de semiotique juridique* 7, no. 2 (1994): 185–200.

———. 'The Return of the Evidencer's Eye: Rhetoric and the Visual Technologies of Proof'. *Griffith Law Review* 8, no. 1 (1999): 86–101.

Hall, Stuart. 'Introduction'. In *Cultural Representations and Signifying Practices*, edited by Stuart Hall, 1–12. London: Sage, 2009.

———. 'The Work of Representation'. In *Cultural Representations and Signifying Practices*, edited by Stuart Hall, 13–74. Sage, 2009.

Hamilton, Sheryl N., Diana Majury, Dawn Moore, Neil Sargent and Christiane Wilke (eds.). *Sensing Law*. London: Routledge, 2017.

Hanne, Michael, and Robert Weisberg (eds.). *Narrative and Metaphor in the Law*. Cambridge: Cambridge University Press, 2018.

Hansen, Thomas Blom. *The Saffron Wave: Democracy and Hindu Nationalism in Modern India*. Princeton: Princeton University Press, 1999.

Hart, H. L. A. *The Concept of Law*. Oxford: Oxford University Press, 2012.

Hasan, Mushirul (ed.). *India's Partition: Process, Strategy and Mobilization*. New Delhi: Oxford University Press, 1997.

———. *Legacy of a Divided Nation: Indian Muslims since Independence*. New York: Routledge, 2018.

Hiebaum, Christian, Susan Knaller and Doris Pichler (eds.). *Law and Literature In-Between*. Bielefeld: Transcript Verlag, 2015.

Hirway, Indira, Amita Shah and Ghanshyam Shah (eds.). *Growth or Development: Which Way Is Gujarat Going?* New Delhi: Oxford University Press, 2014.

Hoenig, Patrick, and Navsharan Singh (eds.). *Landscapes of Fear: Understanding Impunity in India*. New Delhi: Zubaan, 2015.

Hoffheimer, Michael H. 'Awāra and the Post-colonial Origins of the Hindi Law Drama'. *Historical Journal of Film, Radio and Television* 26, no. 3 (2006): 341–59.

———. 'Bollywood Law: Commercial Hindi Films with Legal Themes'. *Law Library Journal* 98, no. 1 (2006): 61–79.

Honore, T. 'The Primacy of Oral Evidence'. In *Crime, Proof and Punishment: Essays in Memory of Sir Rupert Cross*, 172–92. London: Butterworths, 1981.

Horan, Jacqueline, and Shelley Maine. 'Criminal Jury Trials in 2030: A Law Odyssey'. *Journal of Law and Society* 41, no. 4 (2014): 551–75.

Hourigan, Daniel. 'Spectres and Psychoanalysis in the Turn to Law and Affect'. *Law and Literature* 31, no. 1 (2017). https://www.tandfonline.com/doi/abs/1 0.1080/1535685X.2017.1327694.

Human Rights Watch. 'Discouraging Dissent: Intimidation and Harassment of Witnesses, Human Rights Activists, and Lawyers Pursuing Accountability for the 2002 Communal Violence in Gujarat'. https://www.hrw.org/legacy/ backgrounder/asia/india/gujarat/gujarat0904.pdf. Accessed 18 December 2022.

———. *We Have No Orders to Save You.* Human Rights Watch, 2002. http://www. hrw.org/reports/2002/india//. Accessed 18 December 2022.

Humes, Cynthia Ann. 'Hindutva, Mythistory, and Pseudoarcheology'. *Numen* 59, nos. 2–3 (2012): 178–201.

Hunt, Alan. 'The Critique of Law: What Is "Critical" about Critical Legal Theory'. *Journal of Law and Society* 14, no. 1 (1987): 5–19.

International Human Rights and Conflict Resolution Clinic (IHRCRC). *When Justice Becomes the Victim: The Quest for Justice after the 2002 Violence in Gujarat.* Stanford: Stanford Law School, 2014.

International Initiative for Justice in Gujarat (IIJG). *Threatened Existence: A Feminist Analysis of the Genocide in Gujarat.* Mumbai: IIJG, 2003.

Islam, Shamsul. *Religious Dimensions of Indian Nationalism: A Study of RSS.* New Delhi: Media House, 2006.

Iyer, Mani Shankar. *Confessions of a Secular Fundamentalist.* New Delhi: Penguin, 2004.

Iyer, Sriya, and Anand Shrivastava. 'Religious Riots and Electoral Politics in India'. *Journal of Development Economics* 131, no. C (2018): 104–22.

Jaffrelot, Christophe. 'Gujarat 2002: What Justice for the Victims?' *Economic and Political Weekly* 47, no. 8 (2012): 77–89.

———. 'Hindu Nationalism and the (Not So Easy) Art of Being Outraged: The *Ram Setu* Controversy'. *South Asia Multidisciplinary Academic Journal* 2 (2008). https://journals.openedition.org/samaj/1372.

———. 'Refining the Moderation Thesis: Two Religious Parties and Indian Democracy—the Jana Sangh and the BJP between Hindutva Radicalism and Coalition Politics'. *Democratization* 20, no. 5 (2013): 876–94.

——— (ed.). *Sangh Parivar: A Reader.* New Delhi: Oxford University Press, 2005.

———. *The Hindu Nationalist Movement and Indian Politics: 1925 to the 1990s*. New Delhi: Penguin, 1999.

———. 'What "Gujarat Model"? Growth without Development—And with Socio-political Polarisation'. *South Asia: Journal of South Asian Studies* 38, no. 4 (2015): 820–38.

Jaffrelot, Christophe, and Pratinav Anil. *India's First Dictatorship: The Emergency, 1975–77*. New Delhi: HarperCollins, 2021.

Jaffrelot, Christophe, and Charlotte Thomas. 'Facing Ghettoisation in Riot City'. In *Muslims in Indian Cities: Trajectories of Marginalisation*, edited by Laurent Gayer and Christophe Jaffrelot, 43–80. Noida: HarperCollins, 2012.

Jain, Anuja. '"Beaming It Live": 24-Hour Television News, the Spectator and the Spectacle of the 2002 Gujarat Carnage'. *South Asian Popular Culture* 8, no. 2 (2010): 163–79.

Janmohamed, Zahir. 'Kai Po Che and the Reduction of 2002'. *Kafila*, 2 March 2013. https://kafila.online/2013/03/02/kai-po-che-and-the-reduction-of-2002-zahir-janmohamed/. Accessed 18 December 2022.

Jasani, Rubina. 'Violence, Urban Anxieties, and Masculinities: The "Foot Soldiers" of 2002, Ahmedabad'. *South Asia: Journal of South Asian Studies* 43, no. 4 (2020): 675–90.

Jayasankar, K. P., and Anjali Monteiro. *A Fly in the Curry: Independent Documentary Film in India*. New York: Sage, 2016.

Jha, Dhirendra. *Gandhi's Assassin: The Making of Nathuram Godse and His Idea of India*. New Delhi: Vintage, 2022.

———. *Shadow Armies: Fringe Organizations and Foot Soldiers of Hindutva*. New Delhi: Juggernaut, 2017.

Jha, Dhirendra K., and Krishna Jha. *Ayodhya: The Dark Night*. New Delhi: HarperCollins, 2016.

Johns, Fleur, Richard Joyce and Sundhya Pahuja (eds.). *Events: The Force of International Law*. New York: Routledge-Cavendish, 2010.

Josh, Bhagwan. 'Partition and the Rise of Hindutva Movement in Contemporary India'. *Revista Canaria de Estudios Ingleses* 76 (April 2018): 175–95.

Juluri, Vamsee. *Rearming Hinduism*. Chennai: Westland, 2016.

Junaid, Mohamad. 'Death and Life under Occupation: Space, Violence, and Memory in Kashmir'. In *Everyday Occupations: Experiencing Militarism in South Asia and the Middle East*, edited by Kamala Visveswaran, 158–90. Pennsylvania: University of Pennsylvania Press, 2013.

Jung, Berenike. *Narrating Violence in Post-9/11 Action Cinema: Terrorist Narratives, Action Cinema and Referentiality*. Wiesbaden: VS Research, 2010.

Kabeer, Nasreen Munni. 'Playback Time'. *Film Comment* 38, no. 3 (2002): 41–43.

Kabir, Ananya Jahanara. 'The Kashmiri as Muslim in Bollywood's "New Kashmir Films"'. *Contemporary South Asia* 18, no. 4 (2010): 373–85.

Kafka, Franz. 'Before the Law'. Translated by Ian Johnston. *Franz Kafka Online: The Works and Life of Franz Kafka*. http://www.kafka-online.info/before-the-law.html. Accessed 18 December 2022.

Kamir, Orit. *Framed: Women in Law and Film*. Durham: Duke University Press, 2006.

Kannabiran, Kalpana. *Tools of Justice: Non-discrimination and the Indian Constitution*. New Delhi: Routledge, 2012.

Kanungo, Pralay. 'Hindutva's Discourse on Development'. In *Religion, Communities and Development: Changing Contours of Politics and Policy in India*, edited by Gurpreet Mahajan and Surinder S. Jodhka, 83–101. New Delhi: Routledge, 2010.

Kapadia, Shagufa. *Adolescence in Urban India: Cultural Construction in a Society in Transition*. New Delhi: Springer, 2017.

Kapila, Shruti, and Faisal Devji. 'The Bhagavad Gita and Modern Thought: Introduction'. *Modern Intellectual History* 7, no. 2 (2010): 269–73.

Kapoor, Coomi. *The Emergency: A Personal History*. Gurgaon: Viking, 2015.

Kapur, Ratna. 'A Leap of Faith: The Construction of Hindu Majoritarianism through Secular Law'. *South Atlantic Quarterly* 113, no. 1 (2014): 109–28.

———. '"A Love Song to Our Mongrel Selves": Hybridity, Sexuality and the Law'. *Social and Legal Studies* 8, no. 3 (1999): 353–68.

———. *Makeshift Migrants and Law: Gender, Belonging, and Postcolonial Anxieties*. London: Routledge, 2010.

———. 'Normalizing Violence: Transitional Justice and the Gujarat Riots'. *Columbia Journal of Gender and Law* 15, no. 3 (2006): 885–927.

———. 'The "Ayodhya" Case: Hindu Majoritarianism and the Right to Religious Liberty'. *Maryland Journal of International Law* 29 (2014): 305–65.

———. 'Too Hot to Handle: The Cultural Politics of Fire'. *Feminist Review* 64, no. 1 (2000): 53–64.

Karat, Brinda, and Vijay Prashad (eds.). *Delhi's Agony: Essays on the February 2022 Communal Violence*. New Delhi: LeftWord Books, 2021.

Karstedt, Susanne (ed.). *Legal Institutions and Collective Memories*. London: Bloomsbury, 2009.

Katju, Manjari. *Hinduising Democracy*. New Delhi: New Text, 2017.

Kaur, Raminder, and William Mazzarella (eds.). *Censorship in South Asia: Cultural Regulation from Sedition to Seduction*. Bloomington: Indiana University Press, 2009.

Kaur, Raminder, and Ajay J. Sinha (eds.). *Bollyworld: Popular Indian Cinema through a Transnational Lens*. New Delhi: Sage, 2005.

Kaur, Ravinder, and Nayanika Mathur (eds.). *The People of India: New Indian Politics in the 21st Century*. Gurugram: Penguin Random House, 2022.

Kaviraj, Sudipta. *The Imaginary Institution of India: Politics and Ideas*. New York: Columbia University Press, 2010.

Kelsen, Hans. *Pure Theory of Law*. Berkeley: University of California Press, 1967.

Kennedy, Duncan. 'Legal Education and the Reproduction of Hierarchy'. *Journal of Legal Education* 32, no. 4 (1982): 591–615.

Kenny, Paul D. *Populism and Patronage: Why Populists Win Elections in India, Asia, and Beyond*. Oxford: Oxford University Press, 2017.

Khalidi, Omar. 'Hinduising India: Secularism in Practice'. *Third World Quarterly* 29, no. 8 (2008): 1545–62.

Khan, Amir Ullah, and Bibek Debroy. 'Indian Economic Transition through Bollywood Eyes'. Working Paper, August 2002. http://citeseerx.ist.psu.edu/viewdoc/download?doi=10.1.1.200.8312&rep=rep1&type=pdf. Accessed 18 December 2022.

Khetan, Ashish. *Undercover: My Journey into the Darkness of Hindutva*. New Delhi; Bengaluru: Context, 2021.

Khorakiwala, Rahela. *From the Colonial to the Contemporary: Images, Iconography, Memories, and Performances of Law in India's High Courts*. New Delhi: Bloomsbury, 2020.

Kimura, Makiko. *The Nellie Massacre of 1983: Agency of Rioters*. New Delhi: Sage, 2013.

Kinnvall, Catarina. 'Populism, Ontological Insecurity and Hindutva: Modi and the Masculinization of Indian Politics'. *Cambridge Review of International Affairs* 32, no. 3 (2019): 283–302.

Kirmani, Nida. 'History, Memory and Localised Constructions of Insecurity'. *Economic and Political Weekly* 43, no. 10 (2008): 57–64.

Klienman, Arthur, and Klienman Joan. 'The Appeal of Experience; The Dismay of Images: Cultural Appropriations of Suffering in Our Times'. *Daedalus* 125, no. 1 (1996): 1–23.

Kohli, Atul. *Poverty amid Plenty in the New India*. New York: Cambridge University Press, 2012.

Kohli, Pranav. *Memories in the Service of the Hindu Nation: The Afterlife of the Partition of India*. Cambridge: Cambridge University Press, 2023.

Kothari, Urvish. 'Parzania and the Dictator of Gujarat'. *Himal Southasian* 20, no. 3 (March 2007): 68.

———. 'Parzania and the Dictator of Gujarat'. *Himal Southasian*, March 2007. https://old.himalmag.com/component/content/article/1193-parzania-and-the-dictator-of-gujarat.html. Accessed 18 December 2022.

Krishnaswamy, Sudhir. *Democracy and Constitutionalism in India: A Study of the Basic Structure Doctrine*. New Delhi: Oxford University Press, 2011.

Kristeva, Julia. 'Word, Dialogue and Novel'. In *The Kristeva Reader*, edited by Toril Moi, 34–61. New York: Columbia University Press, 1986.

Kuldova, Tereza. 'Designing an Illusion of India's Future Superpowerdom: Of the Rise of Neo-aristocracy, Hindutva and Philanthrocapitalism'. *Unfamiliar: An Anthropological Journal* 4, no. 1 (2014): 15–22.

Kumar, Amrita, and Prashun Bhaumik (eds.). *Lest We Forget: Gujarat 2002*. New Delhi: World Report in association with Rupa, 2002.

Kumar, Ashish. 'Aryans versus Non-Aryans: A Study of Dalit Narratives of India's Ancient Past'. *Contemporary Voice of Dalit* 10, no. 2 (2018): 127–37.

Kumar, Megha. *Communalism and Sexual Violence: Ahmedabad since 1969*. New Delhi: Tulika, 2017.

Kumar, Priya. 'Islamic Terrorism and Visions of Justice'. In *Cinema, Law, and the State in Asia*, edited by C. Creekmur and M. Sidel, 63–82. New York: Palgrave Macmillan, 2007.

Kumar, Rakesh. 'Structural Analysis of the Indian Legal System through the Normative Theory'. *Journal of the Indian Law Institute* 41, nos. 3–4 (1999): 500–12.

Kumar, Sanjay. 'Gujarat Assembly Elections 2002: Analysing the Verdict'. *Economic and Political Weekly* 38, no. 4 (2002): 270–75.

Kumar H. M., Sanjeev. 'Constructing the Nation's Enemy: Hindutva, Popular Culture and the Muslim "Other" in Bollywood Cinema'. *Third World Quarterly* 34, no. 3 (2013): 458–69.

———. 'Metonymies of Fear: Islamophobia and the Making of Muslim Identity in Hindi Cinema'. *Society and Culture in South Asia* 2, no. 2 (2016): 233–55.

Kurian, Alka. *Narratives of Gendered Dissent in South Asian Cinemas*. New York: Routledge, 2014.

———. 'The Politics of Hindutva in Nandita Das' Firaaq, Rahul Dholakia's Parzania, and Rakesh Sharma's Final Solution'. In *Narratives of Gendered Dissent in South Asian Cinemas*, 63–97. New York: Routledge, 2012.

Lacey, Nicola. 'Feminist Legal Theory beyond Neutrality'. *Current Legal Problems* 48, Part 2 (1995): 1–38.

Lal, Vinay, and Ashis Nandy (eds.). *Fingerprinting Popular Culture: The Mythic and the Iconic in Indian Cinema*. New Delhi: Oxford University Press, 2006.

Lalita, K., and Deepa Dhanraj. *Rupture, Loss and Living: Minority Women Speak about Post-conflict Life*. Hyderabad: Orient BlackSwan, 2016.

Laul, Revati. *The Anatomy of Hate*. New Delhi: Context, 2018.

Laungani, Pittu. 'Death in a Hindu Family'. In *Death and Bereavement across Cultures*, edited by Colin Murray, Pittu Laungani and Bill Young, 52–72. New York: Routledge, 2000.

Liang, Lawrence. 'Censorship and the Politics of Micro-fascism'. *Television and New Media* 16, no. 4 (2015): 388–93.

———. 'Cinematic Citizenship and the Illegal City'. *Inter-Asia Cultural Studies* 6, no. 3 (2005): 366–85.

———. 'Media's Law: From Representation to Affect'. *Bioscope: South Asian Screen Studies* 2, no. 1 (2011): 23–40.

Liang, Lawrence, Mayur Suresh and Namita Avriti Malhotra. *The Public Is Watching: Sex, Laws and Videotapes*. New Delhi: Public Service Broadcasting Trust, 2007.

Liddle, Madhulika. 'Writing the Script of Life: The Typewriter in Hindi Cinema'. In *With Great Truth and Regard: The Story of the Typewriter in India*, edited by Sidharth Bhatia, 280–92. Delhi: Roli Books, 2016.

Litowitz, Douglas E. 'Review: Franz Kafka's Outsider Jurisprudence'. *Law and Social Inquiry* 2, no. 1 (2002): 103–38.

Lokhande, Sanjeevini Badigar. *Communal Violence, Forced Migration and the State: Gujarat since 2002*. New Delhi: Cambridge University Press, 2015.

Lothspeich, Pamela. 'The *Kaliyug* of Modernity in Surendra Verma's *Draupadi*'. In *Interpreting Homes in South Asian Literature*, edited by Malashri Lal and Suktara Paul Kumar, 159–67. New Delhi: Pearson, 2007.

Machura, Stefan, Stefan Ulbrich, Francis M. Nevins and Nils Behling. 'Law in Film: Globalizing the Hollywood Courtroom Drama'. *Journal of Law and Society* 28, no. 1 (2001): 117–32.

Maclean, Kama Kellie. 'Embracing the Untouchables: The BJP and Scheduled Caste Votes'. *Asian Studies Review* 23, no. 4 (1999): 488–509.

MacNeil, William P. *Lex Populi: The Jurisprudence of Popular Culture*. Stanford: Stanford University Press, 2007.

Madan, Triloki Nath. 'The Householder Tradition in Hindu Society'. In *The Blackwell Companion to Hinduism*, edited by Gavin Flood. London: Blackwell, 2003.

Mahadevia, Darshini. 'A City with Many Borders: Beyond Ghettoisation in Ahmedabad'. In *Indian Cities in Transition*, edited by Annapurna Shaw, 288–305. Hyderabad: Orient Longman, 2007.

Mahmood, Saba. 'Religious Reason and Secular Affect: An Incommensurable Divide?' *Critical Inquiry* 35, no. 4 (Summer 2009): 858–59.

Mahmudabad, Ali Khan. 'Indian Muslims and the Anti-CAA Protests: From Marginalisation towards Exclusion'. *South Asia Multidisciplinary Academic Journal* 24/25 (2020). https://journals.openedition.org/samaj/6701.

Malhotra, Aanchal. *Remnants of a Separation: A History of the Partition through Material Memory*. New Delhi: HarperCollins, 2017.

Malik, Iftikhar Haider. *Jihad, Hindutva, and the Taliban: South Asia at the Crossroads*. Karachi: Oxford University Press, 2005.

Mamdani, Mahmood. *Good Muslim, Bad Muslim: America, the Cold War, and the Roots of Terror*. New York: Doubleday, 2004.

Mander, Harsh. *Looking Away: Inequality, Prejudice and Indifference in New India*. New Delhi: Speaking Tiger Books, 2015.

Manderson, Desmond. *Danse Macabre: Temporalities of Law in the Visual Arts*. Cambridge: Cambridge University Press, 2019.

———. *Kangaroo Courts and the Rule of Law: The Legacy of Modernism*. New York: Routledge, 2012.

———. *Songs without Music: Aesthetic Dimensions of Law and Justice*. Berkeley: University of California Press, 2000.

Manderson, Desmond, and Cristina S. Martinez. 'Justice and Art, Face to Face'. *Yale Journal of Law and the Humanities* 28, no. 2 (2016): 241–63.

Matsuda, Mari J., Charles R. Lawrence III, Richard Delgado and Kimberlé Williams Crenshaw. *Words that Wound: Critical Race Theory, Assaultive Speech, and the First Amendment*. New York: Routledge, 1993.

Mazumdar, Ranjani. *Bombay Cinema: An Archive of the City*. Minneapolis: University of Minnesota Press, 2007.

———. 'The Bombay Film Poster'. *Seminar* (2003): 525. http://www.india-seminar.com/2003/525/525%20ranjani%20mazumdar.htm. Accessed 18 December 2022.

Mazzarella, William. *Censorium: Cinema and the Open Edge of Mass Publicity.* Durham: Duke University Press, 2013.

McLane, John R. 'Hindu Victimhood and India's Muslim Minority'. In *The Fundamentalist Mindset: Psychological Perspectives on Religion, Violence, and History*, edited by Charles B. Strozier, David M. Terman, and James W. Jones, with Katharine A. Boyd, 195–215. New York: Oxford University Press, 2010.

McQueen, Rob. 'Of Wigs and Gowns: A Short History of Legal and Judicial Dress in Australia'. *Law in Context* 16, no. 1 (1999): 31–58.

Mehta, Deepak. 'The Ayodhya Dispute: The Absent Mosque, State of Emergency and the Jural Deity'. *Journal of Material Culture* 20, no. 4 (2015): 397–414.

Mehta, Nalin. 'Modi and the Camera: The Politics of Television in the 2002 Gujarat Riots'. *South Asia: Journal of South Asian Studies* 29, no. 3 (2006): 395–414.

Mehta, Rini Bhattacharya, and Debali Mookerjea-Leonard (eds.). *The Indian Partition in Literature and Films: History, Politics, and Aesthetics.* New York: Routledge, 2014.

Mehta, Rini Bhattacharya, and Rajeshwari V. Pandharipande (eds.). *Bollywood and Globalization: Indian Popular Cinema, Nation, and Diaspora.* New York: Anthem, 2011.

Menon, Dilip M. *The Blindness of Insight: Essays on Caste in Modern India.* Pondicherry: Navayana, 2005.

Menon, Jisha. *The Performance of Nationalism: India, Pakistan, and the Memory of Partition.* Cambridge: Cambridge University Press, 2013.

Menon, Meena. *Riots and after in Mumbai: Chronicles of Truth and Reconciliation.* New Delhi: Sage, 2011.

Menon, Nirmala, and Reema Chowdhary. 'Muslim Identity and Representation in Deepa Mehta's *Earth* and Abhishek Kapur's *Kai Po Che*'. *Postcolonial Text* 11, no. 2 (2016). http://postcolonial.univ-paris13.fr/index.php/pct/article/viewArticle/2036. Accessed 18 December 2022.

Menon, Nivedita. 'Citizenship and the Passive Revolution: Interpreting the First Amendment'. In *Politics and Ethics of the Indian Constitution*, edited by Rajeev Bhargava, 189–210. New Delhi: Oxford University Press, 2010.

———. 'Foucault and Indian Scholarship: History, Governmentality, Modernity'. In *Trajectory of French Thought*, 61–82. New Delhi: French Information Resource Centre: Rupa, 2004.

———. 'Hindu Rashtra and Bollywood: A New Front in the Battle for Cultural Hegemony'. *South Asia Multidisciplinary Academic Journal* 24, no. 25 (2020). https://journals.openedition.org/samaj/6846.

————. *Secularism as Misdirection: Critical Thought from the Global South*. Ranikhet: Permanent Black, 2023.

Menon, Nivedita, and Aditya Nigam. *Power and Contestation: India since 1989*. London: Zed Books, 2007.

Menon, Ritu, and Kamla Bhasin. *Borders and Boundaries: Women in India's Partition*. New Delhi: Kali for Women, 2007.

Mirza, Saeed Akhtar. 'Outlook for the Cinema'. *Social Scientist* 8, nos. 5–6 (December 1979–January 1980): 121–25.

Mirzoeff, Nicholas. 'On Visuality'. *Journal of Visual Culture* 5, no. 1 (2006): 53–79.

Mishra, Pankaj. 'Kashmir: The Unending War'. *New York Review of Books*, 19 October 2000. https://www.nybooks.com/articles/2000/10/19/kashmir-the-unending-war/. Accessed 18 December 2022.

Mishra, Vijay. *Bollywood Cinema: Temples of Desire*. New York: Routledge, 2013.

————. 'Spectres of Sentimentality: The Bollywood Film'. *Textual Practice* 23, no. 3 (2009): 439–62.

————. 'The Aching Joys of Bollywood Song and Dance'. *Postcolonial Studies* 12, no. 2 (2009): 247–54.

Misri, Deepti. 'The Violence of Memory: Renarrating Partition Violence in Shauna Singh Baldwin's *What the Body Remembers*'. *Meridiens* 11, no. 1 (2011): 1–25.

Misztal, Barbara A. *Theories of Social Remembering*. Maidenhead: McGraw-Hill Education, 2003.

Mitchell, W. J. T. *Iconology: Image, Text, Ideology*. Chicago: University of Chicago Press, 1986.

Mitra, Subrata K. 'Level Playing Fields: The Post-Colonial State, Democracy, Courts and Citizenship in India'. *German Law Journal* 9, no. 3 (2008): 343–66.

Mitta, Manoj. *The Fiction of Fact Finding: Modi and Godhra*. New Delhi: HarperCollins, 2014.

Mitta, Manoj, and H. M. Phoolka. *When a Tree Shook: The 1984 Carnage and Its Aftermath*. New Delhi: Roli Books, 2008.

Modéer, Kjell Å., and Martin Sunnqvist (eds.). *Legal Stagings: The Visualization, Medialization and Ritualization of Law in Language, Literature, Media, Art and Architecture*. Copenhagen: Museum Tusculanum Press, 2012.

Mohammad, Robina. '*Phir Bhi Dil Hai Hindustani* (Yet the Heart Remains Indian): Bollywood, the "Homeland" Nation-State, and the Diaspora'. *Society and Space* 25, no. 6 (2007): 1015–40.

Mondal, Seik Rahim. 'Social Structure, OBCs and Muslims'. *Economic and Political Weekly* 38, no. 46 (2003): 4892–97.

Moodie, Deonnie. 'Retail Religion: Hinduism for a Neoliberal Age'. *Journal of the American Academy of Religion* 89, no. 3 (2021): 863–84.

Mukherjee, Debashree. 'No Time for Grieving—or Why We Should Talk Some More About Kai Po Che'. *Kafila*, 19 March 2013. https://kafila.online/2013/03/19/no-time-for-grieving-or-why-we-should-talk-some-more-about-kai-po-che-debashree-mukherjee/. Accessed 18 December 2022.

Mulcahy, Linda. *Legal Architecture: Justice, Due Process and the Place of Law*. New York: Routledge, 2010.

Muralidhar, S. 'Access to Criminal Justice: Challenges and Prospects'. In *Towards Legal Literacy: An Introduction to Law in India*, edited by Kamala Sankaran and Ujjwal Kumar Singh, 45–60. New Delhi: Oxford University Press, 2008.

Muralidharan, Sukumar. 'Mandal, Mandir aur Masjid: "Hindu" Communalism and the Crisis of the State'. *Social Scientist* 18, no. 10 (1990): 27–49.

Murray, Tania. *The Will to Improve: Governmentality, Development, and the Practice of Politics*. Durham: Duke University Press, 2007.

Murty, Madhavi. 'Representing Hindutva: Nation, Religion and Masculinity in Indian Popular Cinema, 1990 to 2003'. *Popular Communication* 7, no. 4 (2009): 267.

Mussawir, Edward. 'The Cinematics of Jurisprudence'. *Law and Literature* 17, no. 1 (2005): 131–52.

———. 'The Trial'. In *An Aesthetics of Law and Culture: Texts, Images, Screens*, edited by Peter D. Rush and Andrew T. Kenyon, 111–31. Studies in Law, Politics and Society, vol. 34. Bingley: Emerald Group Publishing, 2004.

Muthukkaruppan, Parthasarathi. 'Critique of Caste Violence: Explorations in Theory'. *Social Scientist* 45, nos. 1–2 (2017): 49–71.

Nainar, Vahida, and Saumya Uma (eds.). *Pursuing Elusive Justice: Mass Crimes in India and Relevance of International Standards*. New Delhi: Oxford University Press, 2013.

Nanda, Meera. 'Ambedkar's Gita'. *Economic and Political Weekly* 51, no. 49 (2016): 38–45.

———. 'Hindu Triumphalism and the Clash of Civilisations'. *Economic and Political Weekly* 44, no. 28 (2009): 106–14.

———. 'Secularism without Secularisation: Reflections on God and Politics in US and India'. *Economic and Political Weekly* 42, no. 1 (2007): 39–46.

———. *The God Market: How Globalization Is Making India More Hindu.* Gurgaon: Random House India, 2009.

Nandy, Ashis. 'An Anti-Secularist Manifesto'. *India International Centre Quarterly* 22, no. 1 (1995): 35–64.

———. 'Introduction: Indian Popular Cinema as a Slum's Eye View of Politics'. In *The Secret Politics of Our Desires: Innocence, Culpability and Indian Popular Cinema*, edited by Ashis Nandy, 1–18. London: Zed Books, 1999.

Nandy, Ashis, Shikha Trivedy, Shail Mayaram and Achyut Yagnik. *Creating a Nationality: The Ramjanmabhumi Movement and Fear of the Self.* New Delhi: Oxford University Press, 1998.

Naqvi, Saba. *Shades of Saffron: From Vajpayee to Modi.* Chennai: Westland, 2018.

Narain, Vrinda. 'Law, Gender, Nation: Muslim Women and the Discontents of Legal Pluralism in India'. In *Islam, Gender and Democracy in Comparative Perspective*, edited by Jocelyne Cesari and José Casanova, 188–210. New York: Oxford University Press, 2017.

Narayan, Badri. *Fascinating Hindutva: Saffron Politics and Dalit Mobilization.* New Delhi: Sage, 2009.

Narrain, Arvind. *India's Undeclared Emergency: Constitutionalism and the Politics of Resistance.* Bengaluru: Context, 2022.

———. 'Truth Telling, Gujarat and the Law'. In *Sarai Reader 04: Crisis/Media.* New Delhi: Sarai, 2004. http://archive.sarai.net/files/original/4ac595f03bc91 168e27c97719a12cadc.pdf. Accessed 18 December 2022.

Nayar, Kuldip. *Emergency Retold.* New Delhi: Konark, 2013.

Nayar, Sheila J. 'Dreams, Dharma, and Mrs. Doubtfire: Exploring Hindi Popular Cinema via Its "Chutneyed" Western Scripts'. *Journal of Popular Film and Television* 31, no. 2 (2003): 73–82.

Needham, Anuradha Dingwaney, and Rajeswari Sunder Rajan (eds.). *The Crisis of Secularism in India.* Durham: Duke University Press, 2007.

New Indian Express. '2002 Bilkis Bano Gangrape: Supreme Court for Gujarat's Reply on Compensation'. 10 January 2018. http://www.newindianexpress. com/nation/2018/jan/10/2002-bilkis-bano-gangrape-supreme-court-for-gujarats-reply-on-compensation-1749794.html. Accessed 18 December 2022.

Nigam, Aditya. *Desire Named Development.* New Delhi: Penguin, 2011.

Noorani, A. G. *Destruction of the Babri Masjid: A National Dishonour.* New Delhi: Tulika, 2017.

———. 'Kissa Kursi Kaa Case'. *Economic and Political Weekly* 15, nos. 24–25 (June 1980): 1067–74.

———. *Savarkar and Hindutva: The Godse Connection*. New Delhi: LeftWord, 2004.

———. *The RSS and the BJP: A Division of Labour*. New Delhi: LeftWord, 2000.

Noorani, A. G., and South Asia Human Rights Documentation Centre. *Challenges to Civil Rights Guarantees in India*. New Delhi: Oxford University Press, 2012.

Nussbaum, Martha. 'Body of the Nation: Why Women Were Mutilated in Gujarat'. *Boston Review*, 1 June 2004. http://bostonreview.net/martha-nussbaum-women-mutilated-gujarat. Accessed 18 December 2022.

———. *The Clash Within: Democracy, Religious Violence and India's Future*. Cambridge: Harvard University Press, 2007.

O'Connell, Paul. 'The Death of Socio-economic Rights'. *Modern Law Review* 74, no. 4 (2011): 532–54.

Ohm, Britta. 'Forgetting to Remember: The Privatisation of the Public, the Economisation of Hindutva, and the Medialisation of Genocide'. In *South Asian Media Cultures: Audiences, Representations, Contexts*, edited by Shakuntala Banaji, 123–44. New York: Anthem Press, 2011.

Olick, Jeffrey K. *The Politics of Regret: On Collective Memory and Historical Responsibility*. New York: Routledge, 2007.

Olick, Jeffrey K., Vered Vinitzky-Seroussi and Daniel Levy (eds.). *The Collective Memory Reader*. New York: Oxford University Press, 2011.

Olivelle, Patrick (ed. and trans.). *A Dharma Reader: Classical Indian Law*. New York: Columbia University Press, 2017.

Olson, Greta. 'The Turn to Passion: Has Law and Literature Become Law and Affect?' *Law and Literature* 28, no. 3 (2016): 335–53.

Oommen, T. K. *Reconciliation in Post-Godhra Gujarat: The Role of Civil Society*. New Delhi: Pearson Longman, 2008.

Osiel, Mark. *Mass Atrocity, Collective Memory, and the Law*. New Brunswick: Transaction, 1999.

O'Sullivan, Simon. 'The Aesthetics of Affect: Thinking Art beyond Representation'. *Angelaki: Journal of the Theoretical Humanities* 6, no. 3 (2001): 125–35.

Osuri, Goldie. '"Ma" and a Political Theology of Hindi Cinema'. *Theory, Culture and Society* 31, nos. 7–8 (2014): 343–46.

Oza, Rupal. 'The Geography of Hindu Right Wing Violence in India'. In *Violent Geographies: Fear, Terror, and Political Violence*, edited by Derek Gregory and Allan Pred, 153–74. New York: Routledge, 2007.

Paasche, Marit, and Judy Radul (eds.). *A Thousand Eyes: Media Technology, Law, and Aesthetics*. Berlin: Sternberg, 2011.

Padmanabhan, P. 'Undemocratic Heart of the Indian Constitution'. In *Violation of Democratic Rights in India*, edited by A. R. Desai, 73–78. Bombay: Popular Prakashan, 1986.

Pahuja, Sundhya. 'Laws of Encounter: A Jurisdictional Account of International Law'. *London Review of International Law* 1, no. 1 (2013): 63–98.

Palsetia, Jesse S. *The Parsis of India: Preservation of Identity in Bombay City*. Leiden: Brill, 2001.

Palshikar, Suhas, Sanjay Kumar and Sanjay Lodha (eds.). *Electoral Politics in India: The Resurgence of the Bharatiya Janata Party*. New Delhi: Routledge, 2017.

Pandey, Gyanendra. 'Can a Muslim Be an Indian?' *Comparative Studies in Society and History* 41, no. 4 (1999): 608–29.

———. *Remembering Partition: Violence, Nationalism and History in India*. Cambridge: Cambridge University Press, 2002.

———. 'Which of Us Are Hindus?' In *Hindus and Others: The Question of Identity in India Today*, edited by Gyanendra Pandey, 238–72. New Delhi: Viking, 1993.

Parker, James E. K. *Acoustic Jurisprudence: Listening to the Trial of Simon Bikindi*. Oxford: Oxford University Press, 2015.

Peters, Timothy, and Karen Crawley (eds.). *Envisioning Legality: Law, Culture and Representation*. New York: Routledge, 2017.

Phelan, James. *Narrative as Rhetoric: Techniques, Audiences, Ethics, Ideology*. Ohio: Ohio State University Press, 1996.

Philadelphoff-Puren, Nina, and Peter Rush. 'Fatal (F)laws: Law, Literature and Writing'. *Law and Critique* 14, no. 2 (2003): 191–211.

Philippopoulos-Mihalopoulos, Andreas. 'Atmospheres of Law: Senses, Affects, Lawscapes'. *Emotion Space Society* 7 (May 2013).

Pollock, Sheldon. 'Ramayana and Political Imagination in India'. *The Journal of Asian Studies* 52, no. 2 (1993): 261–97.

———. 'The Death of Sanskrit'. *Comparative Studies in Society and History* 43, no. 2 (2001): 392–426.

Prabhupada, Bhaktivedanta Swami A. C. *Bhagavad-Gita as It Is*. Vaduz: Bhaktivedanta Book Trust, 1983.

Prakash, Aseem. 'Re-imagination of the State and Gujarat's Electoral Verdict'. *Economic and Political Weekly* 38, no. 16 (2003): 1601–10.

Prakash, Gyan. *Emergency Chronicles: Indira Gandhi and Democracy's Turning Point*. New Delhi: Penguin Viking, 2018.

Prasad, M. Madhava. *Ideology of the Hindi Film: A Historical Construction*. New Delhi: Oxford University Press, 2008.

———. 'Surviving Bollywood'. In *Global Bollywood*, edited by Anandam P. Kavoori and Aswin Punathambekar, 41–51. New York: New York University Press, 2008.

PRS Blog. 'An Overview of Fast Track Courts'. 31 December 2012. http://www.prsindia.org/theprsblog/?p=2388. Accessed 18 December 2022.

Puar, Jasbir K. *Terrorist Assemblages: Homonationalism in Queer Times*. Durham: Duke University Press, 2007.

———. *The Right to Maim: Debility, Capacity, Disability*. Durham: Duke University Press, 2017.

Puniyani, Ram. *Contours of Hindu Rashtra: Hindutva, Sangh Parivar and Contemporary Politics*. Delhi: Kalpaz, 2006.

Radstone, Susannah. 'Cinema and Memory'. In *Memory: Histories, Theories, Debates*, edited by Susannah Radstone and Bill Shwarz. New York: Fordham University Press, 2010.

Raghavendra, M. K. *Seduced by the Familiar: Narration and Meaning in Indian Popular Cinema*, 325–42. New Delhi: Oxford University Press, 2015.

Rai, Alok. *Hindi Nationalism*. New Delhi: Orient BlackSwan, 2001.

Rai, Amit. *Untimely Bollywood: Globalization and India's New Media Assemblage*. Durham: Duke University Press, 2009.

Rai, Vibhuti Narain. 'An Open Letter to My Fellow Police Officers'. In, *Gujarat: The Making of a Tragedy*, edited by Siddharth Varadarajan, 212–13. New Delhi: Penguin, 2002.

Rajadhyaksha, Ashish. *Indian Cinema in the Time of Celluloid: From Bollywood to the Emergency*. New Delhi: Tulika, 2009.

———. *John–Ghatak–Tarkovsky: Citizens, Filmmakers, Hackers*. New Delhi: Tulika, 2023.

———. 'The "Bollywoodization" of the Indian Cinema: Cultural Nationalism in a Global Arena'. In *Global Bollywood*, edited by Anandam P. Kavoori and Aswin Punathambekar, 17–40. New York: New York University Press, 2008.

Rajagopal, Arvind. 'Notes on Postcolonial Visual Culture'. *BioScope* 2, no. 1 (2001): 11–22.

———. *Politics after Television: Hindu Nationalism and the Reshaping of the Public in India*. Cambridge: Cambridge University Press, 2001.

———. 'The Gujarat Experiment and Hindu National Realism'. In *The Crisis of Secularism in India*, edited by Anuradha Dingwaney Needham and Rajeshwari Sunder Rajan. Ranikhet: Permanent Black, 2007.

———. 'Urban Segregation and the Special Political Zone in Ahmedabad: An Emerging Paradigm for Religio-political Violence'. *South Asia Multidisciplinary Academic Journal* 5 (2011). https://journals.openedition.org/samaj/3285.

Rajah, Jothie. 'Law as Record: The Death of Osama bin Laden'. *NoFo: An Interdisciplinary Journal of Law and Justice* 13 (2016): 45.

Rajgopal, Shoba Sharad. 'Bollywood and Neonationalism: The Emergence of Nativism as the Norm in Indian Conventional Cinema'. *South Asian Popular Culture* 9, no. 3 (2011): 237–46.

Ramamoorthy, Rakesh. 'Cricket and Majoritarian Nationalism in Chetan Bhagat's "The 3 Mistakes of My Life"'. *Explicator* 74, no. 4 (2016): 202–05.

Ramdev, Rina, Sandhya D. Nambiar and Debaditya Bhattacharya (eds.). *Sentiment, Politics, Censorship: The State of Hurt.* New Delhi: Sage, 2016.

Ramshaw, Sara. 'Deconstructin(g) Jazz Improvisation: Derrida and the Law of the Singular Event'. *Critical Studies in Improvisation* 2, no. 1 (2006). https://www.criticalimprov.com/index.php/csieci/article/download/81/188/. Accessed 18 December 2022.

Ranganathan, Maya, and Usha M. Rodrigues (eds.). *Indian Media in a Globalised World.* New Delhi: Sage, 2010.

Rao, Anupama. *The Caste Question: Dalits and the Politics of Modern India.* Berkeley: University of California Press, 2009.

Rapping, Elayne. *Law and Justice as Seen on TV.* New York: New York University Press, 2003.

Raz, Joseph. 'Kelsen's Theory of the Basic Norm'. *American Journal of Jurisprudence* 19, no. 1 (1974): 94–111.

Read, Alan. *Theatre and Law.* London: Methuen Drama, 2022.

Rege, Sharmila (ed.). *Against the Madness of Manu: B. R. Ambedkar's Writings on Brahminical Patriarchy.* New Delhi: Navayana, 2013.

Robinson, Rowena. 'Indian Muslims: The Varied Dimensions of Marginality'. *Economic and Political Weekly* 42, no. 10 (2007): 839–43.

Robson, Peter, and Jennifer L. Schulz (eds.). *A Transnational Study of Law and Justice on TV.* Oxford: Hart Publishing, 2016.

Robson, Peter, and Jessica Silbey (eds.). *Law and Justice on the Small Screen.* Oxford: Hart Publishing, 2012.

Robson, Ruthann. *Dressing Constitutionally: Hierarchy, Sexuality, and Democracy from Our Hairstyles to Our Shoes.* New York: Cambridge University Press, 2013.

Rodway, Allan. 'Form'. In *A Dictionary of Modern Critical Terms*, edited by Roger Fowler, 99–101. London: Routledge, 1999.

Rose, Jacqueline. *On Not Being Able to Sleep: Psychoanalysis and the Modern World*. London: Chatto and Windus, 2003, 7.

Roy, Abhijit. 'Live(li)ness and Network Publics in Post Liberalization Indian Popular Films'. *Journal of the Moving Image* 5 (2006). http://jmionline.org/article/liveli_ness_and_network_publics_in_post_liberalization_indian_popular_films. Accessed 18 December 2022.

Roy, Arundhati. *Capitalism: A Ghost Story*. London: Verso, 2015.

———. *The Greater Common Good*. Bombay: India Book Distributor, 1999.

Roy, Suryapratim, and Rahul Sambaraju. 'Hindu Zion: The Politics of Constitutional Accommodation'. *SSRN*, 22 March 2023. https://ssrn.com/abstract=4397260. Accessed 22 April 2023.

Rudolph, Lloyd I., and Susanne Hoeber Rudolph. *In Pursuit of Lakshmi: The Political Economy of the Indian State*. Chicago: University of Chicago Press, 1987.

Ruparelia, Sanjay. 'India's New Rights Agenda: Genesis, Promises, Risks'. *Pacific Affairs* 86, no. 3 (2013): 569–90.

———. '"Minimum Government, Maximum Governance": The Restructuring of Power in Modi's India'. *South Asia: Journal of South Asian Studies* 38, no. 4 (2015): 755–75.

Rush, Peter. 'Dirty War Crimes: Jurisdictions of Memory and International Criminal Law'. In *The Hidden Histories of War Crimes Trials*, edited by Kevin Heller and Gerry Simpson, 367–85. Oxford: Oxford University Press, 2013.

Rush, Peter D., and Andrew T. Kenyon. 'Alter Egos: The Mise-en-Scene of Law and Aesthetics'. In *An Aesthetics of Law and Culture: Texts, Images, Screens*, edited by Peter D. Rush and Andrew T. Kenyon. Studies in Law, Politics and Society, vol. 34, 1–30. Bingley: Emerald Group Publishing, 2004.

——— (eds.). *An Aesthetics of Law and Culture: Texts, Images, Screens*. Studies in Law, Politics and Society, vol. 34. Bingley: Emerald Group Publishing, 2004.

Sagar, Arun. 'Law, Honour, Violence: The Supreme Court's Legal and Non-legal Voice'. *Indian Law Review* 2, no. 2 (2018): 119–34.

Sai, Deepak J. *India, That Is Bharat: Coloniality, Civilisation, Constitution*. Delhi: Bloomsbury, 2021.

Samaddar, Ranabir. 'Beyond the Frame of Practical Reason: The Indian Evidence Act and Its Performative Life'. *Diogenes* 60, nos. 3–4 (2015): 58–73.

———. 'Michel Foucault and Our Postcolonial Time'. In *The Biopolitics of Development: Reading Michel Foucault in the Postcolonial Present*, edited by Sandro Mezaddra, Julian Reid and Ranabir Samaddar, 25–44. New York: Springer, 2013.

Sanders, Mark. *Ambiguities of Witnessing: Law and Literature in the Time of a Truth Commission*. Stanford: Stanford University Press, 2007.

Sarat, Austin (ed.). *Imagining Legality: Where Law Meets Popular Culture*. Tuscaloosa: University of Alabama Press, 2011.

———. 'Imagining the Law of the Father: Loss, Dread, and Mourning in "The Sweet Hereafter"'. *Law and Society Review* 34, no. 1 (2000): 3–46.

——— (ed.). *Law, Violence and the Possibility of Justice*. Princeton: Princeton University Press, 2001.

Sarat, Austin D., and Jonathan Simon (eds.). *Cultural Analysis, Cultural Studies, and the Law: Moving beyond Legal Realism*. Durham: Duke University Press, 2003.

Sarat, Austin, Lawrence Douglas and Martha Merrill Umphrey (eds.). *Law and Performance*. Amherst: University of Massachusetts Press, 2018.

———. 'On Film and Law: Broadening the Focus'. In *Law on the Screen*, edited by Austin Sarat, Lawrence Douglas and Martha Merrill Umphrey, 1–26. Stanford: Stanford University Press, 2005.

Sarkar, Bhaskar. *Mourning the Nation: Indian Cinema in the Wake of Partition*. Durham: Duke University Press, 2009.

Sarkar, Jayabrata. *Politics as Social Text in India: The Bahujan Samaj Party in Uttar Pradesh*. New Delhi: Routledge, 2021.

Sarkar, Sumit. 'Intimations of Hindutva: Ideologies, Caste, and Class in Post-Swadeshi Bengal'. *Proceedings of the Indian History Congress* 60 (1999): 665–66.

———. 'The Fascism of the Sangh Parivar'. *Economic and Political Weekly* 27, no. 5 (1993): 163–67.

Sarkar, Tanika. 'Semiotics of Terror'. *Economic and Political Weekly* 37, no. 28 (2002): 2872–76.

Sathe, S. P. *Judicial Activism in India: Transgressing Borders and Enforcing Limits*. 2nd ed. New Delhi: Oxford University Press, 2003.

Savarkar, V. D. *Hindutva: Who Is a Hindu?* New Delhi: Hindi Sahitya Sadan, 2012.

Savelsberg, Joachim J., and Ryan D. King. 'Law and Collective Memory'. *Annual Review of Law and Social Science* 3 (December 2007): 189–211.

Saxena, Saumya. '"Court"ing Hindu Nationalism: Law and the Rise of Modern Hindutva'. *Contemporary South Asia* 26, no. 4 (2018): 378–99.

Scaria, Arul George. *Piracy in the Indian Film Industry: Copyright and Cultural Consonance*. New Delhi: Cambridge University Press, 2014.

Schaefer, David J., and Kavita Karan (eds.). *Bollywood and Globalization: The Global Power of Popular Hindi Cinema*. London: Routledge, 2013.

Schlag, Pierre. 'The Aesthetics of American Law'. *Harvard Law Review* 115, no. 4 (2002): 1047–118.

Schöttli, Jivanta, and Markus Pauli. 'Modi-nomics and the Politics of Institutional Change in the Indian Economy'. *Journal of Asian Public Policy* 9, no. 2 (2016): 154–69.

Scott, David. 'Colonial Governmentality'. *Social Text* 43 (Autumn 1995): 191–220.

Sen, Meheli. '"It's All about Loving Your Parents": Liberalization, Hindutva and Bollywood's New Fathers'. In *Bollywood and Globalization: Indian Popular Cinema, Nation, and Diaspora*, edited by Rini Bhattacharya Mehta and Rajeshwari V. Pandharipande, 145–68. Delhi: Anthem, 2011.

Sen, Ronojoy. *Articles of Faith: Religion, Secularism, and the Indian Supreme Court*. New Delhi: Oxford University Press, 2010.

———. 'Narendra Modi's Makeover and the Politics of Symbolism'. *Journal of Asian Public Policy* 9, no. 2 (2016): 98–111.

Sen, Satadru. 'Fascism without Fascists? A Comparative Look at Hindutva and Zionism'. *South Asia: Journal of South Asian Studies* 38, no. 4 (2015): 690–711.

———. 'History without a Past: Memory and Forgetting in Indian Cricket'. In *Cricket and National Identity in the Postcolonial Age: Following On*, edited by Stephen Wagg, 94–109. Abingdon: Routledge, 2005.

Sengupta, Hindol. *Being Hindu*. New Delhi: Penguin, 2015.

Setalvad, Teesta. *Beyond Doubt: A Dossier on Gandhi's Assassination*. New Delhi: Tulika, 2015.

———. *Foot Soldier of the Constitution: A Memoir*. New Delhi: LeftWord, 2017.

———. 'The Importance of Zakia Jafri's Protest Petition'. *Economic and Political Weekly* 48, no. 21 (2013): 10–13.

———. 'When Guardians Betray: The Role of the Police'. In *Gujarat: The Making of a Tragedy*, edited by Siddharth Varadarajan, 177–211. New Delhi: Penguin, 2002.

Seymour, David M. 'Film and Law: In Search of a Critical Method'. In *Law's Moving Image*, edited by Leslie J. Moran, Elena Loizidou, Ian Christie and Emma Sandon, 107–20. London: Glass House Press, 2004.

Shaban, Abdul (ed.). *Lives of Muslims in India: Politics, Exclusion and Violence*. 2nd ed. New Delhi: Routledge, 2018.

Shah, Alpa. *In the Shadows of the State: Indegenous Politics, Environmentalism, and Insurgency in Jharkhand, India*. Durham: Duke University Press, 2010.

Shah, Amrita. *Ahmedabad: A City in the World*. New Delhi: Bloomsbury, 2015.

Shah, Ghanshyam. 'Middle Class Politics: Anti-reservation Agitations in Gujarat'. *Economic and Political Weekly* 22, nos. 19–21 (1987): 155–72.

Shah, Ghanshyam, and Jan Breman. *Gujarat, Cradle and Harbinger of Identity Politics: India's Injurious Frame of Communalism*. New Delhi: Tulika, 2022.

Shani, Ornit. 'Bootlegging, Politics and Corruption: State Violence and the Routine Practices of Public Power in Gujarat (1985–2002)'. *South Asian History and Culture* 1, no. 4 (2010): 494–508.

———. *Communalism, Caste and Hindu Nationalism: The Violence in Gujarat*. Cambridge: Cambridge University Press, 2007.

Sharafi, Mitra. *Law and Identity in Colonial South Asia: Parsi Legal Culture, 1772–1947*. Cambridge: Cambridge University Press, 2014.

Sharma, Arvind. 'Dr. B. R. Ambedkar on the Aryan Invasion and the Emergence of the Caste System in India'. *Journal of the American Academy of Religion* 73, no. 3 (2005): 843–70.

Sharma, Jyotirmaya. *Hindutva: Exploring the Idea of Hindu Nationalism*. New Delhi: Penguin, 2011.

Sharp, Cassandra, and Marett Leiboff (eds.). *Cultural Legal Studies: Law's Popular Cultures and the Metamorphosis of Law*. New York: Routledge, 2016.

Sheikh, Danish. 'The Students vs Larry Flynt: Bringing Popular Culture into the Law School'. *Asian Journal of Legal Education* 1, no. 1 (2014): 45–55.

Shepherd, Kancha Ilaiah. *Buffalo Nationalism: A Critique of Spiritual Fascism*. New Delhi: SageSamya, 2019.

Sherman, Taylor C. *Muslim Belonging in Secular India: Negotiating Citizenship in Postcolonial Hyderabad*. Cambridge: Cambridge University Press, 2015.

Sherwin, Richard K. 'Anti-Oedipus, Lynch: Initiatory Rites and the Ordeal of Justice'. In *Law on the Screen*, edited by Austin Sarat, Lawrence Douglas and Martha Merrill Umphrey, 106–52. Stanford: Stanford University Press, 2005.

———. 'Imagining Law as Film (Representation without Reference?)'. In *Law and Humanities: An Introduction*, edited by Austin Sarat, Matthew Anderson and Cathrine O. Frank, 241–68. Cambridge: Cambridge University Press, 2010.

———. *Visualizing Law in the Age of the Digital Baroque: Arabesques and Entanglements*. New York: Routledge, 2011.

————. *When Law Goes Pop: The Vanishing Line between Law and Popular Culture.* Chicago: University of Chicago Press, 2000.

Shklar, Judith N. *Legalism: Law, Morals and Political Trials.* Cambridge: Harvard University Press, 1964.

Silbey, Jessica. 'Persuasive Visions: Film and Memory'. *Law, Culture and the Humanities* 10, no. 1 (2014): 24–42.

Simon, Jonathan, Nicholas Temple and Renée Tobe (eds.). *Architecture and Justice: Judicial Meanings in the Public Realm.* London: Routledge, 2013.

Simpson, Edward. *The Political Biography of an Earthquake: Aftermath and Amnesia in Gujarat, India.* New Delhi: Oxford University Press, 2013.

————. 'The State of Gujarat and the Men without Souls'. *Critique of Anthropology* 26, no. 3 (2006): 331–48.

Simpson, Gerry. 'The Sentimental Life of International Law'. *London Review of International Law* 3, no. 1 (March 2015): 3–29.

Singh, Chander Uday (ed.). *Routes of Wrath: Weaponising Religious Processions.* New Delhi: Citizens and Lawyers Initiative, 2023.

Singh, Gurmukh. 'Representations of the 1984 Tragedy in Punjabi Cinema: Ideology and Cultural Politics'. *Sikh Formations: Religion, Culture, Theory* 11, no. 3 (2015): 418–51.

Singh, M. P., and Surya Deva. 'The Constitution of India: Symbol of Unity in Diversity'. *Jahrbuch des öffentlichen Rechts der Gegenwart* 53 (2005): 649–86.

Singh, Mani Shekhar. 'Religious Iconography, Violence, and Making of a Series'. In 'Riot Discourses', edited by Deepak Mehta and Roma Chatterji, special issue, *Domains* 3 (March 2007): 38–65.

Singh, Pritam. 'Hindu Bias in India's Secular Constitution: Probing Flaws in the Instruments of Government'. *Third World Quarterly* 26, no. 6 (2005): 909–26.

Singh, Sujala. 'Terror, Spectacle and the Secular State in Bombay Cinema'. In *Terror and the Postcolonial: A Concise Companion*, edited by Elleke Boehmer and Stephen Morton, 345–60. Chichester: Wiley-Blackwell, 2009.

Singh, Ujjwal Kumar. *The State, Democracy and Anti-terror Laws in India.* New Delhi: Sage, 2007.

Singh, Upinder. *Political Violence in Ancient India.* Cambridge: Harvard University Press, 2017.

Sircar, Oishik. 'Bollywood's Law: Collective Memory and Cinematic Justice in the New India'. *No Foundations: An Interdisciplinary Journal of Law and Justice* 12 (June 2015): 94–135.

———. 'Seductions of the Neoliberal Nation'. *Himal Southasian* 26, no. 4 (October 2013): 80–95.

———. 'Spectacles of Emancipation: Reading Rights Differently in India's Legal Discourse'. *Osgoode Hall Law Journal* 49, no. 3 (2012): 527–73.

———. 'The Silence of Gulbarg: Some Inadequate Images'. *Human Rights Defender* 25, no. 1 (2016): 24–28.

———. *Violent Modernities: Cultural Lives of Law in the New India*. New Delhi: Oxford University Press, 2021.

Sood, Nikita. *Liberalization, Hindu Nationalism and the State: A Biography of Gujarat*. New Delhi: Oxford University Press, 2012.

Spigelman, J. J. 'The Principle of Open Justice: A Comparative Perspective'. *University of New South Wales Law Journal* 29, no. 2 (2006): 147–66.

Spodek, Howard. *Ahmedabad: Shock City of Twentieth-Century India*. Bloomington: Indiana University Press, 2011.

———. 'In the Hindutva Laboratory: Pogroms and Politics in Gujarat, 2002'. *Modern Asian Studies* 44, no. 2 (2010): 349–99.

Srinivas, Lakshmi. 'Active Viewing: An Ethnography of the Indian Film Audience'. *Visual Anthropology* 11, no. 4 (1998): 323–53.

Srinivasan, T. N. (ed.). *The Future of Secularism*. New Delhi: Oxford University Press, 2007.

Srivastava, Sanjay. 'Modi-Masculinity: Media, Manhood, and "Traditions" in a Time of Consumerism'. *Television and New Media* 16, no. 4 (2015): 331–38.

Stone, Matthew, Illan rua Wall and Costas Douzinas (eds.). *New Critical Legal Thinking*. London: Birkbeck Law Press, 2012.

Subramanian, Ajantha. *The Caste of Merit: Engineering Education in India*. Cambridge: Harvard University Press, 2019.

Sud, Atul (ed.). *Poverty amidst Prosperity: Essays on the Trajectory of Development in Gujarat*. New Delhi: Aakar Books, 2012.

Suresh, Appu Esthose, and Priyanka Kotamraju. *The Murderer, The Monarch and the Fakir: A New Investigation of Mahatma Gandhi's Assassination*. New Delhi: HarperCollins, 2021.

Suresh, Mayur, and Siddharth Narrain (eds.). *The Shifting Scales of Justice: The Supreme Court in Neo-liberal India*. Hyderabad: Orient BlackSwan, 2014.

Swamy, Subramanian. *The Ideology of India's Modern Right*. New Delhi: Har-Anand, 2018.

Tarlo, Emma. *Unsettling Memories: Narratives of the Emergency in Delhi*. Berkeley: University of California Press, 2003.

Tatla, Darshan S. 'The Morning After: Trauma, Memory and the Sikh Predicament since 1984'. *Sikh Formations: Religion, Culture, Theory* 2, no. 1 (2006): 57–88.

Teltumbde, Anand (ed.). *Hindutva and Dalits: Perspectives for Understanding Communal Praxis*. New Delhi: Sage, 2020.

Thampu, Valson. *Harvest of Hate: Gujarat under Siege*. New Delhi: Rupa, 2002.

Tharoor, Shashi. *Why I Am a Hindu*. New Delhi: Aleph Book Company, 2018.

Therwath, Ingrid. '"Shining Indians": Diaspora and Exemplarity in Bollywood'. *South Asia Multidisciplinary Academic Journal* 4 (2010). http://samaj.revues. org/3000. Accessed 18 December 2022.

Thobani, Sunera. 'Performing Terror, Mediating Religion: Indian Cinema and the Politics of National Belonging'. *International Journal of Communication* 8, no. 1 (January 2014): 483–505.

Thussu, Daya Kishan. 'Infotainment Inc.'. In *Media Perspectives for the 21st Century*, edited by Stylianos Papathanassopoulos, 68–82. New York: Routledge, 2010.

———. *News as Entertainment: The Rise of Global Infotainment*. London: Sage, 2009, 91–112.

Tomlins, Christopher. '"Law As ..." III—*Glossolalia*: Toward a Minor (Historical) Jurisprudence'. *UC Irvine Law Review* 5, no. 2 (2015): 239–61.

Tranter, Kieran. *Living in Technical Legality: Science Fiction and Law as Technology*. Edinburgh: Edinburgh University Press, 2018.

Twining, William. *General Jurisprudence: Understanding Law from a Global Perspective*. Cambridge: Cambridge University Press, 2009.

Uberoi, Patricia. *Freedom and Destiny: Gender, Family and Popular Culture in India*. New Delhi: Oxford University Press, 2006.

Udayakumar, S. P. 'Historicizing Myth and Mythologizing History: The "Ram Temple" Drama'. *Social Scientist* 25, nos. 7–8 (1997): 11–26.

———. *'Presenting' the Past: Anxious History and Ancient Future in Hindutva India*. Westport: Praeger, 2005.

Ugra, Sharda. 'Play Together, Live Apart: Religion, Politics and Markets in Indian Cricket since 1947'. In *Cricket and National Identity in the Postcolonial Age: Following On*, edited by Stephen Wagg, 77–93. New York: Routledge, 2005.

Vajpayee, Ananya. *Righteous Republic: The Political Foundations of Modern India*. Cambridge: Harvard University Press, 2012.

Valdes, Francisco. 'Outsider Jurisprudence, Critical Pedagogy and Social Justice Activism: Marking the Stirrings of Critical Legal Education'. *Asian American Law Journal* 10, no. 1 (2003): 65–88.

Vanaik, Achin. *Hindutva Rising: Secular Claims, Communal Realities*. New Delhi: Tulika, 2017.

———. 'Making India Strong: The BJP-Led Government's Foreign Policy Perspectives'. *South Asia: Journal of South Asian Studies* 25, no. 3 (2002): 321–41.

Van Marle, Karin. 'Liminal Landscape: Law, Literature and Landscape in Post-apartheid South Africa'. In *Genres of Critique: Law, Aesthetics and Liminality*, edited by Karin Van Marle and Stewart Motha, 109–32. Stellenbosch: African Sun Media, 2013.

Varadarajan, Siddharth (ed.). *Gujarat: The Making of a Tragedy*. Delhi: Penguin, 2002.

Varma, Rashmi. 'Provincializing the Global City: From Bombay to Mumbai'. *Social Text* 22, no. 4 (2004): 65–89.

Vasudevan, Ravi. 'Aesthetics and Politics in Popular Cinema'. In *The Cambridge Companion to Modern Indian Culture*, edited by Vasudha Dalmia and Rashmi Sadana. Cambridge: Cambridge University Press, 2012.

———. 'Bombay and Its Public'. In *Pleasure and the Nation: The History, Politics and Consumption of Public Culture in India*, edited by Rachel Dwyer and Christopher Pinney, 186–211. New Delhi: Oxford University Press, 2001.

——— (ed.). *Making Meaning in Indian Cinema*. New Delhi: Oxford University Press, 2001.

———. 'Neither State nor Faith: The Transcendental Significance of the Cinema'. In *The Crisis of Secularism in India*, edited by Anuradha Dingwaney Needham and Rajeshwari Sunder Rajan, 239–65. Ranikhet: Permanent Black, 2007.

———. *The Melodramatic Public: Film Form and Spectatorship in Indian Cinema*. New York: Palgrave Macmillan, 2011.

Verghese, Ajay. *The Colonial Origins of Ethnic Violence in India*. Stanford: Stanford University Press, 2016.

Verma, Vidhu. 'Secularism in India'. In *The Oxford Handbook of Secularism*, edited by Phil Zuckerman and John R. Shook. Oxford: Oxford University Press, 2017.

Virdee, Pippa. 'Remembering Partition: Women, Oral Histories and the Partition of 1947'. *Oral History* 41, no. 2 (2013): 49–53.

Virdi, Jyotika. *The Cinematic ImagiNation: Indian Popular Films as Social History*. New Brunswick: Rutgers University Press, 2003.

Vismann, Cornelia. *Files: Law and Media Technology*. Stanford: Stanford University Press, 2008.

———. 'Image and Law: A Troubled Relationship'. *Parallax* 14, no. 4 (2008): 1–9.

Viswanathan, Shiv, and Teesta Setalvad. 'Narratives of Vulnerability and Violence: Retelling the Gujarat Riots'. In *Vulnerability in Technological Cultures: New Directions in Research and Governance*, edited by Anique Hommels, Jessica Mesman and Wiebe E. Bijker, 109–30. Cambridge: MIT Press, 2014.

Wagner-Pacifici, Robin. *What Is an Event?* Chicago: University of Chicago Press, 2017.

Wahab, Ghazala. *Born a Muslim: Some Truths about Islam in India*. New Delhi: Aleph Book Company, 2021.

Waldron, Jeremy. 'Lex Talionis'. *Arizona Law Review* 34, no. 1 (1992): 25–52.

Wan, Marco. *Masculinity and the Trials of Modern Fiction*. New York: Routledge, 2016.

Ward, Ian. *Law and Literature: Possibilities and Perspectives*. Cambridge: Cambridge University Press, 1995.

Wardhaugh, Julia. 'The Jungle and the Village: Discourses on Crime and Deviance in Rural North India'. *South Asia Research* 25, no. 2 (2005): 129–40.

Wariavwalla, Bharat. 'Religion and Nationalism in India: Ram the God of the Hindu Nation'. *Round Table: Commonwealth Journal of International Affairs* 89, no. 357 (2000): 593–605.

Warner, Michael. *Publics and Counter Publics*. New York: Zone Books, 2005.

———. 'Uncritical Reading'. In *Polemic: Critical or Uncritical*, edited by Jane Gallop, 13–38. New York: Routledge, 2004.

Waughray, Annapurna. 'The "Best Bakery" Case: Zahira Habibullah H. Sheikh and Another vs State of Gujarat and Others'. *Journal of Islamic Practices in International Law* 2, no. 1 (2006): 18–44.

Weisberg, Robert. 'The Law-Literature Enterprise'. *Yale Journal of Law and the Humanities* 1, no. 1 (1989): 1–67.

West, Robin. 'Jurisprudence as Narrative: An Aesthetic Analysis of Modern Legal Theory'. *New York Law Review* 60, no. 2 (1985): 145–211.

———. 'Law's Emotions'. In *Law, Reason, and Emotion*, edited by M. N. S. Sellers, 32–54. Cambridge: Cambridge University Press, 2017.

White, James Boyd. *Heracles' Bow: Essays on the Rhetoric and Poetics of the Law*. Madison: University of Wisconsin Press, 1989.

———. *The Legal Imagination*. 2nd ed. Chicago: University of Chicago Press, 1987.

Wilkinson, Steven I. *Votes and Violence: Ethnic Riots in India*. Cambridge: Cambridge University Press, 2004.

Williams, Raymond. 'Structures of Feeling'. In *Performance Analysis: An Introductory Coursebook*, edited by Colin Counsell and Laurie Wolf, 193–200. New York: Psychology Press, 2001.

Yagnik, Achyut, and Suchitra Sheth. *The Shaping of Modern Gujarat: Plurality, Hindutva, and Beyond*. New York: Penguin, 2005.

———. 'Whither Gujarat?' *Economic and Political Weekly* 37, no. 11 (2002): 1009–11.

Young, Alison. 'Murder in the Eyes of the Law'. *Studies in Law, Politics and Society* 17 (1997): 31–56.

———. *The Scene of Violence: Cinema, Crime, Affect*. New York: Routledge, 2009.

Ytreberg, Espen. 'Towards a Historical Understanding of the Media Event'. *Media, Culture and Society* 39, no. 3 (2016): 309–24.

Zinn, Howard. 'The Conspiracy of Law'. In *The Rule of Law*, edited by Robert P. Wolff, 15–36. New York: Simon and Schuster, 1971.

Media Sources

Ahmad, Tufail. 'Abrahamic Hindutva: The Religious Fundamentalism That Is a Threat to India's Tolerant and Pluralist Civilisational Order'. *Firstpost*, 18 July 2017. https://www.firstpost.com/india/abrahamic-hindutva-the-religious-fundamentalism-that-is-a-threat-to-indias-tolerant-and-pluralist-civilisational-order-2-3825669.html. Accessed 18 December 2022.

Ahmed, Nehal. 'Q&A: "The Word Hindu Is Arabic. Why Don't They Throw It Out?"' *Aljazeera*, 10 May 2023. https://www.aljazeera.com/news/2023/5/10/qa-the-word-hindu-is-arabic-why-dont-they-throw-it-out. Accessed 25 May 2023.

Ahuja, Naman. 'Can the Historic Art of Our Constitution Look into the Future?'. *Mint Lounge*, 25 January 2020. https://lifestyle.livemint.com/how-to-lounge/art-culture/can-the-historic-art-of-our-constitution-look-to-the-future-111641402068457.html. Accessed 29 May 2023.

Aman. '"Tuhindi Article" ("The Articles Were Yours")'. *Verfassungsblog: On Matters Constitutional*, 29 December 2022. https://verfassungsblog.de/tuhindi-article-the-articles-were-yours/. Accessed 17 May 2023.

Anand, S. 'Hindutva Has More Legitimacy than the Constitution'. *Outlook*, 23 September 2002. https://www.outlookindia.com/website/story/hindutva-has-more-legitimacy-than-the-constitution/217199. Accessed 18 December 2022.

Ashraf, Ajaz. 'Why Memories of Gujarat 2002 Stay'. *The Hindu*, 2 April 2013. http://www.thehindu.com/opinion/op-ed/why-memories-of-gujarat-2002-stay/article4570587.ece. Accessed 18 December 2022.

Aswani, Tarushi. 'Gujarat: Why a Sizeable Number of Dalits Are Joining Hindutva Outfits'. *The Wire*, 20 March 2023. https://thewire.in/communalism/hindutva-leaders-dharma-sansad-muslim-genocide. Accessed 18 December 2022.

Ather, Sara. 'India's Bulldozer War on Muslim Neighbourhoods'. *Middle East Eye*, 6 February 2023. https://www.middleeasteye.net/opinion/india-muslims-undeclared-war-neighbourhoods. Accessed 17 May 2023.

Ayyub, Rana. 'I Tried Watching "The Kashmir Files." I Left the Theatre to Screams of "Go to Pakistan."' *Washington Post*, 29 March 2022. https://www.washingtonpost.com/opinions/2022/03/29/india-movie-kashmir-files-screams-go-to-pakistan/. Accessed 18 May 2023.

———. 'Why an Indian Film's Success at the Box Office Should Worry Us All'. *Washington Post*, 15 November 2021. https://www.washingtonpost.com/opinions/2021/11/15/why-an-indian-films-success-box-office-should-worry-us-all/. Accessed 18 May 2023.

Bal, Hartosh Singh. 'Spare Me the Good Hindu: The Hindu vs Hindutva Battle Is Meaningless in Shaping Our Politics'. *The Caravan*, 6 July 2018. http://www.caravanmagazine.in/politics/hindu-vs-hindutva-battle-meaningless-in-shaping-our-politics. Accessed 18 December 2022.

———. 'The Instigator'. *The Caravan*, 1 July 2017. http://www.caravanmagazine.in/reportage/golwalkar-ideology-underpins-modi-india. Accessed 18 December 2022.

Banaji, Jairus. 'Indian Big Business'. *Phenomenal World*, 20 December 2022. https://www.phenomenalworld.org/analysis/family-business/. Accessed 22 April 2023.

Bandukwala, J. S. 'Why Gujarat "Banned" Parzania'. *Outlook*, 19 February 2007. http://www.outlookindia.com/magazine/story/why-gujarat-banned-parzania/233909. Accessed 18 December 2022.

BBC. 'Fresh Trial for Gujarat Riot Case'. 12 April 2004. http://news.bbc.co.uk/2/hi/south_asia/3619079.stm. Accessed 18 December 2022.

Bhat, Mohsin Alam. 'Stateless and Hyperlegalized'. *The Baffler*, 3 January 2020. https://thebaffler.com/logical-revolts/stateless-and-hyperlegalized-alam. Accessed 23 May 2023.

Bhattacharjya, Satarupa. 'Best Bakery Case: Supreme Court Slams Witness Zahira Sheikh for Flip-Flops'. *India Today*, 12 September 2005. https://

www.indiatoday.in/magazine/indiascope/story/20050912-best-bakery-case-supreme-court-slams-witness-zahira-sheikh-for-flip-flops-787015-2005-09-12. Accessed 18 December 2022.

Bhowmick, Sourjya. 'Census 2011: India's Muslims Are No Better Today Than a Few Decades Earlier'. *Catchnews*, 14 February 2015. http://www.catchnews.com/india-news/census-2011-india-s-largest-minority-muslims-are-no-better-today-than-a-few-decades-earlier-1452283107.html. Accessed 18 December 2022.

Bunsha, Dionne. 'Verdict in Best Bakery Case'. *Frontline* 23, no. 4 (2006). https://www.frontline.in/static/html/fl2304/stories/20060310005611700.htm. Accessed 18 December 2022.

Business Standard. 'BJP, RSS against the Constitution of India, Want to Impose Hindutva: Mayawati'. 6 December 2016. https://www.business-standard.com/article/politics/bjp-rss-against-the-constitution-of-india-want-to-impose-hindutva-mayawati-116120600554_1.html. Accessed 18 December 2022.

———. '"India First" Should Be Govt's Religion and "Constitution" Its Holy Book: Narendra Modi'. 12 January 2015. http://www.business-standard.com/video-gallery/general/india-first-should-be-govt-s-religion-and-constitution-its-holy-book-narendra-modi-3442/india-first-should-be-govt-s-religion-and-constitution-its-holy-book-narendra-modi-6767.htm. Accessed 18 December 2022.

Butalia, Urvashi. 'How Should We Remember the Violence and Suffering of Partition?' *India Forum*, 15 October 2021. https://www.theindiaforum.in/article/how-should-we-remember-violence-and-sufferingpartition?utm_source=website&utm_medium=organic&utm_campaign=featured-articles&utm_content=Homepage. Accessed 18 December 2022.

Chalmers, John. 'In Narendra Modi's Gujarat, a Case of Rule and Divide'. *LiveMint*, 14 May 2014. https://www.livemint.com/Politics/xDcv5reXXuz-WlCMdDBtstI/In-Narendra-Modis-Gujarat-a-case-of-rule-and-divide.html. Accessed 18 December 2022.

Chander, Mani. 'The Rising Intimidation of Indian Muslims and the Criminalisation of Eating, Praying, Loving and Doing Business'. *Article 14*, 16 September 2022. https://article-14.com/post/the-rising-intimidation-of-india-s-muslims-the-criminalisation-of-eating-praying-loving-doing-business-6323ce1e74c10. Accessed 23 May 2023.

Chandran, Rina. 'Fifteen Years after Bloody Riots, Indian Muslims Struggling to Escape Gujarat Ghettos'. *Reuters*, 24 July 2017. https://www.reuters.com/

article/us-india-property-religion/fifteen-years-after-bloody-riots-indian-muslims-struggling-to-escape-gujarat-ghettos-idUSKBN1A91OA. Accessed 18 December 2022.

Chaturvedi, Megha, and Puneet Nicholas Yadav. 'City Questions "Ban" on Parzania'. *DNA*, 30 January 2007. http://www.dnaindia.com/mumbai/report-city-questions-ban-on-parzania-1077095. Accessed 18 December 2022.

Choksi, Mansi. 'Narendra Modi's Shame: Muslim Survivors of the Gujarat Riots Are Still Suffering'. *Vice News*, 7 May 2014. https://news.vice.com/article/narendra-modis-shame-muslim-survivors-of-the-gujarat-riots-are-still-suffering. Accessed 18 December 2022.

Choudhury, Debasish Roy. 'How Bollywood Rolled Over to Hindu Supremacists'. *Time*, 26 January 2023. https://time.com/6250414/bollywood-hindu-supremacists/. Accessed 23 May 2023.

Colvin, Ross, and Sruthi Gottipati. 'Interview with BJP Leader Narendra Modi'. *Reuters*, 12 July 2013. http://blogs.reuters.com/india/2013/07/12/interview-with-bjp-leader-narendra-modi/. Accessed 18 December 2022.

Dabhi, Parimal A. 'Newsmaker: Maya Kodnani Cleared in Second 2992 Gujarat Riots Case, BJP Says No Bar on Return to Politics'. *Indian Express*, 21 April 2023. https://indianexpress.com/article/political-pulse/maya-kodnani-cleared-in-second-2002-gujarat-riots-case-8567706/. Accessed 21 April 2023.

Dahiya, Himanshi. 'Gujarat 2002: Memories of a Riot'. *The Quint*, 7 March 2022. https://www.thequint.com/videos/documentaries/20-years-of-2002-gujarat-riots-documentary#read-more. Accessed 18 December 2022.

Dalrymple, William. 'Narendra Modi: Man of the Masses'. *New Statesman*, 12 May 2014. http://www.newstatesman.com/politics/2014/05/narendra-modi-man-masses. Accessed 18 December 2022.

Daniyal, Shoaib. 'Partition Horrors Day to CAA: BJP Has Tried to Weaponise 1947 for Electoral Politics'. *Scroll*, 20 August 2021. https://scroll.in/article/1003098/partition-horrors-day-to-caa-bjp-has-tried-to-weaponise-1947-for-electoral-politics. Accessed 18 December 2022.

Dasgupta, Manas. 'NHRC Team Report on Best Bakery Case in a Week'. *The Hindu*, 9 July 2003. https://www.thehindu.com/2003/07/09/stories/2003070905651100.htm. Accessed 18 December 2022.

———. 'SIT Finds No Proof against Modi, Says Court'. *The Hindu*, 10 April 2012. http://www.thehindu.com/news/national/sit-finds-no-proof-against-modi-says-court/article3300175.ece. Accessed 18 December 2022.

————. 'Zahira Retracts Statements'. *The Hindu*, 4 November 2004. https://www.thehindu.com/2004/11/04/stories/2004110407510100.htm. Accessed 18 December 2022.

Deccan Herald. 'Hindutva Is Reflected in Indian Constitution, Says Mohan Bhagwat'. 7 February 2022. https://www.deccanherald.com/national/west/hindutva-is-reflected-in-indian-constitution-says-mohan-bhagwat-1078825.html. Accessed 18 December 2022.

Deuskar, Nachiket. 'Why Are Gujarat's Courts Increasingly Acquitting 2002 Riots Accused?' *Scroll.in*, 26 April 2023. https://scroll.in/article/1047905/why-are-gujarats-courts-increasingly-acquitting-2002-riots-accused. Accessed 25 May 2023.

Dhar, Damayantee. 'Disturbed Areas Act in Gujarat: A Tool to Discriminate against Muslims'. *The Wire*, 26 June 2018. https://thewire.in/rights/disturbed-areas-act-in-gujarat-a-tool-to-discriminate-against-muslims. Accessed 18 December 2022.

Dhillon, Amrit. 'Modi Employs New Tools in India's War against the English Language: Hindi Medical Degrees'. *Guardian*, 22 October 2022. https://www.theguardian.com/world/2022/oct/22/modi-employs-new-tool-in-indias-war-against-the-english-language-hindi-medical-degrees. Accessed 25 May 2023.

Dore, Bhavya. 'The Player: Akshay Kumar's Role as Hindutva's Poster Boy'. *The Caravan*, 31 January 2021. https://caravanmagazine.in/reportage/akshay-kumar-role-hindutva-poster-boy. Accessed 18 December 2022.

Dubey, Priyanka. 'Student Days: The Age of ABVP'. *The Caravan*, 1 October 2017. https://caravanmagazine.in/reportage/age-of-abvp. Accessed 18 December 2022.

Dwivedi, Divya, Shaj Mohan and J. Reghu. 'The Hindu Hoax: How Upper Castes Invented a Hindu Majority'. *The Caravan*, 31 December 2020. https://caravanmagazine.in/religion/how-upper-castes-invented-hindu-majority. Accessed 18 December 2022.

Essa, Azad. 'For Indian Muslims the End Times Have Arrived'. *Middle East Eye*, 14 April 2023. https://www.middleeasteye.net/opinion/india-muslims-end-times-arrived. Accessed 23 May 2023.

————. 'How Shahrukh Khan's Pathaan Will Strengthen Hindu Nationalism'. *Middle East Eye*, 3 February 2023. https://www.middleeasteye.net/opinion/india-shah-rukh-khan-pathaan-hindutva-strengthen-how. Accessed 23 May 2023.

ExpressIndia. 'Zaheera Sheikh a "Self-Condemned Liar": SC Panel'. 20 August 2005. expressindia.indianexpress.com/news/fullstory.php?newsid=53608. Accessed 18 December 2022.

Financial Express. 'Narendra Modi Government for Gita as National Scripture'. 8 December 2014. https://www.financialexpress.com/india-news/bhagwad-gita-only-an-announcement-away-from-national-scripture-sushma-swaraj/16757/. Accessed 18 December 2022.

Firstpost. 'Here It Comes: An Apology from Modi for Gujarat Riots'. 1 April 2013. http://www.firstpost.com/politics/here-it-comes-an-apology-from-modi-for-gujarat-riots-680400.html. Accessed 18 December 2022.

———. 'NCRB Data Show Muslims, Dalits, Tribal Population in Prisons Disproportionate to Their Numbers Outside'. 2 September 2020. https://www.firstpost.com/india/ncrb-data-shows-muslims-dalits-tribal-population-in-prisons-disproportionate-to-their-numbers-outside-8775161.html. Accessed 18 December 2022.

Ganghar, Gopi Maniar. 'Bilkis Bano Rape Case: Released Convicts Greeted with Garlands at VHP Office'. *India Today*, 17 August 2022. https://www.indiatoday.in/india/story/bilkis-bano-rape-case-convicts-greeted-garlands-vhp-office-1988996-2022-08-17. Accessed 26 May 2023.

Ghosh, Amitav. 'The Ghosts of Mrs. Gandhi'. *New Yorker*, 17 July 1995.

Grealy, Leam. 'Challenging the Censor: An Interview with Indian Political Documentarian Rakesh Sharma'. *Bright Lights Film Journal*, 2 December 2016. https://brightlightsfilm.com/challenging-censor-interview-indian-political-documentarian-rakesh-sharma/#.YgPdjurMLEZ. Accessed 18 December 2022.

Halarnkar, Samar. 'Inside the Hindu Mind, the Battle for a Hindu Nation'. *Scroll*, 11 June 2017. https://scroll.in/article/840275/the-battle-for-hindu-rashtra-is-raging-inside-the-hindu-mind-and-it-is-no-longer-a-fringe-fantasy. Accessed 18 December 2022.

Hameed, Syeda, Ruth Manorama, Malini Ghose, Sheba George, Farah Naqvi and Mari Thekaekara. 'The Survivors Speak: How Has the Gujarat Massacre Affected Minority Women'. *Outlook*, 2 May 2002. http://www.outlookindia.com/article.aspx?215433. Accessed 18 December 2022.

Hazra, Indrajit. 'The Forgotten Man'. *Hindustan Times*, 4 Match 2012. https://www.hindustantimes.com/columns/the-forgotten-man/story-4ho43qxpcuiWRsJSx5EbcL.html. Accessed 18 December 2022.

Huffington Post. 'At the "Hindu Rashtra" Conclave in Goa, an Open Call for Violence against Beef Eaters and "Seculars"'. 15 June 2017. https://www.huffingtonpost.in/2017/06/15/at-the-hindu-rashtra-conclave-an-open-call-for-violence-again_a_22266930/. Accessed 18 December 2022.

Ilaiah Shepherd, Kancha. 'Swami Shashi'. *The Caravan*, 1 May 2018. https://caravanmagazine.in/reviews-essays/political-hinduism-shashi-tharoor. Accessed 18 December 2022.

India Today. 'India Is a Hindu Rashtra, It Is Non-negotiable: RSS Chief Mohan Bhagwat'. 2 October 2019. https://www.indiatoday.in/india/story/india-is-a-hindu-rashtra-it-is-non-negotiable-rss-chief-mohan-bhagwat-1605313-2019-10-01. Accessed 18 December 2022.

———. 'Modi Asserts India's Secularism, Says Religion a Personal Choice'. 17 February 2015. https://www.indiatoday.in/india/story/modi-secularism-communal-violence-church-attacks-religion-240660-2015-02-17. Accessed 18 December 2022.

Indian Express. 'A "Pakistani" Is Here: Wheelchair-Bound Man Abused for Sitting during National Anthem in Guwahati Theatre'. 2 October 2017. https://indianexpress.com/article/india/arman-ali-disabled-man-called-pakistani-on-not-standing-up-for-national-anthem-in-guwahati-4871021/. Accessed 18 December 2022.

———. 'Gujarat Riots: "Hang Me If I Am Guilty", Says Narendra Modi'. 26 July 2012. https://indianexpress.com/article/news-archive/politics/gujarat-riots-hang-me-if-i-am-guilty-says-narendra-modi/. Accessed 18 December 2022.

———. 'HC Acquits Five in Best Bakery Case, 4 Get Life'. 10 July 2012. http://archive.indianexpress.com/news/hc-acquits-five-in-best-bakery-case-4-get-life/972411/. Accessed 18 December 2022.

———. 'Looking at Legal Aspects to Rename Ahmedabad to Karnavati, Says Gujarat CM'. 8 November 2018. https://indianexpress.com/article/india/looking-at-legal-aspects-to-rename-ahmedabad-to-karnavati-says-gujarat-cm-vijay-rupani-5437309/. Accessed 18 December 2022.

———. 'Patiyawalas Move On but Ghastly Memory Still Lingers'. 30 August 2012. http://indianexpress.com/article/cities/gujarat/patiyawalas-move-on-but-ghastly-memory-still-lingers/. Accessed 18 December 2022.

———. 'PIL Puts Kai Po Che in the Dock in HC'. 3 May 2013. http://archive.indianexpress.com/news/pil-puts-kai-po-che-in-the-dock-in-hc/1110917/. Accessed 18 December 2022.

———. 'Truth Alone Triumphs, Tweets Modi after SC Relief in Gujarat Riots Case'. 9 January 2014. https://indianexpress.com/article/india/india-others/truth-alone-triumphs-tweets-modi-after-sc-relief-in-gujarat-riots-case/. Accessed 18 December 2022.

———. '2002 Riots Case: Gujarat High Court Rejects Zakia Jafri's Plea, Upholds Clean Chit to Narendra Modi, Others'. 6 October 2017. https://indianexpress.com/article/india/2002-post-godhra-riots-case-gulbarg-riots-case-zakia-jafri-petition-rejected-by-narendra-modi-gujarat-high-court-4875374/. Accessed 18 December 2022.

Iyer, Lakshmi. 'Best Bakery Case: SC Verdict before Gujarat Polls Puts Narendra Modi in a Tight Spot'. *India Today*, 26 April 2004. https://www.indiatoday.in/magazine/states/story/20040426-best-bakery-case-sc-verdict-before-gujarat-polls-puts-narendra-modi-in-a-tight-spot-790191-2004-04-26. Accessed 18 December 2022.

Jacob, Nidhi. 'Status Update: Will Centre Achieve or Miss 'New India' Targets 2022'. *Fact Checker*, 8 January 2022. https://www.factchecker.in/explained/status-update-will-centre-achieve-or-miss-new-india-targets-for-2022-796561. Accessed 18 December 2022.

Jaffrelot, Christophe, and Gilles Verniers. 'Absence on the Bench'. *Indian Express*, 10 September 2018. https://indianexpress.com/article/opinion/columns/muslims-in-prison-india-judiciary-supreme-court-5347728/. Accessed 18 December 2022.

Jain, Akshat. 'Setting the Scene: How Hindi Film Adaptations Align with the Hindutva Project'. *Caravan*, 31 August 2022. https://caravanmagazine.in/film/adaptations-foreign-films-hindi-cinema-hindutva. Accessed 23 May 2023.

Jaiswal, Pooja Biraia. 'How RSS Is Furthering the Idea of Hindutva through Bollywood'. *The Week*, 30 April 2023. https://www.theweek.in/theweek/leisure/2023/04/22/rss-hindutva-agenda-in-hindi-films.html. Accessed 23 May 2023.

Janmohamed, Zahir. 'Why Shashi Tharoor's "Move On" Comment on 2002 Riots Is Particularly Disappointing'. *The Wire*, 31 January 2023. https://thewire.in/communalism/shashi-tharoor-bbc-documentary-gujarat-riots-2002. Accessed 19 May 2023.

Jayaram, N. 'Narendra Modi, British Invitation and Universal Jurisdiction'. *open-India*, OpenDemocracy, 16 August 2013. https://www.opendemocracy.net/

openindia/n-jayaram/narendra-modi-british-invitation-and-universal-jurisdiction. Accessed 18 December 2022.

Jha, Lata. 'Ten Bollywood Courtroom Dramas'. *LiveMint*, 19 September 2016. https://www.livemint.com/Leisure/my1ffkZY8BmZVT1ZAQi9ML/Ten-Bollywood-courtroom-dramas.html. Accessed 15 December 2022.

Jha, Satish. 'Gulbarg Society Massacre Verdict: "Mob Dragged Out Ahsan Jafri, Burnt Him Alive"'. *Indian Express*, 18 June 2016. https://indianexpress.com/article/india/india-news-india/gulberg-society-massacre-verdict-details-mob-dragged-out-ahsan-jafri-burnt-him-alive-2859757/. Accessed 18 December 2022.

John, Arshu. 'The Professional Fortunes of Cops, Bureaucrats and SIT Members Associated with the 2002 Godhra Investigation'. *The Caravan*, 22 September 2017. http://www.caravanmagazine.in/vantage/postings-cops-bureaucrats-sit-members-godhra-2002-investigation. Accessed 18 December 2022.

Johri, Aarefa. 'I Was Sick of the Hateful Climate in Gujarat: Judge Explains Why He Quit after the Riots'. *Scroll*, 7 August 2015. https://scroll.in/article/746832/i-was-sick-of-the-hateful-climate-in-gujarat-judge-explains-why-he-quit-after-the-riots. Accessed 18 December 2022.

Jose, Vinod K. 'The Emperor Uncrowned: The Rise of Narendra Modi'. *The Caravan*, 1 March 2012. https://caravanmagazine.in/reportage/emperor-uncrowned-narendra-modi-profile. Accessed 18 December 2022.

———. '"There Was No Question of Help": Zakia Jafri on the Gulburg Society Massacre'. *The Caravan*, 5 October 2017. http://www.caravanmagazine.in/vantage/zakia-jafri-gulburg-society-massacre-modi-2002. Accessed 18 December 2022.

Kadambi, Rajeev. 'Hijab Row: Why Is the BJP Echoing Liberal Playbook by Seeking to Ban Religious Symbols in Public?' *Scroll*, 10 February 2022. https://scroll.in/article/1016862/one-nation-one-uniform-hijab-row-shows-hindutvas-utter-failure-to-accept-cultural-difference. Accessed 18 December 2022.

Kak, Sanjay. 'The Dangerous "Truth" of The Kashmir Files'. *Aljazeera*, 13 April 2022. https://www.aljazeera.com/opinions/2022/4/13/the-dangerous-truth-of-the-kashmiri-files. Accessed 18 May 2023.

Kalra, Vandana. 'The Handcrafter Constitution Is a Work of Art'. *Indian Express*, 27 January 2020. https://indianexpress.com/article/express-sunday-eye/handcrafted-constitution-india-6233517/. Accessed 29 May 2023.

Kamath, Naresh. '150 Hindu Outfits to Meet in Goa to Discuss "Hindu Rashtra" by 2023, BJP, RSS to Stay Away'. *Hindustan Times*, 11 June 2017. https://www.hindustantimes.com/mumbai-news/150-hindu-outfits-to-meet-in-goa-to-discuss-possibility-of-hindu-rashtra-by-2023/story-R8HWIzIvo UdHytWeZZguRI.html. Accessed 18 December 2022.

Katakam, Anupama. 'A Decade of Shame'. *Frontline* 29, no. 4 (February–March 2012). https://www.frontline.in/static/html/fl2904/stories/20120309290 400400.htm. Accessed 18 December 2022.

———. 'Gulberg Society Case: A Verdict and Three Arrests'. *Frontline*, 10 July 2022. https://frontline.thehindu.com/the-nation/gulberg-society-case-a-supreme-court-verdict-and-three-arrests-teesta-setalvad-rb-sreekumar-san-jiv-bhatt/article65615918.ece. Accessed 22 May 2023.

Kaushal, Sweta. '*Jolly LLB*, *Damini*, *Pink*, *Court* and More: Bollywood's 10 Best Courtroom Dramas'. *Hindustan Times*, 27 February 2017. https://www.hindustantimes.com/bollywood/jolly-llb-damini-pink-court-and-more-bollywood-s-10-best-courtroom-drama/story-IYTPwv776wbs64bbNT-wreJ.html-state. Accessed 18 December 2022.

Khan, Ayesha. 'In Best Bakery City, They Are Lining Up to Watch Dev's Aaliya'. *Indian Express*, 21 June 2004. http://expressindia.indianexpress.com/news/fullstory.php?newsid=32798. Accessed 18 December 2022.

Khan, Saeed. 'FIR Brands Ahmedabad's Muslim Area as Pakistan'. *Times of India*, 19 September 2015. http://timesofindia.indiatimes.com/city/ahmedabad/FIR-brands-Ahmedabads-Muslim-area-as-Pakistan/articleshow/49019847.cms. Accessed 18 December 2022.

Kishore, Roshan. 'Do Muslims in India Suffer a Bias When It Comes to Imprisonment, Convictions?' *Mint*, 12 May 2016. https://www.livemint.com/Opinion/93JZlySuxiVURtuqbA61TN/Do-Muslims-in-India-suffer-a-bias-when-it-comes-to-imprisonm.html. Accessed 18 December 2022.

Konnikkara, Aathira. 'The Warrior Queen: Kangana Ranaut's Role in the BJP's Battle for Bollywood'. *The Caravan*, 1 June 2022. https://caravanmagazine.in/film/kangana-ranaut-role-in-bjp-battle-for-bollywood. Accessed 18 May 2023.

Kotwal, Navaz. 'An Omnibus FIR'. *Frontline* 20, no. 21 (2003). https://www.frontline.in/static/html/fl2021/stories/20031024002204000.htm. Accessed 18 December 2022.

Langa, Mahesh. 'Best Bakery Case: Too Little, Too Late'. *Hindustan Times*, 10 July 2012. https://www.hindustantimes.com/india/best-bakery-case-too-little-too-late/story-2uNz1I3qIM5xC00MU7S29H.html. Accessed 18 December 2022.

———. 'Best Bakery Case: When SC Stepped In for Justice'. *Hindustan Times*, 12 February 2012. https://www.hindustantimes.com/india/best-bakery-case-when-sc-stepped-in-for-justice/story-mrksvuqebiynp58bntwntm.html. Accessed 18 December 2022.

———. '2002 Post-Godhra Riots: Gujarat High Court Upholds Conviction of 19 in Ode Massacre Case'. *The Hindu*, 11 May 2018. https://www.thehindu.com/news/national/other-states/2002-post-godhra-riots-gujarat-high-court-upholds-conviction-of-19-in-ode-massacre-case/article23856779.ece. Accessed 18 December 2022.

Liang, Lawrence. 'Jana Gana Mana and the Danger of Passing Sentiment as Law'. *The Wire*, 1 December 2016. https://thewire.in/83606/jana-gana-mana-dangers-passing-sentiment-law/?fromNewsdog=1. Accessed 18 December 2022.

LiveMint. 'SIT Gives Clean Chit to Modi, 57 Others'. 10 April 2012. https://www.livemint.com/Politics/hJNWc0iH34a25I9E6Tpr1K/SIT-gives-clean-chit-to-Modi-57-others.html. Accessed 18 December 2022.

Mahajani, Urvi. 'Best Bakery: Case Was Shifted for Fair Trial'. *Daily News and Analysis*, 10 July 2012. http://www.dnaindia.com/mumbai/report-best-bakery-case-was-shifted-for-fair-trial-1712893. Accessed 18 December 2022.

Mahmudabad, Ali Khan. 'The Kai Po Che Question'. *Outlook*, 8 March 2013. https://www.outlookindia.com/website/story/the-kai-po-che-question/284287. Accessed 18 December 2022.

Mahurkar, Uday. 'Best Bakery Case Hangs in Balance as Key Players Turn against Each Other'. *India Today*, 22 November 2004. https://www.indiatoday.in/magazine/states/story/20041122-zaheera-sheikh-accuses-teesta-setalvad-of-abduction-789216-2004-11-22. Accessed 18 December 2022.

———. 'Best Bakery Case: Nine Accused Get Life Imprisonment'. *India Today*, 13 March 2006. https://www.indiatoday.in/magazine/indiascope/story/20060313-best-bakery-case-nine-accused-get-life-imprisonment-783565-2006-03-13. Accessed 18 December 2022.

———. 'Best Bakery Trial: Zaheera Sheikh Says She Lied under Oath Out of Fear for Her Life'. *India Today*, 21 July 2003. http://indiatoday.intoday.in/story/best-bakery-trial-zaheera-sheikh-says-she-lied-under-oath-out-of-fear-for-her-life/1/205856.html. Accessed 18 December 2022.

Mander, Harsh. 'From Godhra to Una: The Face of the Gujarat Riots Has Attached His Name to the Dalit Cause'. *Scroll*, 28 August 2016. https://scroll.in/article/813919/from-godhra-to-una-the-face-of-the-gujarat-riots-has-attached-his-name-to-the-dalit-cause. Accessed 18 December 2022.

―――. 'Where Are India's Dissenting Hindus?' *The Wire*, 12 April 2017. https://thewire.in/123008/india-hindutva-narendra-modi-rss-muslims/. Accessed 18 December 2022.

Mashal Mujib, Raj Suhasini and Kumar Hari. 'As Officials Look Away, Hate Speech in India Nears Dangerous Levels'. *New York Times*, 8 February 2022. https://www.nytimes.com/2022/02/08/world/asia/india-hate-speech-muslims.html. Accessed 18 December 2022.

McCarthy, Niall. 'Bollywood: India's Film Industry by the Numbers'. *Forbes*, 3 September 2014. https://www.forbes.com/sites/niallmccarthy/2014/09/03/bollywood-indias-film-industry-by-the-numbers-infographic/#1c4c5d7b2488. Accessed 18 December 2022.

Mishra, Pankaj. 'The Big Con'. *London Review of Books*, 4 May 2023. https://www.lrb.co.uk/the-paper/v45/n09/pankaj-mishra/the-big-con. Accessed 19 May 2023.

Misra, R. K. 'Judge Who Convicted Modi's Minister in Riots Case Now Fears for Her Family'. *The Wire*, 23 July 2015. https://thewire.in/law/judge-who-convicted-modis-minister-in-riots-case-now-fears-for-her-family. Accessed 18 December 2022.

Modi, Narendra. 'Should We Run Relief Camps? Open Child Producing Centres?' *Outlook*, 30 September 2002. http://www.outlookindia.com/article/should-we-run-relief-camps-open-child-producing-centres/217398. Accessed 18 December 2022.

Mojo Story. 'Shashi Tharoor on BBC Documentary on PM Modi'. *Youtube*, 24 January 2023. https://www.youtube.com/watch?v=uf8yol0erMU. Accessed 19 May 2023.

Mukherjee, Tatsam. 'The Slow Death of Artistic Freedom in India'. *Slate*, 20 September 2021. https://slate.com/technology/2021/09/india-censorship-films-freedom-netflix-amazon.html. Accessed 18 December 2022.

Muraleedharan, Sruthi. 'Narendra Modi's "Gujarat Model": Re-moulding Development in the Service of Religious Nationalism'. *Commonwealth and Comparative Politics*, 14 May 2023. https://www.tandfonline.com/doi/citedby/10.1080/14662043.2023.2203997?scroll=top&needAccess=true&role=tab&aria-labelledby=cit. Accessed 17 May 2023.

Nair, Janaki. 'Reading the Constitution'. *The Hindu*, 26 January 2018. https://www.thehindu.com/opinion/op-ed/reading-the-constitution/article22524714.ece. Accessed 29 May 2023.

Narla, Shreyas. 'Indians Should Stop Reading Too Much into the Artwork on the Constitution and Instead Heed Its Words'. *Scroll.in*, 26 January 2021. https://scroll.in/article/984978/indians-should-stop-reading-too-much-into-the-artwork-on-the-constitution-and-instead-heed-its-words. Accessed 29 May 2023.

NDTV. '"We Are Here to Change the Constitution", Says Union Minister in New Controversy'. 26 December 2017. https://www.ndtv.com/india-news/we-are-here-to-change-the-constitution-says-union-minister-anant-kumar-hegde-in-new-controversy-1792197. Accessed 18 December 2022.

News18. 'Truth Always Prevails, Says Maya Kodnani on Acquittal in 2002 Gujarat Riots Case'. 21 April 2018. https://www.news18.com/news/politics/truth-always-prevails-says-maya-kodnani-on-acquittal-in-2002-gujarat-riots-case-1725409.html. Accessed 18 December 2022.

———. 'What Is Best Bakery Case?' 9 July 2912. https://www.news18.com/news/india/best-bakery-3-486666.html. Accessed 18 December 2022.

New York Times. 'Timeline of the Riots in Modi's Gujarat'. 19 August 2015. https://www.nytimes.com/interactive/2014/04/06/world/asia/modi-gujarat-riots-timeline.html#/#time287_8514. Accessed 18 December 2022.

Noorani, A. G. 'Modi and Zionism'. *Frontline*, 4 August 2017. https://www.frontline.in/the-nation/modi-amp-zionism/article9774462.ece. Accessed 18 December 2022.

———. 'Muslims and Police'. *Frontline*, 26 December 2014. https://www.frontline.in/the-nation/muslims-and-police/article6672575.ece. Accessed 18 December 2022.

Outlook. 'Court Allows Zaheera to Depose in Narrative Form'. 22 December 2004. https://www.outlookindia.com/newswire/story/court-allows-zaheera-to-depose-in-narrative-form/268910. Accessed 18 December 2022.

———. 'Guj Bar Council for "Reviewing" SC Order in Best Bakery Case'. 14 April 2004. https://www.outlookindia.com/newswire/story/guj-bar-council-for-reviewing-sc-order-in-best-bakery-case/214889. Accessed 18 December 2022.

———. 'Naroda Patiya: Kodnani Bajrangi among 32 Convicted'. 29 August 2012. https://www.outlookindia.com/newswire/story/naroda-patiya-kodnani-bajrangi-among-32-convicted/773493. Accessed 18 December 2022.

———. 'SC Makes the Best Possible History'. 12 April 2004. https://www.outlookindia.com/website/story/sc-makes-the-best-possible-history/223541. Accessed 18 December 2022.

———. 'Zahira a "Self-Condemned Liar": SC Committee'. 29 August 2005. http://www.outlookindia.com/news/article/zahira-a-selfcondemned-liar-sc-committee/319677. Accessed 18 December 2022.

Pandey, Sanjay. 'Now, Uttar Pradesh "Dharm Sansad" Calls for "Hindu Rashtra", Seers Say Gandhi Not Father of the Nation, Nehru Not "First" PM'. *Deccan Herald*, 30 January 2022. https://www.deccanherald.com/national/now-uttar-pradesh-dharm-sansad-calls-for-hindu-rashtra-seers-say-gandhi-not-father-of-the-nation-nehru-not-first-pm-1076216.html. Accessed 18 December 2022.

Pandya, Haresh. 'Govind Nihalani's Dev in Trouble'. Rediff India Abroad, 16 June 2004. http://www.rediff.com/movies/2004/jun/16dev.htm. Accessed 18 December 2022.

———. 'Hindu, Muslim Join Hands, Defend Dev'. Rediff.com, 19 June 2004. http://www.rediff.com/movies/2004/jun/19dev.htm. Accessed 18 December 2022.

Parthasarathy, Adhiraj, and Mohammad Dawood. 'Clean Chit, Taluka, Zilla: How Persian Lingers On in India's Legal and Revenue Language'. *Scroll.in*, 31 December 2022. https://scroll.in/article/1040685/clean-chit-taluka-zilla-how-persian-lingers-on-in-indias-legal-and-revenue-language. Accessed 26 May 2023.

Patel, Aakar. 'Riot Act'. *The Caravan*, 1 April 2013. https://caravanmagazine.in/perspectives/riot-act. Accessed 18 December 2022.

Petersen, Hannah-Ellis. '"A Threat to Unity": Anger over Push to Make Hindi National Language of India'. *Guardian*, 25 December 2022. https://www.theguardian.com/world/2022/dec/25/threat-unity-anger-over-push-make-hindi-national-language-of-india. Accessed 25 May 2023.

Phukan, Sandeep. 'Why Everyone Tiptoes around Memories of 2002 Gujarat Riots'. *The Hindu*, 28 November 2017. https://www.thehindu.com/elections/gujarat-2017/why-everyone-tiptoes-around-memories-of-2002/article21040625.ece. Accessed 18 December 2022.

Poonam, Snigdha. '"Kai Po Che" and the Strange Case of the Vanishing Villain'. *New York Times*, 27 February 2013. https://india.blogs.nytimes.com/2013/02/27/did-chetan-bhagat-scrub-whitewash-the-godhra-riots-in-kai-po-che/. Accessed 18 December 2022.

Prakash, Satya. 'Hindus Can Be Declared "Minority" in States Where They're Numerically Lower Strength: Centre Tells Supreme Court'. *The Tribune*, 27 March 2023. https://www.tribuneindia.com/news/nation/hindus-can-be-declared-minority-in-states-where-theyre-numerically-lower-strength-centre-tells-supreme-court-381292. Accessed 18 May 2023.

Press Trust of India. 'Modi's Decision to Seek Death Penalty for Maya Kodnani a Deadly Attack on Hindus: Shiv Sena'. *Indian Express*, 20 April 2013. http://www.indianexpress.com/news/modis-decision-to-seek-death-for-maya-kodnani-a-deadly-attack-on-hindus-shiv-sena/1105307/. Accessed 18 December 2022.

———. 'Some Convicts in Bilkis Bano Case Are "Brahmins with Good Sanskaar", Says BJP MLA'. *The Hindu*, 19 August 2022. https://www.the-hindu.com/news/national/other-states/some-convicts-in-bilkis-bano-case-are-brahmins-with-good-sanskaar-says-gujarat-bjp-mla/article65786447.ece. Accessed 26 May 2023.

Punwani, Jyoti. 'Bilkis Bano Convicts Felicitated: Why Are We Surprised?' *Deccan Herald*, 19 August 2022. https://www.deccanherald.com/opinion/bilkis-bano-convicts-felicitated-why-are-we-surprised-1137467.html. Accessed 26 May 2023.

Rai, Piyush. 'Hate Crimes Highest in UP, Gujarat Second: Amnesty Report'. *Times of India*, 17 July 2018. https://timesofindia.indiatimes.com/india/hate-crimes-highest-in-up-guj-second-says-amnesty-report/articleshow/65014822.cms. Accessed 18 December 2022.

Raj, Shivangi Mariam. 'The Forsaken Ones'. *Verso Blog*, 10 May 2022. https://www.versobooks.com/en-gb/blogs/news/5348-the-forsaken-ones?_pos=1&_sid=3e3a5626f&_ss=r. Accessed 25 May 2023.

Raja, D. 'A Nation's Conscience'. *Indian Express*, 28 November 2017. https://indianexpress.com/article/opinion/columns/a-nations-conscience-india-constitution-day-hindutva-forces-narendra-modi-4957562/. Accessed 18 December 2022.

Rajagopal, Krishnadas. 'National Anthem Must Be Played before Screening of Films: Supreme Court'. *The Hindu*, 30 November 2016. https://www.thehindu.com/news/national/National-anthem-must-be-played-before-screening-of-films-Supreme-Court/article16729264.ece. Accessed 18 December 2022.

———. 'SC Modifies Order, Says Playing of National Anthem in Cinema Halls Is Not Mandatory'. *The Hindu*, 9 January 2018. https://www.thehindu.com/news/national/sc-modifies-order-says-national-anthem-not-mandatory/article22403095.ece. Accessed 18 December 2022.

Rajendran, Soumya. 'The Kerala Story Review: A No-Nuance Propaganda Film That Thrives on Shock Value'. *News Minute*, 5 May 2023. https://www.thenewsminute.com/article/kerala-story-review-no-nuance-propaganda-film-thrives-shock-value-176794. Accessed 18 May 2023.

Rebbapragada, Pallavi. 'Gujarat Elections: Godhra Muslims Say Godhra Is a Distant Memory, Want Their Daily Needs Addressed'. *Firstpost*, 2 December 2017. http://www.firstpost.com/india/gujarat-assembly-election-2017-godhra-residents-wish-to-forget-2002-want-focus-on-development-4238093.html. Accessed 18 December 2022.

Rediff.com. 'Modi for "Appeasement of None and Justice to All"'. 16 December 2002. http://www.rediff.com/election/2002/dec/16guj4.htm. Accessed 18 December 2022.

———. 'Zaheera Surrenders before Mumbai Court'. 11 March 2006. http://in.rediff.com/news/2006/mar/10godhra.htm. Accessed 18 December 2022.

Rose, Jacqueline. 'Agents of Their Own Abuse'. *London Review of Books* 41, no. 19 (October 2019). https://www.lrb.co.uk/the-paper/v41/n19/jacqueline-rose/agents-of-their-own-abuse. Accessed 24 May 2023.

Roy, Arundhati. 'Modi's Model Is At Last Revealed for What It Is: Violent Hindu Nationalism Underwritten by Big Business'. *Guardian*, 18 February 2023. https://www.theguardian.com/commentisfree/2023/feb/18/narendra-modi-hindu-nationalism-india-gautam-adani. Accessed 22 April 2023.

Roy, Arundhati. 'The Doctor and the Saint: Ambedkar, Gandhi and the Battle against Caste'. *The Caravan*, 1 March 2014. https://caravanmagazine.in/essay/doctor-and-saint. Accessed 18 December 2022.

Sabrang India. 'Lockdown of Memory of Gujarat 2002 Must Be Resisted: Sidharth Bhatia in Conversation with Teesta Setalvad'. Newsclick, 27 February 2017. https://newsclick.in/lockdown-memory-gujarat-2002-must-be-resisted-sidharth-bhatia-conversation-teesta-setalvad. Accessed 18 December 2022.

Roy, Kumkum. 'Cleansing the Past? Creating the Future? Do (History) Books Matter?' *India Forum*, 3 May 2023. https://www.theindiaforum.in/education/cleansing-past-creating-future-do-history-books-matter. Accessed 25 May 2023.

Sagar. 'Biting My Tongue: What Hindi Keeps Hidden'. *The Caravan*, 26 June 2019. https://caravanmagazine.in/caste/what-hindi-keeps-hidden. Accessed 18 December 2022.

Sahni, Diksha. 'Picture Focus: Ansari and the Anatomy of Fear'. *Wall Street Journal*, 28 February 2012. https://blogs.wsj.com/indiarealtime/2012/02/28/picture-focus-ansari-and-the-anatomy-of-fear/. Accessed 18 December 2022.

Salam, Ziya Us. 'Explained: Understanding the Supreme Court Verdict on the Zakia Jafri Protest Petition'. *The Hindu*, 26 June 2022. https://www.thehindu.com/news/national/explained-understanding-supreme-court-verdict-zakia-jafri-protest-petition-ziya-us-salam/article65567152.ece. Accessed 24 April 2023.

Saldanha, Alison, and Karthik Madhavapeddi. 'Our New Hate-Crime Database: 76% of Victims over Ten Years Minorities; 90% of Attacks Reported since 2014'. Fact Checker, 30 October 2018. https://factchecker.in/our-new-hate-crime-database-76-of-victims-over-10-years-minorities-90-attacks-reported-since-2014/. Accessed 18 December 2022.

Saxena, Nikita, and Atul Dev. 'Death of Judge Loya: Government Letter Concealed from the Supreme Court Detailed Purpose of Loya's Visit to Nagpur and Arrangements for His Stay'. *The Caravan*, 12 June 2018. https://caravanmagazine.in/vantage/death-of-judge-loya-government-letter-concealed-supreme-court-detailed-purpose-of-loya-visit-nagpur-arrangements. Accessed 18 December 2022.

Sebastian, John, and Faiza Rahman. 'Improving Preventive Detention Laws'. *India Forum*, 15 May 2023. https://www.theindiaforum.in/law/improving-preventive-detention-laws. Accessed 25 May 2023.

Sengupta, Somini. 'In India, Showing Sectarian Pain to Eyes That Are Closed'. *New York Times*, 20 February 2007. http://www.nytimes.com/2007/02/20/movies/20parz.html?n=Top/Reference/Times%20Topics/People/S/Sengupta,%20Somini&_r=0. Accessed 18 December 2022.

Setalvad, Teesta. 'Contours of a Conspiracy'. *Frontline*, 17 May 2013. https://www.frontline.in/cover-story/contours-of-a-conspiracy/article4660251.ece. Accessed 18 December 2022.

S. F. 'The Silence and Symbolism of Hate'. *India Forum*, 4 August 2022. https://www.theindiaforum.in/article/silence-and-symbolism-hate. Accessed 18 December 2022.

Shah, Jumana. '"Parzania" to Open in Gujarat in February'. *DNA*, 30 January 2007. http://www.dnaindia.com/india/report-parzania-to-open-in-gujarat-in-february-1077047. Accessed 18 December 2022.

Shaikh, Zeeshan. 'Mumbai Riots 1992: Srikrishna Commission Report and Action Taken'. *Indian Express*, 6 December 2017. https://indianexpress.com/article/india/babri-masjid-demolition-mumbai-riots-1992-srikrishna-commission-report-and-action-taken-4970003/. Accessed 18 December 2022.

Sharma, Kamayani. 'Supporting Role: How Bollywood Acted under the Modi Government'. *The Caravan*, 1 April 2019. https://caravanmagazine.in/perspective/how-bollywood-acted-under-modi-government. Accessed 18 December 2022.

Sharma, Sanjukta. 'Scars in Vadodara'. *LiveMint*, 26 July 2013. https://www.livemint.com/Leisure/NS8gvUYS89gfLf1xLEoq9L/Scars-in-Vadodra.html. Accessed 18 December 2022.

Sharma, Shalini. 'India: How Some Hindu Nationalists Are Rewriting Caste History in the Name of Decolonisation'. *The Conversation*, 9 May 2019. https://theconversation.com/india-how-some-hindu-nationalists-are-rewriting-caste-history-in-the-name-of-decolonisation-114133. Accessed 18 December 2022.

Sharma, Supriya. 'How "Kashmir Files" Added to Communal Fires in Khargone That Ended with Bulldozer Injustice'. *Scroll.in*, 29 April 2022. https://scroll.in/article/1022860/how-kashmir-files-added-to-communal-fires-in-khargone-that-ended-with-bulldozer-injustice. Accessed 18 May 2023.

Singh, Karan Deep, Suhasini Raj and Mujib Mashal. 'In India, New Wave of Trauma as 11 Convicted of Rape and Murder Walk Free'. *New York Times*, 20 August 2022. https://www.nytimes.com/2022/08/20/world/asia/india-rape-muslim-hindu.html. Accessed 18 December 2022.

Sircar, Oishik. 'Coffee Shops, Cricket and a Pogrom'. Infochange India, May 2013. http://infochangeindia.org/human-rights/373-human-rights/rights-and-resistance. Accessed 18 December 2022.

———. 'Seductions of the Neoliberal Nation'. *Himal Southasian*, 15 September 2013. https://www.himalmag.com/seductions-of-the-neoliberal-nation/. Accessed 18 December 2022.

Subramanian, Samanth. 'When the Hindu Right Came for Bollywood'. *New Yorker*, 10 October 2022. https://www.newyorker.com/magazine/2022/10/17/when-the-hindu-right-came-for-bollywood. Accessed 18 May 2023.

Takle, Niranjan. 'A Family Breaks Its Silence: Shocking Details Emerge in Death of Judge Presiding over Sohrabuddin Trial'. *The Caravan*, 20 November 2017. https://caravanmagazine.in/vantage/shocking-details-emerge-in-death-of-judge-presiding-over-sohrabuddin-trial-family-breaks-silence. Accessed 18 December 2022.

Taseer, Atish. 'The War on Bollywood'. *The Atlantic*, 10 June 2021. https://www.theatlantic.com/magazine/archive/2021/07/can-bollywood-survive-modi/619008/. Accessed 23 May 2023.

Tehelka. 'The Truth: Gujarat 2002'. 2 November 2007. http://archive.tehelka.com/story_main35.asp?filename%3DNe031107gujrat_sec.asp. Accessed 18 December 2022.

Tewari, Ruhi, and Abhishek Mishra. 'Every Second ST, Every Third Dalit and Muslim in India Poor, Not Just Financially: UN Report'. *The Print*, 12 July 2019. https://theprint.in/india/every-second-st-every-third-dalit-muslim-in-india-poor-not-just-financially-un-report/262270/. Accessed 18 December 2022.

Thapar, Romila. 'If NCERT Has Its Way, the Study of Indian History Will Move Entirely Outside of India'. *The Wire*, 2 May 2023. https://thewire.in/history/ncert-history-textbooks-mughals-india. Accessed 25 May 2023.

The Hindu Bureau. 'Gujarat Assembly Elections: BJP Evokes 2002 Riots to Gain Vote Favour'. *The Hindu*, 25 November 2022. https://www.thehindu.com/elections/gujarat-assembly/bjps-gujarat-campaign-evokes-2002-post-godhra-riots/article66183228.ece. Accessed 24 April 2023.

Times of India. 'AMC Officially Changes Logo, Makes Ahmedabad "Amdavad"'. 10 February 2011. http://timesofindia.indiatimes.com/city/ahmedabad/AMC-officially-changes-logo-makes-Ahmedabad-Amdavad/articleshow/7463751.cms. Accessed 18 December 2022.

———. 'Best Bakery Case: Zahira Sheikh Surrenders in Mumbai'. 10 March 2006. https://timesofindia.indiatimes.com/india/Best-Bakery-case-Zahira-Sheikh-surrenders-in-Mumbai/articleshow/1445736.cms. Accessed 18 December 2022.

———. 'Gujarat IPS Officer Sanjeev Bhatt Who Took On Narendra Modi Arrested'. 1 October 2012. http://timesofindia.indiatimes.com/india/

Gujarat-IPS-officer-Sanjeev-Bhatt-who-took-on-Narendra-Modi-arrested/articleshow/10191519.cms. Accessed 18 December 2022.

———. 'Narendra Modi Gets Clean Chit in SIT Report on Gujarat Riots'. 10 April 2012. https://timesofindia.indiatimes.com/india/Narendra-Modi-gets-clean-chit-in-SIT-report-on-Gujarat-riots-Zakia-Jafri-vows-to-continue-her-fight/articleshow/12612345.cms. Accessed 18 December 2022.

———. 'PIL against Kai Po Che for "Biased" Portrayal of Gujarat Riots'. 3 May 2013. http://articles.timesofindia.indiatimes.com/2013-05-03/news-interviews/39007874_1_po-che-the-3-mistakes-hindi-film. Accessed 18 December 2022.

———. 'Zaheera Sheikh Released from Nasik Jail'. 14 March 2007. https://timesofindia.indiatimes.com/india/Zaheera-Sheikh-released-from-Nasik-jail/articleshow/1762108.cms. Accessed 18 December 2022.

———. 'Zahira Goes Flip, Flop, Flip....' 23 December 2004. https://timesofindia.indiatimes.com/india/Zahira-goes-flip-flop-flip-/articleshow/969471.cms. Accessed 18 December 2022.

The Hindu. 'Best Bakery Case: 5 Acquitted, Life Term for Four Upheld'. 9 July 2012. http://www.thehindu.com/news/national/other-states/best-bakery-case-5-acquitted-life-term-for-four-upheld/article3620604.ece. Accessed 18 December 2022.

———. 'Convictions in Bilkis Bano Case Hailed'. 24 January 2008. https://www.thehindu.com/todays-paper/tp-national/tp-newdelhi/Convictions-in-Bilkis-Bano-case-hailed/article15150118.ece. Accessed 18 December 2022.

———. 'Gujarat Government to Seek Death Penalty for Kodnani, Bajrangi'. 17 April 2013. http://www.thehindu.com/news/national/other-states/gujarat-government-to-seek-death-penalty-for-kodnani-bajrangi/article4626829.ece. Accessed 18 December 2022.

———. 'I Was Warned against Deposing: Sreekumar'. 20 August 2009. http://www.thehindu.com/news/national/article5896.ece. Accessed 18 December 2022.

———. '"India First" Only Religion of Government, Constitution Its Only Scripture: Modi'. 27 November 2015. https://www.thehindu.com/news/national/india-first-only-religion-of-government-and-constitution-its-only-scripture-says-modi/article7923917.ece. Accessed 18 December 2022.

The Telegraph. 'Modi Rethink on Death for Ex-minister'. 15 May 2013. https://www.telegraphindia.com/india/modi-rethink-on-death-for-ex-minister/cid/1312328. Accessed 18 December 2022.

The Wire. 'Hindutva Leaders at Haridwar Event Call for Muslim Genocide'. 22 December 2021. https://thewire.in/communalism/hindutva-leaders-dharma-sansad-muslim-genocide. Accessed 18 December 2022.

TwoCircles. 'BJP's Bid to Rename Ahmedabad as "Amdavad"'. 16 February 2011. http://twocircles.net/2011feb16/bjp%E2%80%99s_bid_rename_ahmedabad_%E2%80%98amdavad%E2%80%99.html#.VvzczuJ96Uk. Accessed 18 December 2022.

Vanaik, Achin. 'By the Book: Does the Constitution Keep its Promises?' *The Caravan*, 1 May 2019. https://caravanmagazine.in/reportage/does-constitution-keep-promises. Accessed 18 December 2022.

Venkataraman, Rajagopalan. 'Courts, Last Bastion of the Good Old Typewriter'. *Indian Express*, 9 November 2013. http://www.newindianexpress.com/cities/chennai/Courts-last-bastion-of-the-good-old-typewriter/2013/11/09/article1879797.ece. Accessed 18 December 2022.

Yechury, Sitaram. 'What Is a Hindu Rashtra?' *Frontline*, 21 July 2017. https://www.frontline.in/cover-story/what-is-hindu-rashtra/article9748316.ece. Accessed 18 December 2022.

Zee News. 'Gujarat Court to Hear Petition Banning Dev on June 28'. 25 June 2004. http://zeenews.india.com/news/nation/gujarat-court-to-hear-petition-banning-dev-on-june-28_165029.html. Accessed 18 December 2022.

Feature Films and Documentaries

Agnihotri, Vivek (dir.). *The Kashmir Files*. 2022.

Das, Nandita (dir.). *Firaaq*. Percept Picture Company, 2010.

Dholakia, Rahul (dir.). *Parzania*. PVR Pictures, 2007.

Kapoor, Abhishek (dir.). *Kai Po Che*. UTV Motion Pictures, 2013.

Kapur, Pankaj (dir.). *Mausam*. Cine Acts, 2011.

Kohli, Ashok (dir.). *Rajdhani Express*. Cine Acts, 2013.

Minhaj, Sharique (dir.). *Chand Bujh Gaya*. F. A. Picture International, 2005.

Nahata, Amrit (dir.). *Kissa Kursi Kaa*. 1978.

Nihalani, Govind (dir.). *Dev*. Udbhav Productions, 2004.

Patwardhan, Anand (dir.). *Father, Son and Holy War*. 1995.

—— (dir.). *Ram ke Naam*. 1992.

Rai, Amit (dir.). *Road to Sangam*. Produced by Amit Chheda, distributed by Shethia Audio Video Productions, 2009.

Ratnam, Mani (dir.). *Bombay*. Aalayam Productions, 1995.

Sen, Sudipto (dir.). *The Kerala Story*. 2023.

Shah, Tejal (dir.). *I Love My India* (documentary). http://www.womanifesto.com/ project/tejal-shah-i-love-my-india/. Accessed 18 December 2022.

Sharma, Rakesh (dir.). *Final Solution*. 2004.

Literary Works

Bhagat, Chetan. *3 Mistakes of My Life*. New Delhi: Rupa, 2008.

Hariharan, Githa. *Fugitive Histories*. Delhi: Penguin, 2009.

Jha, Raj Kamal. *Fireproof.* New Delhi: Picador, 2009.

Kafka, Franz. *The Trial*. Translated by Breon Mitchell. New York: Schocken, 1998.

Manto, Saadat Hasan. 'Tidiness'. *In Bitter Fruit: The Very Best of Saadat Hasan Manto*, edited by Khalid Hasan, 490. New York: Penguin, 2008.

Vassanji, M. G. *The Assassin's Song*. Edinburgh: Canongate, 2007.

Index